# The Rights of Women

**Lenora M. Lapidus** is the director of the American Civil Liberties Union Women's Rights Project. She litigates constitutional and other gender discrimination cases in federal and state courts throughout the country, advocates before international human rights fora, engages in public policy efforts, and speaks on gender equity issues in the media and to the public. Her work focuses on economic justice, violence against women, women and girls in the criminal and juvenile justice systems, and educational equity. Prior to becoming director of the ACLU Women's Rights Project, Lapidus served as the legal director of the American Civil Liberties Union of New Jersey; held the John J. Gibbons Fellowship in Public Interest and Constitutional Law at Gibbons, in New Jersey; was a staff attorney fellow at the Center for Reproductive Rights in New York; and clerked for the Honorable Richard Owen, in the U.S. District Court for the Southern District of New York. In addition to her litigation and public policy experience, Lapidus has taught Gender and the Law, Procreation and the Law, and Women and Public Policy as an adjunct professor at Seton Hall Law School and Rutgers University, and has taught in the Constitutional Litigation Clinic at Rutgers Law School. She has published law review articles and book chapters on gender equality, constitutional law, welfare, reproductive rights, capital punishment, and child custody. Lapidus has received several awards, including the Wasserstein Fellowship from Harvard Law School for outstanding public interest lawyers. She graduated *cum laude* from Harvard Law School and *summa cum laude* from Cornell University.

**Emily J. Martin** is the deputy director of the American Civil Liberties Union Women's Rights Project, where she has worked since 2001. At the ACLU Women's Rights Project, Martin undertakes a variety of litigation, including cases challenging gender discrimination in education, housing, employment, welfare administration, and public accommodations, with a special emphasis on the needs of low-income women and women of color. She also serves as president of the board of the Fair Housing Justice Center in New York City. Martin received her B.A. with highest distinction from the University of Virginia and her J.D. from Yale Law School. Following law school, she clerked for Judge T. S. Ellis, III, of the U.S. District Court for the Eastern District of Virginia and for Judge Wilfred Feinberg of the U.S. Court of Appeals for the Second Circuit. As a recipient of the Rita Charmatz Davidson Fellowship through the Georgetown Women's Law and Public Policy Fellowship Program, she also previously worked as counsel at the National Women's Law Center in Washington, D.C., where she undertook legislative advocacy and policy analysis on issues affecting women's employment and women's economic security.

**Namita Luthra** was a staff attorney at the American Civil Liberties Union Women's Rights Project from 2001 through 2007. She worked on a wide range of litigation, advocacy, and public education efforts to advance the rights of women and girls, including authoring reports on criminal justice matters relating to the effects of overincarceration and drug sentencing policies on women and successfully litigating gender discrimination jury trials in federal court. Prior to joining the Women's Rights Project, Luthra was a staff attorney at the Office of the Appellate Defender in New York representing indigent defendants in criminal state appeals and federal postconviction proceedings, and the Karpatkin Fellow in the ACLU Legal Department. Ms. Luthra graduated from the University of Pittsburgh School of Law and from Bryn Mawr College.

# THE RIGHTS OF
# WOMEN

The Authoritative ACLU Guide to
Women's Rights

Fourth Edition

## Lenora M. Lapidus
## Emily J. Martin
## Namita Luthra

*General Editor of the Handbook Series*
*Eve Carey*

NEW YORK UNIVERSITY PRESS
New York and London

NEW YORK UNIVERSITY PRESS
New York and London
www.nyupress.org

Library of Congress Cataloging-in-Publication Data
Lapidus, Lenora M.
The rights of women : the authoritative ACLU guide to women's rights /
Lenora M. Lapidus, Emily J. Martin, and Namita Luthra. — 4th ed.
p.   cm. — (American Civil Liberties Union handbook)
Rev. ed. of: The rights of women / Susan Deller Ross ... [et al.].
3rd ed., completely rev. and up-to-date. c1993.
Includes bibliographical references and index.
ISBN-13: 978-0-8147-5230-2 (cl : alk. paper)
ISBN-10: 0-8147-5230-6 (cl : alk. paper)
ISBN-13: 978-0-8147-5229-6 (pb : alk. paper)
ISBN-10: 0-8147-5229-2 (pb : alk. paper)
1. Women—Legal status, laws, etc.—United States.   I. Martin, Emily J.
II. Luthra, Namita. III. American Civil Liberties Union. IV. Title.
KF478.L37  2009
346.7301'34—dc22            2008047033

New York University Press books are printed on acid-free paper,
and their binding materials are chosen for strength and durability.
We strive to use environmentally responsible suppliers and materials
to the greatest extent possible in publishing our books.

Manufactured in the United States of America

c 10 9 8 7 6 5 4 3 2 1
p 10 9 8 7 6 5 4 3 2 1

# CONTENTS

# Introduction to the ACLU Handbook Series

## Eve Carey, General Editor

This book is one of a series published in cooperation with the American Civil Liberties Union (ACLU) that is designed to inform individuals about their rights in particular areas of law. A guiding principle of the ACLU is that an informed citizenry is the best guarantee that the government will respect individual civil liberties. These publications carry the hope that individuals informed of their rights will be encouraged to exercise them. In this way, rights are given life. If rights are rarely used, however, they may be forgotten, and violations may become routine.

In order to understand and exercise individual rights, it is important to know something about how our legal system works. The basic document that sets up our legal system is the United States Constitution. The Constitution explains how we elect the government of the United States and provides the government with the specific powers it needs to run the country. These include the power to pass laws that are "necessary and proper" for carrying out the other powers. The government does not have the authority to do anything that the Constitution does not permit it to do. Therefore, a better question to ask than "Do I have the right to do this?" is "Does the government have the right to stop me from doing this?"

Although the government may not deny a citizen the right to do something unless the Constitution gives it the power to do so, the framers of the Constitution thought that certain rights are so critical that they should be specifically guaranteed. Therefore, the framers added ten amendments, known as the Bill of Rights, that are among the most important rights that the government may never deny to its citizens. Four of the amendments to the Constitution are particularly important for individuals seeking to understand their rights in relation to the government.

The First Amendment contains two important statements. The first is that "Congress shall make no law . . . abridging freedom of speech, or of the press; or the right of the people peaceably to assemble, and to petition the government for a redress of grievances." This means that a person cannot be forbidden from or punished for expressing opinions out loud or in print, either individually or with a group of people, as long as he or she does it at a reasonable time and in a reasonable place and manner.

The second statement of the First Amendment is that "Congress shall make no law respecting an establishment of religion, or prohibiting the free exercise thereof." This means that the government may neither prohibit nor encourage the practice of a particular religion; indeed, government may not encourage the practice of religion at all. In short, religion is none of the government's business.

The Fourth Amendment says, "The right of the people to be secure in their persons, houses, papers, and effects, against unreasonable searches and seizures, shall not be violated, and no Warrants shall issue, but upon probable cause, supported by Oath or affirmation, and particularly describing the place to be searched, and the persons or things to be seized." This means that the police may neither search a person, or anything he or she is carrying, nor make an arrest, unless they have a very good reason for believing that the person has committed a crime. Moreover, they may not search a house or other private place without a warrant signed by a judge who has decided it is reasonable to believe that the person involved has committed a crime. (Note that the police have most leeway in searching automobiles.)

The Fifth Amendment says, "No person shall . . . be deprived of life, liberty, or property without due process of law." This means that the government may not punish individuals without giving them a fair chance to defend themselves.

In addition to the rights guaranteed by the Bill of Rights, the Fourteenth Amendment says, "No State shall deprive any person of life, liberty or property without due process of law; nor deny to any person within its jurisdiction the equal protection of the laws." This amendment means that, just as the federal government may not punish individuals without giving them a fair chance to defend themselves, so the government of a state may not do so either. Moreover, all laws must apply equally to all citizens who are in the same situation as one another. For example, the government may not pass a law saying that people of one race or sex or religion are allowed to do something that people of another race or sex or religion are not allowed to do. (It may, however, pass laws that apply to children, but not to adults, for example, since children are not always in the same situation as adults. For example, laws requiring children, but not adults, to go to school are constitutional, as are laws prohibiting children from buying alcohol and cigarettes.)

Before going any further, it is important to understand two things. First, when we talk about "the government" in this book, we mean not only elected officials but also the people who are hired to work for the government, such as police officers and public school principals. All of these people must obey the Constitution when they are performing their jobs.

Second, the Constitution applies *only* to the people who work for the government. It does not apply to private individuals or people who work in the private sector. This means, for example, that while the principal of a public school may not make students say prayers in class because that would violate the First Amendment guarantee of freedom of religion, students in parochial or other private schools may be required to pray.

In addition to the United States Constitution, each state also has its own constitution. Many of the provisions of these state constitutions are the same as those in the United States Constitution, but they apply only to the actions of state officials. Thus, a public school principal in New York is prohibited from holding religious services in school, not just by the federal Constitution but also by the New York State Constitution. While a state may not deny its citizens rights guaranteed by the United States Constitution, it may, and often does, provide more rights. For example, while the Supreme Court has held that the death penalty does not violate the federal Constitution, the Massachusetts Supreme Court has held that it does violate the Massachusetts Constitution.

Although federal and state constitutions do not govern the actions of the private sector, limitations on personal behavior do exist. Both Congress and all of the state legislatures pass laws that apply to the private sector. The laws enacted by Congress are for the entire country. Those passed by the state legislatures are just for the people of that state. Thus, for example, people in New York may have more or fewer or different rights and obligations than do the people in Louisiana. In fact, in Louisiana anyone over the age of eighteen can buy alcohol, while in other states the legal drinking age is twenty-one.

Just as we have separate federal and state governments, we also have separate systems of federal courts and state courts. The job of the federal courts is to interpret laws passed by Congress; the job of the state courts is to interpret laws passed by their own state legislatures. Both courts have the power to interpret the United States Constitution. State courts may, in addition, interpret their own state constitutions.

In this book, you will read about lawsuits that individuals have brought in both federal and state courts asking the courts to declare that certain actions by state officials are illegal or unconstitutional. In the federal system, these suits are filed in a district court, which is a trial court that decides cases in a particular district. The district court hears the evidence and reaches a decision. The losing party may then appeal to one of the thirteen circuit courts of appeals, which hear appeals from several districts. The loser in the circuit court may ask the Supreme Court of the United States to decide the case. Because the Supreme Court agrees to hear only a small fraction of the cases that litigants wish to bring before it, as a practical matter, the circuit court is usually the court of last resort. Each state also has its own court system. All are a little different from one another, but each works in basically the same way as the federal court system, beginning with a trial court, which hears evidence, followed by two levels of appellate courts.

In such a complicated system, it is inevitable that courts may disagree about how to interpret a particular law. When this occurs, the answer to the question, "What are my rights?" may be "It depends where you live." Moreover, the law may change; in some areas of law it is changing very rapidly. An effort has been made in this book to indicate areas of the law in which movement is taking place, but it is not always possible to predict precisely when this will happen or what the changes will be.

If you believe that your rights have been violated, you should, of course, seek legal assistance. The ACLU affiliate office in your state may be able to guide you to the available legal resources. If you consult a lawyer, take this book with you as he or she may not be familiar with the law applicable to your situation. You should be aware, however, that litigation is usually expensive, takes a long time, and carries with it no guarantee of success. Fortunately, litigation is not always necessary to vindicate legal rights. On occasion, government officials themselves are not aware of their legal obligations to respect the rights of individuals and may change their practices or policies when confronted by an individual who is well informed about the law. We hope that this book will help to provide the basic information about the legal principles applicable to this area of law and will, as well, suggest to you arguments that you might make on your own behalf to secure your rights.

This introduction is being written as the United States is engaged in fighting terrorism. It is precisely at times of national stress like these that we see civil liberties coming under attack. It is therefore crucial in such times that Americans rededicate themselves to protecting the precious liberties that our Constitution and laws guarantee us. This book is part of that effort.

The principal purpose of this handbook, as well as the others in this series, is to inform individuals of their legal rights. The authors from time to time suggest what the law should be, but their personal views are not necessarily those of the ACLU. For the ACLU's position on the issues discussed in this handbook, the reader should write to Communications Department, ACLU, 125 Broad Street, 18th Floor, New York, NY 10004-2400 or access http://www.aclu.org.

# PREFACE

When the first edition of *The Rights of Women* was published in 1973, many laws existed that on their face treated women and men differently. These laws, for example, prohibited women from holding certain jobs or working overtime; mandated that if a man and a woman were equally qualified to serve in a position, preference should be given to the man; and barred married women from controlling property jointly owned with their husbands.

Indeed, prior to 1971, the Supreme Court had never struck down as unconstitutional any law that discriminated against women. It was not until the case of *Reed v. Reed*, in 1971, that the Court declared that the Fourteenth Amendment prohibited sex discrimination, just as it prohibited discrimination on the basis of race. In this case, the Court struck down an Ohio law that provided that if a man and a woman were equally qualified to be the administrator of a deceased's estate, the man should be appointed.

Throughout the 1970s, the ACLU Women's Rights Project and other advocates worked strenuously to establish women's equality through court challenges and the enactment of civil rights statutes. They achieved enormous gains, striking down the vast majority of laws that differentiated between women and men, and enshrining in federal and state law prohibitions against discrimination.

Today, few laws explicitly treat men and women differently. Nevertheless, the rights that have been established by court decision and by legislation are still not realized by all women in the United States. For the most marginalized women—poor women, women of color, immigrant women—those rights are still far from a reality. Thus, the fight for women's rights remains critical.

This book addresses the most important women's rights issues today. These rights—and their violations—arise in many contexts: in the work place, in schools, in housing, in public accommodations, in state or federal custody, and in the distribution of government benefits. Reproductive rights continue to be threatened. Women's rights to be free from discrimination and from violence remain at risk. These rights are protected by the U.S.

Constitution, by state constitutions, and by federal and state statutes. In some contexts, the work of the ACLU Women's Rights Project today focuses on enforcing rights that are already established; in others, it is about expanding interpretations of laws so as to provide greater protection.

This book explains how the law can be used to advance women's equality. For the most part, the law now can be used to expand women's opportunities, rather than restricting them as it did in the past. It is essential that women learn and understand how to use the law in this manner. It is our hope that this book will aid in that process.

To help us achieve our goal of gender equality, join the ACLU's Action Network. Go to http://action.aclu.org.

To learn more about efforts to protect women's rights, go to http://www.aclu.org/womensrights, www.aclu.org/reproductiverights, www.aclu.org/lgbt, and www.aclu.org/prison.

# ACKNOWLEDGMENTS

Many people have assisted in researching and writing this book. For their crucial contributions, we would like to thank former ACLU Women's Rights Project staff, including Jennifer Arnett, Claudia Flores, and Jennifer Pasquerella; former ACLU Women's Rights Project contract attorney and writer Camilla Roberson; and ACLU Women's Rights Project legal assistant Eliza Reshefsky. We would also like to thank ACLU Reproductive Freedom Project staff, including Louise Melling and Lorraine Kenny; former ACLU Reproductive Freedom Project staff member Rachel Hart; and ACLU Reproductive Freedom Project consultant Carrie Flaxman for their work on chapter VI, "Reproductive Freedom." This book also would not have been possible without the assistance of numerous past Women's Rights Project interns over many years, including Jennifer Amore, Ginger Anders, Jennifer Arbuse, Caroline Bettinger-Lopez, Rachel Braunstein, Ying Chi, Nusrat Choudhury, Melissa Chua, Alexandra Cira, Adrienne Fowler, Angelina Fryer, Carly Grant, Cynthia Hanawalt, Heidi Hengel, Amy Kapczynski, Gowri Krishna, Romy Lerner, Patty Li, Stacy Lozner, Anna MacCormack, Samantha Marks, Jennifer McAdams, Chloe McRae, Socheatta Meng, Zulma Miranda, Jennifer Mockerman, Aileen Monahan, Cynthia Nagendra, Emi Omura, Karen Paik, Monica Pal, Lisa Rubin, Kristina Scharts, Dorothy Smith, Ann Spence, and Michaele Turnage.

This is the fourth edition of *The Rights of Women*. It is built upon the foundations of the three earlier editions. We are deeply indebted to the authors of those editions: Susan Deller Ross, Ann Barcher, Isabelle Katz Pinzler, Deborah A. Ellis, and Kary L. Moss.

# I

# Constitutional Rights:
# Equal Protection

This chapter explains how the Constitution and evolving judicial interpretations of it may invalidate both state and federal laws and actions that discriminate on the basis of sex. Although such laws and practices have become rarer since the early 1970s when the Supreme Court first held that the Constitution prohibited certain kinds of sex discrimination, many still remain. The United States Constitution is one of a variety of tools that may be used to dismantle discrimination against women; many state constitutions also provide protection against certain kinds of sex discrimination. Unfortunately, in recent years constitutional arguments have also been used successfully to strike down laws meant to advance women's equality.

While many different sections of the Constitution are useful in fighting for important rights for women, this chapter focuses on the Equal Protection Clause of the Fourteenth Amendment. One problem that has pervaded many of the issues facing women has been the unequal treatment under the law of men and women. Thus, it is essential to understand the equal protection doctrine in order to recognize how it is relevant to different problems women face and in order to know how to apply it vigorously when necessary.

**Where does the U.S. Constitution prohibit laws and government practices that discriminate on the basis of sex?**

The Equal Protection Clause of the Fourteenth Amendment to the Constitution provides, "No state shall . . . deny to any person within its jurisdiction the equal protection of the laws." Courts have interpreted this

1

language to prohibit certain kinds of sex discrimination by state governments and agencies.

**What does the Equal Protection Clause mean?**

The Equal Protection Clause requires states to treat their citizens equally, and advocates have used it to combat discriminatory laws, policies, and government actions. Adopted shortly after the Civil War, the Equal Protection Clause has been invoked often to invalidate policies such as racial segregation in public schools, the denial of voting rights to African-Americans, and racially exclusive public accommodations.[1] It also extends to protect the rights of other groups, such as immigrants, ethnic minorities, and women.

Judges deciding cases under the Equal Protection Clause have over time defined what "equal treatment" demands for different classifications. For instance, state legislatures may not pass laws that single out one racial group for unfavorable treatment, because the Constitution has been interpreted to require equal treatment among racial groups. On the other hand, legislatures may deny rights to fifteen-year-olds that are given to fifty-year-olds, such as driving and voting, if they have a rational reason for doing so. A more difficult question for courts has been in what circumstances the Constitution forbids governments from treating men and women differently. Though rare, there may be instances when real differences between men and women justify governmental decisions to treat them differently. Indeed, treating men and women fairly may sometimes require taking these differences into account. On the other hand, mere stereotypes about the differences between men and women cannot justify differential treatment.[2]

**Does the Equal Protection Clause forbid discrimination by private individuals?**

The Constitution's guarantee of equal protection is limited by the concept of *state action*. In other words, the Fourteenth Amendment only forbids federal, state, and local governments from discriminating, not private actors. This prohibition covers a broad range of activities, but it is still limited to action in which the government is substantially involved. For instance, if a public school official decides to bar women from a physics class, even though there is no law requiring him or her to do so, this would be a prohibited *state action*. But if a private school official made the same decision, that action, although blatantly discriminatory, would not violate the Equal Protection Clause.[3]

Occasionally, courts have categorized a private institution's acts as state action when a government has sufficiently involved itself with or supported the acts, for instance through funding. In addition, a private institution fulfilling functions normally considered governmental, such as running a town, may be said to engage in state action. Thus, if the government provides most of the funds for building a private hospital, or if a private company owns a town where all of its employees live, the courts may say that both the hospital and the company are equivalent to state actors and their activities will have to meet the constitutional standard of equal protection.

Understanding the concept of state action is important. First, where there is no state action, there is no constitutional equal protection claim and women will need other laws, such as the Civil Rights Act, to challenge discrimination. Second, where there is state action, women may be able to challenge discriminatory practices even if no law prohibits the specific acts. For instance, even though no law prohibited single-sex colleges, women students succeeded in integrating the once all-male University of Virginia (UVA) by bringing a constitutional equal protection claim.[4] The Equal Protection Clause was applicable because UVA was a state school, and therefore a state actor.

### Does the Equal Protection Clause prohibit all laws or policies that impact women more than men, even if they do not explicitly differentiate between the two?

No. The Supreme Court has interpreted the Constitution as only addressing state laws and actions that explicitly treat men and women differently —i.e., that are discriminatory on their face—or that can be shown to have been motivated by a desire to harm women—i.e., intentional discrimination.[5] It is not enough to show that the legislature knew that a law might affect women negatively. It must be shown that the law was passed *because of* that negative effect on women.[6] Because this is extremely hard to prove, most laws or policies that do not clearly treat women and men differently will not raise constitutional equal protection problems. For instance, the Supreme Court has upheld a state law giving preference in civil service jobs to veterans. This law clearly had a disparate impact on women because it effectively locked them out of many jobs. In spite of the discriminatory effect of the law, however, the Court decided that it did not violate the Constitution because it was passed out of a desire to help veterans, not to hurt women.[7] In this way, a law or policy may be unfair in its impact on women, without necessarily raising constitutional equal protection issues.

**How do courts decide which laws and actions violate the Equal Protection Clause?**

In deciding whether a particular law or action violates the Equal Protection Clause, courts have used three distinct tests. These tests are difficult to describe precisely or apply mechanically and therefore, in practice, the facts of the case may be just as important as the particular test employed by the court. The test a court uses depends on the classification that the law or action makes and/or the rights that are affected. For instance, a law that makes a classification by race will be analyzed under a different test than a law making a classification by gender or age.

The three tests are the "rational basis" test, the "strict scrutiny" test, and the "intermediate" or "heightened scrutiny" test. Each looks at (1) the government's purpose in passing the law and (2) the relationship between that purpose and the classification used to accomplish it.

**1. *The Rational Basis Test.*** The test the Supreme Court has used in a majority of cases is known as the rational basis test. It is basically a test of reasonableness. Courts ask two questions: (1) Did the state have a reasonable purpose (or "rational basis") for passing the law? and (2) Is there some difference between the two classes or groups of people that makes it reasonable to treat them differently? The law is valid only if the answer to both questions is yes. For example, a government has a legitimate interest in regulating adoption to protect parents and children. However, a law arbitrarily prohibiting people named "Jane" from adopting cannot be understood as rationally related to that purpose. Thus such a law would be invalid under the Equal Protection Clause because it fails the rational basis test.

The rational basis test is the most forgiving and most deferential form of review under the Equal Protection Clause and can be used to avoid a real analysis of a law. While the approach sounds fair, it has often proven virtually meaningless because a court can always find a variety of reasonable purposes for a law. In fact, the Supreme Court has even held that if a court can imagine any conceivable way in which a law or action furthers a legitimate purpose, a law subject to the rational basis test will be sustained.[8] As a result, most laws and policies are upheld under this test.

The Court has occasionally been willing to use the rational basis test to invalidate laws that arbitrarily discriminate between groups of people that for all purposes are indistinguishable and deserve equal treatment.[9] The Court will also sometimes invalidate legislation that was passed because of hostility toward a particular group.[10] For instance, in *Romer v. Evans*, the Court applied the rational basis test in considering whether the Equal Protection Clause prevents a state from adopting a constitutional amendment prohibiting any type of governmental action designed to protect lesbians and gay men from discrimination. The Court held that a law that imposes such a broad legal disability on a single group, in this case lesbians and gay men, can serve no legitimate state purpose, and the law was found to be invalid.[11]

Cases such as this suggest that rational basis review can result in a critical review of discriminatory laws, but it is important to remember that the vast majority of legislation challenged under this level of review is upheld. The difference in the cases where the rational basis test has been used to strike down laws may be more in the character of the law and whether the Court perceives its purpose as discriminatory. It is likely that the Court will continue to apply the rational basis test in a way that mixes fact with law, making outcomes difficult to predict.

**2. *The Strict Scrutiny Test.*** The second test developed by the Supreme Court is known as the strict scrutiny test and is the test most likely to invalidate a law. It is generally applied to laws that classify on the basis of race or national origin, as well as laws affecting certain fundamental rights, such as the right to vote or the right to have children. The classifications that trigger strict scrutiny are called "suspect classifications." Under this test, the courts ask (1) does the state have a compelling interest in passing the law? and (2) is the legal classification absolutely necessary to accomplish that purpose? Courts will critically examine the state's purpose in passing the law or instituting a policy, and will look closely at whether using a particular classification is the only way of achieving that purpose.

An example of strict scrutiny is found in the Supreme Court's analysis of a Florida law that made sexual conduct between an African-American person and a white person illegal, although the same conduct was not illegal if the two persons were either both African-American or both white.[12] The state of Florida argued that its purpose in passing the law was to maintain sexual decency, but the Supreme Court could not find any differences between persons engaging in interracial sex and those engaging in intraracial sex that made it necessary to single out the first group for criminal punishment. In other words, the classification between the two groups was not necessary in order for the state to achieve its purpose of maintaining sexual decency.

Therefore, the law was invalid because it denied, without a valid reason, the equal protection of law to persons who engaged in interracial sex.

Unlike the rational basis test, the strict scrutiny test requires rigorous examination of laws and policies. As a result, it is extremely difficult to show that a law is valid under the strict scrutiny test, and courts tend to find laws unconstitutional under it. Women's rights advocates have long pushed the Court to consider sex a "suspect classification" and to apply strict scrutiny when examining laws or practices that discriminate on the basis of sex. The Court, however, has never done so.

**3. *The Intermediate Scrutiny Test.*** In 1976, the Supreme Court announced a third equal protection test that, thus far, has been applied most often in cases challenging classifications made on the basis of sex. This test is more demanding than the rational basis test and more forgiving than strict scrutiny and, consequently, is referred to as the "intermediate scrutiny" or "heightened scrutiny" test. It provides that classifications by sex are constitutional only if they (1) serve important government objectives and (2) are closely and substantially related to the achievement of those objectives. A law will not pass this test if the law could be written to achieve the same purpose without referring to sex. Likewise, if the law serves no "important" objectives, it is unconstitutional.

The Supreme Court first applied the new test in *Craig v. Boren.*[13] Prior to this case, challenges to sex discrimination were examined under the rational basis test and often upheld. *Craig v. Boren* involved an Oklahoma law that allowed women aged eighteen and over to purchase 3.2 percent beer, or "near" beer (beer with a lower alcohol content), but did not allow men to purchase it until they were twenty-one. The male plaintiff argued that it violated the Equal Protection Clause to treat eighteen- to twenty-year-old men and women differently. Oklahoma attempted to justify the law to the Supreme Court as a measure to improve traffic safety—an important state objective. After examining Oklahoma's statistics on "driving while intoxicated," the Court concluded that the statistical differences in the behavior of young men and women were too insignificant to justify denying beer to the young men. Thus, although promoting driving safety might be a purpose important to Oklahoma, treating men and women differently in allowing them to buy 3.2 percent beer was not closely and substantially related to the accomplishment of that purpose. Other efforts—such as improved education about the dangers of drinking and driving, and better enforcement of drunk driving laws—would have a more direct effect on traffic safety. The Supreme Court has applied this same test in considering gender classifications since then.

In 1996, the Court seemed to alter the intermediate scrutiny test established in *Craig* in *United States v. Virginia*, a case that invalidated an all-male admissions policy at Virginia Military Institute (VMI), a state school.[14] In the VMI case, the Court stated that a classification made on the basis of sex was unconstitutional unless the state "at least" demonstrated that the classification was closely and substantially related to an important state purpose, and could show that it had an "exceedingly persuasive justification" for the all-male policy. This language led many observers to conclude that the Court was applying a more demanding standard to gender classifications.

**Why does it matter which equal protection test a court uses?**

When a court applies a higher level of scrutiny to a law, it is more likely to invalidate discriminatory legislation. For this reason, women's rights groups have pressed for the application of strict scrutiny to all gender-based classifications. However, no majority of the Supreme Court has ever declared sex a suspect classification, like race, that would automatically require "strict scrutiny," although in 1973, four of nine Justices voted to apply this stringent standard to a sexually discriminatory military benefits law.[15] A majority did not emerge for this position, perhaps because some Justices at the time were waiting to see whether an equal rights amendment would pass before applying the strict scrutiny standard.[16]

Meanwhile, the intermediate scrutiny test ensures that the Court will take a more critical look at sexually discriminatory laws than it did in the past using the rational basis test. Although it is an improvement over rational basis analysis, the intermediate scrutiny test still allows courts latitude in deciding whether or not a government action that classifies on the basis of sex violates the Equal Protection Clause. It provides no guarantee that sexually discriminatory laws will be struck down, particularly as the courts, especially the Supreme Court, become more conservative and less concerned with the protection of civil rights and civil liberties in general.[17]

**How does the Constitution treat affirmative action programs that classify on the basis of sex in order to help women?**

This is an important question, and it is largely unresolved. In a 1989 case called *Richmond v. J. A. Croson*, the Court held that strict scrutiny applied to all state and local race-based affirmative action programs.[18] Six years later, in *Adarand Construction, Inc. v. Pena,* the Court held that federal race-based affirmative action programs are subject to strict scrutiny.[19] In other words, a race-based affirmative action program is only constitutional if it is narrowly tailored to serve a compelling government purpose. In the context of employment, these cases have been understood to mean that a race-based affirmative action program is generally only permitted to remedy the effects of a government's own previous acts of race discrimination.

Neither *Croson* nor *Adarand* discussed the proper level of review for gender-based affirmative action programs sponsored by governments, and as a result there is some confusion among the different states. *Croson* and *Adarand* have led some lower courts to review gender-based affirmative action programs under a strict scrutiny level of review, such as that applied to race-based programs.[20] Other courts have applied intermediate scrutiny to gender-based affirmative action programs, while applying strict scrutiny to race-based programs. For instance, a government can offer certain preferences to women in order to make up for discrimination women might face elsewhere in society, but can only offer preferences to racial minorities if the government itself has previously discriminated against those minorities.[21]

The resulting confusion demonstrates some of the problems with equal protection jurisprudence. Holding all remedial affirmative action programs to the requirements of the strict scrutiny test leads to a very strange result, for under such a system state actions discriminating against women will be subject to a lower level of review than gender-conscious state actions meant to *remedy* that discrimination. However, if gender-based affirmative action is subject to less strenuous review than race-based programs, gender-based remedial programs will probably be upheld more often than those remedying race discrimination. This would be inconsistent with a long history of case law that has defined race discrimination as the most serious and malignant form of discrimination, and would be inconsistent with the purposes of the Fourteenth Amendment. The confusion over which standard of review to use for affirmative action programs also leaves unclear what standard should be applied to programs designed to assist women of color.

### Does the Equal Protection Clause prohibit discrimination on the basis of pregnancy?

No. The Equal Protection Clause does not protect women against one of the most persistent forms of sex discrimination—pregnancy discrimination.

In fact, in 1974, the Supreme Court did an extraordinary thing. In a case called *Geduldig v. Aiello*, it held that under the Constitution discrimination on the basis of pregnancy is *not* sex discrimination.[22] The case involved a California state-mandated disability program that replaced workers' wages for every type of physical disability that prevented them from working except for disability periods arising from normal pregnancy and delivery. The Court found that the program did not discriminate between men and women, but rather between pregnant and nonpregnant persons, and thus was sex-neutral and subject only to rational basis review.[23] Fortunately, Congress has passed laws that define pregnancy discrimination as a form of sex discrimination in the employment context and in some education contexts. These laws will protect against pregnancy discrimination in many situations. See chapter 2, "Employment: Discrimination and Parenting Issues," and chapter 4, "Education."

### Is it possible to assert the constitutional right to equal treatment without bringing a lawsuit?

Legal rights can be asserted in informal discussions and negotiations with officials or even in demonstrations and other public events. Merely raising a question of the constitutionality of the actions of public officials will sometimes have an effect on those actions because most public officials do not like to be accused of discrimination. Furthermore, on occasion officials will choose to act in order to avoid being sued. An indication that a woman is ready to pursue a lawsuit may convince officials that she is serious about a claim for fair treatment.

## STATE EQUAL RIGHTS PROVISIONS

### Are there any state constitutional provisions that offer more protection from gender discrimination than the U.S. Constitution?

Yes. Just as the United States has a constitution that guarantees certain rights to its citizens, so do all the states. As of this writing, twenty-three states[24] have constitutions that either explicitly prohibit gender discrimination or contain provisions that have been interpreted to offer more protection from gender discrimination than the U.S. Constitution. Some state constitutional provisions addressing gender discrimination take the form of an equal rights amendment specifically affirming the equality of men and women. Others do not specifically refer to gender, but have been interpreted by state courts to prohibit gender discrimination along with other forms of differential treatment.

Because of these state constitutional guarantees, a woman may enjoy additional protection from discrimination by governments than that offered by the U.S. Constitution. Whether a particular law or action violates a state constitution, however, turns on how that state's courts have interpreted its constitution and the provision prohibiting discrimination. These interpretations vary widely from state to state.

### How do state constitutional protections differ from those of the federal Constitution?

Federal constitutional rights can be understood as a floor rather than a ceiling. In other words, states are free to offer more protection to individual rights than the federal government does as long as state rights do not conflict with the federal provisions. For example, although currently there is no Equal Rights Amendment (ERA) in the federal Constitution, states are free to enact similar provisions in their own state constitutions, and several states have done so. State courts are also free to interpret their own constitutions in ways that provide more protection against gender discrimination than the federal Constitution. For instance, several state courts have held that their constitutions require a higher level of review than the intermediate scrutiny demanded by the federal Constitution. As a result, those courts are more likely to strike down gender-based laws under their state constitutions, and have gone beyond the federal constitutional standard to ban almost all gender distinctions in their laws.

### What level of review do state courts use in gender discrimination cases?

It depends on the state. As mentioned above, many state courts employ a higher standard of review in gender discrimination cases brought under the state constitutional provisions than the federal courts use in equal protection cases. The higher standard of review used by those courts makes it easier to challenge discrimination in those states, because those states are more likely to strike down gender-based laws.

### Absolute Prohibition on Legal Classifications Based on Gender

High courts in five states—Colorado, Maryland, Oregon, Pennsylvania, and Washington[25]—have ruled that practically *all* gender-based classifications are prohibited because their state constitutions impose an absolute standard that eliminates gender as a factor in determining legal rights. This standard is higher even than the strict scrutiny standard in federal cases and the only exception to it is in cases of discrimination based on physical characteristics. For instance, the Pennsylvania Supreme Court declared in one of the first cases interpreting its state ERA that "[t]he thrust of the Equal Rights Amendment is to insure equality of rights under the law and to eliminate gender as a basis for distinction. The gender of citizens . . . is no longer a permissible factor in the determination of their legal rights and responsibilities."[26]

### Strict Scrutiny of Legal Classifications Based on Gender

In eight states—California, Connecticut, Hawaii, Illinois, Massachusetts, New Hampshire, Texas, and Vermont—courts applying the strict scrutiny standard have ruled that gender discrimination should be treated in the same way as race discrimination is treated in federal cases. These states consider gender a suspect classification and apply a strict scrutiny test to gender classifications.[27] A court employing this standard of review will uphold a state legislature's gender-based classification only when the state's "compelling interest justifies the classification and if the impact of the classification is limited as narrowly as possible consistent with its proper purpose."[28] Vermont does not use the federal language of "strict scrutiny" or "suspect class" but has afforded broad protections against gender-based classifications.[29]

Not all states employing strict scrutiny of gender discrimination under their constitutions have traditional ERAs. Strong gender discrimination prohibitions may also stem from less specific constitutional provisions that have been interpreted by state courts to require gender equality.

### Standards Mirroring Federal Intermediate Level of Review

Three states that have adopted ERAs explicitly prohibiting gender discrimination interpret these provisions to mirror the intermediate level of protection afforded by the U.S. Constitution for gender-based classifications. The Louisiana Constitution effectively codifies federal equal protection standards of strict scrutiny for race and intermediate scrutiny for gender,[30] and courts employ the language of intermediate scrutiny in equal protection cases involving classifications based on gender.[31] Alaska uses a "sliding scale" ranging from "relaxed scrutiny to strict scrutiny," with the level of scrutiny being determined by how the court assesses the importance of the rights asserted and how suspiciously the court views the classification scheme.[32] The Virginia Supreme Court has stated that it applies the federal intermediate level of protection to gender classifications.[33] In addition, many states that do not have ERAs also follow the federal standard in interpreting their state constitution's antidiscrimination provisions.

### Unresolved Standards of Review for Legal Classifications Based on Gender

In six states with an ERA—Florida, Iowa, Montana, New Mexico, Utah, and Wyoming—state courts have not definitively settled on a standard of review. The Supreme Courts of Florida and Iowa have not heard any cases brought under their ERAs and, thus, have not had a chance to interpret them. Montana recognizes that the Supreme Court applies intermediate scrutiny to cases involving gender classifications, and has applied a similar "middle tier" test in some cases. It has not clearly articulated a standard of review for sex discrimination challenges under its state constitution, although the fact that Montana's courts have consistently followed the lead of the Supreme Court in analyzing equal protection cases is a strong indication that it will probably continue to do so if faced with a gender discrimination claim.[34] New Mexico uses a sliding scale standard for cases brought under the state's equal protection clause, and has held that "classifications based on gender" trigger an intermediate review.[35] However, New Mexico's Supreme Court has not reconciled this level of review with the state ERA, which expressly prohibits denial of equal protection on the basis of gender.[36] The Utah Court of Appeals has stated, without further explanation, that the state standard is "at least as stringent as the [federal] equal protection intermediate review for gender discrimination."[37] Finally, Wyoming's Supreme Court has limited the civil rights guaranteed by its state ERA to certain circumstances, including "property, marriage, protection by the laws, freedom of contracts, trial by jury, etc.," but has not settled on a level of review.[38]

### Do any state constitutions prohibit nongovernmental gender discrimination?

Some states limit their ERAs to prohibit only gender discrimination by state actors. The reach of these provisions in part depends on how state courts define state actors. For instance, some states understand "state actor" to include state agencies, contract agencies that work for the state, and recipients of state funding. Several states, including Hawaii, New Hampshire, and Virginia, have equal rights amendments that expressly apply only to instances where governmental action is involved.[39] Other state constitutional prohibitions on gender discrimination, however, reach discrimination by private individuals and institutions. For instance, Illinois has two antidiscrimination provisions: one applies only to state action,[40] but the other prohibits discrimination "[by] any employer or in the sale or rental of property."[41] Montana's ERA is very broad and specifically prohibits discrimination by "any person, firm, corporation or institution."[42] Similarly, Pennsylvania has concluded that no state action is necessary to invoke the state ERA,[43] and both Massachusetts[44] and California[45] have found that sexual discrimination in private employment also violates their ERAs.

Sometimes it is hard to tell from the wording of a state constitutional provision whether it reaches private acts of gender discrimination or not. Occasionally a state constitutional provision expressly reaches some kinds of private action and prompts the assumption that it does not reach others. A constitutional provision may appear to require state action, but state courts will nevertheless interpret it to have a broader reach.[46] Finally, in those cases where a state constitutional provision does not expressly require governmental action, some advocates have successfully argued that state equal rights provisions may regulate private conduct that usually cannot be reached under the Fourteenth Amendment.[47]

### Do any state constitutions prohibit discrimination that is unintentional?

Perhaps. As noted, the Equal Protection Clause of the U.S. Constitution applies only to situations of intentional discrimination or facial discrimination. It is not yet clear whether the same limitation applies to all state constitutional antidiscrimination provisions. Some state courts have suggested that policies that are not intended to discriminate against women, but that nonetheless disproportionately burden women, may be challenged under state constitution ERAs. However, there have not yet been any instances where such a theory has been successful.[48] There have been very few cases brought under state equal rights amendments using the disparate impact theory, but some courts have suggested that such a claim may be possible,[49] and Oregon's court of appeals has indicated that its constitution also protects its citizens from unintentional discrimination.[50] Therefore, advocates should not abandon disparate impact as evidence of discrimination under state constitutional equal rights provisions.

## What kinds of gender discrimination cases have been brought under state constitutional provisions?

### Family Law

Most cases have arisen in the area of family law, perhaps because family law is considered the domain of state courts and state laws. For example, state ERAs have been used to invalidate different age minimums for marriage for men and women,[51] to provide reciprocal grounds for divorce for husbands and wives,[52] and to invalidate common law presumptions that property acquired during marriage belongs to the husband.[53]

### Discrimination in Education

State ERAs have also been used to improve girls' educational opportunities, both in the classroom and in school athletic programs. For example, advocates used the Pennsylvania ERA to successfully challenge the "men only" admissions policy of a city high school.[54] The Pennsylvania ERA was also used to challenge the exclusion of women from the Pennsylvania Interscholastic Athletic Association.[55] Washington's ERA was also used to obtain better funding for female athletic programs at a state university.[56] See chapter 4, "Education."

### Economic and Employment Discrimination

State ERAs have also been used to fight economic discrimination against women. For example, in Pennsylvania the ERA was used to eliminate gender differences in insurance rates,[57] and in Colorado the state ERA was used to challenge an employer health insurance policy that did not cover medical expenses associated with normal pregnancy.[58] In employment discrimination, states have differed on whether their ERAs cover sexual harassment. In Pennsylvania, a district court decided that the state constitutional ERA does not provide protection against sexual harassment,[59] but in Montana, the state Supreme Court held that the state's equal protection provision in conjunction with the Human Rights Commission provides the only remedy for sexual harassment.[60] Maryland has invalidated prohibitions on women holding certain jobs,[61] while California's ERA focuses specifically on employment and has been used to invalidate many different forms of gender discrimination.[62] See chapter 2, "Employment."

### Affirmative Action

State constitutional equal rights provisions create an interesting dilemma for courts when they review affirmative action programs. Affirmative action programs generally give some assistance to a historically disadvantaged group, such as women. On the other hand, ERAs and other equal rights provisions generally require formal equality, meaning that politicians, state actors, and some private actors are unable to take actions that categorize people on the basis of gender, race, or another protected characteristic. Affirmative action programs, however, depend on such categories in order to remedy years of discrimination and institutionalized prejudice. Because affirmative action programs categorize people by race or gender, the Equal Protection Clause of the federal Constitution has been used to strike down some affirmative action programs as illegally discriminatory.[63] Surprisingly, few affirmative action programs have been challenged under state constitutions. California has found that an affirmative action program in the Department of Corrections did not violate the equal rights provision of its state constitution,[64] but the state later amended its constitution to specifically prohibit any affirmative action by state actors.[65] Washington used an alternative approach to reconcile equal rights and affirmative action by holding that affirmative action programs do not implicate the state's ERA so long as the law favoring one gender is intended solely to ameliorate the effects of past discrimination.[66]

### Can state constitutions be used to expand reproductive rights?

Yes, state constitutional ERAs can be a source of expanded protections for reproductive rights, as detailed in chapter 6, "Reproductive Freedom." As that chapter notes, state constitutional protections for privacy, liberty, and ERAs can all be sources of expanded rights, where the courts are willing to see their state constitutional protections as independent of the federal Constitution.

### Can ERAs be used in other forms of advocacy besides litigation?

Yes. In some states the passage of the ERA spurred the state legislature to reform state laws to make sure they conformed with the requirements of the ERA. For example, after the ERA was enacted in New Mexico, the legislature established an equal rights committee that reviewed all New Mexico laws and recommended revisions to eliminate discriminatory provisions. Most of the recommendations were eventually adopted.[67]

Furthermore, the presence of an equal rights amendment in a state can be a valuable tool in legislative and administrative advocacy. For example, the women's coalition in Montana, the first (and so far only) state to pass a law prohibiting gender-based insurance rates, used that state's Equal Rights

Amendment as one of the policy reasons why the legislation should be adopted.

State court interpretations of state constitutional provisions may influence other states.[68] For instance, Vermont cited Oregon's interpretation of its constitutional prohibition of gender discrimination when deciding that Vermont's constitution required a high strict scrutiny standard of review for gender distinctions.[69]

State courts' interpretations of their constitutions may also influence the federal judiciary in its interpretation of the U.S. Constitution.[70] For instance, California's adoption of strict scrutiny review for gender classifications in 1971 is considered to be one of the decisions that led the way for the U.S. Supreme Court to begin invalidating laws that discriminated on the basis of gender.[71]

As more states enact their own equal rights amendments and their courts use a higher level of review for gender-based discrimination, federal courts, including the Supreme Court, may feel some pressure to improve the constitutional protections afforded to women. In the absence of a federal Equal Rights Amendment, this may be the best alternative to ensure equality for women across the country.

## CONSTITUTIONAL LIMITS ON ANTIDISCRIMINATION LAWS

**Other than the Equal Protection Clause, what other constitutional provisions affect women's rights and women's equality?**

The Equal Protection Clause is not the only constitutional provision that affects women's rights. The right to privacy is derived from several constitutional amendments and has been used to establish women's rights to decide when and if to have a child, use birth control, and choose an abortion, and thus control their own bodies.[72] See chapter 6, "Reproductive Freedom." The Nineteenth Amendment guarantees a woman's right to vote. Additionally, the Due Process Clause of the Fourteenth Amendment, which says that no person may be deprived of life, liberty, or property without due process of law, may also be used to protect women against discrimination in some situations. For example, this provision has been used to invalidate mandatory leave policies for pregnant women.[73]

In recent years, however, the Supreme Court has made clear that while the Constitution can be an important weapon to fight discrimination against women, it can also be used to invalidate federal laws meant to promote women's equality. Several Supreme Court cases have held that under the Eleventh Amendment of the Constitution, states cannot be sued under various federal antidiscrimination laws. The text of the Eleventh Amendment states that federal courts cannot hear cases brought against a state by citizens of another state or a foreign country, but over the years, many judges have interpreted it more broadly to mean that states cannot be sued by anyone in federal court or under federal law without their consent, with a few important exceptions. One of these exceptions occurs when the federal law is directed at remedying and preventing discrimination that violates the Equal Protection Clause. In such a circumstance, the federal law may be enforced against a state without its consent, if Congress is clear about its intention to do so and the remedy against the state is proportional to the discrimination the law addresses. So far, however, the Supreme Court has held that state employees cannot sue their employer for damages under the Age Discrimination in Employment Act or the employment discrimination provisions of Title I of the Americans with Disabilities Act.[74]

Fortunately, laws designed to remedy discrimination against women have fared somewhat better. In 2003, the Supreme Court decided that state employees denied their rights to take leave to care for family members under the Family and Medical Leave Act (FMLA) could sue the state for money damages.[75] This was an important decision that reaffirmed Congress's power to design laws addressing discrimination at the state level and the federal level and ensured that some victims of discrimination could still have their day in court.

In *Nevada Department of Human Resources v. Hibbs*, the Court acknowledged that the FMLA was passed with the recognition that the burdens of caring for infants and for sick family members fall disproportionately on women, making it more difficult for them to succeed in the workforce. It reasoned that the FMLA attempted to address this reality by protecting the jobs of individuals who needed time off work to tend to certain family responsibilities, and by ensuring that such leave was available to men as well as to women. The Court then went on to hold that the federal court remedy was an appropriate exercise of congressional power given evidence of the persistence of the stereotypes among employers that caregiving was a woman's responsibility, not a man's, and the accompanying discrimination, in spite of previous attempts to address sex discrimination through Title VII of the Civil Rights Act and the Pregnancy Discrimination Act. With this decision, the rights of state employees to enforce the FMLA and certain other laws seeking to ensure that state employers treat their employees in a nondiscriminatory way have been preserved.

## Are there other constitutional limits on federal laws meant to promote women's equality?

Yes. The federal government is a government of limited powers. This means that Congress can only pass a law if the Constitution specifically gives it the power to do so. The Equal Protection Clause, as mentioned above, is one provision often interpreted to allow legislation affecting state practices. The Commerce Clause,[76] which gives Congress the power to pass laws regulating interstate commerce, has also been used to provide the authority for many different kinds of legislation on issues affecting the economy and thus, by extension, interstate commerce. Antidiscrimination laws such as Title VII of the Civil Rights Act of 1964 were enacted under Congress's Commerce Clause power.

In the 1990s, however, for the first time in over fifty years, a bare majority of the Supreme Court began to strike down some federal legislation as exceeding Congress's powers under the Commerce Clause.[77] This new trend in jurisprudence has limited to some extent the federal government's power to pass many sorts of social legislation. For instance, in 2000 the Supreme Court invalidated a portion of the federal Violence Against Women Act (VAWA), a decision of great concern to women's rights advocates throughout the country.

The VAWA,[78] passed in 1994 and reauthorized in 2005, stated that individuals had a civil right to be free from gender-motivated violence[79] and provided a means for victims of such violence, most often women, to go to court to seek damages from their attackers. In *United States v. Morrison*,[80] the Supreme Court held that the VAWA civil rights remedy was simply beyond Congress's powers and therefore unconstitutional. Even after noting that Congress had made extensive findings as to the economic costs of violence against women, the Court held that gender-motivated violence did not substantially affect interstate commerce, and thus the Commerce Clause did not give Congress the power to pass laws on the subject. The Court also reasoned that questions of violence and of family law, like that addressed by the VAWA civil rights remedy, were "truly local" and inappropriate subjects of federal legislation.

This case remains disturbing for women's advocates, for it limits the power of the federal government, which has traditionally been the protector of civil rights in this country. By categorizing matters related to the family as "truly local" and suggesting that the federal government has no power to legislate in these areas, the Supreme Court may be cordoning off from federal law issues that are very important to women's equality, such as domestic violence.

## NOTES

1. *See, e.g.,* Brown v. Bd. of Educ., 347 U.S. 483 (1954).

2. Stanton v. Stanton, 421 U.S. 7 (1975).

3. The decision might violate other laws. See chapter 4, "Education," for a discussion of Title IX of the Education Amendments of 1972.

4. Kirstein v. Rector & Visitors of Univ. of Va., 309 F. Supp. 184 (1970).

5. Pers. Adm'r of Mass. v. Feeney, 442 U.S. 256 (1979), *remanded to* 475 F. Supp. 109 (D. Mass. 1979), *aff'd,* 445 U.S. 901 (1980).

6. Such actions or laws may violate other federal laws, but not the Constitution. See chapter 2, "Employment," and chapter 4, "Education."

7. *Feeney,* 442 U.S. at 281.

8. FCC v. Beach Commc'ns, 508 U.S. 307 (1993) ("[E]qual protection is not a license for courts to judge the wisdom, fairness, or logic of legislative choices. . . . [A] statutory classification that neither proceeds along suspect lines nor infringes fundamental constitutional rights must be upheld against equal protection challenge if there is any reasonably conceivable state of facts that could provide a rational basis for the classification.").

9. Jimenez v. Weinberger, 417 U.S. 628 (1974) (equal protection clause is violated by discriminatory laws relating to the status of birth where classification is justified by no legitimate state interest, compelling or otherwise).

10. Dep't of Agric. v. Moreno, 413 U.S. 528 (1973) ("bare congressional desire to harm a politically unpopular group [in this case "hippies"] cannot constitute a legitimate governmental interest" such as will sustain a legislative classification against an equal protection challenge).

11. Romer v. Evans, 517 U.S. 620 (1996); *see also* City of Cleburne v. Cleburne Living Ctr., 473 U.S. 432 (1985) (using the rational basis test to strike down a zoning ordinance that required special use permits for group homes for the mentally retarded, when the requirement appeared to rest solely on an irrational bias against the mentally retarded).

12. McLaughlin v. Florida, 379 U.S. 184 (1964).

13. 429 U.S. 190 (1976).

14. 518 U.S. 515 (1996).

15. Frontiero v. Richardson, 411 U.S. 677 (1973). The Court invalidated the requirement that women in the military prove their husbands' dependency in order to get medical and housing benefits, while men received them automatically for their wives. The decision's sweeping language—"women's legal status was once like that of slaves"; "romantic paternalism" has "put women not on a pedestal, but in a cage"—should have added to its impact but was never accepted by the full Court.

16. *Id.* at 692 (Powell, J., concurring).

17. *See, e.g.,* Nguyen v. Immigration and Naturalization Serv., 533 U.S. 53 (2001) (finding reasons to differentiate citizenship requirements for children born abroad to unmarried male and female citizens); Michael M. v. Superior Court of Sonoma County, 450 U.S. 464 (1981) (upholding California statutory rape law criminalizing sex with underage girls, but not underage boys).

18. City of Richmond v. J.A. Croson, 488 U.S. 469 (1989).

19. 515 U.S. 200 (1995).

20. Vogel v. Cincinnati, 959 F.2d 594, 599 (6th Cir. 1992) (applying strict scrutiny to a program designed to remedy both race and gender discrimination).

21. Concrete Works of Colo., Inc. v. City & County of Denver, 36 F.3d 1513, 1519 (10th Cir. 1994) (finding two levels of review: one for race and one for gender).

22. 417 U.S. 484 (1974).

23. It is less clear how the Court would rule on a state law that specifically burdens pregnant women, as opposed to one that denies them a benefit. Even if such a law were held not to violate the Equal Protection Clause, in certain circumstances it might still violate the Constitution. In Cleveland Bd. of Educ. v. LaFleur, 414 U.S. 632 (1974), the Supreme Court held that a school board violated the Due Process Clause of the Fourteenth Amendment when it required all pregnant school teachers to take unpaid maternity leave beginning in their fifth month of pregnancy because such a requirement arbitrarily burdened exercise of fundamental decisions about having a family. Other burdens imposed only on pregnant women might also constitute Due Process Clause violations.

24. Alaska, California, Colorado, Connecticut, Florida, Hawaii, Illinois, Iowa, Louisiana, Maryland, Massachusetts, Montana, New Hampshire, New Jersey, New Mexico, Pennsylvania, Oregon, Texas, Utah, Vermont, Virginia, Washington, and Wyoming.

25. *See, e.g.,* Colo. Civil Rights Comm'n v. Travelers Ins. Co., 759 P.2d 1358, 1363 (Colo. 1988) (en banc) ("This constitutional provision . . . requires that legislative classifications based exclusively on sexual status receive the closest judicial scrutiny."); State v. Burning Tree Club, Inc., 554 A.2d 366 (Md. 1989); *see also* Burning Tree Club, Inc. v. Bainum, 501 A.2d 817, 840 (Md. 1985); Rand v. Rand, 374 A.2d 900, 903 (Md. 1977); Hewitt v. State Accident Ins. Fund Corp. (*In re* Williams), 653 P.2d 970, 977–78 (Ore. 1982); Henderson v. Henderson, 327 A.2d 60, 62 (Pa. 1974) (per curiam); Darrin v. Gould, 540 P.2d 882, 888 (Wash. 1975).

26. *Henderson*, 327 A.2d at 62.

27. Sail'er Inn, Inc. v. Kirby, 485 P.2d 529, 539–41 (Cal. 1971); Paige v. Welfare Comm'r, 365 A.2d 1118 (Conn. 1976); Baehr v. Lewin, 852 P.2d 44, 67–68 (Haw. 1993), *reconsideration granted in part* 875 P.2d 225 (Haw. 1993), *superseded by constitutional amendment* HAW. CONST. ART. I, § 23; People v. Ellis, 311 N.E.2d 98 (Ill. 1974); Att'y Gen. v. Mass. Interscholastic Athletic Assn, Inc., 393 N.E.2d 284 (Mass. 1979); Buckner v. Buckner, 415 A.2d 871 (N.H. 1980); In Interest of McLean, 725 S.W.2d 696, 698 (Tex. 1987); Baker v. State, 744 A.2d 864 (Vt. 1999).

28. Lowell v. Kowalski, 405 N.E.2d 135, 139 (Mass. 1980); *see also McLean*, 725 S.W.2d at 698 ("Our reading of the Equal Rights Amendment elevates gender to a suspect classification.").

29. *Baker*, 744 A.2d at 864.

30. LA. CONST. art I, § 3 (2005) ("No person shall be denied the equal protection of the laws. No law shall discriminate against a person because of race or religious ideas, beliefs, or affiliations. No law shall arbitrarily, capriciously, or unreasonably discriminate against a person because of birth, age, gender, culture, physical condition, or political ideas or affiliations.").

31. Pace v. State, 648 So.2d 1302, 1305 (La. 1995) (finding a classification on the basis of gender unconstitutional unless that classification "substantially furthers an important government objective").

32. Keyes v. Humana Hosp. Alaska, Inc., 750 P.2d 343, 357 (Alaska 1988).

33. Archer v. Mayes, 194 S.E.2d 707, 710 (Va. 1973) (holding that equal protection provision under Virginia state constitution is no broader than the Equal Protection Clause of the Fourteenth Amendment of the U.S. Constitution); Schilling v. Bedford City Mem'l Hosp., Inc., 303 S.E.2d 905 (Va. 1983).

34. Butte Cmty. Union v. Lewis, 712 P.2d 1309, 1312–14 (Mont. 1986), *superseded by amendment as stated in* Zempel v. Uninsured Employers' Fund, 938 P.2d 658 (Mont. 1997); *see also* Arneson v. State, 864 P.2d 1245, 1247 (Mont. 1993) (discussing state's intermediate scrutiny test).

35. Marrujo v. N.M. Highway Transp. Dep't, 887 P.2d 747, 751 (N.M. 1994).

36. N.M. CONST., art. 2, § 18 (2006).

37. *In re* Scheller v. Pessetto, 783 P.2d 70, 76 (Utah Ct. App. 1989) (citing Pusey v. Pusey, 728 P.2d 117 (Utah 1986)).

38. *See* Ward Terry & Co. v. Henson, 297 P.2d 213, 215 (Wyo. 1956) (defining civil rights covered by the Wyoming ERA); Johnson v. State Hearing Exam'rs Office, 838 P.2d 158, 164–67 (Wyo. 1992) (discussing the various levels of review); *see also* Paul Linton, *State Equal Rights Amendments: Making a Difference or Making a Statement?* 70 TEMPLE L. REV. 907, 911–15 (1997) (discussing state standards of review).

39. *See generally* Judith Avner, *Some Observations on State Equal Rights Amendments*, 3 YALE L. & POL'Y REV. 144, 149–50 (1984) [hereinafter Avner, *Some Observations*]; Majorie Heins, *The Marketplace and the World of Ideas: A Substitute for State*

*Action as a Limiting Principle under the Massachusetts Equal Rights Amendment,* 18 SUFFOLK U. L. REV. 347 (1984).

40. ILL. CONST. ART. I, § 18 (2006).

41. ILL. CONST. ART. I, § 17 (2006).

42. MONT. CONST. ART. II, § 4 (2005).

43. Bartholomew *ex rel.* Bartholomew v. Foster, 541 A.2d 393, 396 (Pa Commw. Ct. 1988) (concluding that the Pennsylvania ERA has no state action requirement).

44. O'Connell v. Chasdi, 511 N.E.2d 349 (Mass. 1987).

45. Rojo v. Kliger, 801 P.2d 373, 388 (Cal. 1990).

46. *Colo. Civil Rights Comm'n,* 759 P.2d at 1358 (finding private employer and insurance company discriminated on basis of sex in violation of state equal rights amendment and discrimination statute).

47. *See, e.g.,* Burning Tree Club v. Bainum, 554 A.2d at 822; *Darrin,* 540 P.2d at 891 (finding state action because the interscholastic sports system used public funds); Hartford Accident & Indemn. Co. v. Ins. Comm'r, 482 A.2d 542, 549 (Pa. 1984). There are strong policy reasons why a state constitutional provision might be interpreted to prohibit more private discrimination than the federal Constitution. The federal state action doctrine is based in part on federalism concerns and is narrowly construed to protect the states' traditional jurisdiction over private actions. That rationale is arguably irrelevant to the interpretation of a state constitution. *See* LAURENCE H. TRIBE, AMERICAN CONSTITUTIONAL LAW 1691 (1988).

48. One scholar has persuasively argued that all state ERAs should apply to intentional and unintentional types of discrimination. In support of her position, she points to the fact that commissions established by states to ensure statutory compliance with constitutional equal rights provisions have defined the scope of their mandate to include facially neutral laws that have a potentially discriminatory impact. *See* Phyllis Segal, *Sexual Equality, the Equal Protection Clause, and the ERA,* 33 BUFF. L. REV. 85 (1984). For examples of cases where disparate impact theory has to date been unsuccessful *see, e.g.,* Commonwealth v. King, 372 N.E.2d 196 (Mass. 1997) (rejecting equal protection challenge to prostitution statute based on argument that most prostitutes are female); Wendt v. Wendt, 757 A.2d 1225 (Conn. App. Ct. 2000) (establishing an equal protection challenge requires a showing of intentional or purposeful discrimination); *see generally* William C. Duncan, *"The Mere Allusion to Gender": Answering the Charge That Marriage Is Sex Discrimination,* 46 ST. LOUIS U. L.J. 963, 968–70 (2002) (discussing equal protection caselaw and theory).

49. E.g., Snider v. Thornburgh, 436 A.2d 593, 601 (Pa. 1981).

50. Tanner v. Or. Health Scis. Univ., 971 P.2d 435, 447 (Ore. Ct. App. 1988) (regarding denial of insurance policies to same-gender couples).

51. Phelps v. Bing, 316 N.E.2d 775 (Ill. 1974).

52. George v. George, 409 A.2d 1 (Pa. 1979).

53. DiFlorido v. DiFlorido, 331 A.2d 174 (Pa. 1975).

54. Newberg v. Bd. of Pub. Educ., 26 Pa. D. & C.3d 682 (Pa. Com. Pl. 1983). This case illustrates the usefulness of a state ERA as the same admissions policy at the same school had been unsuccessfully challenged previously under the federal Equal Protection Clause. Vorchheimer v. Sch. Dist. of Philadelphia, 532 F.2d 880 (3d Cir. 1976), *aff'd by an equally divided court*, 430 U.S. 703 (1977).

55. Commonwealth v. Pa. Interscholastic Athletic Ass'n., 334 A.2d 839 (Pa. Commw. Ct. 1975).

56. Blair v. Wash. State Univ., 740 P.2d 1379 (Wash. 1987).

57. Bartholomew *ex rel.* Bartholomew v. Foster, 563 A.2d 1390 (Pa. 1989).

58. *Colo. Civil Rights Comm'n*, 759 P.2d at 1358.

59. Hawthorne v. Kintock Group, No. 99 Civ. 3763 (GDH), 2000 WL 199356 (E.D. Pa. Feb 14, 2000).

60. Chance v. Harrison, 899 P.2d 537 (Mont. 1995).

61. Turner v. State, 474 A.2d 1297 (Md. 1984) (invalidating prohibition on female "sitters" at bars).

62. Hardy v. Stumpf, 112 Cal. Rptr. 739 (Cal. Ct. App. 1974) (invalidating height and weight requirements for the Police Department); Badih v. Myers, 43 Cal. Rptr.2d 229 (Cal. Ct. App. 1995), *review denied* Oct. 19, 1995.

63. Adarand Constructors, Inc. v. Pena, 515 U.S. 200 (1995); *Croson*, 488 U.S. 469; Regents of Univ. of Cal. v. Bakke, 438 U.S. 265 (1978).

64. Minnick v. Dep't of Corr., 157 Cal.Rptr. 260 (Cal. App. Ct. 1979).

65. CAL. CONST., art. I, § 31 (Known as Proposition 209, its name under state referendum, it states that "the state shall not discriminate against, or give preferential treatment to, any individual group on the basis of race, gender, color, ethnicity, or national origin in the operation of public employment, public education, or public contracting.").

66. Sw. Wash. Chapter, Nat'l Elec. Contractors Ass'n v. Pierce County, 667 P.2d 1092 (Wash. 1983) (en banc).

67. *See* Avner, *Some Observations, supra* note 39 at 146 n.8.

68. *See Baker*, 744 A.2d at 878 n.10 (citing Oregon's standard of review in Hewitt).

69. *See Baker*, 744 A.2d at 892 (Dooley, J., concurring).

70. *Craig*, 429 U.S. at 208 (discussing different states' review of gender discrimination when shifting from rational basis review to intermediate scrutiny).

71. *Id.* (citing *Sail'er Inn v. Kirby*, 485 P.2d at 539 (striking down a provision of the state's business and professional code that prohibited the hiring of women as bartenders under strict scrutiny review)).

72. Roe v. Wade, 410 U.S. 113 (1973); *see generally* Laurence H. Tribe, *The Abortion Funding Conundrum: Inalienable Rights, Affirmative Duties, and the Dilemma of Dependence*, 99 HARV. L. REV. 330 (1985); Ruth Bader Ginsburg, *Some Thoughts on Autonomy and Equality in Relation to Roe v. Wade*, 63 N.C.L. REV. 375 (1985).

73. Cleveland Bd. of Educ. v. LaFleur, 414 U.S. 632 (1974) (finding mandatory leave policies for pregnant women unconstitutional under the Due Process Clause of the Fourteenth Amendment); *see also* T. B. DeLouth, *Pregnant Drug Addicts as Child Abusers: A South Carolina Ruling*, 14 BERKELEY WOMEN'S L.J. 96 (1999) (discussing due process concerns as relating to the criminalization of substance abuse while pregnant).

74. Kimel v. Fla. Bd. of Regents, 528 U.S. 62 (2000); Bd. of Trs. of Univ. of Ala. v. Garrett, 531 U.S. 356 (2001).

75. Nev. Dept. of Human Res. v. Hibbs, 538 U.S. 721 (2003).

76. U.S. CONST, art. I, § 8 (2006).

77. United States v. Lopez, 514 U.S. 549 (1995).

78. Violence Against Women Act of 1994, Pub. L. No. 103-322, 108 Stat. 1902 (codified as amended in scattered sections of 8, 16, 20, 28, and 42 U.S.C.).

79. 42 U.S.C.A. § 13981 (2005).

80. 529 U.S. 598 (2000).

# II

# Employment: Discrimination and Parenting Issues

Women have made many advances in the American workplace since the enactment of the Civil Rights Act of 1964,[1] yet they continue to experience gender, race, and other forms of discrimination in employment. Statistics on the sex segregation of workers and on the undervaluation of women's wages, as well as the individual experiences of many women, suggest that many employers in the United States continue to discriminate against female employees on a regular basis. Data on race discrimination also show that employment policies and practices continue to harm women of color. Such discrimination significantly reduces women's earnings and is illegal.

When it was passed, one of the goals of Title VII of the Civil Rights Act of 1964 ("Title VII") was to eliminate this pervasive employment discrimination against women. Indeed, women today represent half of the paid workforce. Yet many women, particularly women of color and immigrant women, remain confined to low-paying, low-status jobs that provide little or no opportunity for advancement. This chapter will discuss types of unlawful discrimination under Title VII and the Equal Pay Act, the right to take medical time off to care for oneself or a close family member, including a new child, under the Family Medical Leave Act (FMLA), and how to enforce those rights.

## What is employment discrimination?

In legal terms, employment discrimination occurs when one employee is treated worse than other employees on the basis of an inherent characteristic, such as gender, race, national origin, or religion. In practice, gender discrimination takes many forms. The most conspicuous kind of gender discrimination exists when an employer openly states that he or she pays female employees less than male employees, or tells a talented secretary that she'll never be promoted to a managerial position unless she engages in sexual relations with the manager. But such blatant examples only begin to tell the story. Rather, discrimination today tends to be a far more complex and pervasive phenomenon.

### Haven't women already achieved on-the-job equality?

No. Although women have come a long way in establishing their equal rights on the books, many women, especially poor women, women of color, and immigrant women, do not enjoy these rights in practice. Little change has been made for women in the most precarious employment situations, where they are often sexually harassed, are given lower-paying "women's work," are paid less than men for performing equivalent jobs, and face other workplace abuses. Additionally, women across the economic spectrum still face obstacles in acquiring access to and maintaining positions in traditionally male fields. In fact, in 2006, women were still over 97 percent of all secretaries, 92 percent of all receptionists, and 92 percent of all registered nurses.[2] Men, on the other hand, were 94 percent of all mechanics and repairers, 97 percent of all electricians, 96 percent of all firefighters, 94 percent of all pilots, and 85 percent of all police officers.[3] With some occasional exceptions, women also tend to be excluded from upper-level positions in administration and management.

### Under what laws is it illegal to discriminate against women workers?

Several major federal laws and many state and city laws forbid such discrimination. The federal laws are (1) Title VII of the 1964 Civil Rights Act, as amended by the Pregnancy Discrimination Act of 1978, and by the Civil Rights Act of 1991; (2) the Equal Pay Act; and (3) Executive Order No. 11,246 (as amended by Executive Order No. 11,375). Teachers have additional relief under Title IX of the Education Amendments of 1972.[4]

## The Basics of Title VII of the Civil Rights Act

**What is Title VII?**

Title VII of the 1964 Civil Rights Act is a federal law that was enacted to protect employees from workplace discrimination.

**What types of discriminatory conduct are prohibited?**

Title VII prohibits discrimination on the bases of gender, pregnancy, color, race, national origin, and religion. It prohibits discrimination in hiring, termination, promotion, compensation, and any other condition or privilege of employment. Employers are also not permitted to segregate or classify employees in a manner that would limit opportunities because of the abovementioned characteristics.

**Which employees are covered by Title VII?**

The protections of Title VII apply to everyone who works at a place with at least fifteen employees, employment agencies, and labor organizations. Title VII also protects teachers and employees of state and local governments. A woman may file a charge of discrimination on her own, or an organization can file on her behalf. Workers afraid that their employer will find out and fire them if they file charges should ask an organization to file for them. However, the organization filing the charge must get the employee's authorization. If an organization files, the Equal Employment Opportunity Commission ("EEOC") will ask for the worker's name and address, but will keep this information confidential.

Under Title VII, unions are also considered "persons."[5] Since any injured "person" can file a charge, a union can file a charge on its own behalf or on behalf of one or more of its members. A union may therefore file a charge against a female member's employer challenging a discriminatory action or policy that has affected her without getting her authorization or submitting her name to the EEOC. In addition, Title VII applies to United States citizens working for American companies abroad, but only where it would not violate foreign law to prohibit discrimination.[6]

**Who can be held legally responsible for discriminatory conduct?**

Four kinds of entities can be held responsible for discrimination under Title VII: an employer, a labor union, an employment agency, and, in some cases, a joint labor-management committee controlling apprenticeship or training. Title VII requires that the employer have at least fifteen employees and that the labor union have at least fifteen members. Finally, an employer is defined as the company, not individuals who work at that company. For example, if Supervisor Smith at ACME Corporation discriminates against female employees, ACME Corporation, *not* Supervisor Smith, is the entity to be charged with discrimination.

### How do women prove that they have suffered discrimination on the basis of their sex?

To have a legal claim of workplace discrimination, a woman must be able to point to her sex, or other inherent characteristic, as the reason for the discriminatory treatment. The methods by which a plaintiff must prove discrimination are different for an intentional discrimination claim than for a disparate impact claim. For instance, discrimination in hiring can result from an *intent* to keep women out of the workplace (intentional discrimination), or from seemingly neutral hiring criteria, such as physical strength, that operate to exclude more women than men from the job (disparate impact).

To succeed on a claim of intentional discrimination, a plaintiff must prove that gender played a role in the decision-making process. This is all that is necessary even in a "mixed-motive" case, in which the employer may have one or more permissible reasons, in addition to the impermissible consideration of gender, for refusing to hire or promote, or for dismissing, a woman.[7] The woman will win her case by showing that her gender affected her treatment; however, she will not be able to recover any monetary damages if the employer can show that it would have made the same decision even had it not been influenced by her sex. Regardless of whether the employer makes this showing, the woman is still entitled to a court order against the discrimination, in addition to attorneys' fees. There may be severe limits on the plaintiff's ability to recover attorneys' fees, however. See the section on Title VII enforcement, below, for a discussion.

In alleging disparate impact discrimination, a plaintiff may point to a specific policy or practice that has an adverse or negative impact on women compared to men, or show that the various elements of the employer's decision-making process are "not capable of separation for analysis."[8] Once the plaintiff has done this, the employer has the burden of proving that the challenged employment practice is "job related for the position in question and required by business necessity."[9] The Civil Rights Act of 1991 does not define "business necessity," so courts may interpret the requirement with varying degrees of strictness. One formulation that is widely followed is that there must be an "*overriding legitimate business purpose* such that the practice is necessary to the safe and efficient operation of the business."[10]

### Is it unlawful to retaliate against an individual who opposes unlawful discriminatory practices?

Yes. Under Title VII, it is unlawful to retaliate against an individual for objecting to any form of illegal discrimination, or for filing a discrimination claim.

### What about people who face discrimination for more than one characteristic?

Discrimination on the basis of at least two of the protected classes within Title VII, such as race and sex, or sex and national origin, is often called "intersectional discrimination." For instance, discrimination against an African-American woman based on her race and sex is intersectional discrimination.

In 1980, an appeals court held for the first time that black women could sue their employers for discrimination against a class of black female employees, even though the employer in question did not discriminate against black men or white women.[11] For many years, courts refused to recognize intersectional discrimination: it was not considered sex discrimination because the employer treated white women well, and was not race discrimination because black men did not suffer discrimination. Even now, many courts are reluctant to allow women of color to base their claims on discrimination against them as women of color, and not all courts will accept the theory.

## PREGNANCY DISCRIMINATION

### What rights does the Pregnancy Discrimination Act of 1978 cover?

The Pregnancy Discrimination Act (PDA), an amendment to Title VII, expanded the definition of discrimination "on the basis of sex" to prohibit employers from making pregnancy-based distinctions, which include distinctions based on women's fertility, past abortions or contemplation of abortion,[12] or single status with children.[13] Thus, if women are capable of performing the major functions necessary to the job, employers with fifteen or more employees may not

- **refuse to hire** women because they are or may become pregnant.[14] (In general, employers may not question a female applicant about her prior pregnancies, childcare arrangements, marital status, or other such concerns if they do not make similar inquiries of male applicants.)[15]
- **fire** employees because they are or may become pregnant.[16]
- **deny a promotion or demote** employees because they are or may become pregnant.
- **force the taking of pregnancy or maternity leave**.
- **provide less favorable disability benefits** to employees based on pregnancy than to nonpregnant employees who are temporarily disabled.[17] Employers must give pregnant women the same level of rights and benefits given to other workers with medical conditions that prevent them from working for a short period of time. For example, if an employer grants an employee undergoing heart surgery paid sick leave or light duty upon return, pregnant employees are also entitled to paid leave or light duty.[18] In short, disabled pregnant women must be treated like all other sick or disabled employees in all employment policies relating to sickness or disability, whether they include modified tasks, alternative assignments, extended unpaid leaves, disability leave, paid leave, or insurance coverage.[19]
- **discriminate against welfare recipients**. Welfare recipients who are employed through certain welfare-to-work programs, such as a workfare program, or placed in jobs by a job placement agency or state welfare office, also have a right to be free from pregnancy discrimination.

### May an employer fire a pregnant employee for no longer being able to perform certain job duties?

If an employee can no longer perform her job in a satisfactory manner because of pregnancy or pregnancy-related complications, an employer may fire or take some other adverse employment action against her, but only if the employer would have done the same for other nonpregnant employees in a comparable situation.

However, an employer *may not* refuse to hire, or take adverse employment action against, a pregnant employee because the employer *thinks* she will be unfit to perform her job duties.[20] "The Pregnancy Discrimination

Act addresses 'the stereotype that women are less desirable employees because they are liable to become pregnant' and 'insure[s] that the decision whether to work while pregnant [is] reserved for each individual woman to make for herself.' "[21] For example, in one case, a department store violated the PDA when it withdrew a job offer to a woman in the sixth month of pregnancy after it wrongfully assumed that she "would be absent from work for an indeterminate period sometime in the future."[22] Likewise, a security company was found to have violated the PDA when it fired a security guard who was nine months pregnant. The employer could not show that the employee was no longer capable of performing her job duties, which included checking hourly each of twelve floors of an apartment complex, detaining troublemakers until the police arrived, and assisting tenants in distress.[23]

Courts have drawn a fine line between employers' ability to fire a pregnant woman because of a perception that pregnant women could not perform the job, and firing a pregnant woman because she actually cannot perform the job at a satisfactory level. In general, if an employer would have fired a comparable nonpregnant employee for the same level of performance, it may fire a pregnant woman for no longer being able to perform her duties as before. Under the PDA, an employer need not accommodate a pregnant woman's needs, even if it can easily do so. For example, in one case where a pregnant employee missed eight days of work, worked less than full days on six other days, and was late on three days within a three-month probationary period, the employer could fire her for absenteeism and lateness even though her absences were pregnancy related.[24] Similarly, a university could legally fire a graduate assistant whose performance was good before her pregnancy but dropped when she returned to her studies after childbirth.[25] Some courts will consider an employer's intent in firing a pregnant employee who can no longer perform her duties well. For instance, where an employer daycare center fired a pregnant employee because she was "too ho-hum" and walked around with her head down, not smiling, the employer could have violated the PDA depending on the motive for the dismissal.[26]

### Do pregnant employees or working parents have the right to light duty, or reasonable accommodations in workload?

Yes, if other similarly situated, nonpregnant employees have access to light duty or reasonable accommodations in workload. The PDA grants pregnant women freedom from discrimination, but does not require "preferential treatment." Therefore, unless it can be shown that the employer treated similarly situated, nonpregnant employees more favorably, an employer has no obligation to grant pregnant women light duty at the workplace. Courts generally have upheld employers' refusals to accommodate pregnant employees with light duty assignments. For example, in *Brinkman v. Kansas Department of Corrections,* a court did not find pregnancy discrimination when the State Department of Corrections failed to accommodate a corrections officer's arthritic pain in the ankles caused by pregnancy.[27] While her physician recommended that she be placed on light duty because of medical aggravation due to prolonged walking and standing, the Department of Corrections continued to place her on assignments not considered light duty, including escorting prisoners and staffing a maximum security visiting room and a tower that required climbing stairs and walking around.[28] The court noted that the plaintiff failed to prove disparate treatment because she lacked evidence that other employees requesting accommodations had been treated more favorably.[29]

Where employers have policies granting light duty assignments only to workers injured on the job, courts have split over whether the same accommodation should extend to pregnant employees. In *Ensley-Gaines v. Runyon,* the Sixth Circuit Court of Appeals held that a pregnant employee could show illegal sex discrimination if an employer permits workers injured on the job to perform light duty, but excludes workers disabled from pregnancy from doing so.[30] The court dismissed the distinction for on-site or off-site injury as irrelevant in the pregnancy context, holding that:

When Congress enacted the PDA, instead of merely recognizing that discrimination on the basis of pregnancy constitutes unlawful sex discrimination under Title VII, it provided additional protection to those "women affected by pregnancy, childbirth or related medical conditions" by expressly requiring that employers provide the same treatment of such individuals as provided for "other persons not so affected but similar in their ability or inability to work."[31]

In contrast, the Fifth and Eleventh Circuit courts of appeals have upheld employers' policies excluding pregnant employees from light duty because the nature of their "injury" occurred off the job and only a limited number of light-duty positions existed. In doing so, the courts held that the proper comparison group for employees disabled by pregnancy is the class of workers injured off the job, not on the job. For instance, in *Spivey v. Beverly Enterprises, Inc.,* the employer fired a pregnant certified nurse's assistant because her physician had restricted her from heavy lifting.[32] The

Eleventh Circuit held that it was not discriminatory for the employer to provide modified duty to workers injured on the job, but not to workers suffering from pregnancy-related conditions, where only a limited number of light-duty tasks were available.[33]

### Can an employer exclude women from jobs involving fetal risk?

No. Employers may not exclude pregnant employees from jobs out of fear of harm to pregnant employees or fetuses.[34] In occupations that involve manual labor like heavy lifting, serving tables where floors are slippery, or exposure to dangerous chemicals, courts have held employers liable for any discriminatory, pregnancy-based distinctions. For example, in *Schneider v. Jax Shack, Inc.,* a court held that an employer could not legitimately demote a pregnant employee from bartender to part-time cocktail waitress out of fear that she would slip on the floor or be injured from heavy lifting.[35]

In addition, employers may not prohibit fertile or pregnant women from working in jobs that entail substantial risk of harm to fetuses via exposure to hazardous substances. In 1991, the Supreme Court ruled in *International Union, UAW v. Johnson Controls* that an employer's policy of excluding all fertile women, regardless of their childbearing intentions, from jobs because of potential fetal injury due to lead exposure, was illegal discrimination based on sex.[36] The Court found that instead of improving workplace conditions for all workers, the company chose to disregard risk of lead exposure to fertile male workers while "protecting" women by denying them jobs.[37] The Court held that women—not their employers—should be the ones to choose between their reproductive and economic roles.[38]

For employers to sustain a policy barring all pregnant women from the workplace, the employer must show a "bona fide occupational qualification" (BFOQ)—i.e., that "substantially all" pregnant workers are incapable of performing the job, and that the duties at stake are not only central to the employee's job performance but the "essence" of the particular business.[39] This is a very difficult standard to meet.

State job discrimination laws may further expose employers to liability for implementing discriminatory fetal protection policies. In California, for instance, a court found that an employer's sex-based policies violated the state's Fair Employment and Housing Act.[40] Overall, court decisions seem to recommend that employers facing liability make the workplace safer for all workers, or adopt neutral fetal protection policies applicable to both fertile male and fertile female employees.

**May an employer require a pregnant woman to sign a release limiting an employer's liability for injury?**

As long as an employer treats a pregnant employee the same as any other employee with medical restrictions, it may require her to sign a release limiting the employer's liability in the event of a workplace injury. For instance, a hospital that asked a pregnant employee to sign a statement agreeing to work with a risk of injury because she had a medical restriction from heavy lifting was not found liable under the PDA.[41] The court reasoned that the employee could not prove discrimination because she presented no evidence that the employer treated pregnancy differently from other conditions limiting employees' ability to lift.[42] The court noted that another pregnant employee, who had no medical restriction on lifting, continued to work despite her pregnancy and was not asked to sign a release.[43]

**Can a pregnant employee refuse specific assignments that involve fetal risk?**

While employers may not exclude women from work based on the risk of harm posed to the women or their fetuses, employers are not required to accommodate pregnant employees who request alternative, safer work. This is the case because courts have held that pregnant employees are not entitled to "preferential treatment."[44]

Several cases have arisen in the health-care context, where pregnant employees have feared risk of exposure to infectious diseases. In *Armstrong v. Flowers Hospital*, a pregnant nurse was fired because she refused to care for an HIV-positive patient.[45] She argued that she felt forced to choose between her job and the health of her fetus because she was afraid of contracting infections. The Eleventh Circuit held that her employer was not required to make alternative work available to pregnant employees.[46] Similarly, in *EEOC v. Detroit-Macomb Hospital Corp.*, the Sixth Circuit held that a hospital could legitimately place pregnant nurses on involuntary leave if they were medically restricted from entering isolation rooms.[47] In holding as it did, the court noted that all employees on temporary medical restrictions were placed on similar leave.[48]

**Do pregnant employees or working parents have a right to refuse to work overtime or during nights or weekends?**

No. Under the PDA, pregnant women who are able to work must be permitted to work under the same conditions as other employees. Therefore, most employers who hire employees with the expectation that they will work overtime or during nights or weekends have not been held liable under the PDA for firing employees unable to work such shifts due to pregnancy. In addition, where employers offer to demote pregnant employees to non-overtime positions, or require similarly situated employees to work nights and weekends, courts have declined to find pregnancy discrimination. For example, in *Haas v. Phoenix Data Processing, Inc.,* where an employee refused to work overtime due to childcare concerns and pregnancy, the court held that the company's proposed alternatives—demotion to a position that didn't require overtime, or discharge—did not violate the PDA.[49] Similarly, in *Elie v. K-Mart Corp.,* the court held that a manager at a K-Mart store did not violate the PDA when, after reassigning a pregnant employee to light duty due to medical restrictions, he demoted her to a service desk job that required her to work during some nights and weekends, and then fired her because she could not work those hours due to childcare difficulties.[50] The court noted that the employer had also required other, nonpregnant employees with similar medical restrictions to work nights and weekends while on light duty.[51]

However, when plaintiffs have shown that employers previously accommodated the needs of nonpregnant employees or discharged the plaintiffs with discriminatory intent, courts have found illegal sex discrimination. In one case, an advertising agency fired a secretary who submitted a physician's recommendation that she work fewer than forty hours a week due to pregnancy-related back pain, nausea, and headaches.[52] Even though her position entailed working overtime, the court found that the employer engaged in illegal pregnancy discrimination, in part because the employer had never inquired into the physical conditions of other employees who had requested accommodation.[53]

**Do pregnant employees or working parents have a right to flex-time?**

No. Employees wishing to care for a newborn or a newly adopted child may work part-time *only if their employer agrees to the arrangement.* If the employer refuses to let an employee work less than full-time, courts generally have not found pregnancy discrimination, unless the employer has accommodated the work schedules of other similarly situated male or nonpregnant employees. For instance, in *Spina v. Management Recruiters of O'Hare,* a court found that a business's refusal to allow an employee to reduce her schedule from a four-day workweek to a three-day workweek to care for her young child did not constitute sex discrimination under the PDA.[54] The plaintiff could not prove that other, similarly situated employees received more favorable treatment: one temporarily disabled employee still worked the same number of hours per week before and after surgery, while another remained a full-time employee while missing days "here and there" for medical reasons.[55] Similarly, a court found that a campaign committee did not violate the PDA when it fired an employee who was working part-time due to pregnancy and childcare concerns.[56] The court observed that the campaign had launched a new program that demanded the plaintiff's full-time attention and that the plaintiff was not incapable of working full-time.[57]

### May an employer fire pregnant employees or working parents for excessive absences?

Yes. Under the PDA, many courts have found that employers may legitimately fire an employee for excessive absences due to pregnancy or childbirth, as long as they do not overlook comparable absences of nonpregnant employees or violate company policy.[58] In *Troupe v. May Department Stores Company*, the Seventh Circuit found no pregnancy discrimination in a pregnant employee's discharge for chronic lateness, even though the discharge occurred one day before the employee's maternity leave, and despite evidence that she was being fired because of the suspicion that she would not return to work after childbirth.[59] The court held that employees could not successfully bring pregnancy discrimination claims unless they could show that employers had treated nonpregnant employees with similar problems in a more favorable manner.[60] The court noted that "[t]he Pregnancy Discrimination Act does not . . . require employers to offer maternity leave or take other steps to make it easier for pregnant women to work—to make it as easy, for example, as it is for their spouses to continue working during pregnancy. Employers can treat pregnant women as badly as they treat similarly affected but nonpregnant employees. . . ."[61]

However, in *Byrd v. Lakeshore Hospital*, the Eleventh Circuit took a different approach and held that if a pregnant employee has accumulated enough sick leave to cover her extensive absences, an employer may not discharge her for excessive absenteeism.[62] Discrimination was found even in the absence of specific information that nonpregnant employees were not fired, or otherwise treated differently, for availing themselves of the company's sick leave benefits.[63]

In cases where a pregnant employee is absent, but not *excessively* absent, many courts have found that discharge constitutes illegal pregnancy discrimination. For instance, in *Troy v. Bay State Computer Group, Inc.*, the First Circuit held that evidence of a supervisor's discharge of a pregnant employee because of stereotypical attitudes about pregnancy, rather than for poor attendance, supported a finding of gender discrimination.[64] In *Gallo v. John Powell Chevrolet, Inc.*, a trial court likewise found that a pregnant salesperson's absences could not be considered excessive under any reasonable standard, and that the reasons given by the car dealer for termination were merely pretextual.[65] In another case, a court held that because the evidence showed that the person fired was an able and competent employee who missed no deadlines, there was sufficient evidence to support a finding of pretext for illegal discrimination.[66] Moreover, in *Nichols v. Electronic Crystals Corp.*, the court recognized that if, as a fired pregnant employee alleged, her company permitted insufficient sick leave, and such a policy had a disparate impact on pregnant women, this would constitute pregnancy discrimination.[67]

Additionally, the PDA prohibits an employer from causing a pregnant employee to be absent with the intent of eventually discharging her for excessive absenteeism. In *Kelber v. Forest Electric Corp.*, a pregnant employee who had already had a substantial number of absences from work was transferred from a heated, indoor job site to an outdoor job site in the middle of winter.[68] The court held that the employer engaged in illegal discrimination under the PDA if the employer had changed the working conditions with the intent of increasing the employee's absences so that the employer would have an excuse to fire the employee.[69]

## Wage Discrimination

### What federal laws forbid wage discrimination?

Title VII and the Equal Pay Act are both used to combat wage discrimination.

### What is wage discrimination?

There are two main types of wage discrimination. The more straightforward form of discrimination, prohibited by the Equal Pay Act,[70] consists of paying women less than men for doing the same job. While this practice is blatantly illegal, women must satisfy the technical requirements of the Equal Pay Act, detailed below, in order to sue successfully.

The less obvious form of wage discrimination arises from the segregation of men and women into different jobs. When men and women perform technically different jobs, employers can pay them different wages without violating the Equal Pay Act.[71] Despite the fact that job segregation itself is illegal, it persists.

The practice of setting salaries lower for predominantly female jobs than for predominantly male jobs is quite prevalent, and results in an average female worker still earning roughly eighty-one cents for every dollar earned by a man.[72] Further breakdown of these statistics by race reveals even greater disparities: in 2003, for every dollar earned by a white male, African-American women earned sixty-six cents, and Hispanic women earned fifty-four cents.[73] Many discrimination experts believe the reason is the historic and systematic undervaluation of wages in predominantly female jobs, on the basis of sex and race. Whether this is unlawful or not is unclear, although the Supreme Court removed one important stumbling block to the goal of making it illegal in a 1981 case, *County of Washington v. Gunther*.[74] In this case, the Supreme Court held that Title VII does not require a showing that a man and woman are performing the same job, or "equal work," before a plaintiff can prove the existence of sex-based discrimination in her wages.[75]

## Challenging Wage Discrimination under the Equal Pay Act

### What does the Equal Pay Act forbid?

The name of this law suggests the answer: companies may not pay women who are doing the same work as men less than they pay those men. However, "equal pay for equal work" is not as simple as it first appears; the work of the men and women must be compared against certain standards to determine whether it is equal work requiring equal pay.

First, both the men and the women must work in the same "establishment"—that is, a distinct place of business or location (such as a complex of buildings). The job of each must require equal skill, equal effort, and equal responsibilities, with each factor to be examined separately. The work must be performed under similar working conditions. Finally, the work itself must be "equal," which means that the tasks involved in a woman's job are substantially equal, even if not identical, to those in a man's job. If any one of these standards is not fulfilled, a company does not violate the Equal

Pay Act when it pays women less than men, which leaves companies with a lot of loopholes.

### May a company avoid complying with the Equal Pay Act by transferring all the men who receive higher wages into another job so that only women are left doing the first job at the lower rate?

No. Once the company establishes a higher rate for men, it must pay women that rate even after the men are transferred out. It would also violate Title VII to transfer workers, women or men, out of a job on the basis of sex.

### May a company comply with the Equal Pay Act by lowering the wages of the more highly paid men?

No. One of the provisions in the law says that companies must always raise the wages of the lower-paid sex (almost always women) and not lower the wages of the other sex.[76]

### May a company avoid the Equal Pay Act by giving men extra duties, such as heavy lifting?

No, although several companies have tried to do this. The Equal Pay Act requires that women must compare their jobs to "substantially equal," but not necessarily *identical*, jobs held by men.[77] Extra job duties that take little time or are of peripheral importance do not make a man's job different for purposes of the law.[78] For example, when the Wheaton Glass Company was sued, in order to try to justify higher wages for men it listed seventeen extra tasks its male selector-packers had to perform, but the court found that the work of both male and female workers was substantially equal and warranted equal pay.[79]

### What kinds of jobs have been found to be equal under the Equal Pay Act, forcing companies to raise the wages of women workers?

Jobs found to be equal include those of nurses' aides and orderlies in hospitals; assembly line workers in factories, where some of the men do a little heavy lifting; janitors and maids in colleges; and salesclerks in department stores, no matter what kind of merchandise they sell. Other "female" jobs that courts have held to be the same as men's are bank teller, laboratory technician, inspector, press operator, machine operator, and packer. Conversely, jobs found to be unequal include math professors and science professors, where the science professor had extra lab responsibilities, or where one job included more supervisory responsibility than another. In any case, women who suspect they are being paid less than men for doing the same work should consider challenging the practice and consult with an attorney.

**May a company avoid responsibility for paying unequal wages if it is done in response to a union's threat to strike?**

No. It is just as illegal for a union to try, by any method, to force un-equal wages on the company as it is for the company to pay them. In such a situation, both the union and the company have violated the law.[80]

**Which federal agency enforces the Equal Pay Act?**

The Equal Employment Opportunity Commission (EEOC) administers this law.

### Challenging Wage Discrimination under Title VII When Women and Men Have Different Jobs

**Can an employment practice be legal under the Equal Pay Act, but illegal under Title VII?**

Yes. As the previous section indicated, the Equal Pay Act covers one very narrowly defined form of wage discrimination. In contrast, Title VII covers a wide range of discriminatory practices and can be used to force changes in employment practices that the Equal Pay Act cannot. For instance, a com-pany that assigns all its assembly line work to men and all its clerical work to women, with the men receiving higher salaries than women, does not violate the Equal Pay Act because the jobs are not equal. But this practice does violate Title VII because the company has assigned jobs on the basis of sex and denied women higher-paying jobs. The women could sue under Title VII to force the company to integrate the two jobs and to recover the income lost in the past. Integration would be a major change in employ-ment patterns, and it would probably lead to other changes as well. The male workers in the clerical jobs might well force the wage scale up—which would also benefit the female clerical workers. Viewed in this light, Title VII offers a far greater chance for meaningful change in employment practices than the Equal Pay Act.

**How can women prove that they are being underpaid on the basis of gender when they are doing different work from that of men?**

Although the Supreme Court's *Gunther* decision seemed to pave the way for further action on a variety of forms of wage discrimination, the problem that remains is how to prove that particular "women's jobs" are worth the same as the more highly paid "men's jobs" and that some portion of the wage differential is due to gender discrimination. On this issue, the Court expressed no opinion except to mention various statistical and comparative methods.

Two primary methods for proving equal worth have emerged since the *Gunther* decision. One method is the use of job evaluation studies, which allot points for various factors of a job and permit comparisons between jobs. Court decisions since the *Gunther* ruling, however, have not been particularly encouraging where women have sought to prove discrimination through the use of job evaluation studies. A second method, which may prove more successful, is regression analysis, a statistical method of sorting out the effects of various factors on salary. In 1986, the Supreme Court in *Bazemore v. Friday* accepted the use of regression analysis for proving wage discrimination in a case involving black employees who had been underpaid because of their race.[81] The plaintiffs' regression analysis examined the influence of race, education, tenure, and job title, and showed that race affected salary.[82] After the *Bazemore* decision, female faculty at Yeshiva University's College of Medicine also used a multiple regression analysis to prove that they were underpaid on the basis of their gender as compared to male faculty doing work in a different kind of department.[83] Men were concentrated in higher-paid clinical departments while women were in lower-paid preclinical departments.[84] Given these cases, this method may offer hope to other women trying to address systemic wage discrimination through litigation.[85]

**What steps can be taken by women who want to challenge wage discrimination?**

Women can file charges with the EEOC and initiate lawsuits. See the section on enforcement in this chapter for detailed information.

On the national level, advocates can lobby for an amendment to broaden the scope of Title VII. Many countries, including the United Kingdom, Canada, Australia, Germany, France, and Finland, explicitly require and enforce equal pay for work of equal value (a broader concept than equal pay for equal work). On the state level, female workers can file lawsuits under state fair employment practice laws and advocate for amended state laws. They can also push their unions to take action or, in the absence of unions, organize with other women to bargain with their employer.

Another suggestion would be for an individual or advocates to request a job evaluation plan if none exists, and make sure that there is close review of existing job evaluation plans. Oversight of a job evaluation plan is useful to determine whether some job elements common to "men's jobs" (e.g., heavy lifting) have been overrated in value while other job elements common to "women's jobs" (e.g., the manual dexterity and speed in typing) have been underrated. Close attention is also needed to ensure that all elements of women's jobs are given points or that men are not given points for tasks they do not perform.

## SEXUAL HARASSMENT

**What is the definition of sexual harassment on the job?**

The EEOC has issued guidelines that define sexual harassment as follows:

Unwelcome sexual advances, requests for sexual favors, and other verbal or physical conduct of a sexual nature constitute sexual harassment when this conduct explicitly or implicitly affects an individual's employment, unreasonably interferes with an individual's work performance, or creates an intimidating, hostile, or offensive work environment.[86]

Thus, under the guidelines, a woman must show that she was subjected to unwelcome sexual conduct that adversely affected her employment. To demonstrate that the conduct was unwelcome, a woman must prove that she said no, asked the harasser to stop, or otherwise made clear her disapproval of the conduct. In addition, there are two ways to show the required adverse employment effect: by proving that some tangible adverse job action was taken against the woman as part of the harassment; or, if no tangible job action was taken, by showing that the harassment was severe or pervasive enough to create an abusive environment.[87]

**Is sexual harassment in the workplace illegal?**

Yes. Working women have been aware of this pervasive problem for a long time. Unwanted sexual advances, employment decisions based on acceptance or rejection of sexual favors, and offensive remarks or pictures in the workplace are all too common in women's employment. A survey done in 1976 showed that 88 percent of working women who responded had experienced sexual harassment on the job.[88] More recent studies have shown little, if any, improvement in this picture.[89] The problem is especially serious for women entering nontraditional employment with mostly male coworkers.

Sexual harassment is prohibited under Title VII. It is considered a form of sex discrimination because the harasser has targeted the employee because of her sex. Under Title VII, employees who confront harassment must show that it was triggered by their sex.[90] Additionally, women who are harassed by other women will succeed under Title VII if they can show that the harassment was based on sex, and that it produced a hostile work environment.[91] However, courts generally have regarded harassment based on sex as distinct from harassment based on sexual orientation, which is not protected by Title VII.

The Supreme Court addressed this problem in a case called *Meritor Savings Bank v. Vinson*,[92] where it clearly articulated that the forms of sexual harassment mentioned above are violations of Title VII. In a later case, *Burlington v. Ellerth*,[93] the Supreme Court clarified that the forms of sexual harassment that are sometimes referred to as quid pro quo harassment (employment decisions based on acceptance or rejection of an employer's sexual advances) and hostile environment harassment (offensive remarks or pictures) should be analyzed in the same manner; the ultimate question is whether female workers are treated differently because they are women.

**What type of conduct constitutes sexual harassment?**

If a woman has suffered an adverse employment action, such as demotion or termination, and can show that the action was taken because of her refusal to submit to her employer's sexual demands, she has proven discrimination under Title VII.[94]

If the woman has not suffered a tangible adverse job action, she must prove that she was subjected to sexual conduct that was sufficiently severe or pervasive to constitute an abusive working environment. In *Harris v. Forklift Systems*, the Supreme Court held that a woman does not have to show psychological injury resulting from the harassment, but only that she reasonably perceived the environment to be hostile or abusive.[95] In *Harris*, the plaintiff alleged that her supervisor repeatedly made sexual comments to her, suggested that they go to a hotel to negotiate her raise, and told her that she was stupid because she was a woman.[96] Harris later won an injunction forbidding the defendant from engaging in hostile conduct towards women, as well as $150,000 in damages and attorneys' fees.[97] Other conduct that has been held to create a hostile working environment has included repeated physical touching and comments about a plaintiff's body over a two-year period,[98] and repeated vulgar remarks and requests for sexual favors.[99] Women may also allege hostile environment sexual harassment even if the conduct was directed at their coworkers but not at them.[100]

Circumstances that courts have held do not constitute a hostile working environment include a formerly polite doctor calling his nurses "castrating bitches" and "Medea" when angry;[101] and a supervisor's repeatedly asking out a female employee, without making hostile comments or punishing her for her refusal.[102]

### What steps can women take to protect themselves against sexual harassment?

First, a woman who receives unwanted sexual attention should express her displeasure in very clear terms to the harasser. If the first refusal does not eliminate the problem, she then must inform management in writing of the problem, asking them to take steps to end the harassment and indicating that the conduct in question violates Title VII. A lawyer should be consulted at the earliest possible stage. Copies of all correspondence to and from management and immediate, detailed, and clear notes about conversations with anyone about the subject should be kept. These documents and notes may be important later if the situation comes down to her word against his, or if the company tries to deny knowledge of the problem.

Finally, charges can be filed with the EEOC as soon as the victim is denied a promotion, is fired, is given a bad evaluation, or perceives the environment to be hostile. Even if a woman is not sure that the treatment she has received is "bad enough" to constitute hostile-environment sexual harassment, she should utilize her employer's grievance procedures and, if necessary, file charges with the EEOC because she may be able to change her working conditions without going to court.

### Can an employer be held liable for harassment by supervisors and coworkers even if he or she was unaware of it?

Yes. When a woman is harassed by a supervisor, the employer can be vicariously liable for the harassment, meaning that the employer is responsible for the actions of its supervisor, even if the woman did not suffer any adverse employment action and the employer did not know about the harassment. If the woman has suffered an adverse action such as termination or demotion, the employer is automatically liable. If there was no adverse action, the employer has the opportunity to show that it took reasonable care to prevent the harassment, and that the woman unreasonably failed to take advantage of any corrective opportunities offered by the employer.[103]

### If a woman is subjected to sexual harassment but does not lose her job, can she still get some kind of monetary award?

Yes. In the Civil Rights Act of 1991, Congress provided that women could get damages for intentional employment discrimination, including sexual harassment. This is especially important in cases where the woman suffered no loss of wages.

The law, codified at 42 U.S.C. § 1981a (2007), allows women to sue for both compensatory damages and punitive damages. Punitive damages are awarded solely to punish the employer, so they do not depend on the degree of plaintiff's injury. Congress set a maximum on the amount of damages an individual woman can recover. The caps are based on the number of covered employees in the employer's workforce, as follows: 15 to 100 employees —$50,000 per employee; 101 to 200—$100,000; 201 to 500—$200,000; over 500—$300,000.[104] It should be noted that no caps apply to race or national-origin discrimination, or to most religion claims.

In some states, women can recover full damages for sexual harassment, without any cap, under local statutes. For example, women working as flag persons on an Iowa road construction crew were awarded $35,000 in damages under the Iowa Civil Rights Act for a "barrage of offensive conduct" waged by their male coworkers.[105]

### What protections do domestic workers have from sexual harassment on the job?

Title VII only applies to domestic workers whose employers have at least fifteen people working for them. However, domestic workers may be able to rely on local or state laws to hold an employer liable for unwanted touching and other forms of physical harassment.

## WORK CONDITIONS

**May a company give "light work" to women and "heavy work" to men?**

No. Companies historically engaged in this practice because many employers assume that women are less capable of performing heavy work. Because light work is generally lower-paid than heavy work, the effect of the practice is discriminatory. Indeed, this practice was one of the first that female workers successfully attacked under Title VII.

**Is it legal for a company to forbid transfers between departments when it once segregated those departments by gender in initial hiring, but no longer does so?**

No. Usually the "men's" department will have higher pay scales than the "women's" department. Although no-transfer policies may appear to be evenhanded because they apply equally to all workers, very few men will want to transfer to a department where the pay is less; conversely, many women will want to transfer to more highly paid work. This is an example of a neutral rule that has a disparate impact on women.

**Can a company and a union negotiate a seniority system that discriminates against women?**

No, but there is one severe limitation to women's ability to challenge discriminatory seniority plans. The Supreme Court has held that discriminatory seniority plans are illegal only if the parties that negotiated them *intended* for them to discriminate. In other words, it is not enough to show that a seniority system has a disparate impact.[106]

Under the Civil Rights Act of 1991, the cause of action arises when an individual is actually injured by the seniority system's application, either when the system is adopted or when a person becomes subject to it. In other words, women do not have to try to anticipate the discriminatory effect of the system when it is first instituted, but can wait to see how the new system will actually affect them.

**May an employer require its employees to speak only English at the workplace?**

Sometimes. When employers forbid their employees from speaking any language other than English (even on breaks and when not interacting with customers), the practice may have an illegal disparate impact on employees from non-English-speaking countries. Because Title VII prohibits discrimination on the basis of race and national origin, it can be used to challenge these practices.

The law is somewhat unsettled on the validity of English-only rules. On the one hand, the EEOC has taken the position that such rules are presumptively invalid because of their disparate impact, so that the employer must prove that the rule is a business necessity for it to be valid.[107] On the other hand, several courts have rejected the EEOC's guideline asserting that the guideline violates Title VII by shifting the burden of proof from the plaintiff to the defendant. At least one court has specifically followed the guideline,[108] but the Supreme Court has not yet resolved the issue.

## HIRING

### Is it ever legal to limit jobs to persons of one gender?

Rarely, unless an employer can prove that being a person of that sex is a "bona fide occupational qualification" (BFOQ), meaning the particular position requires that only men or only women can perform it. The BFOQ defense is extremely limited.[109] In general, the employer must show that the job duties are part of the very "essence" of the business, and that all or substantially all of the members of the excluded sex cannot perform these job duties, or that it is impossible to make individual determinations.[110] A BFOQ is the only legal justification for limiting a job to members of one gender.

BFOQ defenses have been rejected in many contexts, including police and fire department jobs, construction work, and teaching. The BFOQ defense has been successful, however, in a few cases where the employer asserted that it based its decision on considerations of the privacy and modesty of its customers or other third persons. These include jobs such as washroom attendants or certain kinds of nurses.[111] In a variation on the privacy theme, prison officials successfully argued that the exclusion of male guards in a women's prison was necessary to the rehabilitation of the female inmates, many of whom had suffered sexual abuse at the hands of men.[112] Apart from these exceptions, courts have taken a very narrow view of the BFOQ defense.

### May a company or employment agency give job applicants employment tests if the test is applied to men and women in the same way?

It depends. If the proportion of women who pass the test is roughly the same as the proportion of men who pass, the test is perfectly legal. However, if significantly fewer women than men pass, the test may be illegal under the disparate impact doctrine. Under the rule established in *Griggs v. Duke Power Co.*,[113] and EEOC guidelines,[114] a court can order a company to stop using a test unless it can validate the test, or prove that the test validly predicts who would perform well on the job. In conducting a validation study, the employer must consider alternative methods of employee selection that will help select capable employees without eliminating a disproportionate number of women.

The EEOC definition of tests has been extremely broad and basically includes any formal, scored technique to assess job suitability. Women have launched several major challenges to the use of tests. While testing is usually viewed solely as a problem for racial minorities, women on average test less well than men in areas such as mathematics, science, weight lifting, and mechanical aptitude—areas that women and girls systematically have been discouraged from pursuing. In addition, Title VII prohibits employers from correcting for women's and minorities' lower scores on tests by utilizing different cut-off points or by adjusting scores—even though, according to studies, these lower scores do not correlate with poorer job or academic performance.

### May an employer refuse to hire job applicants who fail a physical test, if that test is applied to men and women alike?

It depends. Physical tests present problems because they can often have severely disparate impacts on women, and can keep women out of traditionally male occupations such as firefighting and policing. Whether a test will be valid depends largely on how close a relationship the court requires between the attributes tested and the job responsibilities. Because such tests often help maintain the all-male status of many occupations, women should challenge them if they believe that the requirements of the test are not representative of the actual demands of the job.

A recent case, however, illustrates the difficulty of bringing such a challenge. In 2002, an appeals court upheld an entry-level test imposed by the Philadelphia transit police department of the Southeastern Pennsylvania Transportation Authority (SEPTA), requiring applicants to run 1.5 miles in twelve minutes.[115] Female applicants challenged the test, arguing that it discriminated against them and was neither job-related nor consistent with business necessity. The court, however, found that the test appropriately measured the minimum qualifications necessary for successful performance on the job, even though it had the effect of disqualifying 90 percent of female applicants.[116]

**Can an employer refuse to hire employees below a certain height or weight if the standard is applied to men and women alike?**

No. Such a standard is an example of the disparate impact doctrine and one the Supreme Court specifically declared illegal in the case of *Dothard v. Rawlinson*.[117]

In *Dothard*, in addition to an explicit ban on female guards in some prisons, there was a requirement that all guards be at least five feet two inches tall and weigh 120 pounds. Over 41 percent of all women could not meet this standard, but less than 1 percent of all men were similarly ineligible.[118] The Supreme Court ruled that the requirement discriminated against women because of this differential impact, and then rejected Alabama's defense that the height-weight standard was needed to pick strong guards.[119] If strength is required, the Court stated, employers should test directly for strength, rather than rely on the inexact proxies of height and weight requirements.[120] Since that decision, many other courts have invalidated height and weight rules, especially for police jobs.

**What affirmative steps can an employer take to insure an integrated pool of applicants?**

The EEOC issued guidelines on affirmative action in 1979,[121] and despite repeated attacks on the concept of affirmative action in the decades since, they have remained intact. The EEOC guidelines outline the steps employers may take to overcome the effects of any past or present discriminatory employment practice. The Supreme Court has upheld the EEOC's position that employers need not be found in violation of Title VII before they can implement these affirmative action programs.[122] The EEOC's guidelines set forth a three-step process for employers: (1) self-analysis of employment patterns by the employer; (2) determination of a reasonable basis for taking action; and (3) reasonable action designed to solve the problem.[123]

There are no hard and fast rules as long as the remedy is adequate. Affirmative action plans are designed to accomplish the desired result. This may mean changing advertising and recruiting methods and training company personnel about effective recruitment and retention of a diverse staff. For instance, if the company's advertising and brochures show men and women segregated by sex in different jobs, the company should change the materials.

In practice, however, many companies will not elect to correct the effects of past discrimination and implement affirmative action unless a court makes a finding of discrimination. In fact, the decision of one company to implement an affirmative action plan was challenged by a white man in 1979 on the theory that voluntary race-based affirmative action resulted in reverse discrimination and was forbidden by Title VII. The Supreme Court upheld the company's action as legal because it was within the objectives of Title VII.[124] This result was reaffirmed in 1987 in a challenge by a white man to a sex-based affirmative action plan by a county government.[125] Nevertheless, reverse discrimination challenges are becoming more common.

### Can training programs exclude women?

No, but in practice this is often done. Training programs are a good place to begin a challenge to segregated jobs because they can ensure that women, as well as men, are qualified for the higher-paying jobs.

Indeed, the Supreme Court explicitly approved of affirmative action in the training context.[126] In an effort to correct the absence of African-Americans in higher-paying jobs, a company in Louisiana started a new training program for both whites and African-Americans, with a guarantee that the African-Americans would get some of the training slots. When the company chose an African-American person who had less seniority than a white person for this training program, the white person sued, calling the company's action reverse discrimination. The Supreme Court disagreed and found that the company's action was a reasonable way to correct the results of past discrimination against African-Americans that had led to their virtual absence in the higher-skilled jobs.[127] Although this case involved race discrimination, the same theory would probably apply to gender discrimination.

### Is it illegal for a company to hire or promote a higher percentage of male employees than female employees?

It depends. A statistical difference in the percentage of women compared to men who are hired or promoted by a certain employer, taken alone, is not enough to prove a violation of Title VII. Women wishing to challenge the employment practices of such an employer would have to also show that women were not hired or promoted in proportion to their representation in the available qualified pool, or that there was some sort of unjustified neutral rule or practice causing women to be eliminated from the pool. In fields where more men than women have the necessary qualifications, the hiring and promotion practices would probably survive. In fields that require only a general background equally available to men and women in our society, these practices should not survive. Employers in some jobs for which they have only hired men often argue that women are not interested in these jobs and do not apply for them in numbers equal to men. In such cases, it is important to show that women have applied, tried to apply, or been deterred from applying, and have been discouraged or turned away.

### If a woman wins a discrimination suit and the company agrees to change its hiring or promotion practices, can white male employees attack the judgment?

Yes, but only under certain circumstances. The Civil Rights Act of 1991 amended Title VII to address the issue of white males' lawsuits (known as collateral attacks or reverse discrimination claims) against court orders or court-approved settlements designed to resolve claims of discrimination by other employees. The statute prohibits such challenges to employment practices that implement the terms of a court order if the interests of the plaintiffs attacking the consent order were or could have been represented in the original discrimination suit.[128] Persons barred from bringing a new lawsuit to challenge an affirmative action plan include (1) those who had notice that the outcome of the proceeding might affect them and who had a reasonable opportunity to object; or (2) those whose interests were already adequately represented in the proceedings. A person's interests were adequately represented if the defendants to the discrimination suit had common interests with that person and there was no possible conflict of interest. For instance, a class of unsuccessful applicants for police jobs was allowed to attack a consent decree that had been negotiated by the city and the police union, because the union had only represented the interests of already-employed police officers.[129]

The purpose of this provision is to ensure finality in employment discrimination cases that include hiring or promotion orders that may affect the rights of white men. The main effect of the amendment appears to have been to encourage the parties to hold open hearings in which all interested persons may object to consent decrees before they are finalized.[130] Thus, the amendment has been litigated only infrequently since its adoption ten years ago.

### Can an employment agency choose to deal with individuals of one gender only?

No. This would be legal only for those rare jobs in which one's gender is a BFOQ.

**If a company requests an employment agency to send a man to fill a certain job, is it legal for the agency to comply with this request?**

No. The fact that someone else urges the agency to discriminate does not give it license to do so. The agency must consider and refer female applicants for the job as well as male applicants. Other illegal agency practices include discriminating in employment counseling, accepting discriminatory job orders, and publishing discriminatory ads.[131]

## UNIONS

**May a labor union limit its membership by gender?**

No. Unions are subject to Title VII and therefore may not discriminate on the basis of sex.

**May a labor union use its bargaining power to negotiate contracts that discriminate against women?**

No. Besides suing such labor unions, another remedy is for female members of the union to participate fully in all decision making and work to gain power within the unions.

## RETIREMENT AND INSURANCE

**Are different retirement ages or benefits for men and women legal?**

No. There have been several court decisions requiring equal treatment in retirement,[132] and the EEOC guidelines take the same position.[133] Policies that have been declared illegal include companies forcing women to retire earlier than men, to the disadvantage of women who want to continue working; or companies giving only women an option to retire earlier, to the disadvantage of men who would like to leave earlier.

**Is it legal to provide health insurance coverage only to employees who are "head of household"?**

Although the practice excludes more women than men from health benefits, the lower courts that have dealt with the issue have permitted it as a business necessity, despite the fact that it is a neutral rule that often has a discriminatory effect on women. Although the Supreme Court has not spoken on this issue, the lower courts have ruled that the cost of providing health insurance to all workers is so prohibitive that employers may make this sort of distinction.[134]

**If an employer or insurance company can show that it costs more money to provide some kinds of insurance to women than to men, may it give women smaller benefits than men?**

No. Under a Supreme Court decision and EEOC guidelines,[135] Title VII forbids averaging costs by gender, just as it would forbid averaging costs by race. Averaging is a way of attributing to an individual the experience of the group even when the individual does not conform to average group behavior. Title VII says that women are to be judged as individuals, and the cost for the group is therefore irrelevant. Although employers and insurance companies have contested this concept, the EEOC guidelines have prevailed.

## SPECIAL REQUIREMENTS FOR FEDERAL CONTRACTORS

**What are the rights of female employees of companies that contract with the federal government?**

In addition to Title VII, women who work for federal contractors may take advantage of Executive Order Nos. 11,246 and 11,375, which together prohibit gender and race discrimination by contracting employers.[136] In most respects, any executive order has the force and effect of a law. In the case of these executive orders, discrimination is generally measured by the same standards as discrimination under Title VII. Therefore, if something is illegal under Title VII, it is almost always a violation of these orders.

**Which employers are covered by Executive Order Nos. 11,246 and 11,375?**

Any company or institution that has any contract for more than $10,000 with the federal government, subcontractors of eligible contractors, and anyone applying for federal construction money is subject to the orders. The executive orders apply to all divisions of a company that has a contract with the government, not just the division that has the contract. They do not apply to the union involved with the company, but strong pressure is exerted on unions indirectly.

**What action must the executive branch take under the executive orders?**

Every agency or department in the executive branch must obtain a promise from any contractor with which it has a contract that the company will not discriminate against its workers. The agency also must demand that applicants for federal construction money agree to put the same promise in their contract with the construction company doing the actual work. This promise is generally called the Equal Employment Opportunity (EEO) clause.[137]

A contractor or applicant who refuses to include the EEO clause cannot get the contract or federal money.

**Does the EEO clause require the contractor to do anything other than refrain from discriminating?**

Yes. The EEO clause requires contractors with fifty or more employees and a yearly aggregate of $50,000 or more in federal government contracts to take "affirmative action" to insure fair treatment of female workers.[138] All contractors have this obligation if they want the federal contract.

**What is an affirmative action plan?**

An affirmative action plan is the formal plan a contractor must draw up to meet its affirmative action requirements. Generally, the contractor must analyze those jobs in which it underutilizes women or racial minorities, set goals and a specific timetable for increasing those numbers, and describe in detail the methods it will use to do so. Setting goals and timetables constitutes the heart of the program.

All that the government usually requires is that the contractor make an effort in good faith to meet the goals. If the contractor fails but can demonstrate it took action in good faith, it will not be penalized.

## Employment and Parenting Issues: The FMLA

**What is the Family and Medical Leave Act of 1993?**

The Family and Medical Leave Act of 1993 (FMLA) is a federal law that was designed to "help employees balance their work and family responsibilities" by entitling employees to take up to twelve weeks of unpaid, job-protected leave in a twelve-month period for specified family and medical reasons, and to continue receiving employer-funded health benefits during that time.[139]

Under the FMLA, employees may take family or medical leave to care for a newborn child, to legally adopt or accept into foster care a new child, to care for an immediate family member (spouse, parent, or child) with a serious health condition, or to care for oneself when the employee is unable to work because of a serious health condition, including pregnancy or pre-natal care.[140] In a major victory for all employees—men and women—the Fourth Circuit Court of Appeals ruled in *Knussman v. Maryland*[141] that the FMLA requires employers to provide leave to *any* employee to care for a newborn or newly adopted child, for a seriously ill family member, or for himself or herself when suffering a serious illness, and not to apply gender stereotypes to decide that mothers, but not fathers, are entitled to that leave. The court held that the Maryland State Police could not escape liability for their discriminatory treatment of a male state trooper who was denied leave from work to care for his newborn baby.[142] The court rejected the police de-partment's argument that the department's parental leave policy was limited to "mothers only." Instead, it stated,

Government classifications drawn on the basis of gender have been viewed with sus-picion for three decades. . . . [G]ender classifications that appear to rest on nothing more than conventional notions about the proper station in society for males and females have been declared invalid time and again by the Supreme Court.[143]

The court's decision was an important step toward gender equality in Amer-ica.

### Who is eligible to take leave under the FMLA?

In order for employees to be eligible for FMLA leave, both the em-ployer and the individual employee wishing to take leave must fulfill specific criteria.

First, covered employers include companies with fifty or more employ-ees; all public agencies, including state, local, and federal employers; and all public and private elementary and secondary schools.[144] Second, employ-ees must have worked for their employer at least twelve months, must have worked at least 1,250 hours over the past twelve months,[145] and must work at a location where the company employs fifty or more employees within a 75-mile radius of the employee's worksite.[146]

### What protections does the FMLA provide to eligible employees?

In general, the FMLA protects the jobs and benefits of employees who request or take leave. Employees on FMLA leave are entitled to the same job they had prior to leave, or to a position with equivalent benefits, pay, working conditions, and seniority. Employers may not take adverse employment action against employees on the basis of their taking leave. At the same time, the FMLA does not protect the jobs of qualifying "key employees" or the positions of employees who would have been eliminated or downgraded had they stayed at work.[147]

The FMLA also grants employees the unilateral right to decide when to take leave. Employers may not delay a decision on a request for FMLA leave, grant the leave request for a different time period, or force disabled employees to return to work early by requiring them to accept "light duty" assignments or any other job that is not equivalent.[148]

Additionally, the FMLA protects employees' benefits while they are on leave. An employer may not take away any employment benefit that the employee was entitled to before using FMLA leave, may not count FMLA leave against the employee under a "no-fault" attendance policy, must automatically give the employee the same benefits upon return as she had before, and may not require employees to meet any new criteria.[149] Most importantly, employers must maintain employees' group health insurance coverage by continuing to pay the premiums of employees on FMLA leave. On the other hand, there is no entitlement to accrue benefits during leave.

There are important limitations to the right to health insurance. First, if an employee contributes to the health insurance plan, he or she may be required to continue making the usual payments while on leave. In addition, if an employee informs the employer that he or she will not return to work after the leave, or doesn't return after twelve weeks, the employer may stop making health insurance payments. The employer may even recover premiums for employees who fail to return from leave unless the employee could not return to work because of a serious health condition or circumstances beyond the employee's control. If the job is eliminated while an employee is on leave, the employer may stop making payments at the point at which employment would have ended. Finally, while an employer is under no obligation to continue payments for benefits such as life insurance while an employee is on leave, the employer may do so with the expectation of reimbursement by the employee at a later date.

Some states, cities, unions, and employment contracts offer greater protections than the FMLA.

**What must an employee do to obtain family or medical leave under the FMLA?**

Employees who know ahead of time that they will be taking leave for a new child or for a planned medical treatment (for themselves or a family member) must provide thirty days' advance notice. If the nature of the health condition makes advance notice impossible, employees should generally request FMLA leave within one or two working days of taking leave. The notice should contain enough information to alert the employer that the FMLA applies, and should state the reason for the leave.

In addition, employers may require employees to provide medical certification that either the employee or an immediate family member (spouse, parent, or child) is seriously ill,[150] second or third medical opinions (at the employer's expense) and periodic recertification, and periodic reports during the leave regarding the employee's status and intent to return to work.

**Do employees have to take all the FMLA leave at once?**

No. Under the FMLA an employee is entitled to twelve weeks of leave in total, in a twelve-month period. There is no requirement that the leave be taken all at once. So, for instance, an eligible individual may be able to take two weeks off to care for a sick parent, and several months later take six weeks' maternity leave. All of that time would be covered under the FMLA.

Furthermore, under the FLMA, employees have a right to work "intermittently"—that is, reduce their weekly or daily work schedules, or take their leave in blocks of time—if they are seriously ill and unable to work, or when "medically necessary" to care for a seriously ill family member.[151] Thus, for instance, if a pregnant employee experiences severe morning sickness, she may use six weeks of unpaid leave under the FMLA to work half-time for twelve weeks, and use the remaining six weeks of leave for after childbirth.

**May employees use paid leave, such as vacation or sick leave, for family or medical leave?**

Under the FMLA, employees may use paid leave for family or medical leave depending on the category of paid leave they wish to use. For vacation or "annual" leave, employees have the right to use the paid time for their own serious health condition, including pregnancy or prenatal care, or for the care of a newborn or seriously ill parent, spouse, or child. For sick leave, employees must gain their employer's consent to use the paid time for family leave—that is, leave to care for a newborn or seriously ill parent, spouse, or child. Some states may grant employees greater rights of substitution. The Wisconsin Family and Medical Leave Act, for example, allows employees to "substitute, for portions of family leave or medical leave, paid or unpaid leave of any other type provided by the employer."[152]

### May an employee take FMLA leave in addition to the maternity leave granted by an employer?

Depending on the reasons for taking time off, employers may count paid leave against an employee's entitlement to twelve weeks of FMLA.[153] Thus, an employer may count maternity leave against an employee's entitlement to twelve weeks of FMLA leave because the FMLA defines "serious health condition" to include any absences relating to pregnancy or prenatal care. If an employee uses two weeks of paid leave to recover from childbirth, she may then have ten weeks of unpaid FMLA leave remaining.

While employers have the power to designate paid leave as FMLA leave, they need not insist on it and may permit employees to use up accrued paid leave first before counting against their unpaid leave entitlement under the FMLA. Under the Pregnancy Discrimination Act, employers with permissive policies regarding FMLA leave may not discriminate on the basis of pregnancy by counting paid leave against unpaid leave only for pregnancy and childbirth but not for other health conditions.[154] For example, if male employees get paid leave plus twelve weeks of unpaid leave for serious health conditions like heart attacks, female employees must also get paid leave plus twelve weeks of unpaid leave for pregnancy or childbirth-related conditions.

Some states offer longer leaves for pregnancy or childbirth. In California, for instance, a pregnant employee may take a maternity leave for up to four months and then take an additional twelve weeks of leave due to the birth of a child under the California Family Rights Act of 1991.[155] In California, the right to take a pregnancy disability leave is separate and distinct from the right to take a "family and medical leave."[156] A woman working in California can thus take a total of seven months off for the birth of her child.

### Can employers exclude women based on the perception that their leaves will continue longer than originally requested?

No. Under the Pregnancy Discrimination Act, an employer may not take adverse employment action based on the concern that an employee might need to take a leave of absence longer than originally requested due to pregnancy and childbirth, if the employer did not consider such future possibilities when deciding whether to grant medical leave to nonpregnant employees.[157]

### May an employer fire an employee for requesting additional medical leave for pregnancy or childbirth?

Under the FMLA, employees are entitled to no more than twelve weeks of unpaid leave per year, no matter how urgent the need is for additional time.[158]

Under the PDA, an employer may not require employees on maternity leave to undergo a different procedure than other employees for additional leave, nor may it grant longer leave to temporarily disabled male or non-pregnant employees while denying similar leave extensions to employees who are pregnant, or have childbirth-related conditions. In one case, a court found that an employer violated the PDA when it discharged an employee who requested additional leave due to childbearing-related complications, because she had failed under its policy to give notice of "desire to return to work and the anticipated date of return to work, no later than 30 days after delivery of [her] child. . . ."[159] In another case, however, where an employer denied a pregnant employee additional medical leave after she had exhausted all paid leave, a court did not find pregnancy discrimination because the employer had been dissatisfied with the employee's work prior to pregnancy and had reprimanded her in a memo stating that any further infractions of the work rules would be cause for immediate dismissal.[160]

Employees should find out whether their state or city laws, as well as their collective bargaining agreement or employment contract, offer leave extensions or greater protections.

### May an employer fire an employee for failing to return from leave at the agreed-upon date because the employee can't find childcare?

Yes. The FMLA only provides employees with up to twelve weeks of un-paid leave per year, regardless of how urgent the need is for more time. An employee forfeits the protections if he or she remains on leave longer than the FMLA time, either under alternate employer policies or simply by not returning to work at the end of the twelve-week period.[161] Furthermore, under the PDA, courts have generally defended employers' discharge of em-ployees failing to return to work due to problems with childcare arrange-ments. In one case, a court held that the employer's actions were in response to the employee's parental leave, rather than to her maternity leave, and thus did not violate the PDA.[162] The court declared that there is a point at which pregnancy and immediate postpartum requirements—clearly gender-based in nature—end, and gender-neutral childcare activities begin.[163] The court indicated that the parental leave in this case fell into the latter category because the children's medical needs could have been taken care of by the child's father as well as by the employee.[164] In another case where an employee failed to return from maternity leave at the agreed-upon time due to problems finding childcare, a court held that the employee's refusal to return to work when she was physically able to do so had nothing to do with her pregnancy or pregnancy-related condition.[165]

### Is an employer allowed to have a policy of short leaves, or prohibit leaves of absence altogether?

Under the FMLA, a covered employer must grant eligible employees a minimum of twelve weeks of unpaid family or medical leave per year. However, if employees are ineligible for FMLA leave, they may still get longer leave under the PDA if they can prove sex discrimination if more women than men at the company lose their jobs because leave periods are too short. For example, in one case, an employer who imposed a ten-day limit on disability leave due to the short duration of the project was found to have violated the PDA when it fired a pregnant temporary employee who requested maternity leave.[166] The court found that such a short leave policy had a discriminatory impact on female employees of childbearing age—an impact no male would ever encounter.[167]

### May an employer place an employee returning from family or medical leave in a position that, while different, pays the same amount?

Under the FLMA, eligible employees returning from FMLA leave are entitled to positions that provide equivalent benefits, pay, working conditions, and seniority.[168] "Equivalent," under the FMLA means "substantially equal or similar, not necessarily identical or exactly the same."[169] Under the Pregnancy Discrimination Act, however, courts have generally held that while an employer may have engaged in sex discrimination by offering returning employees less desirable jobs, employees were not eligible for back pay or reinstatement to their original jobs because they were still allowed to work for the same pay. For example, in *Garner v. Wal-Mart Stores,* the court found that an employer violated both Title VII and the employer's own handbook, which required assurance of a similar position after return from leave, when it demoted an employee returning from maternity leave from her position as department manager.[170] The court noted that the employer had previously held a male manager's position open while he was on sick leave.[171] Nevertheless, because the plaintiff received the same rate of pay, and was not forced to quit, the court awarded her only nominal damages of one dollar.[172]

**May an employer fire an employee on family or medical leave because a replacement has been promoted to fill the position?**

Under the FMLA, covered employers may not permanently replace employees on FMLA leave, unless the company needed to replace a highly paid "key employee" and failure to do so would otherwise cause the company "substantial and grievous economic injury."[173] For instance, in *Oby v. Baton Rouge Marriott*,[174] the court held that the Baton Rouge Marriott Hotel had not violated the FMLA when it replaced the executive housekeeper while she was on FMLA leave to care for her sick father. She was a key employee as defined by the state, being the third highest paid employee and in charge of the housekeeping staff at the hotel, and the hotel had informed her of the intent to replace her.[175] By the time the employee was ready to return from leave, the employer had hired a replacement and reinstating her would have caused the employer substantial and grievous injury.[176] Furthermore, the hotel had offered her a position of equivalent rank, pay, and benefits once she returned from leave, but she had declined.

Under the PDA, courts have generally found pregnancy discrimination only when employers had treated other male or nonpregnant employees on disability leave more favorably, or when employers had no valid reason for permanently replacing an employee on maternity leave. In *Garner v. Wal-Mart Stores*, the court held that the reason given by an employer for discharging a female department manager was merely pretextual, because the employee on maternity leave had more relevant experience than her male replacement and the employer could at least have assured her that she would get the next opening for department manager.[177] In a case where a company's office was short-staffed during the manager's maternity leave, however, a court found that an employer did not violate the PDA when it promoted a lower-paid employee to the managerial position, leaving open only the lower-paid office position for the employee on maternity leave.[178] The court noted that the employer acted only when the lower-paid employee threatened to resign.[179] Another court denied relief to a plaintiff who was fired while on maternity leave during her tenure as property manager of an apartment complex, because she had no evidence that the real estate company had treated nonpregnant employees on disability leave any differently.[180]

**During an economic downturn, may an employer lay off employees
based on the fact that they are on family or medical leave relating to
pregnancy, childbirth, or childcare?**

Under the FMLA, the employer may lay off employees on family or
medical leave only if the job would have been eliminated had the employee
not taken leave. Where courts have ruled under the PDA, they have allowed
employers to discharge employees on maternity leave when employers have
an independent basis for eliminating the position. For instance, a travel
company was found not to have engaged in pregnancy discrimination when
it eliminated plaintiff's position during an economic downsizing: its policy
of not providing job protection for employees on all leaves lasting more than
twelve weeks served as an independent basis for eliminating the plaintiff's
position while the plaintiff happened to be on maternity leave lasting more
than twelve weeks.[181] Likewise, an employer's discharge of a pregnant employee was held to be permissible because the employee was highly paid, she
had little client contact, and her duties could readily be distributed among
other employees.[182]

## ENFORCEMENT

### *Enforcing Title VII*

#### How is a Title VII claim pursued?

Employees who have faced workplace discrimination, and who want to
initiate a federal action, must file a charge of discrimination with the Equal
Employment Opportunity Commission (EEOC). An employee cannot initiate a lawsuit under Title VII directly in court. As explained below, the employee must receive a "right to sue" letter from the EEOC before she may
proceed to court.

#### How does a woman enforce her rights under Title VII?

The first step is to contact the nearest EEOC field office—in person,
in writing, or by phone. The EEOC's website has a listing of field offices
at http://www.eeoc.gov/offices.html. One can also call 1-800-669-4000 to
reach the nearest office.

A complainant or charging party (the employee) who contacts the EEOC
in person will be asked to fill out a Charge of Discrimination form. The

type of information requested will include the employee's name, address, and telephone number, the name of the respondent (the employer or union), its address, phone number, and number of employees, the basis of the alleged discrimination (sex, race, etc.), the date of the most recent discriminatory act, whether the discrimination is continuing, and the details of the discrimination. The charge may be amended at any time to correct technical defects or to allege new acts of discrimination. The EEOC will send the employer a copy of the charge within ten days. It will then begin an investigation of the charge.

### What action does the EEOC take after receiving the charge?

In a state or city that passed a law against gender discrimination in employment, usually called a fair employment practice law (FEP law), the commission's first step will normally be to "dual file" by sending a copy of the charge to the state or city FEP agency. The EEOC dual files because Title VII requires that any person filing a charge with the EEOC must first file the charge with her local or state FEP agency. To ensure that this is done, the EEOC files the charge for the complainant.

The EEOC and most state and local agencies have work-sharing agreements that divide the charges and investigations into various categories. These divisions of responsibility are different in various parts of the country. If the EEOC has primary responsibility for the kind of charge a complainant has filed, it will notify the state agency of the charge and will proceed to investigate without waiting to allow the state or local agency to act first. If the state agency has primary responsibility for the kind of charge the complainant has filed, the EEOC will allow the state or local agency to investigate the charge first. The EEOC usually takes no further action until it reviews the findings and orders of the state agency. However, if the state agency does not begin investigation or if it begins to investigate but it appears that there will be a long delay before the matter is resolved, the complainant should request that the EEOC take over responsibility as the law provides. The EEOC will also take over from the beginning if the charge is against the state agency itself or if it is necessary to get immediate or temporary court action while the charge is being investigated and processed. The practical result of many work-sharing agreements is that, regardless of the category of the charge, whichever agency receives the complaint first investigates it.

Depending on the reputations of the EEOC and state agency nearest the complainant's area, the complainant may have a preference about which agency conducts the investigation of her charge. A local women's legal organization can explain how the work-sharing agreement between the EEOC and local state agency operates. If the office that first receives the charge investigates, the next step is to ask which agency is more responsive. This information will help a woman decide whether to file her complaint with the EEOC or state agency first. If she files with the state first, she should file also with the EEOC to protect her rights.

If a woman decides to file with the state agency, or if her charge is sent there, she should cooperate fully with the investigators. The agency's final findings and orders are considered very seriously when the EEOC reviews them, and they are almost always adopted without further investigation. If she is not satisfied with the state investigation, she can and should ask for the EEOC's review (otherwise, the EEOC probably will not conduct one). A request for review must be placed within fifteen days of the state agency's determination.

### How does the EEOC investigate a charge?

An EEOC investigator is assigned to the case and will interview the respondent. The investigator may talk to witnesses and may review records. The complainant may be requested to give additional information, including the identity and whereabouts of any witnesses who will support the details of incidents that gave rise to the charge or preceded it, the complainant's work history with the respondent, a job description, ways in which the complainant was treated differently from others, and the reasons the complainant was given or the respondent will give for its action(s).

In the course of an investigation, the respondent (the employer) will also be asked to provide specific information about the issues raised in the charge, as well as the identity and whereabouts of witnesses who will support its version of the facts, information about the business operation and the workplace, and personnel records. If the respondent is uncooperative, the EEOC has the power to issue a subpoena to obtain the necessary evidence. If the respondent still refuses to comply, the subpoena may be enforced in court. The investigator may also hold a fact-finding hearing with the parties in order to determine the disputed and undisputed issues.

Based on the evidence gathered, the investigator may prepare a recommended determination for the office director as to whether there is cause to believe that there was discrimination. On the basis of that recommendation, the director will issue, and the complainant will receive, a Letter of Determination that will state whether the EEOC believes the charge of discrimination is supported by the evidence.

If the EEOC does find cause to believe the discrimination occurred, the letter will say this and will invite the respondent to meet with the EEOC to work out an agreement for providing relief. If such an agreement cannot be reached, the investigative file will be reviewed at EEOC headquarters, and the EEOC (or, in cases of state or local employers, the Department of Justice) either will bring a suit on the complainant's behalf or will formally notify her of her right to sue on her own behalf.

If the director does not believe that the charge amounts to discrimination, the Letter of Determination will say this and will notify the complainant of her right to sue in federal court. The complainant has no right to request that the EEOC review its no-cause determination, but the agency itself does initiate review of some such determinations.

### What other actions can the EEOC take?

The EEOC may attempt to reach a settlement between the employee and employer at any time. It is the parties' decision whether they want to pursue settlement. If the EEOC recommends that parties pursue settlement, either the claimant or the respondent can decline. If a woman is unsure whether settlement would be advantageous to her, she should contact an attorney.

Alternatively, the EEOC may select a charge for mediation, if both the claimant and respondent express an interest. Mediation is an alternative to an investigation and can provide a quicker solution. As with settlement, though, parties are not required to pursue mediation and can request that the EEOC continue with its investigation.

### What is a notice of right to sue?

A notice of right to sue, or a right to sue letter, gives an employee permission to file her case in federal district court. A complainant has only ninety days from the day she receives the notice to file a lawsuit. This is a strict deadline—a claimant will not be permitted to pursue a Title VII claim in court if she files more than ninety days after receiving the right to sue letter.

There are basically four different situations in which a charging party may receive a right to sue letter from the EEOC. EEOC regulations call for the dismissal of a charge if (1) the investigation shows that Title VII does not apply to the case;[183] (2) the EEOC cannot complete the investigation because it cannot locate the charging party; (3) the charging party does not cooperate in the investigation; or (4) the charging party does not accept a settlement offer that the EEOC deems would afford full relief from the harm alleged. This last one can be tricky if the complainant and the EEOC have very different views about what would constitute full relief. If such a problem arises, a complainant should consult an attorney.

The second reason for receiving a right to sue letter is that the EEOC finds no violation with respect to the allegations in the charge. Before this happens, the complainant should be given an opportunity to provide more evidence and then fourteen days to request that EEOC headquarters review the determination. A complainant has ninety days to file suit from the day that the determination becomes final—either after the fourteen-day period ends if she does not ask for a review, or after the final EEOC action at a later date if she does ask for review.

The third reason for receiving a right to sue letter occurs when the EEOC does find a violation but either fails to obtain relief through voluntary compliance and/or decides not to bring a suit on the charging party's behalf. Whether to bring a lawsuit is the EEOC commissioners' decision, and may or may not have anything to do with the merits of the case.

The fourth way to receive a right to sue letter is to ask for one. A complainant has a right to receive a right to sue letter at any time after 180 days have passed from the date the charge was filed or the EEOC took jurisdiction over it from the state FEP agency, whether or not the investigation is complete.

### How long does it take the EEOC to resolve a complaint?

The resolution time will vary with the complaint and the type of relief that is requested. In 2001, the average time taken to resolve a complaint through voluntary mediation was eighty-four days.[184] Once a complainant's charge has been assigned to an investigator, she can contact that investigator and find out about the progress of the case.

### If the EEOC is not handling a complaint rapidly enough or to the complainant's satisfaction, is there any action she can take?

Yes. A charging party has an automatic right to request a right to sue letter 180 days from the time she filed a charge with the EEOC. If a state agency first handled the charge, a complainant may request the right to sue letter 180 days after the EEOC assumes responsibility for the charge. If a complainant can find a lawyer to take her case, she should ask the EEOC to give her the right to sue letter. This Notice of Right to Sue should not be requested until a complainant has a lawyer, because the lawyer must start the lawsuit within ninety days of the complainant's receipt of the notice and will need time to prepare the case. Although a complainant may pursue her case in federal court without an attorney, it is advisable to proceed with an attorney.

### Are there time limits to watch out for?

Yes, and they are extremely important. A person can lose a lawsuit simply by failing to comply with certain time requirements under Title VII, regardless of the facts of the case.

The first time limit involves the date a complainant files her charge with the EEOC. A Title VII charge must be filed within 180 days of the act of discrimination, if there is no state or local FEP agency. If there is a state or local agency, a complainant must file with the EEOC within thirty days after the state or local agency finishes with her case *or* within three hundred days of the date of the act of discrimination, whichever is earlier. It is best to file with the EEOC right away, even when filing with the state or local agency first.

Another time limit imposed by Title VII involves going to court. A complainant has only ninety days after the day she receives her EEOC right to sue letter to file the court complaint that starts the lawsuit. Therefore, the right to sue letter should not be requested until she has a lawyer and makes certain that the lawyer understands that the complaint must be filed within the time period.

### Will a woman's employer or union find out if she files a charge?

Yes. Within ten days after someone files a charge, the EEOC sends a notice of the charge to the employer or union, and the notice will probably include the name of the person filing the charge. To avoid this, women can have an organization file on their behalf, but the employer will usually find out her name at some point because the EEOC will have to discuss remedies with the employer.

### If a company fires someone who files a charge against it, or if some other retaliatory action is taken, is there anything that can be done about it?

Yes. Retaliation for filing a charge of discrimination is as illegal as the discrimination itself. Retaliation includes firing, demotions, changing work shifts, and other negative actions in response to the filing of a Title VII charge. If a woman's company retaliates, she can file another charge with the EEOC. In addition, the commission has the authority to bring lawsuits for what is called "temporary or preliminary relief"—i.e., relief pending final disposition of the initial charge. Therefore, if she needs to get her job back or end any other retaliation immediately, she can request that the EEOC bring a lawsuit to accomplish this. If the EEOC will not assist, she can ask her lawyer about bringing a lawsuit.

## Enforcing Executive Order Numbers 11,246 and 11,375

**What government agency enforces Executive Order No. 11,246 (as amended by Executive Order No. 11,375)?**

The order is enforced by a special office in the Department of Labor, called the Office of Federal Contract Compliance Programs (OFCCP).

**How does the OFCCP enforce the executive orders?**

There are two basic methods: compliance reviews and complaint procedures. In theory, the OFCCP conducts periodic reviews of contractors to see whether they discriminate or have fulfilled their duty to take affirmative action. When the OFCCP uncovers major violations, the contractor and the OFCCP must negotiate an agreement that will bring the contractor into compliance. In addition, OFCCP regulations require reviews of certain large contractors before they are awarded a contract. In practice, however, compliance reviews (either before or after contracts are awarded) are not conducted regularly.

The OFCCP also has a complaint procedure under which a job applicant or employee of a contractor can charge the contractor with discrimination by writing to the OFCCP. For information on how to file a complaint, look at OFCCP's website: http://www.dol.gov/esa/regs/compliance/ofccp/pdf/pdfstart.htm.

## Enforcing the Equal Pay Act

**How can women enforce their rights under the Equal Pay Act?**

They must contact a local or area office of the EEOC and explain the circumstances in which they and/or other women are being paid less than men, and they must then give their name and address in order to be contacted for further information. In addition, a lawsuit can be brought against the company immediately without the employeee going to the EEOC at all.[185]

### Will the EEOC keep the employee's name confidential on request?

Yes, in an equal pay investigation, the EEOC is supposed to go to great lengths to protect the anonymity of anyone who fears exposure. For example, if the only female faculty member in the English department of a university files an Equal Pay Act charge and wants to remain anonymous, the EEOC should investigate a number of departments. This way, the investigation will include a number of female faculty, not just the complainant, and the complainant can remain unidentified.

If the charge includes both an Equal Pay Act and a Title VII violation, it will be more difficult to protect a woman's anonymity.

### Will the EEOC refer an Equal Pay Act charge to a state FEP agency for initial investigation?

No. There is no requirement that the EEOC give state agencies a chance to act first under the Equal Pay Act. If a charge claims a violation of Title VII in addition to a violation of the Equal Pay Act, the state agency gives up any right it may have to investigate first the Title VII part of the charge. This allows the EEOC to begin processing both parts of the charge immediately.

### What steps will the EEOC take to enforce a woman's rights?

The EEOC investigative procedures for Equal Pay Act complaints are very similar to those used for Title VII cases.

### Which companies are covered by the Equal Pay Act?

The official definition is that a company must be "engaged in [interstate] commerce" or "engaged in the production of goods for commerce," meaning the employer has some sort of out-of-state connection. The courts have interpreted this definition broadly to reach many companies and even some public institutions like schools and hospitals. When in doubt, it is wise to assume that an employer is covered until it is determined otherwise. Even if the company itself is not engaged in commerce, it may have to comply with the Equal Pay Act with regard to any employees who *are* engaged in commerce. For example, a business whose overall work is completely within one state will be bound by the Equal Pay Act as to an employee who, as part of her job, needs to cross state lines.[186]

**Are there any time limits under the Equal Pay Act?**

Only one. A lawsuit must be brought in court within two years of the discrimination, or within three years if the company discriminated "willfully," that is, the employer meant to pay women less for equal work. If a company that was underpaying its female workers begins to comply with the law, the lawsuit must be filed within two years from the time the company stopped discriminating.

It is important also to remember that going to the EEOC is not the same as starting a lawsuit. In one case, a woman complained to the EEOC about wage discrimination immediately but did not start her lawsuit until more than three years later. She lost her case under the Equal Pay Act because of this delay.[187] So the two- or three-year deadline for starting an equal pay lawsuit must be kept in mind, even if a Title VII complaint is filed with the EEOC about the same incident.

**What are women in a successful lawsuit under the Equal Pay Act entitled to recover?**

Women can receive back wages—the difference between the amount they should have earned if they had been paid the same as men and the amount they actually earned. They may win up to two years' worth of back wages or, in the case of willful violations, three years' worth of back pay. They are also entitled to an equal amount in "liquidated damages," plus attorneys' fees and costs.

*Enforcing the FMLA*

**What should employees do if an employer violates their rights under the FMLA?**

If an employer denies an employee's request for FMLA leave, or fires or demotes an employee upon return from FMLA leave, employees should ensure that they complied with their obligations under the FMLA, which include clear advance notice if possible, and any medical certification. Then, employees should furnish information about the FMLA to their employer (fact sheets are available from the Labor Department's Wage and Hour Division). If the employer still won't comply, employees should contact their regional office of the Labor Department's Wage and Hour Division to file a complaint by phone, by mail, or in person. Most problems are resolved by a phone call from the Labor Department to the employer. If the employer persists in its practices, the Labor Department may sue the employer on an employee's behalf after investigating the complaint.

Employees may also sue their employers in federal or state court.[188] Generally, they must bring the suit within two years of the FMLA violation (three years if the violation is willful). Employers found guilty of violating employees' rights must restore their jobs or compensate them for up to double their lost wages and benefits, as well as pay legal fees and costs.

To get more information about enforcing the FMLA, call or write the U.S. Department of Labor, Wage and Hour Division, 200 Constitution Ave. N.W., Washington, D.C. 20210, (866) 487-9243 (toll-free) or call the regional office of the U.S. Labor Department, Wage and Hour Division, which has written materials about the FMLA, including free copies of the law and regulations. Other helpful materials are also available on the Labor Department's web site at http://www.dol.gov.

## STATE ANTIDISCRIMINATION LAWS

**What are state fair employment practice laws?**

Most states have passed one or more laws forbidding employment discrimination, often using language or concepts parallel or identical to the federal laws discussed in this chapter. The federal and state laws cover many of the same practices, although state courts may interpret state laws differently than federal courts interpret similar federal laws. State laws may provide that victims of discrimination are entitled to full damages for pain and suffering or punitive damages. It may be beneficial to check state law before filing a complaint with the EEOC in order to compare potential damages.

It is particularly important to consider using state laws, because some states may have stronger laws and judges who are willing to enforce them, such that women there may wish to consider proceeding in state court rather than federal court.

## GENERAL CONSIDERATIONS

**Why is it important to understand the differences among all these laws?**

Different laws prohibit different practices and help different workers. For instance, Title VII forbids segregating jobs by sex; the Equal Pay Act does not. On the other hand, Title VII does not protect workers in companies with fewer than fifteen employees, but many state fair employment laws do.

If a woman turns to the wrong law, she will not succeed in changing her situation, even though another law may offer her protection; thus, it is crucial that women and their advisors know the available range of laws and the details of their application. Sometimes, too, there is overlap among the various laws. When more than one prohibits the same practice, women can maximize the pressure on their employer or union by relying on all the applicable laws to try to end the discrimination.

Women have made dramatic strides in the workplace over the past few decades. Nonetheless, they have not yet achieved true equality in job opportunities, compensation, and treatment. In order to improve working conditions and opportunities for themselves and others, women must be aware of their rights and the organizations that exist to help enforce them. Change in the workplace will occur only if all women—including poor women, women of color, and immigrant women—have the legal tools to enforce their rights and advocate for greater protections.

## Notes

1. 42 U.S.C. § 2000e (2007) *et seq.*

2. Dep't of Labor & Bureau of Labor Statistics, Women in the Labor Force: A Databook, tbl. 11 (Sept. 2006), *available at* http://www.bls.gov/cps/wlf-databook. htm.

3. *Id.*

4. *See* chapter 4, "Education," for general information on Title IX. In 1982, the Supreme Court ruled that Title IX prohibits sex-based discrimination not only against students but also against employees in federally funded education programs. North Haven Bd. of Educ. v. Bell, 456 U.S. 512 (1982).

5. 42 U.S.C. § 2000e(a) (2007).

6. 42 U.S.C. § 2000e(f); 42 U.S.C. § 2000e-1(b).

7. Price Waterhouse v. Hopkins, 490 U.S. 228 (1989), *superseded by statute*, Civil Rights Act of 1991, Pub. L. No. 102-166, 105 Stat. 1074, *as recognized in* Landgraf v. USI Film Products, 511 U.S. 244 (1994).

8. Civil Rights Act of 1991, 42 U.S.C. §2000e-2(k)(1)(B)(i) (2007).

9. 42 U.S.C. § 2000e-2(k)(1)(A)(i).

10. Hamer v. City of Atlanta, 872 F.2d 1521, 1533 (11th Cir. 1989) (citing Pettway v. Am. Cast Iron Pipe Co., 494 F.2d 211, 245 (5th Cir. 1974)) ("The test is whether

there exists an overriding legitimate business purpose such that the practice is necessary to the safe and efficient operation of the business. Thus, the business purpose must be sufficiently compelling to override any racial impact; the challenged practice must effectively carry out the business purpose it is alleged to serve; and there must be available no acceptable alternative policies or practices which would better accomplish the business purpose advanced, or accomplish it equally well with lesser differential racial impact.").

11. Jefferies v. Harris County Cmty Action Ass'n, 615 F.2d 1025 (5th Cir. 1980).

12. Women who have had or are contemplating abortions are protected against employment discrimination in the same way as pregnant workers. *See* Turic v. Holland Hospitality Inc., 85 F.3d 1211, 1213–14 (6th Cir. 1996) (holding that the PDA forbids employers from treating an employee differently on the basis of an employee's consideration or use of abortion, because this constitutes a medical aspect of pregnancy). Employers must give employees who have used, or are contemplating using, abortion the same paid sick leave, temporary disability payments, or other fringe benefits that others workers receive. However, Congress wrote one exception into the law: employers are not required to pay for health insurance benefits for abortion unless the woman's life would be endangered if the pregnancy were continued until term or unless there are complications. 42 U.S.C. § 2000e(k).

13. In Phillips v. Martin Marietta Corp., the Supreme Court rejected the employer's decision not to hire Ms. Phillips as an assembly trainee because she had pre-school-aged children, even though it would hire fathers who had such young children. The Court said that it is illegal to have "one hiring policy for women and another for men—each having pre-school-age children." 400 U.S. 542, 544 (1971). *See generally* 45A Am. Jur. 2d *Job Discrimination* § 135 (2006).

14. Under the PDA, an individual need not in fact be pregnant in order to show pregnancy discrimination. *See* Jolley v. Phillips Educ. Group of Cent. Fla. Inc., 71 Fair Empl. Prac. Cas. (BNA) 916, 1996 WL 529202 (M.D. Fla. 1996).

15. King v. Trans World Airlines, Inc., 738 F.2d 255 (8th Cir. 1984).

16. Even before the PDA was passed, it was considered an unlawful employment practice to terminate an employee merely because she became pregnant. 45A Am. Jur. 2d *Job Discrimination* § 135 (2005).

17. The EEOC published guidelines that state the following:

Disabilities caused or contributed to by pregnancy, childbirth, or related medical conditions, for all job-related purposes, shall be treated the same as disabilities caused or contributed to by other medical conditions, under any health or temporary disability insurance or sick leave plan available in connection with employment. Written or unwritten employment policies and practices involving matters such as the commencement and duration of leave, the availability of extensions, the accrual of seniority and other benefits and privileges, reinstatement, and payment under any health or temporary disability insurance or sick leave plan, formal or informal, shall be applied to disability due to pregnancy, childbirth, or related medical conditions on the same terms and conditions as they are applied to other disabilities. 29 C.F.R. § 1604.10(b) (2007).

The EEOC guidelines apply only to "disabilities *caused or contributed to by*" pregnancy and childbirth, not to the entire period of pregnancy (unless a woman is disabled from doing her job during the entire pregnancy). A pregnant woman who is *not* disabled from working is not entitled to sick benefits.

18. There are exceptions, however, if the employee is injured at the workplace and workers' compensation requires employers to accommodate the employee. Many courts do not consider pregnancy to be an occupational injury. *See, e.g.*, Urbano v. Cont'l Airlines, Inc., 138 F.3d 204, 206 (5th Cir. 1998).

19. *See* 45A Am. Jur. 2d *Job Discrimination* § 138 (2006). But if a plan exclusion treats pregnancy no less favorably than any other medical condition, it does not violate the PDA. Vance v. Aetna Life Ins. Co., 714 F. Supp. 203 (E.D. Va. 1989).

20. 42 U.S.C.A. § 2000e(k). *See* Wagner v. Dillard Dept. Stores, Inc., 17 Fed. Appx. 141 (4th Cir. 2001) (finding direct evidence of discriminatory attitude against pregnant women where employer refused to hire plaintiff because she was pregnant).

21. Wagner, 17 Fed. Appx. at 149 (quoting Maldonado v. U.S. Bank, 186 F.3d 759, 762 (7th Cir. 1999)).

22. *Id. See also* Deneen v. Northwest Airlines, Inc., 132 F.3d 431, 434 (8th Cir. 1998) (affirming jury's verdict that plaintiff was subjected to pregnancy discrimination when, despite her doctor's approval to return to work, she was placed on medical leave by her supervisors, who were "acting on an assumption that she had a pregnancy-related complication that would not allow her to perform her job functions.").

23. EEOC v. Old Dominion Sec. Corp., 41 Fair Empl. Prac. Cas. (BNA) 612, (E.D. Va. 1986). *See also* Carney v. Martin Luther Home, Inc., 824 F.2d 643 (8th Cir. 1987) (employer's requirement that plaintiff take unpaid leave of absence when she presented medical note recommending that she refrain from pushing or lifting without assistance violated PDA); *see also* EEOC v. Corinth, Inc. 824 F. Supp. 1302 (N.D. Ind. 1993) (waitress's termination because she was "too big" and might fall down constituted pregnancy discrimination).

24. Armindo v. Padlocker, Inc., 71 F. Supp. 2d 1238 (S.D. Fla. 1998).

25. Ivan v. Kent State Univ., 863 F. Supp. 581 (N.D. Ohio 1994).

26. Thompson v. La Petite Acad., 838 F. Supp. 1474 (D.C. Kan. 1993). *See also* Stanton v. Tower Ambulance Serv., 1994 WL 424127 (N.D. Ill. Aug. 11, 1994) (unpublished opinion) (where employer ambulance company refused to accommodate pregnant employee who could no longer lift due to doctor's restriction, discharge may be discriminatory if employer's reason for refusal of accommodation was because of pregnancy). *See also* Sussman v. Salem, Saxon & Nielsen, P.A., 818 F. Supp.

1510 (M.D. Fla. 1993) (recognizing that, under some circumstances, law firm might violate the PDA by requiring pregnant employee to produce eight billable hours per day, where her physician recommended that she work no more than eight hours per day in total).

27. Brinkman v. Kan. Dep't. of Corr., 863 F. Supp. 1479 (D. Kan. 1994).

28. *Id.* at 1483.

29. *Id.* at 1487.

30. 100 F.3d 1220, 1226 (6th Cir. 1996).

31. *Id.* (citing to the PDA, 42 U.S.C. § 2000e(k)).

32. Spivey v. Beverly Enters, Inc., 196 F.3d 1309 (11th Cir. 1999) (holding that employer did not violate the PDA when it denied request of pregnant certified nurse's assistant to go on modified duty when her physician restricted her from lifting for medical reasons).

33. *Id.* at 1313 (citing Urbano v. Cont'l Airlines, Inc., 138 F.3d 204, 205 (5th Cir. 1998)) (concluding, "it was not a violation of the PDA for an employer to deny light duty assignments to pregnant employees even though employees who were injured on the job were provided with such an opportunity").

34. *See Corinth, Inc.*, 824 F. Supp. at 1306 (employer's discharge of waitress in sixth month of pregnancy because she was "too big" and "might fall down" violated PDA).

35. Schneider v. Jax Shack, Inc., 794 F.2d 383 (8th Cir. 1986). *See also* EEOC v. Red Baron Steak Houses, 47 Fair Empl. Prac. Cas. (BNA) 49 (N.D. Cal. Jun. 3, 1988) (unpublished opinion) (holding that employer restaurant violated the PDA when, out of stated belief that it was in the best interest of waitress and child, it reduced her hours, then replaced her).

36. Int'l Union, United Auto., Aerospace & Agr. Implement Workers of Am., UAW v. Johnson Controls, Inc., 499 U.S. 187 (1991).

37. *Id.* at 210 ("Johnson Controls attempts to solve the problem of reproductive health hazards by resorting to an exclusionary policy. Title VII plainly forbids illegal sex discrimination as a method of diverting attention from an employer's obligation to police the workplace."). The Supreme Court did not accept the employer's assertion that hazardous conditions could not be improved.

38. *Id.* at 211 ("It is no more appropriate for the courts than it is for individual employers to decide whether a woman's reproductive role is more important to herself and her family than her economic role. Congress has left this choice to the woman as hers to make.").

39. *Id.* at 206.

40. Johnson Controls, Inc. v. Cal. Fair Employment & Housing Comm'n., 267 Cal. Rptr. 158 (Cal. Ct. App. 1990) (employer failed to show fertile women could not efficiently perform jobs in question or that essence of business would be undermined by fertile women workers).

41. Porter v. Kansas, 757 F. Supp. 1224 (D. Kan. 1991).

42. *Id.* at 1229.

43. *Id.* at 1230.

44. Armstrong v. Flowers Hosp. Inc., 33 F.3d 1308, 1317 (11th Cir. 1994).

45. *Id.*

46. *Id.* at 1316.

47. EEOC v. Detroit-Macomb Hosp. Corp., Nos. 91-1088, 91-1278, 1992 WL 6099 (6th Cir. Jan. 14, 1992) (unpublished opinion).

48. *Id.* at *1.

49. No. 89 C 0305, 1990 WL 44515 (N.D. Ill. Apr. 5, 1990) (unpublished opinion).

50. No. 93-1077, 1994 WL 50250 (E.D. La. Feb. 11, 1994) (unpublished opinion).

51. *Id.* at *3.

52. EEOC v. Ackerman, Hood & McQueen, Inc., 956 F.2d 944 (10th Cir. 1992).

53. *Id.* at 948.

54. 764 F. Supp. 519, 536 (N.D. Ill. 1991).

55. *Id.* at 531.

56. Gleklen v. Democratic Cong. Campaign Comm., Inc., 38 F. Supp. 2d 18 (D.D.C. 1999).

57. *Id.* at 21.

58. Armindo v. Padlocker, Inc., 209 F.3d 1319 (11th Cir. 2000) (holding that employer's reason for firing probationary employee, namely her poor attendance record, was not discriminatory because employee failed to show that employer violated company policy by firing her, or that similarly situated nonpregnant employees who missed comparable amount of work were treated differently); Stout v. Baxter Healthcare Corp., 282 F.3d 856 (5th Cir. 2002) (holding that employee who had suffered a miscarriage with complications during her ninety-day probationary period and was subsequently fired for exceeding three absences failed to prove pregnancy discrimination: even though "all or substantially all" pregnant women who gave birth during the probationary period would be terminated, the PDA did not guarantee medical leave for pregnant employees). *But see,* Minott v. Port Auth. of N.Y. & N.J., 116 F. Supp. 2d 513, 521 (S.D.N.Y. 2000) (finding that probationary police officers for the Port Authority of New York and New Jersey with more absences, but who were not fired, were not similarly situated to pregnant female officer terminated for excessive absenteeism because the nonpregnant officers' absences were due primarily to work-related injuries, which were exempt for purposes of absenteeism-related discipline).

59. 20 F.3d 734 (7th Cir. 1994).

60. *Id.* at 737–38.

61. *Id.* at 738.

62. 30 F.3d 1380 (11th Cir. 1994).

63. *Id.* at 1383.

64. 141 F.3d 378 (1st Cir. 1998).

65. 765 F. Supp. 198, 210 (M.D. Pa. 1991).

66. Stockard v. Red Eagle Resources Corp., Nos. 90-6393, 91-6226, 1992 WL 180131 (10th Cir. July 27, 1992) (unpublished opinion).

67. Nichols v. Elec. Crystals Corp., No. 87-2381-0, 1988 WL 139496, at *4 (D. Kan. Dec. 19, 1988) (unpublished opinion). However, the court stated that the evidence in this case did not support such an allegation.

68. 799 F. Supp. 326, 334–35 (S.D.N.Y. 1992).

69. *Id.* at 335.

70. Equal Pay Act of 1963, 29 U.S.C. § 206(d) (2007).

71. *See* County of Washington v. Gunther, 452 U.S. 161, 169 (1981).

72. U.S. Dep't of Labor & U.S. Bureau of Labor Statistics, Highlights of Women's Earnings in 2005 (2006), *available at* http://www.bls.gov/cps/cpswom2005.pdf.

73. The National Women's Law Center, *The Paycheck Fairness Gap: Helping to Close the Gap for Women*, *available at* http://www.pay-equity.org/PDFs/PaycheckFairness Act_April2005.pdf.

74. *Gunther*, 452 U.S. at 161; *see also* Int'l Union of Elec., Radio, & Mach. Workers, AFL-CIO-CLC v. Westinghouse Elec. Corp., 631 F.2d 1094 (3rd Cir.), *cert. denied*, 452 U.S. 967 (1981); Christensen v. Iowa, 563 F.2d 353 (8th Cir. 1977); Lemons v. City & County of Denver, 620 F.2d 228 (10th Cir. 1980), *cert. denied*, 449 U.S. 888 (1980).

75. *Gunther*, 452 U.S. at 179–80.

76. 29 U.S.C. § 206(d)(1).

77. E.g., Mickelson v. N.Y. Life Ins. Co., 460 F.3d 1304, 1311 (2d Cir. 2006); Beck-Wilson v. Principi, 441 F.3d 353, 359–60 (6th Cir. 2006). *See generally* Corning Glass Works v. Brennan, 417 U.S. 188 (1974).

78. *Id.* at 1110.

79. Schultz v. Wheaton Glass Co., 421 F.2d 259 (3d Cir. 1970), *cert. denied*, 398 U.S. 905 (1970).

80. Hodgson v. Baltimore Reg'l Joint Bd., Amalgamated Clothing Workers of Am., AFL-CIO, 462 F.2d 180 (4th Cir. 1972).

81. 478 U.S. 385 (1986).

82. *Id.* at 398–99.

83. Sobel v. Yeshiva Univ., 839 F.2d 18 (2d Cir. 1998), *cert. denied*, 490 U.S. 1105 (1989).

84. *Id.* at 22.

85. For further information on the use of regression analysis to prove gender or race discrimination in wages, consult Carin Ann Clauss, *Comparable Worth: The*

*Theory, Its Legal Foundation, and the Feasibility of Implementation*, 20 U. Mich. J.L. Reform 7 (1986).

86. 29 C.F.R. § 1604.11 (2007).

87. *See* Burlington Indus. Inc. v. Ellerth, 524 U.S. 742, 768 (1998).

88. Claire Safran, *What Men Do to Women on the Job: A Shocking Look at Sexual Harassment*, Redbook, Nov. 1976, at 148.

89. *See, e.g.*, U.S. Merit Sys. Protection Bd. Office of Policy & Evaluation, Sexual Harassment in the Federal Government: An Update (1988), *available at* http://www.mspb.gov/studies/rpt_june1988_harupdate/1988%20sexual%20harassment%20report.htm; *see also* Joann S. Lublin, *Thomas Battle Spotlights Harassment*, Wall St. J., Oct. 9, 1991, at B1 (sexual harassment complaints filed with the EEOC rose 25 percent between 1986 and 1990); Judith Havemann, *Evaluating Sexual Harassment in the Workplace*, Wash. Post, July 4, 1988, at A19; Eric Schmitt, *Two Out of Three Women in Military Study Report Sexual Harassment Incidents*, N.Y. Times, Sept. 12, 1990, at A22; EEOC, Sexual Harassment Charges: EEOC & FEPAs Combined: FY 1992–FY 2003 (2004) *available at* http://www.eeoc.gov/stats/harass.html.

90. *See* Oncale v. Sundowner Offshore Svcs., Inc., 523 U.S. 75, 81 (1998).

91. *Id.* at 79.

92. 477 U.S. 57 (1986).

93. *Burlington*, 524 U.S. at 752.

94. *Id.* at 753–54.

95. Harris v. Forklift Sys. Inc., 510 U.S. 17, 22 (1993).

96. *Id.* at 19.

97. Harris v. Forklift Sys. Inc., No. 3:89-0557, 1994 WL 792661 (M.D. Tenn. Nov. 9, 1994).

98. Anderson v. Reno, 190 F.3d 930 (9th Cir. 1999), *overruled in part on other grounds*, Nat'l R.R. Passenger Corp. v. Morgan, 536 U.S. 101 (2002).

99. Burrell v. Star Nursery, Inc., 170 F.3d 951 (9th Cir. 1999).

100. Hicks v. Gates Rubber Co., 833 F.2d 1406 (10th Cir. 1987).

101. Kortan v. Cal. Youth Auth., 217 F.3d 1104 (9th Cir. 2000).

102. Dayes v. Pace Univ., No. 00-7641, 2 F. App'x. 204 (2d Cir. Feb. 5, 2001) (unreported summary order).

103. Faragher v. City of Boca Raton, 524 U.S. 775, 807–8 (1998).

104. 42 U.S.C. § 1981a(b)(3).

105. Hall v. Gus Constr. Co., Inc., 842 F.2d 1010, 1018 (8th Cir. 1988).

106. Am. Tobacco Co. v. Patterson, 456 U.S. 63 (1982).

107. 29 C.F.R. § 1606.7(a) (2007).

108. EEOC v. Synchro-Start Prods., Inc., 29 F. Supp. 2d 911 (N.D. Ill. 1999).

109. *See Johnson Controls*, 499 U.S. at 201 ("The BFOQ defense is written narrowly, and this Court has read it narrowly.").

110. *Id.* at 188, 216.

111. *See* Brooks v. ACF Indus., 537 F. Supp. 1122 (S.D. W.Va. 1982); Fesel v.

Masonic Home of Del. Inc., 447 F. Supp. 1346 (D. Del. 1978), *aff'd*, 591 F.2d 1334 (3d. Cir. 1979); Backus v. Baptist Med. Ctr., 510 F. Supp. 1191 (E.D. Ark. 1981), *vacated on other grounds*, 671 F.2d 1100 (8th Cir. 1982). For a discussion of the competing rights of privacy and equal employment opportunity, *see* Deborah A. Calloway, *Equal Opportunity and Third Party Privacy Interests: An Analytical Framework for Reconciling Competing Rights*, 54 FORDHAM L. REV. 327 (1985).

112. Torres v. Wis. Dep't of Health & Soc. Servs., 859 F.2d 1523 (7th Cir. 1988) (en banc), *cert. denied*, 489 U.S. 1017, 489 U.S. 1082 (1989). This case illustrates the difficulty of this issue. While this result seems advantageous to the women inmates, it sets a precedent that may someday be used against women seeking jobs where men's privacy interests are at stake.

113. 401 U.S. 424 (1971).

114. 29 C.F.R. § 1607.6A (2007).

115. Lanning v. Se. Pa. Transp. Auth., 308 F.3d 286 (3rd Cir. 2002).

116. *Id.* at 292–93.

117. 433 U.S. 321 (1977).

118. *Id.* at 329–30.

119. *Id.* at 332.

120. *Id.*

121. 29 C.F.R. § 1608.1 (2004).

122. United Steelworkers AFL-CIO-CLC v. Weber, 443 U.S. 193 (1979), *reh'g. denied*, 444 U.S. 889 (1979).

123. 29 C.F.R. § 1608.4 (2007).

124. *Weber*, 443 U.S. at 193.

125. Johnson v. Transp. Agency, Santa Clara County, 480 U.S. 616 (1987).

126. *Id.* at 638–40.

127. *Weber*, 443 U.S. 193 (1979).

128. 42 U.S.C. § 2000e-2(n).

129. Rutherford v. Cleveland, 137 F.3d 905 (6th Cir. 1998).

130. *See, e.g.*, Edwards v. Houston, 78 F.3d 983 (5th Cir. 1996).

131. Ruhe v. Phila. Inquirer, No. 72-2423, 1975 WL 130 (E.D. Pa. 1975) (unpublished opinion).

132. Ariz. Governing Comm. for Tax Deferred Annuity & Deferred Comp. v. Norris, 463 U.S. 1073 (1983); Los Angeles Dept. of Water & Power v. Manhart, 435 U.S. 702 (1978); Bartmess v. Drewry's U.S.A. Inc., 444 F.2d 1186 (7th Cir. 1971), *cert. denied*, 404 U.S. 939 (1971); Rosen v. Pub. Servs. Elec. & Gas Co., 409 F.2d 775 (3d Cir. 1969), *following remand*, 477 F.2d 90 (3d Cir. 1973).

133. 29 C.F.R. § 1604.9(f) (2007).

134. Lissak v. United States, 49 Fed. Cl. 281 (Ct. Cl. 2001); Wambhein v. J.C. Penney Co., 642 F.2d 362 (9th Cir. 1981), *cert. denied*, 467 U.S. 1255 (1984); EEOC v. J.C. Penney & Co., 843 F.2d 249 (6th Cir. 1988).

135. *Manhart*, 435 U.S. at 702; 29 C.F.R. § 1604.9(e) (2007).

136. Exec. Order No. 11,246, 30 Fed. Reg. 12319 (Sept. 24, 1965); Exec. Order No. 11,375, 32 Fed. Reg. 14303 (Oct. 13, 1967).

137. 41 C.F.R. § 60-1.4 (2007).

138. *Id.* § 60-1.4(a)(1).

139. The Family and Medical Leave Act of 1993, Pub. L. 103-3, 107 Stat. 6 (2007) (codified as amended in scattered sections of 5, and 29 U.S.C.). For more information, *see* Department of Labor, Family and Medical Leave, *available at* http://www.dol.gov/esa/whd/fmla/; *see also* Department of Labor, Fact Sheet #28: The Family and Medical Leave Act, *available at* http://www.dol.gov/esa/regs/compliance/whd/whdfs28.htm ("The employer may elect to use the calendar year, a fixed 12-month leave or fiscal year, or a 12-month period prior to or after the commencement of leave as the 12-month period.") (hereinafter Fact Sheet #28).

140. 29 U.S.C. § 2612(a). "Family leave" refers to an employee taking time off to care for a family member, including care for a newborn and adoption, while "medical leave" refers to an employee taking time off for his or her own serious health condition.

141. 272 F.3d 625 (4th Cir. 2001).

142. *Id.* at 635.

143. *Id.* at 635–36.

144. *See* Fact Sheet #28, *supra* note 139. The Fact Sheet states, Covered employers must post a notice approved by the Secretary of Labor explaining rights and responsibilities under FMLA. An employer that willfully violates this posting requirement may be subject to a fine of up to $100 for each separate offense. Also, covered employers must inform employees of their rights and responsibilities under FMLA, including giving specific written information on what is required of the employee and what might happen in certain circumstances, such as if the employee fails to return to work after FMLA leave.

145. *See id.* ("Whether an employee has worked the minimum 1,250 hours of service is determined according to FLSA principles for determining compensable hours or work.").

146. For more information, *see* Department of Labor website, *available at* http://www.dol.gov.

147. *See* Fact Sheet #28, *supra* note 139 ("A 'key' employee is a salaried 'eligible' employee who is among the highest paid ten percent of employees within 75 miles of the work site.").

148. In Sherry v. Protection, Inc., 981 F. Supp. 1133, 1136 (N.D. Ill. 1997) the district court found that delaying a decision on an employee's requests for FMLA leave constituted denial of the employee's FMLA rights, even where the employer ultimately granted the request. Similarly, in Williams v. Shenango, the court held that where the employee requested a particular week off to care for his seriously ill spouse, the employer's denial of the request interfered with the employee's FMLA

rights, despite the fact that the employer granted the request for leave during a different week.

149. Furthermore, an employer may not force an employee to surrender his or her other benefits in order to take FMLA leave. In Mardis v. Cent. Nat'l Bank & Trust of Enid, No. 98-6056, 1999 WL 218903 (10th Cir. Apr. 15, 1999) (unpublished decision), the court held that forcing an employee to forfeit her other employee benefits, such as accrued paid sick leave and vacation time, violated the employee's FMLA rights to care for her seriously ill husband.

150. A sample medical certification form is available from the Labor Department's Wage and Hour Division, *available at* http://www.dol.gov/esa/whd/. It is important to note that employees who don't provide medical certification upon request are not protected by the FMLA unless another law or collective bargaining agreement applies.

151. *See* 29 U.S.C. § 2612(b); 29 CFR 825.203.

152. Wis. Stat. Ann. § 103.10(5)(b) (2005); *see also* Aurora Med. Group v. Dep't. of Workforce Dev., 602 N.W.2d 111, 114 (Wis. Ct. App. 1999); Sinai Samaritan Med. Ctr., Inc. v. Dep't. of Workforce Dev., No. 98-2119, 1999 WL 1139479 (Wis. Ct. App. Dec. 14, 1999) (unpublished opinion).

153. *See* Department of Labor, elaws—FMLA Advisor: Frequently Asked Questions and Answers, *available at* http://www.dol.gov/elaws/esa/fmla/faq.asp.

154. *See generally* 42 U.S.C. § 2000e(k).

155. Cal. Gov't Code § 12945.2 (2006).

156. *Id.* § 12945.2(s).

157. *See* EEOC v. Lutheran Family Servs. in the Carolinas, 884 F. Supp. 1022 (E.D.N.C. 1994) (rejecting the employer's arguments that it needed to replace the worker due to a staff shortage and due to the difficulty of temporarily filling plaintiff's absence, because other employees had been allowed to take medical leave when the employer was similarly short of staff, and a permanent replacement had been hired only after two months of the pregnant employee's absence, on what would have been the final day of her leave).

158. 29 CFR § 825.214 (2007); *see, e.g.,* Johnson v. Morehouse Coll., Inc., 199 F. Supp. 2d 1345, 1358 (N.D. Ga. 2002) (employer did not violate FMLA when it fired employee who did not return to work after twelve weeks of FMLA leave time expired); Dube v. J.P. Morgan Investor Servs., No. Civ.A.02-12290-GAO, 2005 WL 1140766 (D. Mass. May 13, 2005) (no violation of FMLA where employee fired after fifteen weeks' leave time, in excess of FMLA statutory requirements); LaCoparra v. Pergament Home Ctrs., Inc., 982 F. Supp. 213, 223 (S.D.N.Y. 1997), *overruled on other grounds*; Kosakow v. New Rochelle Radiology Assocs., P.C., 274 F.3d 706 (2d Cir. 2001) (employee's discharge after she exhausted the twelve weeks of maternity leave that employer, pursuant to the FMLA, allowed to its employees constitutes a legitimate, nondiscriminatory rationale for termination); Cormier v. Littlefield, 112

F. Supp. 2d 196, 200 (D. Mass. 2000) (employer is not required to hold an employee's position open beyond the twelve-week period when that employee is unable to return at its expiration).

159. Lunsford v. Leis, 686 F. Supp. 181, 182 (S.D. Ohio 1988).

160. Conners v. Univ. of Tenn. Press, 558 F. Supp. 38 (E.D. Tenn. 1982).

161. *See, e.g.* Farina v. Compuware Corp., 256 F. Supp. 2d 1033 (D. Ariz. 2003) (employee who took longer than twelve weeks' leave due to pregnancy with triplets was only entitled under FMLA to restoration to equivalent position if she was prepared to return to work during time designated as FMLA leave); Palao v. Fel-Pro., Inc., 117 F. Supp. 2d 764 (N.D. Ill. 2000) (where employee took eight weeks of maternity leave, and eleven weeks of disability leave for shoulder surgery five months earlier, employer was under no obligation under the FMLA to reinstate the employee after that twelve-month period is exceeded); Hill v. Underwood Mem'l Hosp., 365 F. Supp. 2d 602 (D.N.J. 2005) (employer's failure to rehire terminated employee was not retaliation for her taking FMLA leave, where her inability to work extended for eight months, far beyond twelve-week maximum provided by FMLA).

162. Barnes v. Hewlett-Packard Co., 846 F. Supp. 442 (D. Md. 1994).

163. *Id.* at 445.

164. *Id.*

165. Baffuto-Fein v. Pfizer, Inc., No. 91-3063, 1993 WL 312277 (S.D.N.Y. Jul. 1, 1993) (unpublished opinion).

166. Abraham v. Graphic Arts Int'l Union, 660 F.2d 811 (D.C. Cir. 1981).

167. *Id.* at 819. This case was decided less than three years after the PDA was enacted, and later cases do not appear to have followed its reasoning. *See* Davidson v. Franciscan Health Sys. of Ohio Valley, Inc., 82 F. Supp. 2d 768 (S.D. Ohio 2000) (holding that former employee alleging her discharge—for exceeding her employer's medical leave allotment—violated the PDA failed to show that employer's leave policy had a disparate impact on pregnant women; terminating twenty-one women for exceeding the leave allotment, out of twenty-two terminations in total, in a work force comprised of approximately 80 percent women, was not statistically significant, and not one of the twenty-one women was on leave because of pregnancy); *see also* Honegger v. Wickes Furniture Co., No. 94-4584, 1995 WL 625196 (N.D. Ill. Oct. 23, 1995) (unpublished opinion) (finding that plaintiff, who alleged that she was discharged from her employment while she was on a medical leave of absence due to her pregnancy was not discriminated against under the PDA; plaintiff failed to show that employer's stated reasons for her termination were a mere pretext, since the employer had a written, company-wide policy for all of its employees under which pregnant employees were entitled to the same period of disability as nonpregnant disabled employees, and that, pursuant to that policy, no employee who wished to return to work more than thirty days after taking a medical leave of absence was guaranteed a job).

168. *See generally* 175 A.L.R. Fed. 1.

169. *See* Watkins v. J & S Oil Co., 164 F.3d 55 (C.A.1 (Me.), 1998) ("equivalent," for purposes of requirement that employer restore employee to his or her previous position or an equivalent position upon employee's return from FMLA leave, means substantially equal or similar, not necessarily identical or exactly the same); Montgomery v. Maryland, 72 Fed. App'x 17 (4th Cir. 2003) (unpublished opinion) (state employee who was reassigned to new position while on extended medical leave was not entitled to reinstatement to her former position under FMLA, where jobs were at same pay grade and increment level, her classification was same, and she received significant raise within two months of transfer); Dirham v. Van Wert County Hosp., No. 3:99CV7485, 2000 WL 621139 (N.D. Ohio Mar. 3, 2000) (hospital employee had a valid claim when she alleged that hospital violated FMLA by failing to reinstate her to the same or an equivalent position after her maternity leave).

170. Garner v. Wal-Mart Stores, 807 F.2d 1536 (11th Cir. 1987).

171. *Id.* at 1538.

172. *Id.* at 1537; *see also* Fancher v. Nimmo, 549 F. Supp. 1324 (E.D. Ark. 1982) (finding that because employer did not exert pressure upon the employee to resign, and employee did not find work in the new position "hateful," there was no constructive termination under the PDA despite the presence of sex discrimination).

173. Fact Sheet #28, *supra* note 139. A "key" employee is a salaried "eligible" employee who is among the highest paid 10 percent of employees within seventy-five miles of the work site.

174. Oby v. Baton Rouge Marriott, 329 F. Supp. 2d 772 (M.D. La., 2004).

175. *Id.* at 783.

176. *Id.*

177. *Garner*, 807 F.2d at 1538.

178. Crnokrak v. Evangelical Health Sys. Corp., 819 F. Supp. 737 (N.D. Ill. 1993).

179. *Id.* at 739.

180. Soreo-Yasher v. First Office Mgmt., 926 F. Supp. 646 (N.D. Ohio 1996).

181. Ulloa v. Am. Express Travel Related Servs. Co., 822 F. Supp. 1566 (S.D. Fla. 1993).

182. Luongo v. Lawner Reingold Britton & Partners, No. 93-10777, 1995 WL 96901 (D. Mass. Mar. 6, 1995) (unpublished opinion), *aff'd by* No. 95-1341, 1995 WL 697316 (1st Cir. Nov. 22, 1995) (unpublished opinion).

183. This might occur, for example, if the employer has fewer than fifteen employees or if charges are not filed within the time allowed.

184. EEOC, *EEOC Issues Fiscal 2001 Enforcement Data* (Feb. 22, 2002), *available at* http://www.eeoc.gov/press/2-22-02.html.

185. The EEOC and the Department of Labor have signed an agreement that Wage and Hour Division offices of the Department of Labor will continue to take

complaints under the Equal Pay Act. After taking the complaint, the Wage and Hour Division office will transfer the complaint to the EEOC. This arrangement was made because there are many more Wage and Hour offices than EEOC offices around the country and because workers are familiar with filing Equal Pay Act complaints at Wage and Hour offices. Although the arrangement is to continue indefinitely, complainants should file directly with the EEOC whenever possible because most Wage and Hour employees who used to handle equal pay complaints have been transferred and soon very few Wage and Hour employees will be familiar with the Equal Pay Act.

186. Johnson-Medlana v. Bethanna, 72 Fair Empl. Prac. Cas. (BNA) 1482 (1996).

187. Wells v. Pioneer Wear, Inc., 19 Empl. Prac. Dec. (CCH) P9244 (10th Cir. 1979).

188. If the Labor Department files a lawsuit on an employee's behalf, the employee can no longer file an individual suit.

# III

## Trafficking and Forced Labor of Women Workers

Trafficking in persons is a worldwide form of labor exploitation in which women, men, and children are held against their will in slave-like conditions through force, fraud, or coercion. The inequalities women face in status and opportunity worldwide make women particularly vulnerable to trafficking.

The U.S. Constitution prohibits slavery, but until the passage of the Trafficking Victims Protection Act in 2000 (TVPA), U.S. law did not adequately address the myriad forms of coercion that enable trafficking. As a result of the TVPA, U.S. law now contains robust mechanisms to prevent trafficking, protect victims of trafficking, and punish their traffickers. Notably, the TVPA provides victims of trafficking a variety of forms of relief and assistance. This chapter will discuss trafficking and other slave-like practices, the rights of survivors of trafficking, and their ability to enforce those rights.

### Wasn't slavery eradicated in the United States?

No. Despite efforts to abolish slavery, unscrupulous employers continue to find ways to subject workers to slave-like conditions both in the United States and worldwide. Although the United States outlawed chattel slavery and involuntary servitude with the ratification of the Thirteenth Amendment to the U.S. Constitution in 1865,[1] today modern forms of slavery, such as trafficking, persist in the United States.

A prominent feature of American society until it was finally outlawed, chattel slavery was characterized by the absolute and permanent control of one person over another. This type of slavery is defined in international law as "the status and/or condition of a person over whom any or all of the powers attaching to the right of ownership are exercised."[2] Since its abolition, however, other insidious forms of slavery-like practices have continued to emerge in the United States. Following the American Civil War, thousands of freed slaves and indigent people were subjected to peonage and debt bondage as sharecroppers in the American South.[3] In response, in 1872, the U.S. Supreme Court in the *Slaughter-House Cases* ruled that the Thirteenth Amendment's prohibition of slavery was intended to eliminate "any other kind of slavery, now or hereafter."[4] Subsequently, as other slave-like practices surfaced in the United States, the U.S. Congress responded in 1948 by criminalizing peonage (the practice of debt servitude) and involuntary servitude (the practice of holding a person in a condition of compulsory service or labor against her will).[5] Still, these laws were insufficient. United States courts narrowly interpreted involuntary servitude to only impose criminal penalties on perpetrators who used physical force or threats of force in subjecting an individual to peonage or involuntary servitude.[6] Until 2000, when the U.S. Congress passed the TVPA, it was not a criminal offense to hold an individual in bondage through the use of other tactics amounting to psychological or legal coercion.

In recent years, modern manifestations of slavery in the United States have become widespread and tenacious. Globalization and the increasing migration of workers for economic reasons have resulted in a growing population of workers vulnerable to exploitation.[7] Today, the newest pernicious incarnation of slave-like practices is trafficking in persons, forced labor, and debt bondage. These modern-day forms of slavery are analogous to traditional slavery but are characterized by much more subtle, but equally insidious, forms of coercion and control that compel an individual to work against her will.

### What is forced labor and trafficking in persons?

Under U.S. law, "forced labor" is defined as labor compelled through the use of physical, psychological, and legal forms of coercion.[8] This definition is rooted in, but more specific than, international law, which defines forced labor as "all work or service which is exacted from any person under the *menace of any penalty* and for which the said person has not offered himself *voluntarily*."[9] As with the U.S. definition, international law recognizes that an individual can be forced to work against her will through physical and psychological threats, including economic and legal coercion.[10]

U.S. law defines "severe forms of trafficking in persons" as

- *Sex Trafficking*: a commercial sex act[11] that a person is induced to perform by force, fraud, or coercion, or in which the person forced to perform such an act is under the age of eighteen years; or
- *Labor Trafficking*: the recruitment, harboring, transportation, provision, or obtaining of a person for labor or services, through the use of force, fraud, or coercion for the purpose of subjection to involuntary servitude,[12] peonage, debt bondage,[13] or slavery.

Similarly, international law defines trafficking in persons as

recruitment, transportation, transfer, harbouring or receipt of persons, by means of the threat or use of force or other forms of coercion, of abduction, of fraud, of deception, of the abuse of power or of a position of vulnerability or of the giving or receiving of payments or benefits to achieve the consent of a person having control over another person, for the purpose of exploitation.[14]

### What are the typical characteristics of trafficking in the United States?

Traffickers use force, fraud, or coercion to compel individuals to labor against their will. Trafficking victims do not freely consent to the conditions of their employment. Sometimes victims of trafficking do not consent to the employment in the first place. At other times, victims give their initial consent to the employment relationship, but once the employment begins, they are subjected to conditions they did not consent to and become coerced into remaining in the employment of their trafficker.

At the extreme, victims may be *forced or coerced into entering* an employment relationship, such as if a victim is sold by a family member to traffickers, threatened with harm to her or her family, or actually kidnapped or abducted by traffickers.[15] More commonly, however, traffickers *lure* their victims into an employment relationship by making false promises about the nature and conditions of their future employment.[16] Once the victim agrees to enter the employment relationship, then the trafficker employs coercion or force to compel the victim *to stay in* the relationship.

If a person has not freely consented to her actual conditions of employment and is forced to labor against her will, she is a victim of trafficking. This is so regardless of whether the victim initially consented to her employment conditions.

### How do traffickers force or coerce other people to work against their will?

Traffickers use a variety of tactics to compel the labor of trafficking victims. These tactics range from physical and sexual abuse to psychological and legal coercion. On the more extreme end, an employer may simply tell a victim that she will be killed or harmed if she does not do as she is told. Similarly, an employer may threaten to have a victim's loved one or family member harmed or killed.

However, many equally effective coercive tactics are much more subtle. Employers or traffickers commonly deprive victims of freedom of movement by, for example, confiscating passports and other identification documents or isolating them in the workplace and cutting off their contact with the outside world. Employers often threaten that if trafficking victims try to escape they will be arrested or deported. Employers also may subject victims to debt bondage by, for example, withholding their wages to cover alleged travel or living expenses. Trafficking victims in such situations may receive little or none of the wages they are supposed to earn and may never know the specific amount of their purported debt.

Other forms of coercion employed by traffickers include complex psychological coercion, which occurs, for example, when a trafficker gains control of a victim by inflicting on the victim a pattern of behavior intended to cause fear and disorientation through the use of tactics like verbal abuse, humiliation, and deprivation of food, sleep, and medical care.

### Why are women particularly vulnerable to trafficking?

Worldwide, poverty, gender discrimination, illiteracy and low levels of education, regional conflicts, and a lack of job opportunities disproportionately affect women. Such conditions pressure women to migrate for employment and make them particularly vulnerable to trafficking. Accordingly, 80 percent of trafficking victims worldwide are women and children.[17]

In the United States, migrant women are extremely vulnerable to the deceptive and coercive tactics of traffickers because of their low levels of education, their inability to speak English, their immigration status, their lack of familiarity with U.S. labor protections, and the nature of their jobs, which are often hidden from the public view.

### How extensive is the problem of trafficking and forced labor worldwide?

Using the international definition of forced labor, which is broader than the U.S. definition and encompasses the various forms of coercive labor, the International Labor Organization (ILO) estimates that at least 12.3 million people are victims of forced labor worldwide.[18] According to this estimate, the ILO calculates that there are at least two victims of forced labor per thousand global inhabitants.[19] Forced labor exacted by private agents for the purpose of economic exploitation accounts for 64 percent of all forced labor, while forced commercial sexual exploitation accounts for 11 percent.[20]

Of the estimated 12.3 million victims of forced labor, the ILO estimates that more than 2.4 million people toil in forced labor as a result of human trafficking, according to the international definition of trafficking.[21] By contrast, the U.S. Department of State estimates that, according to the U.S. definition of trafficking, six to eight hundred thousand victims are annually trafficked across international borders.[22] The hidden nature of trafficking makes it extremely difficult to calculate the actual number of victims.[23]

As the number of people subjected to trafficking grows, so do the profits and networks associated with it. Today, according to the Department of Health and Human Services, trafficking in persons is the second largest criminal industry in the world after drug trafficking and the fastest growing criminal industry.[24] Large organized criminal networks are often responsible for trafficking, but small-scale networks and individuals also perpetrate trafficking in persons. Trafficking violations usually rely on some level of illicit networks of recruiters, document forgers, transporters, and purchasers to complete the offense.[25]

**How extensive is the problem in the United States?**

The U.S. Department of State estimates that between 14,500 and 17,500 people are trafficked into the United States each year.[26] These numbers, however, are criticized as overly conservative and unreliable estimates based on questionable methodology.[27] These numbers, also, do not include the many victims who are trafficked within U.S. borders.[28] Another study, released by the University of California at Berkeley and Free the Slaves, estimated that ten thousand or more people are working as forced laborers in the United States at any given time.[29]

Increasingly, forced labor operations have been discovered throughout the country and in a range of industrial sectors. According to the UC-Berkeley study, forced labor operations were uncovered in at least ninety U.S. cities between 1998 and 2003.[30]

**Why is trafficking and forced labor such a problem in this country?**

Trafficking and forced labor are endemic in those industries that are unregulated or poorly regulated and that fail to comply with U.S. labor laws.

As the "informal economy" grows in the United States—that is, remunerative work that is not recognized, regulated, or protected by existing laws or regulations—so do the occurrences of trafficking and forced labor.[31] Trafficking and forced labor are particularly prevalent in those poorly regulated occupations that are removed from the public view.

**What kinds of jobs are victims trafficked into in the United States?**

According to a recent study, victims of trafficking are most frequently found, in the order of prevalence, in prostitution, domestic work, agriculture, sweatshop factories, restaurant and hotel work, and entertainment.[32]

**What is the United States government doing to address trafficking abuses?**

In the United States, local and federal law enforcement work to identify persons who have committed trafficking, investigate allegations of trafficking, locate and apprehend traffickers, and carry out prosecutions against traffickers. The federal government provides grants to states, local governments, and nonprofit organizations that provide services to victims of trafficking to develop and strengthen trafficking victim services programs.[33]

In its efforts to combat trafficking internationally, the United States, through the Trafficking in Persons office of the U.S. Department of State, produces an annual trafficking in persons report describing the extent of severe forms of trafficking occurring in foreign countries and evaluating the efforts made by foreign governments to combat trafficking.[34] These reports rank foreign governments' compliance with minimum standards for the elimination of trafficking.[35] Pursuant to such findings, the president is authorized to withhold nonhumanitarian, non-trade-related foreign assistance to governments until those governments comply with minimum standards to eliminate trafficking.[36]

**Are trafficking and forced labor crimes?**

Yes. The TVPA makes trafficking in persons and forced labor federal crimes. Sections 1,589 and 1,590 of Title 18, United States Code, prohibit forced labor and trafficking in persons, respectively, and assign a fine and/or prison sentence up to twenty years to anyone convicted of forced labor or trafficking. Under this section, an individual convicted of committing a forced labor or trafficking violation in which a death, kidnapping, or aggravated sexual assault occurred may be sentenced to any term of years or life in prison.[37]

In addition, the TVPA assigns criminal penalties to anyone convicted of sex trafficking of children or who destroys or confiscates a passport or identification document in furtherance of trafficking. The TVPA also provides mandatory restitution for victims of convicted traffickers.[38]

### Does trafficking require movement across international borders?

No. Under the TVPA, trafficking may occur solely within United States borders. Victims are not required to have physically moved from one place to another in order to qualify as victims of severe forms of trafficking. A victim of sex trafficking simply must be induced to perform a commercial sex act under force, fraud, or coercion or must be under the age of eighteen.[39] A victim of labor trafficking must be "recruited, harbored, transported, provided, or obtained" for her labor or services under force, fraud, or coercion and subjected to forced labor.[40]

### Can someone who is smuggled into the United States be a victim of trafficking?

Yes, but smuggling is not the same as trafficking. Migrant smuggling involves the unauthorized transport of persons across national borders, whereas trafficking can occur without the physical movement or transport of a person and is for the purpose of labor or sexual exploitation. In addition, individuals may consent to being smuggled, whereas victims of trafficking do not consent to their coercive employment situations. Under U.S. law, smuggled persons can be prosecuted under criminal law, whereas trafficked persons are considered victims who merit protection. However, it is important to note that an individual who is smuggled across borders *can also* be a victim of trafficking if she is forced, deceived, or coerced for the purpose of being placed into a forced labor situation.

### What forms of assistance are available to victims of trafficking?

Victims of trafficking in the United States, including labor and sex trafficking, are eligible for immigration relief—that is, the ability to lawfully remain in the United States.[41] Victims can receive "continued presence"[42] or apply for a Trafficking Visa ("T-Visa"), which confers nonimmigrant status to victims, on the condition that they agree to cooperate with law enforcement in a criminal investigation.[43] Continued presence and the T-Visa enable victims of trafficking to legally remain in the United States once they escape their traffickers and provides them access to social services and employment authorization.[44]

Continued presence is a more immediate form of relief for a trafficking victim as the application can be processed within a couple of weeks, whereas an application for a T-Visa can take months to process.[45] Continued presence, however, can only be requested on behalf of a victim by a federal law enforcement agency (LEA).[46] As a result, continued presence is only an option for those victims whose cases the government has an interest in prosecuting. In addition, continued presence is issued to individuals for no more than one-year increments and it does not convey immigration status to the victim other than the right to legally remain in the United States for the designated period of time.[47]

By contrast, victims may self-petition for a T-Visa. The T-Visa offers temporary lawful immigration status and the option of adjusting to legal permanent resident status in the United States.[48] T-Visa recipients may also apply to bring their eligible family members to the United States on derivative immigration status.[49]

Victims of severe forms of trafficking—who are granted either continued presence or a T-Visa—are also eligible for the benefits and services available to refugees in the United States, such as cash assistance, Food Stamps, Medicaid, and SSI.[50]

### What makes a victim of trafficking eligible for immigration relief?

A victim of trafficking is eligible for immigration relief—either continued presence or a T-Visa—if she is a victim of trafficking in the United States and is willing to cooperate with law enforcement in the prosecution of her traffickers.[51] In order to obtain continued presence, a law enforcement agency must take interest in a victim's case and request continued presence on her behalf.

The requirements for a victim to be eligible for a T-Visa are much more rigorous. A victim of trafficking must (1) demonstrate that she is a victim of a severe form of trafficking in persons; (2) be physically present in the United States or other U.S. territories due to trafficking; (3) demonstrate that she has been willing to comply with any reasonable request for assistance in the investigation or prosecution of acts of trafficking in persons; and (4) demonstrate that she would suffer extreme hardship involving unusual and severe harm if removed from the United States.[52] Additionally, a victim must not have committed a trafficking offense[53] and must not otherwise be inadmissible under the immigration exclusion criteria of Section 212 of the Immigration and Nationality Act,[54] unless the Attorney General waives her inadmissibility.[55]

**What challenges do trafficking victims experience in acquiring immigration relief?**

Victims of trafficking face significant obstacles to obtaining continued presence or a T-Visa. Chief among these obstacles is the requirement that victims cooperate with law enforcement in the investigations and prosecutions of their traffickers. Victims of trafficking are often unwilling or reticent to cooperate with law enforcement for various reasons. Victims of trafficking often distrust law enforcement officials because of bad experiences with police in their home countries. They also sometimes fear that if they cooperate with law enforcement in investigating or prosecuting their traffickers, they or their family members will suffer retribution by their traffickers.

In addition, victims of trafficking commonly suffer significant psychological trauma, such as Post-Traumatic Stress Disorder. As a result, victims of trafficking sometimes have difficulty remembering details about their trafficking experiences or responding to all of the demands for information by law enforcement.[56] As a result, law enforcement sometimes misperceives victims' statements or actions as indicating a lack of willingness to cooperate with law enforcement.[57] However, in 2005, Congress amended the law so that victims of trafficking who suffer psychological or physical trauma can receive a waiver of the requirement that they cooperate with law enforcement.[58]

Another significant obstacle to victims' ability to acquire immigration relief is law enforcement agents' lack of responsiveness in many cases. If law enforcement is unresponsive to an individual's allegations of trafficking, then a victim cannot obtain continued presence because it is law enforcement that must make a continued presence request. In addition, individuals face challenges to obtaining a T-Visa when law enforcement is nonresponsive to their cases. Determinations on T-Visa applications are made considering "all credible and relevant evidence,"[59] but endorsements from law enforcement agencies that an individual is a victim of trafficking carry significant weight. Such endorsements are considered "primary evidence" and are "strongly encouraged" in determining an individual's eligibility for a T-Visa.[60] Without such endorsements, victims must rely on "secondary evidence," such as a personal statement and supporting documentation, to prove their eligibility for a T-Visa.[61]

**How many victims in the United States have received immigration relief?**

Although the U.S. government estimates that there are tens of thousands of individuals trafficked into the United States each year, the number of victims whom the government has managed to assist pales in comparison.

In the TVPA, Congress capped the number of T-Visas issued each year at five thousand, estimating that that many visas would be needed each year to assist large numbers of victims and secure victim witnesses in government prosecutions of traffickers.[62] Between the passage of the TVPA in October 2000 and March 2005, however, the U.S. Citizenship and Immigration Services (USCIS), the agency that adjudicates all T-Visa applications, had only granted a total of 478 T-Visas and had denied 496 applications.[63] By the end of fiscal year 2003, only 374 victim witnesses had been granted continued presence status, but most likely many of these victims were also granted T-Visas.[64] Compared to the tens of thousands of trafficking victims in the United States, only hundreds have actually received the immigration relief and other benefits authorized for victims under the TVPA.

### Can trafficking victims pursue redress for their abuse in United States courts?

Yes. When the U.S. Congress reauthorized the TVPA in 2003, it amended the law to include a civil cause of action for trafficking and forced labor abuses.[65] This civil cause of action grants victims of trafficking the right to pursue damages in federal court for the trafficking and forced labor they experienced, regardless of whether the U.S. government chooses to prosecute their traffickers criminally. A victim of trafficking can seek damages for unpaid wages, emotional damages, and other forms of compensatory damages if she demonstrates by a preponderance of the evidence that she has been trafficked to the United States.[66] Moreover, trafficking victims, like other exploited workers, may also seek redress under federal and state labor and employment laws that prohibit discrimination and sexual harassment, set minimum wages and overtime, require minimum health and safety standards in the workplace, and protect the right to organize for improved working conditions.[67]

### Must a minor be coerced into providing sexual services to qualify as a victim of trafficking?

No. Under the TVPA, any person under the age of eighteen who performs a commercial sex act is considered a victim of sex trafficking; such persons do not need to prove force, fraud, or coercion.[68]

### What is the difference between sex trafficking and prostitution?

Under the TVPA, sex trafficking is any commercial sex act induced by force, fraud, or coercion.[69] Prostitution, however, is any commercial sex act that an individual chooses to perform. However, the prostitution of minors constitutes per se sex trafficking regardless of the presence of force, fraud, or coercion.[70]

## What should I do if I am or know a victim of trafficking and forced labor in the United States?

- To report a trafficking situation, obtain information, and access supportive services available to a victim of trafficking, contact the Trafficking Information and Referral Hotline of the Department of Health and Human Services at (888) 373-7888.
- To report a trafficking situation to law enforcement, contact the police at 911 or the Trafficking in Persons and Worker Task Force complaint line at (888) 428-7581 or your district attorney's office.
- To file a complaint for violations of wage and hour laws, contact the Wage and Hour Division of the Department of Labor at (866) 487-9243.
- To file a complaint for violations of antidiscrimination laws, contact the EEOC at 1-800-669-4000.

To obtain legal or social services for a trafficking victim from a nongovernmental organization, contact your local ACLU affiliate, your local Legal Aid chapter, or one of the local member organizations of the Freedom Network, an umbrella group of organizations that serve trafficking victims. A list of member organizations of the Freedom Network is available at http://www.freedomnetworkusa.org/members.htm.

## NOTES

1. U.S. Const. amend. XIII, § 1. "Neither slavery nor involuntary servitude, except as a punishment for crime whereof the party shall have been duly convicted, shall exist within the United States, or any place subject to their jurisdiction."

2. Slavery, Servitude, Forced Labour and Similar Institutions and Practices Convention of 1926 (Slavery Convention of 1926), September 25, 1926, art. 1(1), 60 L.N.T.S. 253, entered into force March 9, 1927.

3. FREE THE SLAVES AND HUMAN RIGHTS CENTER, UNIVERSITY OF CALIFORNIA, BERKELEY, HIDDEN SLAVES: FORCED LABOR IN THE UNITED STATES 19 (2004).

4. Slaughter-House Cases, 83 U.S. 36, 72 (1872).

5. 18 U.S.C. § 1581; 18 U.S.C. § 1584; *see* Free the Slaves, *supra* note 3, at 19.

6. *See, e.g.,* United States v. Kozminski, 487 U.S. 931 (1988) (interpreting the involuntary servitude statute to require actual physical force or the threat of physical force to compel labor); United States v. Shackney, 333 F.2d 475 (2d Cir. 1964) (holding that an employer's threats of deportation did not constitute holding employees in involuntary servitude under the statute).

7. *See* ILO, Report of the Director-General, A Global Alliance against Forced Labour 9, 93rd Sess., Report I(B) (2005).

8. TVPA, 22 U.S.C. § 7109; 18 U.S.C. § 1589 ("Whoever knowingly provides or obtains the labor or services of a person—(1) by threats of serious harm to, or physical restraint against, that person or another person; (2) by means of any scheme, plan, or pattern intended to cause the person to believe that, if the person did not perform such labor or services, that person or another person would suffer serious harm or physical restraint; or (3) by means of the abuse or threatened abuse of law or the legal process. . . .").

9. Convention Concerning Forced or Compulsory Labour (ILO No. 29), June 28, 1930, art. 2(1), 39 U.N.T.S. 55, *entered into force* May 1, 1932 (emphasis added).

10. *Id.*

11. Under the TVPA, a commercial sex act means "any sex act on account of which anything of value is given to or received by any person." § 7102(3).

12. Under the TVPA, involuntary servitude is defined as "a condition of servitude induced by means of—(A) any scheme, plan, or pattern intended to cause a person to believe that, if the person did not enter into or continue in such condition, that person or another person would suffer serious harm or physical restraint; or (B) the abuse or threatened abuse of the legal process." § 7102(5).

13. Under the TVPA, debt bondage is defined as "the status or condition of a debtor arising from a pledge by the debtor of his or her personal services or of those of a person under his or her control as a security for debt, if the value of those services as reasonably assessed is not applied toward the liquidation of the debt or the length and nature of those services are not respectively limited and defined." § 7102(4).

14. Protocol to Prevent, Suppress and Punish Trafficking in Persons, Especially Women and Children, Supplementing the United Nations Convention Against Transnational Organized Crime of 2000, Dec. 13, 2000, G.A. res. 55/25, annex II, 55 U.N. GAOR Supp. (No. 49) at 60, U.N. Doc. A/45/49 (Vol. I) (2001), *entered into force* Dec. 25, 2003.

15. *See* ILO, Global Alliance, *supra* note 7, at 6.

16. *Id.*

17. Both the International Labor Organization and the U.S. Department of

State estimate that 80 percent of trafficking victims are women and girls. *See* Government Accountability Office, Human Trafficking: Better Data, Strategy,
and Reporting Needed to Enhance U.S. Antitrafficking Efforts Abroad 12,
GAO-06-825 (2006).

18. *See* ILO, Global Alliance, *supra* note 7, at 5–10.

19. *Id.* at 12.

20. *Id.*

21. *Id.*

22. U.S. Dep't of State, 2005 Trafficking in Persons Report 6 (2005).

23. The reliability of U.S. estimates of the number of victims of trafficking is
questionable, according to the U.S. Government Accountability Office (GAO). In a
report released in July 2006, the GAO details the methodological weakness, gaps in
data, and numerical discrepancies in the U.S. statistics on trafficking. *See generally*
GAO, Human Trafficking, *supra* note 17.

24. Department of Health and Human Services, Human Trafficking Fact Sheet
(2004), *available at* http://www.acf.hhs.gov/trafficking/about/fact_human2004.pdf.

25. *See* Kathleen Kim and Kusia Hreshchyshyn, *Human Trafficking Private Right
of Action: Civil Rights for Trafficked Persons in the United States*, 16 Hastings Wom-
en's L.J. 1, 6 (2004).

26. U.S. Dep't of State, 2004 Trafficking in Persons Report 23 (2004).

27. *See* GAO, Human Trafficking, *supra* note 17, at 10–21; Women's Commission for Refugee Women and Children, The U.S. Response to Human Trafficking: An Unbalanced Approach 10–13 (2007).

28. *See* Women's Commission, *supra* note 27, at 11.

29. Free the Slaves, *supra* note 3, at 10.

30. *Id.* at 10.

31. *Id.* at 9.

32. *Id.* at 14.

33. TVPA, § 7105(b)(2).

34. TVPA, § 2151n.

35. TVPA, § 7107(b).

36. TVPA, § 7107(d).

37. In addition to federal laws outlawing trafficking and forced labor, many
states also have separate criminal provisions under state law.

38. 18 U.S.C. § 1593.

39. TVPA, § 7102(8)(A).

40. TVPA, § 7102(8)(B).

41. TVPA, § 7105(b).

42. TVPA, § 7105(c)(3).

43. TVPA, § 7105(e)(1).

44. TVPA, § 7105(e)(4).

45. *See* Suzanne Seltzer et al., NYC Anti-Trafficking Network Legal Subcommittee, *Identification and Legal Advocacy for Trafficking Victims* at A-9, 2nd ed. (2005), *available at* http://www.urbanjustice.org/pdf/publications/IDLegalAdvocacy.pdf.

46. "Law Enforcement Agency (LEA) means any Federal law enforcement agency that has the responsibility and authority for the detection, investigation, or prosecution of severe forms of trafficking in persons. LEAs include the following components of the Department of Justice: the United States Attorneys' Offices, the Civil Rights and Criminal Divisions, the Federal Bureau of Investigation (FBI), the Immigration and Naturalization Service, and the United States Marshals Service. The Diplomatic Security Service, Department of State, also is an LEA." 8 C.F.R. § 214.11(a).

47. *See* Seltzer, *Advocacy for Trafficking Victims*, *supra* note 45, at A-9.

48. TVPA, § 7105(f).

49. 8 U.S.C. § 1101(a)(15)(T)(ii). T-Visa recipients who are over twenty-one years of age can bring their spouses and children to the United States on derivative immigration status, while recipients who are under twenty-one years old can bring their parents, spouses, children, and unmarried siblings under eighteen years of age.

50. TVPA, § 7105(b)(1)(A); *see* Seltzer, Advocacy for Trafficking Victims, *supra* note 45, at A-9.

51. TVPA, § 7105(c)(3) ("Federal law enforcement officials may permit an alien individual's continued presence in the United States, if, after an assessment, it is determined that such individual is a victim of a severe form of trafficking and a potential witness to such trafficking in order to effectuate prosecution of those responsible. . . .").

52. TVPA, § 7105(e)(1).

53. TVPA, § 7105(e)(2)(B).

54. TVPA, § 7105(e)(3); *see* Seltzer, Advocacy for Trafficking Victims, *supra* note 45, at A-10.

55. TVPA, § 7105(e)(3).

56. Jose Hidalgo et al., Human Trafficking in the United States: Expanding Victim Protection beyond Prosecution Witnesses, 16 STAN. L. POL'Y REV. 379, 398; interview with Catherine Griebel, Trafficking Case Manager, Safe Horizon, Brooklyn, NY (Feb. 14, 2007).

57. *Id.*

58. Violence Against Women and Department of Justice Reauthorization Act of 2005 § 801(a)(3); 8 U.S.C. § 1101(a)(15)(T)(iii).

59. 8 C.F.R. § 214.11(f)(3).

60. 67 Fed. Reg. 4784, 4788 (2002); *see* Seltzer, Advocacy for Trafficking Victims, *supra* note 45, at A-12.

61. 8 CFR § 214.11(f)(3); *see* Seltzer, Advocacy for Trafficking Victims, *supra* note 45, at A-12.

62. TVPA, § 7105(e)(2).

63. Hidalgo, Expanding Victim Protection, *supra* note 56, at 392–93.

64. *Id.* at 393.

65. Trafficking Victims Protection Reauthorization Act of 2003, Pub. L. No. 108-193, 1595, 117 Stat. 2875, 2878 (2003).

66. *See generally* Kim, Trafficking Private Right of Action, *supra* note 25.

67. *See, e.g.,* National Labor Relations Act, 29 U.S.C. § 152(3); Fair Labor Standards Act, 29 U.S.C. § 213(b)(21); Occupational Safety and Health Act, 29 C.F.R. § 1975.6 (1972).

68. TVPA, § 7102(8)(A).

69. TVPA, § 7102(8)(A).

70. TVPA, § 7102(8)(A).

# IV

# Education

In 1837, Oberlin College made history by becoming the first college in the United States to admit women. Later, in 1862, the first African-American woman to earn a college degree graduated from Oberlin. Yet women's admission, while a historic step forward, did not ensure women's equality. In the early years of their attendance at Oberlin, women were considered too weak-minded to take the same courses as men. Female students were also required to wash the male students' clothes, care for their rooms, and serve them at meals. Nor were women permitted to speak publicly at the college. Lucy Stone, the famous feminist and an early Oberlin graduate, refused to write a commencement essay because a male student would have read it to the audience.[1]

The early history of women at Oberlin illustrates that access to educational institutions, while critical, does not alone guarantee that women will achieve true equality in education. The same is true today, as educational programs and institutions, while in most cases formally open to women, in many cases continue to be afflicted with deep-seated sexism that is largely unrecognized and sometimes unconscious. This sexism harms both male and female students, but there are legal weapons available to challenge it.

### Are there laws against gender discrimination in education?

Yes, although they do not reach every form of gender discrimination. As discussed in chapter 1, "Constitutional Rights," the Equal Protection Clause of the Fourteenth Amendment of the Constitution prohibits gender discrimination carried out by government. As a result, women can rely on this constitutional guarantee to challenge intentional gender discrimination by public elementary, junior high, and senior high schools, as well as state colleges and universities and government-run training programs.

In addition to the Constitution, various federal statutes forbid gender discrimination in education. In the 1970s, Congress for the first time focused on the problem of gender discrimination in the nation's schools and colleges and passed a variety of federal laws designed to end gender discrimination in education. These laws, however, include some limitations that do not exist in the federal employment discrimination laws.

The most far-reaching of the education antidiscrimination laws is Title IX of the Education Amendments of 1972, usually referred to as "Title IX."[2] Title IX provides,

No person in the United States shall, on the basis of sex, be excluded from participation in, be denied the benefits of, or be subject to discrimination under any education program or activity receiving Federal financial assistance.[3]

In other words, it forbids gender discrimination in public and private schools and educational programs receiving federal money, and thus provides important protections to girls and women in education. Once an institution receives federal funding for one of its programs or activities, it is prohibited from discriminating in *any* of its programs or activities. As initially passed, however, Title IX specifically allowed gender discrimination to continue in certain areas, such as military academies and private college admissions, a list that Congress has added to over the years. Also, the federal agency that enforces the law (today, the Department of Education; previously, the Department of Health, Education, and Welfare) has permitted some forms of gender discrimination. Finally, recent court decisions threaten to further limit Title IX's reach.

Other laws passed by Congress are much narrower in scope than Title IX or suffer from other limitations. The Public Health Service Act,[4] for instance, forbids discrimination on the basis of sex, but only with respect to health-related schools and training programs. Title IV of the 1964 Civil Rights Act allows the U.S. Attorney General to sue public elementary schools, secondary schools, and colleges for practices that discriminate on the basis of gender in violation of the Constitution or Title IX. In a rare exercise of this authority, in 1990 the Attorney General challenged the all-male admissions policy of the Virginia Military Institute, a state college, and ultimately succeeded in overturning the policy.[5]

In another federal law, the Equal Educational Opportunities Act of 1974 (EEOA), Congress acted more ambiguously. In its preface, the EEOA declares that "all children enrolled in public schools are entitled to equal educational opportunity without regard to race, color, sex, or national origin."[6] It explicitly prohibits "the assignment by an educational agency of a student to a school, other than the one closest to his or her place of residence within the school district in which he or she resides, if the assignment results in a greater degree of segregation of students on the basis of race, color, sex, or national origin."[7] However, other sections of the legislation nevertheless fail to address various forms of gender discrimination, such as situations in which students in a particular school are segregated by sex for the purpose of specific classes.[8]

Several states also have statutes[9] or constitutional provisions[10] forbidding discrimination in education, many of which are more expansive or specific than federal law. Alaska, for instance, specifically forbids sex-biased textbooks and outlaws discrimination in areas ranging from guidance and counseling services to the scheduling of athletic events. Similarly, Florida prohibits sex discrimination in course and program admissions as well as in vocational opportunities. Many of these state laws apply only to public schools or to educational institutions receiving state and/or federal education funding, meaning that private schools that do not receive such funding can legally discriminate against girls or women.[11]

Although many laws forbid discrimination in education, there is still much work to be done to achieve true educational equality between men and women. Some important examples of persisting inequality are the *de facto* gender segregation in many vocational, professional, and graduate education programs, which in turn leads to and reinforces gender segregation in employment; the small number of women in top administrative and faculty positions at colleges and universities; the lack of support for and funding of truly equal athletic opportunities for girls and women; and excessive reliance on standardized tests that underpredict girls' and women's achievement.

This chapter discusses the rights of women and girls to receive equal educational opportunities, as protected by the Equal Protection Clause and various federal statutes. Although the chapter focuses on Title IX, it is important to keep in mind that in some instances, other state and federal laws may provide protection against discrimination in education.

## PRIVATE SCHOOLS

**Is it illegal for private schools or training programs to discriminate against women or girls?**

Often, but not always. Both public and private schools and training programs play a vital role in education in this country and both frequently discriminate on the basis of gender, in spite of the many differences in ideology, educational philosophy, and affiliation. However, not all laws apply equally to all schools and training programs, and distinctions must be kept in mind when considering whether a particular practice at a particular school or program is illegal.

The Equal Protection Clause applies to public education but does not apply to private schools because the Constitution only restricts government action. Similarly, Title IV of the 1964 Civil Rights Act (which empowers the U.S. Attorney General to sue a school system that is discriminating on the basis of gender in violation of the Constitution or Title IX) and the Equal Educational Opportunities Act of 1974 apply only to public schools.

On the other hand, Title IX applies to any education program or activity that receives federal funds, including private schools. In practice, this includes most elementary and secondary schools, colleges, and universities, as well as activities affiliated with schools that receive federal funds, such as internship programs. Additionally, Title IX applies to federally funded education programs run by other organizations, such as prisons, unions, and businesses. Title IX therefore reaches not only discriminatory practices in public schools but also those in many private schools and education programs. Similarly, the Public Health Service Act, which prohibits federal funding of health-related schools and training programs that discriminate on the basis of sex, applies to any institution that receives federal health professions education funding. However, under federal law, private educational institutions that receive no federal money are permitted to discriminate on the basis of gender. (State law may prohibit some forms of discrimination by these schools.) In addition, Title IX does not apply to specific practices of gender discrimination in religious schools, even if they receive federal funds, if the particular religion's tenets require the gender discrimination. (If the religion's tenets do not require gender discrimination and the school receives federal funding, then Title IX forbids discriminatory practices.)

## Sex-Segregated Schools and Classes

**Do public schools violate the Constitution when they only admit students of one gender?**

In many instances, public schools' single-sex admissions policies violate the Equal Protection Clause of the U.S. Constitution. In 1970, for example, women scored an important early victory when they succeeded in opening the doors to the previously all-male University of Virginia, the most prestigious school in Virginia's state university system.[12] In the same year, a lawsuit initiated by a thirteen-year-old girl persuaded the New York City Board of Education to abandon its all-male policy at nationally renowned Stuyvesant High School.[13] Two years later, a federal court held that Boston's two single-sex academic high schools must use the same admissions standards for boys and girls, thus allowing some girls to attend the over-300-year-old, formerly all-male Boston Latin.[14]

Yet not all challenges to the constitutionality of all-male public schools during the 1970s were successful. In 1976, a Philadelphia girl, Susan Vorchheimer, was denied admission to the all-male Central High, one of the city's two single-sex academic high schools. Although the all-female Girls High was well regarded, Vorchheimer preferred to attend Central because of its superior reputation and academic atmosphere. Unfortunately, almost no factual record setting out the differences between the two schools was ever developed in the case; a federal appellate court ruled that the two schools were comparable in quality, academic standing, and prestige, and that Vorchheimer therefore was not denied her constitutional rights by the single-sex policy.[15] The Supreme Court later upheld the conclusion of the appellate court without giving its reasons for doing so.[16] (Because the Supreme Court was equally divided, this case does not have the status of controlling Supreme Court precedent.) Despite this setback, in 1983, girls ultimately won the right to attend Central. Armed with a more complete record of the differences between the two schools, a new set of plaintiffs successfully argued in *Newberg v. Board of Public Education* that Central's all-male admissions policy violated the Equal Rights Amendment of the Pennsylvania Constitution.[17]

In 1982, the Supreme Court issued its first opinion on the constitutionality of single-sex schools in *Mississippi University for Women v. Hogan*.[18] Justice O'Connor, the first woman to sit on the Supreme Court, wrote the Court's opinion, holding that the Equal Protection Clause prohibited the exclusion of men from Mississippi's School of Nursing. While Justice O'Connor acknowledged that a policy favoring one sex can be justified if it "intentionally and directly assists members of the sex that is disproportionately burdened" by "a disadvantage related to the classification,"[19] she noted that the nursing school's policy did not operate in such a way because most nurses are women. Rather than compensating for past discrimination, Justice O'Connor asserted, Mississippi's exclusion of men simply reinforced traditional stereotypes of nursing as a woman's field.[20] Finally, Justice O'Connor pointed out that the exclusion of men from nursing helps to depress nurses' wages—in other words, that the all-female policy may actually have worked to women's disadvantage.[21] Therefore, the Court decisively rejected Mississippi's argument that its admissions policy constituted "educational affirmative action" and found the policy unconstitutional.

Fourteen years after its decision in *Hogan*, the Supreme Court returned to the issue of single-sex admissions policies in public schools when it considered whether the Virginia Military Institute's (VMI) male-only admissions policy violated the Equal Protection Clause.[22] In this case, the United States sued VMI after a female high school student who had been denied admission to the all-male military academy filed a complaint with the Attorney General. In an opinion written by Justice Ginsburg, who twenty years earlier as director of the ACLU Women's Rights Project argued and won many seminal Supreme Court cases prohibiting gender discrimination, the Court found that VMI's all-male policy violated the Equal Protection Clause because it deprived women of the opportunity to take advantage of the unique educational program offered by VMI.[23] The Court also held that Virginia's attempt to remedy the situation by establishing a women's "leadership program" at another college in the state failed to satisfy constitutional requirements because the women's program differed substantially from that offered at VMI and lacked most of the tangible and intangible benefits of a VMI education, ranging from curricular and athletic opportunities to the school's powerful alumni network.[24]

### Are single-sex public schools constitutional if they are designed to address the special needs of low-income students?

After the Supreme Court's decision in *Hogan*, at least two lower courts dealt with the creation or maintenance of single-sex schools for the benefit of disadvantaged students. In 1986, a group of parents sued to preserve the all-female status of Washington Irving High School, then New York City's last public single-sex school. Over 90 percent of Washington Irving's students came from low-income families, and the parents believed that the school's unusually low dropout rate and high rate of enrollment in postsecondary education directly resulted from the school's female-only policy.[25] A federal district court responded that while Title IX forbids discrimination, it does not prohibit coeducation.[26] The court held that "nothing in Title IX establishes either [the parents'] right to send their daughters to an all-girls school" or the right to prevent New York City from converting Washington Irving to a coed school.[27] The court further stated that even if Washington Irving provided girls with an education superior to that of coed programs, making the school coed did not violate the Constitution. While the Constitution may *allow* some single-sex schools, the court held that it does not *require* the provision or maintenance of such schools.[28] Of course, the case, while finding that single-sex schools are never required, left open the important question of when they are permitted.

In 1991, a federal district court in Michigan considered this question and blocked the Detroit Board of Education from opening three all-male academies designed to address the particular needs and problems of urban African-American boys.[29] The Board of Education attempted to justify its policy of sex segregation by arguing that the academies were experimental and that data collected from the three-year project would benefit female students as well. In addition, the board argued that coeducational programs had failed to adequately meet the needs of young urban males. Yet the court was not persuaded because the Board of Education offered "no evidence that the educational system is failing urban males *because* females attend schools with males."[30] In fact, the court found that the board had acknowledged an "equally urgent and unique crisis facing . . . female students."[31] The court held that the operation of the proposed academies would probably violate the federal and Michigan constitutions, as well as Title IX and several state laws. However, the court did not consider whether separate-but-equal schools for boys and girls would have been constitutional, because no all-female academy was available to students in Detroit. Instead, it simply concluded that by barring girls from the new academies, the board was unconstitutionally failing to provide equal educational opportunities to males and females.

Detroit's desire to open public single-sex schools is far from unique. In fact, in the last decade, there has been a national resurgence of interest in public single-sex elementary and secondary schools, particularly in low-income, inner-city environments. Often arguing that "poor students, minorities, and girls stand to profit most from a single-sex environment,"[32] at least ten school districts across the country have established public single-sex schools since 1996.[33] In 1997, the state of California even provided pilot funding for six districts to establish single-sex academies.[34] All of these schools were in urban areas, and most aimed to improve academic performance of at-risk students and/or those from low-income backgrounds. However, the program was eventually discontinued, in part because of a lack of political support for gender-based reform, limited financial resources, high teacher and administrator turnover, and concerns around possible Title IX challenges.[35]

### Given the VMI decision, as well as prior cases, are public single-sex schools ever constitutional?

The VMI case holds that sex-based classifications, such as all-male admissions policies, are permissible only when there is "an exceedingly persuasive justification" for excluding women. The VMI case also makes clear that conclusions that certain types of instruction are inappropriate for the "average woman" do not constitute an exceedingly persuasive justification for single-sex education. However, the VMI Court also expressly noted that the Constitution may permit classifications on the basis of gender to "'compensate women for particular economic disabilities they have suffered,'[36] 'to promote equal opportunity,'[37] [and] to advance full development of the talent and capacities of our Nation's people."[38] In the aftermath of the VMI case, some have argued that the Constitution allows single-sex programs "that are compensatory and will help to overcome barriers to equal educational opportunity and historic gender stereotypes that have limited the prospects for girls and women."[39] No courts have yet addressed this question.

The VMI opinion also suggests that if sex-segregated public schools are ever allowable, the Constitution requires that they be provided "evenhandedly."[40] Given that in most cases challenging single-sex schools, the school system did not provide an identical counterpart for the other sex, the Supreme Court has not yet directly addressed the question of whether separate public schools for males and females that provide truly equal educational opportunities would violate the Equal Protection Clause. The VMI case makes clear, however, that when a single-sex public program for women provides opportunities arguably comparable to but significantly different from those provided in a single-sex public program for men, the constitutional guarantee of equal protection is not satisfied. In other words, at the very least, separate but equal programs for females must be *truly* equal in terms of tangible and intangible benefits, or they are unconstitutional.

### Does Title IX prohibit single-sex schools?

Title IX prohibits gender discrimination in admissions in all levels of vocational education, in professional education, in graduate schools, and in public undergraduate institutions that have not traditionally been sex-segregated, if the schools receive federal funding. However, the statute's prohibitions on gender discrimination in admissions do not apply to single-sex admissions or admissions procedures that otherwise discriminate on the basis of gender in preschool, elementary, or secondary schools, whether public or private; in private undergraduate institutions; in public undergraduate institutions that have traditionally been single-sex; or in military schools.[41] (One court has concluded that this provision was only meant to apply to single-sex schools in existence at the time of Title IX's passage and that Title IX prohibited the creation of *new* single-sex schools.)[42]

The regulations that implement Title IX further clarify when single-sex schools are permissible under the statute.[43] They state that a school district may operate a public single-sex elementary or secondary school only if the district "provide[s] students of the excluded sex a substantially equal single-sex school or coeducational school."[44] In determining whether one school is substantially equal to another, relevant factors include curriculum, instructional materials, technology, extracurricular offerings, faculty qualifications and reputation, geographic accessibility, and the quality and availability of facilities and resources.[45] Some public charter schools, however, are exempted from this rule, leaving open the possibility that (for example) only boys in a particular geographic area might be able to take AP Physics, if the only school in the area offering the class was an all-male charter school.[46] Regardless of what Title IX permits, however, public single-sex schools may be prohibited by the Constitution, as described above.

In addition to Title IX, the EEOA prohibits a school district from *assigning* students to a single-sex school.[47] A student's attendance at a single-sex school must be voluntary, or else a school district violates the EEOA. The EEOA was adopted when some school districts, motivated by a desire to keep the races from mixing sexually when faced with court orders to end racial segregation, put all the girls (black and white) in separate schools from all the boys (black and white). Under the EEOA, federal courts have struck down such plans by southern school districts to use sex segregation to avoid complete racial integration.[48]

### Other than excluding one gender entirely, how else are schools likely to discriminate in admissions?

Institutions whose admissions policies are covered by Title IX not only cannot limit admissions to a single gender; they also cannot set up quota systems to limit their enrollment of students of one gender or require students of one gender to meet higher admissions standards than students of the other gender. The Constitution also prohibits this type of discrimination in public schools unless it is substantially and directly related to an important state interest. For example, in 1974, a federal court considered whether imposing different admission standards to equalize the number of male and female students at Lowell, San Francisco's premier public high school, implicated the Equal Protection Clause.[49] After finding the school's justification —that an equal number of male and female students is an essential element in a good high school education—to be "unsupported,"[50] the Court held that its actions violated the Fourteenth Amendment.

In recent years, there has been growing concern about gender bias in collegiate admissions. While there are many educational disciplines in which women remain underrepresented, women have become an increasing majority of those students seeking a college education. Some schools, concerned that the larger number of women in their entering classes has produced a gender imbalance, have started to award preferences to male applicants, in an attempt to ensure that approximately half of the students are male and half are female. At least one federal court of appeals has found that this practice violates Title IX and, when undertaken by a public university or college, may implicate the Equal Protection Clause of the Constitution as well.[51]

### Does Title IX prohibit coeducational schools from excluding girls from certain courses or otherwise segregating classes by sex?

The Title IX statute provides that "no person in the United States shall, on the basis of sex, be excluded from participation in . . . any education program or activity receiving Federal financial assistance."[52] It does not contain any exception authorizing sex-segregated courses in coeducational schools. As a result, for over thirty years, Title IX regulations prohibited sex segregation in coeducational schools, with narrow exceptions for contact sports and sex education classes. In 2006, however, these regulations were amended to permit elementary and secondary schools to segregate nonvocational classes by sex in many more circumstances.[53]

Schools may continue to group students in physical education classes according to physical ability measured without regard to gender, as was permitted under the previous regulations.[54] Schools may continue to separate girls and boys for participation in wrestling, boxing, rugby, ice hockey, football, basketball, and other contact sports. Additionally, while postsecondary sex education classes may not be single-sex, elementary and secondary sex education classes may segregate by gender. The regulations further provide that choruses that are selected on the basis of vocal range may be made up of one (or predominantly one) gender, as was previously permitted.[55]

The new regulations go far beyond these narrow exceptions to the integration rule, however, and provide that a school may also institute many other sorts of sex-segregated classes or extracurricular activities as long as it does so (1) "to improve educational achievement of its students, through a recipient's overall established policy to provide diverse educational opportunities" or (2) "to meet the particular, identified educational needs of its students."[56] According to the Department of Education's explanation of the regulations, a school will be understood to meet the first of these objectives if it has a policy of offering "diverse" options to students, of which sex-segregated classes form one part—for instance, a school that offers a range of elective courses, or the opportunity to take classes at other schools, would have a sufficient justification for offering sex-segregated courses as well. According to the Department of Education, schools will meet the second objective if they identify limited or deficient student educational achievement and determine on the basis of an analysis of evidence that a sex-segregated class would be substantially related to addressing that problem.[57]

While the new regulations definitely represent a far more permissive approach to sex segregation in public schools, some important protections for equal educational opportunity remain. Most importantly, participation in a sex-segregated class or activity must be *completely* voluntary. The regulations make clear that participation in a sex-segregated class is not voluntary unless a school offers a substantially equal coeducational class in the same subject to all students. (There is no absolute requirement under the regulations, however, that a school providing a single-sex class for boys also provide one for girls, or vice versa.)[58]

Vocational classes still may not be segregated by sex in any instance.[59] Schools also remain prohibited from assigning a teacher to a particular school or class (whether single-sex or not) on the basis of the teacher's sex. According to the new regulations, if a school district or school relies on overly broad sex-based generalizations in creating or teaching sex-segregated classes, this is sex discrimination and remains impermissible. Schools or school districts implementing sex-segregated classes or activities must conduct evaluations at least once every two years to ensure that the sex segregation is based on genuine justifications and does not rely on overbroad generalizations about the talents, capacities, or preferences of either sex.[60]

It is also important to keep in mind that the Equal Protection Clause probably prohibits sex-segregated classes in many or most instances. Prior to the adoption of Title IX, some girls succeeded in challenging discriminatory course assignments—such as metal working for boys and home economics for girls—under the Equal Protection Clause. Although federal courts have not dealt with such cases in recent years, there is good reason to believe that sex-segregated classes still violate the Equal Protection Clause. However, if the class was somehow compensatory, and helped girls or women overcome barriers to educational opportunity, and if equal opportunities were provided to boys and girls, the legal questions might be more complex.

### Is single-sex education better for girls' and women's achievement?

Researchers and women's advocates are divided on this issue. In previous decades, the debate about single-sex education revolved around the impact of single-sex colleges on women's achievement. The argument that women who go to women's colleges are more successful than women who go to coeducational colleges stems in part from studies in the 1970s demonstrating that women graduates of single-sex colleges had achieved a disproportionate number of leadership roles later in life.[61] However, these studies did not control for important factors ranging from socioeconomic status and career aspirations to test scores and the selectivity of the colleges. Moreover, in the 1960s, when the women studied attended women's colleges, many of the nation's most prestigious institutions—including Harvard, Yale, and Princeton, as well as many smaller selective colleges and the military service academies—did not admit women at all. Thus, the most talented women of previous generations who desired to attend highly selective colleges often had little choice but to attend women's colleges, such as the so-called Seven Sisters, many of which are now coed.

Today fewer than 2 percent of women earning bachelor's degrees receive them from women's colleges.[62] In fact, the number of women's colleges in the United States has shrunk from 298 in 1960 to 65 as of 2001,[63] and more than a dozen women's colleges have closed or become coed just since 1990.[64] While the number of women's colleges has dramatically declined, enrollment at these colleges rose by nearly thirty thousand during the 1990s.[65] In addition, between 1991 and 2004, the total enrollment in schools belonging to the National Coalition of Girls' Schools rose by 43 percent.[66] Thus, the debate about single-sex education rages on, fueled in part by the new interest in single-sex elementary and secondary schools, particularly in urban areas.

Some of the recent interest in single-sex education may stem from evidence supporting what girls and women have long known from their own experiences: that sex stereotyping and discrimination are still facts of life in schools. In 1992, for example, the American Association of University Women (AAUW) published *How Schools Shortchange Girls,* a report finding that girls received less attention and encouragement in classrooms than boys, felt less comfortable participating in class than boys, and were increasingly exposed to sexual harassment in school.[67] These findings led many to wonder whether girls might be better off in single-sex classrooms.

Yet research is at best inconclusive as to whether single-sex education is the solution. In 1998, for example, AAUW followed up on its earlier research by evaluating the impact of single-sex education and concluded that factors such as small classes and schools, equitable teaching practices, and a focused curriculum are far more influential in and predictive of student achievement for both boys and girls than is single-sex education. Perhaps more importantly, the study found no evidence that single-sex education generally leads to better outcomes for girls than coeducation. Nevertheless, the AAUW study did acknowledge some benefits of all-female education, including girls' heightened regard for math and science and an increase in academic confidence.[68]

A more recent study examined California's experiment with public single-sex academies in the late 1990s and concluded that single-sex schools offer the potential to advance gender equity, "but the organizational arrangement alone does not ensure it."[69] In fact, the authors found that rather than promoting gender equity, the schools often reinforced traditional gender stereotypes about boys' and girls' needs and abilities. Equally troubling was the study's assessment that single-sex public schools can have serious consequences for those not enrolled. In at least two California school districts with single-sex academies, remaining coed classes were left with gender imbalance, less motivated students, and/or less experienced teachers.

Given such conflicting and incomplete evidence as to the impact of sex segregation on education, there are good reasons to be cautious about encouraging or expanding single-sex education for girls and women, especially when one takes into account the strides by women in closing what was a huge gender gap in education in America made since Title IX's prohibition on sex discrimination and many forms of sex segregation.

## SCHOOL ORGANIZATIONS

**Does Title IX permit any school organizations to discriminate on the basis of gender?**

A few. Under Title IX, most school organizations and activities are forbidden from discriminating on the basis of gender. A 1974 amendment to Title IX, however, permitted college sororities and fraternities to limit membership to one sex and allowed such groups as the YMCA, YWCA, Girl Scouts, Boy Scouts, and Camp Fire Girls to exclude members of the opposite sex.[70] Congress amended the law once again in 1976 to exempt certain American Legion activities, such as Boys State, Boys Nation, Girls State, and Girls Nation. The 1976 amendment also permits schools to sponsor mother-daughter and father-son activities with the condition that if such activities are provided for boys, girls must be given the opportunity for "reasonably comparable" activities.[71] Although Title IX does not outlaw such single-sex organizations, it does not protect these policies from constitutional attack under the Equal Protection Clause if the relevant organizations or activities receive enough support from public schools or other public entities to qualify as government actors or government actions.

Moreover, the new Title IX regulations addressing sex-segregated classes, described above, also apply to extracurricular activities other than athletics, and permit single-sex activities in many instances as long as a substantially equal coeducational activity is available.[72]

## CAMPUS LIVING

**Does Title IX permit schools to discriminate in providing housing for students?**

Yes and no. Title IX specifically allows schools to segregate living facilities by gender.[73] Many students prefer sex-segregated dormitories. Others want coed dorms, however, and they will not be helped by Title IX, which does not provide any right to coed housing, although the law does not limit the school's option to provide integrated living facilities either for all students or for students who choose this sort of accommodation.

On the other hand, Title IX's implementing regulations require schools that provide housing for one sex to provide housing for the other sex that is comparable in quality and cost.[74] For instance, a university cannot house its male students in two-room private suites while crowding its female students into dormitory doubles. The regulations also provide that schools may not impose different rules, fees, services, or benefits related to housing on the basis of gender, such as offering free cleaning for male students only or imposing curfews or on-campus residency requirements only on female students. Housing provided to female students must be proportionate in quantity to housing provided to male students. In addition, schools must take steps to ensure that off-campus housing is available to men and women on the same terms.

## FINANCIAL AID AND TUITION

**May schools award scholarships that are explicitly restricted to students of one gender or otherwise discriminate in awarding financial aid?**

With a few exceptions, the Title IX regulations forbid gender discrimination in financial aid.[75] Schools may not give similarly situated male and female students different types and amounts of financial aid, nor may they use different financial aid eligibility requirements for males and females. For instance, a school may not give scholarships to all men with a 3.0 grade point average but only to women who have a 3.5 grade point average, nor may it award larger scholarships to men than to women with the same financial need.

Again, however, the regulations permit certain forms of gender discrimination. A school may administer scholarships and fellowships restricted to students of one gender that are established by will or trust or by foreign governments. For instance, when the Rhodes Scholarships were restricted to male students, Title IX did not prevent schools from participating in the scholarship application process. However, the Title IX regulations require that the overall effect of the award of these sex-restricted scholarships must not discriminate against female students. In addition, female students who are otherwise eligible for financial aid must not be denied aid simply because of a shortage of funds that are not restricted to male students. Thus, a school cannot make scholarships available to men with less need or lower academic qualifications simply because there are more endowed scholarships for men.

The Title IX statute also explicitly permits scholarships or other financial assistance awarded by colleges or universities based on participation in beauty pageants that are limited to individuals of a single gender.[76]

**What about athletic scholarships? Are schools permitted to spend more on scholarships for male athletes than scholarships for female athletes?**

Schools can only spend more on scholarships for male athletes if there are more male athletes at the school. Title IX regulations require that schools' athletic scholarships be distributed in amounts proportional to the number of male and female athletes at the school. Thus, if 40 percent of athletes on a college's varsity teams are women, the college should spend about 40 percent of its athletic scholarship dollars on women.[77]

**If a woman who is married to a nonresident attends a state university in her home state, can she be forced to pay nonresident tuition rates because of her husband's out-of-state residence?**

No, not if she can show that she is in fact a resident of the state. State universities usually charge nonresidents higher tuition rates than residents pay. In determining residency, some universities once applied the common-law rule that a married woman's residence follows that of her husband, instead of the modern view that each spouse may establish his or her own residence. As a result, married women students sometimes discovered they were classified as nonresidents for tuition purposes although they may have lived in the state since birth. This practice is today forbidden by Title IX and the state laws and has been held unconstitutional.[78]

## COURSES AND TEXTBOOKS

**May school counselors steer girls into courses "suitable" for females or advise them to prepare only for jobs that women have traditionally held?**

No. Such steering is today far more common than explicit restrictions on the coursework that girls and women may take. This common practice, while more subtle than a "no girls allowed" rule, is extremely destructive in that it perpetuates limited opportunities and low wages for girls and women. Such steering violates Title IX regulations and probably (when undertaken by public schools or other state actors) the Equal Protection Clause as well.

The Title IX regulations provide that counselors may not indirectly preserve male-only courses, like auto mechanics or computer programming, by encouraging females to pursue more "feminine" courses or fields, and may not discourage females from taking what may be considered masculine subjects, like physics or calculus.[79] However, such discrimination is often insidious and far more difficult to eradicate than are rules prescribing one set of classes for females and another for males, because counselors are often unaware of their own biases or honestly believe they are merely being realistic about the job opportunities for women or responding to student preferences.

Title IX's regulations forbid the use of standardized vocational interest tests and counseling materials with built-in gender biases. Parents' and women's groups should investigate the tests used in their community schools and job training programs to make sure such discriminatory tests are not being used.

In an attempt to address these problems, the Title IX regulations require schools or educational programs that find a disproportionate number of males or females enrolled in particular courses or programs of study to investigate their counseling and testing programs. It is unlikely that such self-monitoring alone is very effective. Thus it is important for students, parents, and advocates to push for full enforcement of the Title IX regulations (and the Constitution's equal protection guarantee) whether through advocacy with local school boards and job training programs or through legal action.

### May schools use textbooks that show women only in traditionally female jobs or that contain other gender stereotypes?

Yes. Although gender-stereotyped textbooks tend to reinforce the stereotypes of women as (for instance) passive, dependent, and emotional, the regulations issued under Title IX specifically exempt textbooks and other curricular materials from coverage under the law.[80] The reason is a possible conflict with the First Amendment to the Constitution, which protects freedom of speech and the press from government interference.

However, there may be other avenues to address this issue. Many women's groups work to develop unbiased textbooks, educational materials, and courses, and to eliminate sex-role stereotyping in schools. In response to their efforts, some states have adopted laws or directives to replace, forbid, or supplement discriminatory textbooks and other course materials.

## Pregnant and Parenting Students

**May a school exclude pregnant students or unwed mothers?**

No. Title IX regulations forbid schools from excluding pregnant students or students who have had a child or an abortion.[81] Pregnant students may choose to attend special schools or educational programs, but their request to do so must be truly voluntary. In other words, schools are not permitted to pressure pregnant students into withdrawing from regular courses and may not refuse to allow them to return after their babies are born. A pregnant student must also be allowed to take a medical leave of absence for as long as her physician thinks necessary and later resume school attendance, even if the school does not usually permit leaves of absence. If the school maintains a separate, voluntary program for pregnant students, it must be comparable in educational quality to that afforded to other students.

In addition to laws prohibiting discrimination on the basis of sex (which are usually interpreted to include discrimination on the basis of pregnancy), a number of states—including California, Florida, Illinois, Iowa, Michigan, Oregon, Rhode Island, and Wisconsin—also have laws specifically prohibiting discrimination against pregnant or parenting students and/or programs designed to encourage such students to remain in school.[82]

Several decisions rendered before the passage of Title IX concluded that students' equal protection and due process rights under the Constitution were violated when they were excluded from public school solely on account of pregnancy, marital status, or familial status. In lawsuits seeking reinstatement to educational programs after expulsion or suspension on account of pregnancy or parenthood, plaintiffs usually won.[83] Other courts have rejected, on constitutional grounds, efforts to punish students or teachers for their decisions concerning parenting and marriage.[84] Today, Title IX provides a statutory basis to buttress the earlier case law.

**May students who are pregnant, married, or parents be excluded from extracurricular activities?**

This practice is forbidden by Title IX regulations,[85] and a number of courts have ruled that pregnant, married, or parenting students cannot be barred from extracurricular activities.[86] The issue has sometimes arisen when schools attempt to keep pregnant girls from joining the National Honor Society, arguing that pregnancy evidences premarital sex and thus bad character. Courts have generally indicated that at the very least, such a rule cannot be applied unless boys who are known to have engaged in premarital sex are also excluded.[87] The most recent case to address the issue held that even if boys known to have engaged in premarital sex *were* excluded from the National Honor Society, such a rule would probably have an impermissible disparate impact on female students. The court reasoned that pregnancy demonstrates that a female student has engaged in sexual relations, while there is no similar way to know, absent reliance on interrogation, rumor, or innuendo, that a male student has had sex.[88]

Courts have also found that rules that bar married students (whether male or female) from participating in extracurricular activities in public schools (in an effort to discourage early marriage or to curb discussions of sex) violate the Equal Protection Clause or the Due Process Clause of the Constitution. For instance, a federal judge in Texas decided that a sixteen-year-old girl who had been married and divorced and had given up a child for adoption could not be excluded from such extracurricular activities as chess, choir, drama, and the National Honor Society. He emphasized that she was an exceptionally good student and that success in these activities would enhance her chances of getting into college or winning a scholarship.[89] Similarly, in another case, a school was ordered to allow a married high school senior to participate in extracurricular activities and other school functions. The judge decided that the school regulation, the sole purpose of which was to punish students for entering into perfectly legal marriages, infringed upon the student's fundamental right to marry.[90] Several married male high school students have won the right to play on school athletic teams.[91]

### Must health insurance benefits offered by educational institutions provide coverage for pregnancy and pregnancy-related conditions?

Yes, except that they are not required to cover abortions. Title IX regulations require that pregnancy and childbirth be treated the same as other medical conditions under health insurance plans offered by covered educational institutions.[92] However, the Civil Rights Restoration Act of 1987, which was otherwise necessary to the continued vitality of Title IX, included a provision that permits institutions not to cover abortions in such plans. Schools may not discriminate against a student on the basis of the fact or suspicion that she has had an abortion.

## Sexual Harassment

### Is sexual harassment a significant problem in schools?

Yes. A study conducted in 1993 by the AAUW showed that sexual harassment affects nearly 80 percent of girls in elementary and secondary schools and more than 75 percent of women in colleges and universities.[93] While a large percentage of male students also reported experiencing sexual harassment, women reported more frequent and more severe harassment.[94] A 2001 AAUW study produced similar findings: over 80 percent of girls in eighth through eleventh grades reported having experienced sexual harassment.[95] This more recent study also demonstrated that significant numbers of male students experience harassment, but girls reported higher rates of self-consciousness, embarrassment, and loss of confidence following incidences of harassment.[96] Girls were also more likely to alter their behavior, such as not raising their hand in class and going out of their way to avoid their harasser, after suffering sexual harassment.[97]

Experiencing sexual harassment may affect a student's education in a number of ways. First, as the 2001 AAUW study suggests, a girl may avoid the places and thus the classes where the conduct occurs. Second, the emotional impact may reduce her self-esteem generally and her confidence in her academic ability in particular. In fact, the 1993 AAUW study showed that 33 percent of girls experiencing sexual harassment reported that they did not want to attend school and 32 percent reported not wanting to participate in class. That study also revealed the impact of the harassment on students' academic performance: 20 percent of girls reported earning lower grades after the harassment occurred.[98]

### Are students protected against sexual harassment in schools and training programs under Title IX?

Yes, they are protected against sexual harassment by teachers. Federal courts have uniformly ruled that Title IX prohibits sexual harassment of students. Title IX also prohibits sexual harassment by students against a classmate, if that harassment is "sufficiently serious to limit or deny a student's ability to participate in or benefit from the school's program."[99] Furthermore, the Supreme Court has ruled that Title IX allows victims of harassment to recover monetary damages to compensate them for their losses. The case *Franklin v. Gwinnett County School District*[100] involved a Georgia high school student, Christine Franklin, who alleged she was "subjected to a continuing course of intentional sexual harassment, culminating in forced intercourse" by a teacher.[101] Although school officials initially ignored her complaint, their eventual investigation concluded that the sexual harassment allegations were true, and the teacher was forced to resign. The federal Department of Education, which is charged with enforcing Title IX, concluded that his resignation and the school's implementation of grievance procedures were enough to achieve compliance with Title IX. Franklin disagreed and successfully brought a lawsuit establishing harassment victims' right to receive money damages under Title IX as well.

In 1998, in *Gebser v. Lago Vista Independent School District*, the Supreme Court clarified the circumstances under which a school would be liable for monetary damages when a teacher sexually harasses a student.[102] The Court said that a school is only responsible for the teacher's actions and liable for damages when a school official who actually knows about the teacher's conduct and who has the authority to take corrective measures is deliberately indifferent to that teacher's misconduct.

In addition to its rulings on sexual harassment by teachers, the Supreme Court has also held that Title IX requires schools to protect students from sexual harassment by other students. In *Davis v. Monroe County Board of Education*,[103] the mother of a fifth-grade student brought suit on her daughter's behalf after the girl was harassed by a classmate over the course of six months. Although the student reported each harassing incident to a teacher and although her mother was informed that the school principal had been notified, no disciplinary action was taken against the perpetrator. The Supreme Court said that the school's responsibility for the harassment, and thus its liability in damages, would be analyzed under the same standard as *Gebser*: when a school official with actual notice of the student's misconduct and the authority to take corrective measures acts with deliberate indifference to the student's misconduct, the school district is liable for damages under Title IX. (For a more detailed discussion of sexual harassment generally, see chapter 2, "Employment: Discrimination and Parenting Issues.")

### Does federal law protect students from same-sex harassment?

Title IX explicitly protects against discrimination only "on the basis of sex" and does not include sexual orientation discrimination. However, since 1996, several courts have held that same-sex harassment by either teachers or students may violate Title IX.[104] In the first case to do so, *Kinman v. Omaha Public School District*, a female teacher made sexual advances toward and ultimately engaged in a sexual relationship with a female high school student. The court held that such harassment could violate Title IX as the teacher targeted the student because she was female and "directed no similar attentions toward male students."[105]

Later cases have emphasized that same-sex harassment violates Title IX only where the harassment is motivated by gender, not sexual orientation. Nevertheless, at least one court has held that harassment based on an individual's failure to meet gender stereotypes violates Title IX.[106] In *Montgomery v. Independent School District No. 709*, Jesse Montgomery alleged that he had been sexually harassed by fellow students over eleven years and provided an extensive list of examples, ranging from continual name calling to physical assaults, including the grabbing of his buttocks and simulated anal rape. The court concluded that it was "plausible that the students began tormenting him based on feminine personality traits that he exhibited and the perception that he did not engage in behaviors befitting a boy."[107] The court found that if the school had notice that other students were harassing the boy because he failed to meet gender stereotypes, and took no action to stop it, it violated Title IX.

In addition to these cases, Title IX guidance supplied by the Department of Education states that sexual harassment directed at gay and lesbian students can violate Title IX where the harassment consists of sexual advances or assaults. According to the department, mere comments based on a student's actual or perceived orientation do not violate Title IX. The department also acknowledges that harassment based on gender stereotyping but not involving sexual conduct can also violate Title IX.

In addition to Title IX, the Equal Protection Clause may also provide gay and lesbian students protection against sexual harassment, as in a 1996 case, *Nabozny v. Podlesny*.[108] For five years, Jamie Nabozny, a gay student, endured harassment and assault at the hands of fellow students, even suffering a mock rape and a beating that resulted in severe internal bleeding. While he repeatedly reported the incidents to school officials, his complaints were ignored or dismissed despite the school district's policy against both gender and sexual orientation discrimination. The court concluded that the school district's nonenforcement of its policy with respect to Nabozny's complaint violated the Equal Protection Clause.

## ATHLETIC PROGRAMS

One of the great successes of Title IX has been in increasing opportunities for female student athletes. According to the National Coalition for Women and Girls in Education, today women account for 43 percent of college athletes—an increase of more than 403 percent since 1971, when Title IX became law.[109] Girls' participation in high school athletics has skyrocketed at an even faster rate: girls now represent 41.5 percent of varsity athletes in American high schools, an increase of more than 847 percent since 1971.[110]

Many inequities remain. For instance, while women made up over half of the student body at Division I colleges in 1999, they received only 43 percent of athletic scholarship dollars, 32 percent of athletic recruiting dollars, and 36 percent of athletic budgets.[111] Less than 25 percent of these schools provided women with numbers of athletic opportunities within five percentage points of female student enrollment.[112] While data regarding athletic opportunities for girls in elementary and secondary schools are not as widely available, "the available statistics and anecdotal information indicate that discrimination against girls and young women in athletics is every bit as much of a problem in middle and high schools as it is in colleges and universities."[113] Parents and students report inequities in girls' athletic opportunities ranging from discriminatory scheduling to inferior coaching, equipment, and facilities.[114] In addition, women working in coaching and athletic administration continue to suffer from gender discrimination. Women coaches led only 44 percent of women's intercollegiate athletics teams during the 2001–2002 academic year, down from 90 percent in the early 1970s.[115] Moreover, women continue to hold only 2 percent of coaching positions in men's college sports, a percentage that is typical of the past thirty years.[116] A comparison of the salaries for men and women collegiate basketball head coaches shows that women coaches earn sixty-one cents to every dollar that men earn.[117] In light of these persisting inequities, vigorous enforcement of Title IX and its implementing regulations remains important.

### Do girls and women have a right to equal participation in school athletic programs?

Yes. The Department of Education has issued regulations implementing Title IX that state, "No person shall, on the basis of sex, be excluded from participation in, be denied the benefits of, be treated differently from another person or otherwise be discriminated against in any interscholastic, intercollegiate, club or intramural athletics offered by a recipient. . . ."[118] The regulations also direct all recipients of federal education funds to "provide equal athletic opportunity for members of both sexes." To provide equal athletic opportunity to both genders, the sports selected and the levels at which they are played must "effectively accommodate the interests and abilities of members of both sexes."

Women and girls seeking equal opportunity in athletics have been victorious in lawsuits under both Title IX and the Equal Protection Clause. For example, female high school students in Kentucky sued the state board of education and athletics association under Title IX both for offering fewer sports for girls than boys and for failing to "recognize and sponsor a state tournament in" fast-pitch softball.[119] The federal appellate court agreed with the girls that Kentucky high schools failed to provide them equal athletic opportunity and reversed the lower court's dismissal of the case. In another case, parents sued on behalf of their daughters, female high school students who were varsity wrestlers but were denied the opportunity to compete in mixed-gender matches at a tournament.[120] The court agreed that plaintiffs had a claim for gender discrimination under the Equal Protection Clause of the Constitution.

### What does Title IX require schools to do in regard to athletics?

Title IX mandates that schools that receive federal funding (including elementary schools, secondary schools, and colleges) provide girls and boys equal opportunities to participate in sports. In addition, Title IX's mandate applies to nonprofit athletic associations representing public high schools in interscholastic sports competitions.[121]

Whether a school is in compliance with Title IX requirements in its treatment of girls' athletic opportunities can be evaluated in terms of three factors: opportunities for girls to participate in athletics, treatment of female athletes, and funding and scholarships allotted to girls' sports.[122]

### How do colleges ensure equal opportunities for female athletes under Title IX?

With respect to intercollegiate athletic programs, a policy interpretation issued by the Department of Education states that a college complies with Title IX if it meets any *one* of the following three tests:

• The college offers athletic opportunities for male and female students "substantially proportionate" to the numbers of male and female students enrolled.

• Where members of one gender (usually women) have been underrepresented among intercollegiate athletes, the college has demonstrated a history and continuing practice of expanding athletic opportunities for those students.

• Where members of one gender (usually women) have been under-represented among intercollegiate athletes, the college has nevertheless fully and effectively accommodated the athletic interests and abilities of those students.[123]

While this guidance is directed at colleges, it is probably relevant to elementary and secondary schools as well.

In applying the proportionality test, courts and others have understood it to require a comparison of the gender breakdown of participating athletes to the gender breakdown of student enrollment.[124] Thus, a college achieves proportionality when, for example, 52 percent of athletes are male and 48 percent are female, while 52 percent of the student body is male and 48 percent of students are female.[125] However, the proportionality test does not require "strict numerical equality between the gender balance of a college's athletic program and the gender balance of its student body."[126] One federal court found that a 10.5 percent disparity between the percentage of women students and the percentage of women participating in athletics was not proportional.[127]

Alternatively, a college can show that it has a history and continuing practice of expanding women's athletics. In making this showing, it is not enough for an institution to demonstrate that it once expanded the athletic program for women. This was illustrated in a 1993 case in which women students at Colorado State University claimed discrimination when the university cut the women's fast-pitch softball team. Although the university had created a women's athletics program "out of nothing in the 1970s," the fact that opportunities for women to participate in sports declined in the 1980s belied the university's claim that it had continued to expand sports programs for women.[128] The women students won reinstatement of the softball team.

Finally, a college may demonstrate Title IX compliance by showing that it has "fully and effectively accommodated" the "interests and abilities" of women. To do so, a college must assess whether there is unmet interest among female students requiring the college to create new programs. The Office of Civil Rights ("OCR") of the U.S. Department of Education suggests that, in determining whether there is unmet interest, a college consider students' requests that a sport be added; students' participation in a particular club or intramural sport; and information gathered from student interviews or questionnaires.[129] Additionally, OCR suggests that colleges take into consideration "the athletic experience and accomplishments" of interested students and the opinions of coaches and student athletes regarding interested students' abilities.[130]

Courts have rejected universities' arguments that women are less interested in athletics so schools may provide them with fewer opportunities. In one such case, members of the women's volleyball and gymnastics teams sued Brown University when the school cut off funding and support services for the teams.[131] Although Brown also cut two men's teams—golf and water polo—at that time, the university cut substantially more from the women's athletic budget than from the men's. Because women at Brown did not participate in athletics proportionate to their enrollment and Brown had not been expanding the women's athletic program, the court looked to the third part of the test—effective accommodation of students' interests and abilities—to determine whether the university violated Title IX. Brown argued that it could provide athletic opportunities on the basis of the ratio of men with demonstrated interest to women with demonstrated interest, whether or not that resulted in women's interests going unmet, and still comply with Title IX. The court illustrated Brown's argument with an example: the school is made up of 1,000 men and 1,000 women; 500 men and 250 women demonstrate interest in participating in athletics. Brown asserted it could comply with the third part of the test—full and effective accommodation—by offering athletic opportunities for men and women in a 2:1 ratio, reflecting the differences in interest: for example, 100 positions for men and 50 for women. The court found that, because this method would not accommodate the interests of 200 women, Brown did not "*fully* and effectively accommodate" the female students' interests and thus it violated Title IX.[132]

In 2003, the Department of Education reaffirmed its commitment to the three-part test for Title IX compliance,[133] but a surprise "clarification" of the Title IX policy issued in 2005 allows schools to meet the third prong using easily ignored email surveys to gauge female students' interest in athletics, instead of conducting a broad analysis as to whether the schools are effectively meeting the interests and abilities of the underrepresented gender.[134] The clarification permits colleges to claim lack of interest based solely on a low rate of response to the survey, and that in turn would lead to a presumption that the schools are in compliance with Title IX, unless students can provide "direct and very persuasive evidence to the contrary." This new policy in effect undermines Title IX protections and threatens to reverse the gains women and girls have made in sports, by creating a major loophole through which schools could conceivably evade their obligation to provide equal opportunity in sports.

### How can colleges and other schools ensure equal treatment of male and female athletes in regard to equipment, scheduling, and publicity?

In assessing whether schools are providing equal athletic opportunities to male and female students, not only the number of teams or the number of slots on teams is important. According to the regulations implementing Title IX, the following factors are also important to determining whether athletic opportunities are equal: the provision of equipment and supplies, the scheduling of games and practices, the financial support offered for travel and other expenses, the quality of coaching, and the quality of facilities such as playing fields and locker rooms.[135] Superior budgets for travel, facilities, and athletics training personnel for men's teams and greater compensation for coaches of men's teams than for women's have been found to demonstrate a school's discriminatory treatment of women's teams.[136] Courts may also look to whether schools treat girls' and boys' teams differently through press coverage, trophies and awards, and other sorts of public recognition.[137]

### How does Title IX require colleges and high schools to provide equal funding for male and female athletics?

A Title IX regulation states that "unequal aggregate expenditures for members of each sex or unequal expenditures for male and female teams if a recipient operates or sponsors separate teams will not constitute noncompliance with [Title IX], but the Assistant Secretary may consider the failure to provide necessary funds for teams for one sex in assessing equality of opportunity for members of each sex."[138] In other words, while unequal spending on boys' and girls' sports is not in itself a Title IX violation, it may be relevant to whether a violation exists. As a result, "if funding creates a lack of opportunities for girls, the school must increase funding-related benefits to the girls' programs, reduce benefits for the boys' programs, or both."[139]

Devoting disproportionate amounts of outside funding to the activities of one gender can also violate Title IX's mandate that both genders be given equal athletic opportunity. In *Chalenor v. University of North Dakota*,[140] male student wrestlers argued that the university violated Title IX when it cut the men's wrestling team. In fact, the university had cut the team to maintain proportional opportunities for male and female students in order to comply with Title IX's gender equity mandate. In their claim, the male wrestlers asserted that because there was "outside funding" available for the wrestling team that the university chose not to use, the university's motivation was dubious in eliminating the team.[141] The court rejected this argument, stating that a university could not justify inequities in opportunities for men and women athletes by supporting men's athletics programs through outside funding.

### Do girls and women have a right to play on all-male teams under Title IX?

Although Title IX demands that schools provide equal athletic opportunities for girls and boys, the implementing regulations specifically permit schools to have gender-segregated teams "where selection . . . is based upon competitive skill or the activity involved is a contact sport"[142] and thus to bar girls from membership on some male teams. One or the other of these exceptions covers most teams. Therefore, Title IX offers little protection to girls who are barred from some all-male teams. The regulation does provide, however, that if the sport involved is not a contact sport, there is no team in the sport for girls, and girls' athletic opportunities at the school have previously been limited, interested girls must be given an opportunity to try out for the boys' team.

In addition, Title IX as applied in a recent lawsuit may offer girls and women some relief with respect to their exclusion from contact sports. In a landmark decision, Duke University graduate and football place kicker Heather Sue Mercer sued her alma mater for gender discrimination in violation of Title IX and won.[143] Mercer, who had been a successful place kicker on her high school football team, made Duke's team during her first year of college, but was discouraged from participating on the team in numerous ways, such as not being allowed to attend preseason camp and not being issued a uniform or pads. Duke's coach also made several discriminatory remarks to Mercer, such as suggesting that she try out for the cheerleading squad instead. Ultimately, Mercer became the first Duke football player ever to be cut from the football team.[144]

While noting that "Duke was not required by Title IX to afford females the opportunity to play football,"[145] a federal court held that "once a member of the opposite sex is given the opportunity to participate on a same-sex contact sports team, that member of the opposite sex must be treated equally and given the same types of opportunities that other members of the team are given."[146] A jury subsequently awarded Mercer $2 million due to Duke's nearly two-year-long indifference to her rights under Title IX, and a federal district court judge upheld the verdict.[147]

### Do girls and women have a constitutional right to play on all-male teams?

When public schools exclude girls from all-male teams in either contact or noncontact sports, they may violate the Equal Protection Clause. Given the historic lack of athletic opportunities for girls and women, the athletically talented girls of previous generations often had no choice but to attempt to join boys' teams if they wanted to play sports. Thus, in the 1970s, a number of young women—from Colorado to Tennessee—sued over their exclusion from all-male teams and won the right to join all-male tennis, skiing, cross-country, soccer, golf, and baseball teams.[148] During this era, the absence of a comparable girls' team seemed to be a critical factor in decisions allowing girls to play with boys. These suits also usually dealt with girls' desire to play noncontact sports, such as tennis or track. Under these cases, if a public school only has an all-male team in a noncontact sport, girls must be allowed to try out for the team.

A public school's exclusion of girls from participating in contact sports such as football or wrestling may also violate the Equal Protection Clause. For instance, in a case brought by the New York Civil Liberties Union in 1985, Jacqueline Lantz wanted to try out for her high school's junior varsity football team but could not do so under New York state rules forbidding mixed-gender competition in basketball, boxing, football, ice hockey, rugby, and wrestling.[149] The federal district court that heard the case found no Title IX violation, but it determined that the prohibition on mixed competition was premised on averages and generalities about the physical development of female students as compared to male students and that decision making based on these conclusions about the average female violated Lantz's constitutional rights.[150] Hence, the court held that Lantz was entitled to an opportunity to try out for the team. Similarly, in 1998, two parents sued the Texas Interscholastic Wrestling Association for preventing their daughters from competing at a wrestling tournament on the basis of a rule prohibiting intergender matches. Deeming wrestling "the quintessential contact sport," a federal district court ruled that there was no Title IX violation but refused to eliminate the plaintiffs' constitutional claims.[151]

While some girls have successfully challenged their exclusion from all-male contact teams, others have failed, especially where a separate girls' team exists. For example, in 1982, Karen O'Connor wanted to try out for the junior high school boys' basketball team because of her exceptional skill level even though a girls' team existed. A federal district court held that denying O'Connor the opportunity to try out for the boys' team did not violate her constitutional rights.[152] Courts have also relied on arguments about women's and men's physical differences to validate separation of men and women's contact sports teams, even when the women's teams play by less stringent rules. A federal appellate court's reasoning in a 1977 Tennessee case exemplifies this discriminatory justification for gender-segregated teams in contact sports. In that case, a female basketball guard wanting her high school team to play by "boys'" rules, persuaded the trial court judge that special girls' basketball rules in force at that time denied her equal protection of the law and handicapped her in competing for a college athletic scholarship.[153] However, the appellate court reversed and upheld the rules in a decision based on the perceived necessity of maintaining separate male and female basketball teams, reasoning that

[w]hen the classification, as here, relates to athletic activity, it must be apparent that its basis is the distinct difference in physical characteristics and capabilities between the sexes and that the differences are reflected in the sport of basketball by how the game itself is played. It takes little imagination to realize that were play and competition not separated by sex, the great bulk of the females would quickly be eliminated from participation and denied any meaningful opportunity for athletic involvement. Since there are such differences in physical characteristics and capabilities, we see no reason why the rules governing play cannot be tailored to accommodate them without running afoul of the Equal Protection Clause.[154]

Thus, women and girls have had mixed success in suing for the constitutional right to participate in all-male teams.

### What about bringing lawsuits under state laws to protect the rights of women and girls in athletics?

State laws may also offer relief to girls who have been discriminated against in athletics. In the 1970s, at least two state courts struck down restrictions on girls' participation in contact sports based on state constitution equal rights amendments. A Pennsylvania court found unconstitutional under the state's Equal Rights Amendment a bylaw of an interscholastic athletic association that prohibited high school girls from practicing or competing with boys in football, basketball, wrestling, soccer, baseball, and several other sports. The court ruled that girls must be permitted to play on boys' teams, even when there were separate girls' teams.[155] Similarly, in Washington, two high school girls who had qualified for the football team won the right to play when a state court ruled that the athletic association regulation barring their participation violated the state's Equal Rights Amendment.[156]

Challenges to unequal treatment of girls in athletics programs have also raised state constitutional claims. In Montana, for example, high school girls and their parents contested the inferior playing time, facilities, sports offerings, and support given to girls' sports.[157] The court found that the program treated girls inequitably under the Montana state constitution, which guarantees "equality of educational opportunity . . . to each person of the state" and "prohibits discrimination by the state or by private individuals on the basis of sex."[158]

Women and girls have also invoked state civil rights laws to challenge unequal treatment of girls' sports. An organization and parents of female student athletes in Michigan sued the Michigan High School Athletic Association claiming that the association discriminated on the basis of gender, scheduling girls' sports during nontraditional and undesirable times of the school year.[159] In particular, the challengers relied on Michigan's civil rights statute in arguing discriminatory treatment. The federal district court held that the association violated the state civil rights law by scheduling six girls' sports and tournaments—basketball, volleyball, soccer, golf, swimming and diving, and tennis—and no boys' athletic events during disadvantageous times of the year.[160]

### Does either Title IX or the Equal Protection Clause give boys the right to try out for girls' teams?

Male students have sued for the right to play on all-female teams under Title IX, but have been largely unsuccessful. In *Williams v. School District*,[161] fourteen-year-old John Williams, a student at a high school that did not sponsor a boys' or coed field hockey team, tried out for and won a spot on the all-girls interscholastic field hockey team. After John began to practice with the team, the school district informed him that he was ineligible to participate on the all-girls team according to a policy that limited field hockey team membership to girls. His parents sued on his behalf, alleging that since the district offered no boys' field hockey team, John's exclusion from the girls' team violated Title IX.[162] In its analysis, the court referred to the language of the Title IX implementing regulations,[163] which indicated that a school must provide the opportunity for a student to try out for a gender-segregated team if (1) the sport is noncontact; and (2) members of the student's gender have previously suffered restricted opportunities in athletics.[164] With respect to Williams's claim, the court found first that field hockey was not a contact sport.[165] Next, the court examined whether athletics opportunities for boys had previously been limited. On the basis of its review of the number of teams for which boys were invited to try out (twelve) as compared with the number of teams available to girls (twenty-two), the court concluded that boys' athletics opportunities at the school had been previously limited.[166] Thus, it held that the school district violated John Williams's rights to equal athletic opportunity under Title IX.

On appeal, the Court of Appeals for the Third Circuit reversed the district court's decision and sent the case back to the lower court for further factual development.[167] The Third Circuit rejected the district court's conclusion that field hockey was not a contact sport. The court also took issue with the district court's view of boys' opportunities in sports as previously limited. It reasoned that the school district's emphasis on the greater number of try-out opportunities for girls, who were permitted to try out for boys' teams while boys were not permitted to try out for girls' teams, was misplaced because " '[a]thletic opportunities' means real opportunities, not illusory ones."[168] On this issue, it directed the district court to take into account "whether meaningful physiological differences between boys and girls of high school age negate the significance of allowing girls to try out for boys' teams but not allowing the reverse."[169] The *Williams* case is an example of the hurdle that male students must overcome in seeking membership on girls' teams.[170]

Boys have also failed in challenging their exclusion from girls' teams under the Equal Protection Clause. In *Clark v. Arizona Interscholastic Association*, high school-aged boys claimed a constitutional right to play on girls' volleyball teams where there were no boys' volleyball teams.[171] The Ninth Circuit upheld the Arizona Interscholastic Association's policy excluding boys from girls' teams and reasoned that such segregation was justified because physical differences between the genders meant that allowing boys to play on a girls' team might diminish girls' opportunities to play volleyball. Moreover, excluding boys from the team was substantially related to the important government objective of remedying historical discrimination against women in athletics and thus the policy was held constitutional.

**Has Title IX otherwise affected boys' athletic opportunities?**

Opponents of Title IX are arguing more and more frequently that Title IX has a negative impact on boys' athletics opportunities. For instance, they claim that males are losing athletic opportunities because colleges have cut men's teams or have reduced the numbers of spots on men's teams in their efforts to ensure proportional opportunities for members of both genders under Title IX. Representatives of male athletes made this argument in a recently filed case, *National Wrestling Coaches Association v. United States Department of Education*. The Wrestling Association argued that Title IX is unconstitutional because it requires schools to cut men's teams to inflate the proportion of female athletes at a school. According to the association, Title IX limits men's opportunities by requiring provision of equal opportunities for women, because (the association argues) women are less interested in sports than men. The National Women's Law Center filed a brief on behalf of various coaches and women's advocates that defended the policy behind Title IX and argued that the association's claims were premised on the discriminatory and wrong-headed notion that girls and women are inherently less interested in athletics than men.[172] In its brief, the center pointed out that since the passage of Title IX, "Women have gone from being almost totally excluded from intercollegiate athletics to having a disproportionately small but important share of athletic opportunities." The huge increase in female athletes since the passage of Title IX shows that when opportunities for women and girls in sports expanded, women demonstrated more interest in sports. According to the center, it follows that arguments about women's and girls' lack of interest in athletics is "obviously nothing more than an attempt to continue an outmoded stereotype." The court dismissed the Wrestling Association's case in 2003, concluding that nothing in Title IX required schools to eliminate men's teams and that the law provided schools significant flexibility in achieving gender equity.[173]

In similar cases brought against individual colleges, courts have consistently rejected the argument that Title IX creates quotas and the notion that women lack interest in athletics. In *Pederson*, the Court of Appeals for the Fifth Circuit stated, "[Louisiana State University's] hubris in advancing [such an] argument is remarkable, since of course fewer women participate in sports, given the voluminous evidence that LSU has discriminated against women in refusing to offer them comparable athletic opportunities to those it offers its male students."[174] Similarly, in *Cohen v. Brown University*, the Court of Appeals rejected Brown's argument that it is legally permissible for universities to offer women disproportionately fewer athletic opportunities because women are less interested than men in athletics, stating that "interest and ability rarely develop in a vacuum; they evolve as a function of opportunity and experience."[175]

### What strategy is best for women and girls who seek equal athletic opportunities?

Women and girls must make some difficult strategy decisions in seeking to establish equal rights to participate in athletic programs. Should they ask for equal funding for separate male and female sports, integrated sports programs, or a combination of the two? The last option is probably the most desirable. Integrated sports provide the opportunity for the most athletically talented girls to compete with athletically talented boys. By also asking the schools to fund sports diverse enough to attract most girls and by insisting (in the political arena) that the average per student expenditure be equal for boys and girls, advocates would also provide opportunities for those girls who are not interested in, or lack the muscular development for, some of the traditionally male sports. More adequate funding of different sports than are currently emphasized would also help those boys with a similar lack of interest in or muscular development for sports like football. Eventually the schools might find themselves providing meaningful athletic programs for all students, sorting individuals into sports roughly by interest and skill rather than by gender.

## VOCATIONAL EDUCATION

### What laws protect women from discrimination in vocational education?

Gender bias and segregation in vocational education have long helped to exclude women from skilled-craft jobs in trade and industry and to keep them in domestic, clerical, and other low-wage, low-status positions. To remedy this situation, beginning in 1976, Congress amended the Vocational Education Act (now known as the Perkins Act) on several occasions to require states to address sex discrimination in vocational education. To qualify for federal money, states had to collect data on women's enrollment in training programs, reduce sex bias and stereotyping in vocational education, and assist schools in making vocational education opportunities available to women. The law also provided grants for job training for single parents, single pregnant women, homemakers, and women seeking employment in "male" fields. By the late 1990s, national funding for these programs exceeded $100 million.[176]

In 1998, however, Congress substantially reduced its commitment to gender equity in vocational education by amending the Perkins Act.[177] In addition to eliminating the grants for programs specifically serving single parents and homemakers, the 1998 amendments also terminated funding for gender equity programs. While the Perkins Act still requires states to report on single parents' and homemakers' progress in areas such as participation in vocational education programs and subsequent placement, achieving such progress without the help of federal funding will be significantly more challenging.

The elimination of gender equity provisions from the Perkins Act is particularly troubling given the persistence of gender bias and stereotyping in vocational education. According to a recent study by the National Women's Law Center, vocational education programs remain highly gender segregated.[178] Its evaluation of vocational education programs in twelve states across the country found that female students make up 96 percent of those enrolled in cosmetology courses, 87 percent of those in childcare courses, and 86 percent of those in courses that prepare them to be health assistants. Male students, on the other hand, make up over 90 percent of students in training programs for plumbers, electricians, welders, carpenters, and automotive technologies.[179] An earlier study of fourteen vocational education programs for high school students found similarly dramatic sex segregation: more than 90 percent of the young women were trained in traditionally female fields such as health, teaching, and office technology.[180]

Such sex segregation has serious consequences for the range and quality of educational opportunities that women receive. In New York City, for instance, even as late as 2002, "none of the four predominantly female vocational schools . . . [offered] any AP classes in calculus, statistics, biology, chemistry, physics, or computer science—including those schools that purport to prepare their students for careers in the health field or the business world."[181] As late as 2005, in the entire state of Maryland only a single girl was studying electrical engineering in a high school technical program.[182] In addition, sex segregation within vocational education programs leads to significant disparities in the wages earned by male and female graduates. The National Women's Law Center study reveals, for example, that the wages of the *top ten percent* of cosmetologists, childcare workers, and medical assistants do not even begin to approach the *median* wages of those in predominantly male occupations.[183] Girls who take up traditionally female occupations can expect to earn half—or less—what they could make if they went into such traditionally male fields as auto repair, welding, or engineering.[184]

Many other federal laws can be used to fight sex discrimination in vocational education. Most notably, Title IX forbids sex discrimination in those vocational schools that receive federal money, and most do. Thus, women should be able to challenge all-male or all-female vocational schools under Title IX, as well as challenge integrated schools with single-sex or discriminatory vocational programs. Moreover, federal regulations stipulate that any institution receiving federal education funding and providing vocational education may not discriminate in admissions, recruitment, or counseling on the basis of sex.[185] It may also be possible to use the Equal Protection Clause to challenge public vocational education policies or programs that discriminate on the basis of sex.

### Do students in the health professions have any additional protection against discrimination by their schools?

Yes. Two sections of the Public Health Service Act specifically prohibit schools and training programs in the health professions from discriminating on the basis of sex in admissions.[186] These sections apply only to schools and programs receiving financial assistance under Titles V and VI of the Public Health Service Act, but the vast majority of health-related schools do receive such assistance. The prohibition also applies to hospitals insofar as they operate medical schools, training programs, or internships. These laws provide a remedy if a hospital refuses to hire women interns, if a medical school limits its enrollment of women or refuses to admit people over thirty (which affects women more than men as women are more likely to delay their education because of childbearing), or if a nursing school refuses to admit men.

Though the Public Health Service Act refers only to sex discrimination in admissions, the accompanying federal regulations also outlaw sex discrimination in health professions training programs *after* students are selected and extend to undergraduate programs involving health professions training.[187] Like Title IX, the regulations address discrimination in the areas of student housing, student financial aid, equal benefits and services to men and women, and the treatment of pregnant and married students.[188]

## TESTING

### Does Title IX prohibit the use of tests that have the effect of discriminating on the basis of sex?

Yes. Although the Title IX statute does not address testing, a federal regulation implementing Title IX prohibits reliance on admissions tests or criteria that have a disproportionate impact on one sex unless they are proven to predict success in the program or activity at issue and alternative tests that do not have such an effect are unavailable.[189]

On the basis of this regulation, in 1989, ten female high school seniors —with the help of the ACLU—sued their state education department for awarding merit scholarships solely on the basis of Scholastic Aptitude Test (SAT) scores. All of the women possessed outstanding academic records but did not have high enough SAT scores to qualify for the coveted scholarships. In court, they demonstrated that women, on average, scored sixty points below men on the SAT despite the fact that women, on average, earned slightly superior grades in both high school and college. The case also showed that women made up 53 percent of scholarship competitors in 1987 but only 28 percent of recipients. As a result, the district court ruled that the SAT had a discriminatory impact on New York's young women and prohibited the Department of Education from relying exclusively on the SAT in awarding scholarships.[190]

Today, women's scores continue to lag behind men's on a number of standardized tests, including the SAT, GMAT, MCAT, and GRE. For instance, in 2005, women averaged thirty-four fewer points on the math section of the SAT and eight fewer points on the verbal section than their male counterparts.[191] Although gender differences in standardized test scores have declined, their persistence should trouble all who believe that women deserve equal educational and professional opportunities.

It is worth noting that a 2001 Supreme Court decision, *Alexander v. Sandoval*,[192] may limit individuals' ability to sue under Title IX to challenge educational practices, such as the overreliance on standardized test scores, that have a discriminatory impact on women. For more information on how this could affect testing-related lawsuits, consult this chapter's discussion of remedies.

## FACULTY

**Are teachers, other school employees, and students protected against employment discrimination by the sex discrimination provisions of Title IX?**

Yes. In 1982, the Supreme Court ended a long controversy on this issue in *North Haven Board of Education v. Bell*.[193] In *Bell,* the Court ruled that Title IX forbids federally funded educational institutions from discriminating on the basis of sex in their employment.[194] Thus, Title IX protects teachers, administrators, and other school employees, as well as students.

However, federal courts have since disagreed about whether school employees can sue under Title IX given the existence of Title VII of the Civil Rights Act, which prohibits discrimination on the basis of sex by any employer, private or public, with more than fifteen employees.[195] While the Supreme Court has never considered this issue, some courts have held that Title VII precludes school employees from bringing employment discrimination claims under Title IX.[196] One district court in New York held that "the remedies of Title IX are limited to student plaintiffs, and Title VII is meant to offer the exclusive remedy for employment discrimination based on sex."[197] In the view of this court, the *Bell* case simply meant that the government could revoke federal education funds because of employment discrimination on the basis of sex, not that employees could themselves sue to enforce this prohibition. Another district court in New York held that a university employee could not bring a Title IX claim to contest sexual harassment by her supervisor, the director of the school's security services. In doing so, the court reasoned that to do otherwise would provide some individuals with "an additional remedy not available to Title VII claimants whose employers are not educational institutions to pursue a private right of action."[198]

On the other hand, a number of courts have directly or indirectly held that school employees may bring a claim of sex discrimination under Title IX.[199] For instance, in *Henschke v. New York Hospital-Cornell Medical Center,* a federal district court stated that Congress intended for Title IX to serve as "an additional protection against gender-based discrimination in educational programs receiving federal funding regardless of the availability of a remedy under Title VII."[200]

The Public Health Service Act also protects those teachers and employees in medical and health professions who work directly with students. Both the Equal Pay Act and Title VII, which also protect against employment discrimination in schools, are discussed in detail in chapter 2, "Employ-ment: Discrimination and Parenting Issues."

## REMEDIES

A right that exists only in theory does no one any good. For example, a school principal may be acting illegally by preventing a young woman from enrolling in a course just because she is a woman, but until the principal has been forced to stop, the woman merely has a theoretical right not to be dis-criminated against. She has not gotten the results she needs. Occasionally, a woman can change the situation by telling the principal (or other authority) that she has a right to do certain things and by referring the official to the ap-propriate law or appropriate enforcement agency; if the official then changes his or her actions, the woman has achieved her result. All too often, however, a lawsuit or some other legal action is required to enforce her rights.

The rights guaranteed by Title IX, the Equal Protection Clause, and other laws are enforced in different ways. These are briefly described below.

### Title IX

#### How are discriminatory schools punished under Title IX?

Any federal agency that awards money—whether grants, loans, or con-tracts—to a school can cancel that assistance if it finds that the school dis-criminates. The agency may also refuse to award such assistance in the future or refer the case to the Justice Department for a lawsuit against the school. Although many federal agencies administer grant programs to educational institutions, the Department of Education is the main grantor and as such is the chief enforcement agency for Title IX.

The threat of a cutoff of federal money is a powerful weapon as many schools depend on this money for a major portion of their budget. Of course, for this threat to be effective, the Department of Education must be willing to carry it out in the event of noncompliance. In the more than thirty years since Title IX was passed, the agency has never done so.

#### Can a woman bring her own lawsuit to enforce Title IX?

Yes. In 1979, in *Cannon v. University of Chicago,*[201] the Supreme Court ruled that women may bring their own Title IX suits in federal court, and do not have to depend on federal agencies threatening to cut funding to schools for Title IX enforcement. Since then, women have successfully sued under Title IX to contest a variety of discriminatory practices, ranging from their exclusion from athletic programs to sexual harassment. A woman need only find a lawyer to bring suit for her; the amount of time a woman has after she has been discriminated against to file a lawsuit varies from state to state. Furthermore, there is no requirement that the woman file anything with the Department of Education before suing. In bringing a suit, the woman plaintiff will be able to present her own case through her lawyer in court. Plaintiffs may win damages and defendants may have to pay the attorneys' fees of plaintiffs who win their cases.

Individuals can also bring lawsuits to contest any retaliation against them by a school for asserting their rights under Title IX. Title IX regulations make clear that not only can schools not discriminate against girls and women but also they cannot punish girls and women for complaining about discrimination. Until recently, however, federal courts had split as to whether women could go to court to enforce that right. Some courts had previously held that this regulation created a "new right" different from the right to be free from discrimination set out in the statute and that individuals could not enforce this new right in court.[202] Others had concluded that the right to be free from retaliation for complaining about discrimination is an essential part of the right to be free from discrimination.[203] The Supreme Court settled the conflict in 2005 when it held in *Jackson v. Birmingham*[204] that retaliation against a person who had complained of sex discrimination is a form of intentional sex discrimination prohibited by Title IX. Therefore, an individual who complained of sex discrimination and was punished for her complaint has a right to bring a lawsuit under Title IX to challenge the retaliatory actions. The court also added that the individual could assert a retaliation claim if he or she was punished for protesting discrimination against others, thus protecting from mistreatment witnesses of discrimination who dared to speak up.[205]

### Are there any limitations to a woman's right to bring her own lawsuit under Title IX?

Unfortunately, recent court decisions leave open the possibility that not all rights guaranteed by Title IX and the regulations implementing it can be enforced by a woman bringing her own lawsuit. One open question is whether individuals can bring lawsuits under Title IX challenging actions that have a disproportionate *effect* on one sex, even if they were not motivated by a desire to discriminate against women or girls. While the Supreme Court has never decided that Title IX covers only intentional discrimination, some courts have assumed as much based on cases involving similar civil rights laws.[206] Other courts, however, have held that because Title VII, which addresses workplace discrimination based on sex, can be violated even where there is no intentional discrimination but only a policy with a disproportionate effect on one sex, Title IX can be as well.[207]

In addition, several of Title IX's implementing regulations forbid practices, ranging from admissions tests to recruitment systems, that have a disparate impact on one sex. Therefore, on a few occasions, federal courts have held that recipients of federal education funding violate Title IX's implementing regulations when their policies have a disparate impact on one sex.[208] For instance, as discussed earlier, a federal district court held in 1989 that New York State's merit scholarships, which were awarded solely on the basis of SAT scores, violated Title IX regulations forbidding testing practices that disproportionately affect one sex.[209] (The court found that women consistently scored lower than men on the test and that the test underpredicted women's collegiate achievement.)

Yet in the wake of a recent Supreme Court ruling, it is unclear whether individuals can bring their own lawsuits regarding educational practices that have a disproportionate effect on one sex. In *Alexander v. Sandoval*,[210] the Court held that individuals cannot sue to enforce disparate impact regulations under Title VI, a civil rights law prohibiting race and national origin discrimination in programs receiving federal funds. The Court explained that the statute itself does not specifically allow individuals to sue under this theory and has been interpreted to forbid only intentional discrimination. Because the Supreme Court previously stated that Congress intended to enforce Title IX and Title VI in the same way,[211] a few courts have concluded that individuals have also lost the right to enforce Title IX regulations forbidding practices with a disparate impact on one sex.[212] On the other hand, many women's rights organizations, including the ACLU, have asserted that *Sandoval* does not prevent women from bringing Title IX claims concerning disparate impact. According to this view, the language and history of Title IX, which courts have accorded "a sweep as broad as its language,"[213] differ substantially from those of Title VI and render *Sandoval* inapplicable in Title IX cases.

If courts decide that *Sandoval* applies to Title IX, the question they must then answer when deciding whether a woman can bring a suit to enforce a right described in Title IX's regulations is whether a particular regulation simply implements and effectuates the right set out in the statute (i.e., the right to be free from discrimination on the basis of gender), or whether it creates a wholly new right. If the latter, individuals may not be able to enforce these rights in court.

In coming years, the Supreme Court will probably have to deal directly with whether or not the *Sandoval* decision precludes individuals from enforcing any of the Title IX regulations. However, in the interim, it is important to remember that *Sandoval* did not change women's right to bring claims of intentional discrimination under Title IX. Indeed, in *Sandoval* itself, the Court noted "that Title IX created a private right of action to enforce its ban on intentional discrimination."[214] Moreover, as most Title IX suits involve intentional discrimination, some predict that the impact of *Sandoval* on Title IX enforcement will be minimal.[215]

**Are there any other ways to enforce rights under Title IX?**

If a woman wants a Department of Education investigation, which threatens the school with a possible cutoff of federal funds, she should send a letter detailing her charges of discrimination and the name and address of the school involved to the nearest regional office of the Department of Education. She can also file a complaint online, at http://www.ed.gov/ocr/complaintprocess.html.

The complaint must be filed within 180 days of the discriminatory action complained of, and should include as many facts as possible about the discrimination. For example, it could give statistical evidence of discrimination, such as percentages of men and women enrolled in different programs. Charges need not be limited to those the complainant is sure she can prove; she should add those she thinks might be true. It is the responsibility of the Department of Education to investigate and prove or disprove the charges. Likewise, the complaint should address practices the complainant only suspects are discriminatory, whether or not legal authority already supports her. Only if new issues are raised will new law be made. If possible, the name of the federal program that gives money to the school should be included. However, if the complainant isn't sure, the Department of Education will find out which agency gives grants to the school. The department will also send the letter to the proper federal agency if it is not in charge of the grant program (or programs) at the school.

Once the Department of Education receives the charge, it must investigate and may hold a hearing to find out whether the school discriminates. The woman who complained of the discrimination may participate in these hearings only as a witness or as a "friend of the court." She may not present her side of the matter by having her attorney call witnesses or present evidence. Only Department of Education lawyers do these things unless a special arrangement is made. Furthermore, she cannot recover any damages through a complaint to the Department of Education.

However, if a woman is unhappy with the results, she can ask a United States Court of Appeals to review the Department of Education action. Sometimes women's organizations may also be allowed to participate as "friends of the court," which means they can offer their opinion as to what the result should be, but they cannot present evidence or control the course of the hearing unless they are invited to do so.

The Justice Department, through the Attorney General, can also bring lawsuits to enforce Title IX.

### If a woman files a complaint with the Department of Education, how can she assist (or pressure) the Department of Education while it is handling her complaint?

Nothing is guaranteed to work, but the following steps may help mobilize the bureaucracy. First, the initial letter to the department should provide as much information as possible, especially such useful items as the names, addresses, and phone numbers of people who should be interviewed. If several people have suffered from the same discrimination (for example, five other girls were excluded from the same shop class), all of them should join in the complaint. This guarantees that if the situation of one of the complainants changes before the department takes action, there will be someone else who can assist in correcting the discriminatory practice.

Any letters received from department officials should be answered quickly. If the department does not get a reply within a reasonable time, it will conclude that the complainant is no longer interested in pursuing the complaint and will close the investigation.

The complainant should call the department regional office to find out the name and phone number of the investigator assigned to the complaint and should maintain friendly contact with this person. The department still has a great deal of discretion over which cases it handles and how thoroughly it investigates them. A complainant who is cooperative and remains interested in resolving her case may receive more attention. If nothing seems to be happening on a complaint, she can call the department to find out what action is being taken or planned. She can also contact the congressperson for her district and tell him or her about the discrimination and the lack of action on it. A letter from a congressperson to the department's regional office may work wonders.

## *The Equal Protection Clause*

### How can women challenge a discriminatory practice under the Equal Protection Clause?

A woman can enforce rights under the Equal Protection Clause by bringing a lawsuit against the discriminating school or official. She will need a lawyer, preferably one experienced in the area of women's rights.

Usually a woman in this type of situation sues for an injunction—a court order telling someone to do something or ordering someone to stop doing something. For instance, a judge can order a school to admit women or to stop enforcing a rule that applies only to female students. Occasionally a woman also sues for money damages or some other award. An equal protection claim against officials may be brought in a single lawsuit with a challenge to the discriminatory practice under one of the other federal laws discussed here, although some courts will not permit an equal protection claim, if a remedy under Title IX is available. In some cases a constitutional equal protection claim may also be combined with a claim under state law. It is important to remember, however, that the Equal Protection Clause prohibits discrimination only by public schools and colleges.

## *The Equal Educational Opportunities Act*

### How can women enforce rights under the Equal Educational Opportunities Act?

This statute is enforced in two ways: a woman may bring a lawsuit in a federal district court to enforce her rights, or the U.S. Attorney General may begin one on her behalf. The Attorney General is also authorized to intervene in lawsuits begun by private individuals.[216]

## *Title IV of the 1964 Civil Rights Act*

### How can women enforce rights under Title IV?

This law only permits the Justice Department to sue a discriminatory school or college. Thus, a woman's role is limited to requesting that the

Justice Department bring such a lawsuit when she has been discriminated against or is aware of a discriminatory practice. In the past, Title IV has been used principally to desegregate racially segregated public schools. In 1990, the department sued the Virginia Military Institute over its refusal to admit women and ultimately prevailed when the case went to the Supreme Court, as discussed above.

Women should request that the Justice Department continue to fight other forms of educational discrimination unrelated to racial segregation, if for no other reason then to help educate Justice Department lawyers on other sex discrimination issues.

### How can women request that the Attorney General or Justice Department bring such lawsuits?

They can send a letter to Department of Justice, Civil Rights Division, 950 Pennsylvania Ave. NW, Educational Opportunities Section, PHB, Washington, D.C. 20530.

In the letter, the complainant should describe the school system and the discriminatory practices and give as many facts as possible. It also helps to identify others who share the same problem. The Justice Department will be more interested if it is a widespread problem. Although it is impossible to know whether the Justice Department will follow through, it is probably worthwhile to make the effort—certainly so for women who cannot find or afford their own lawyers. Even for those who have access to counsel, requests for Justice Department intervention may serve as a means of publicizing the discrimination and of awakening government officials to its existence and effects.

### *The Public Health Service Act*

### How are the antidiscrimination provisions of the Public Health Service Act enforced?

The Department of Health and Human Services (HHS) must cancel any federal financial assistance—whether in the form of a grant, a loan guarantee, or a subsidy on interest payments—under Titles VII or VIII of the Public Health Service Act for a school or program that discriminates. Theoretically, cancellation can occur in three ways. If the school fails to give HHS a written assurance that it will not discriminate, HHS must cut off or refuse to award the funds. HHS also conducts routine reviews to check for discrimination. Finally, someone can file a complaint with HHS, charging a program with discrimination. HHS would then conduct a hearing and cancel any financial assistance if it finds discrimination. Although the women discriminated against will not be allowed to participate in these hearings except as witnesses or "friends of the court," they will be able to ask a federal court to review HHS action.

A complaint can be filed by sending a letter describing the charges to the nearest Health and Human Services Office for Civil Rights regional office.

Although there has been no court ruling on the point, it may also be possible for a woman who has been discriminated against to sue the discriminatory schools in federal court, under the Public Health Service Act, under the same theory used to allow private lawsuits under Title IX.

## NOTES

1. ELEANOR FLEXNER, CENTURY OF STRUGGLE: THE WOMAN'S RIGHTS MOVEMENT IN THE UNITED STATES 29–30 & n.13 (1970).

2. 20 U.S.C. §§ 1681–1688 (2007).

3. 20 U.S.C. § 1681(a).

4. 42 U.S.C. §§ 295m, 42 U.S.C. §§ 296g (2007).

5. *See* United States v. Virginia, 518 U.S. 515 (1996).

6. 20 U.S.C. § 1701(a)(1).

7. 20 U.S.C. § 1703(c).

8. *See* Galen Sherwin, *Single-Sex Schools and the Antisegregation Principle*, 30 N.Y.U. REV. L. & SOC. CHANGE 35, 51–54 (2005). Not surprisingly, the EEOA has been used only in a handful of sex discrimination cases, all of which occurred in the 1970s. *See, e.g.*, United States v. Hinds County Sch. Bd., 560 F.2d 619 (5th Cir. 1977); Vorchheimer v. Sch. Dist. of Phila., 532 F.2d 880 (3d Cir. 1976), *aff'd by an equally divided court*, 430 U.S. 703 (1977).

9. *See, e.g.*, ALASKA STAT. §§ 14.18.010–18.110 (2006); CAL. EDUC. CODE § 66270 (West 2005); CONN. GEN. STAT. ANN. §10-15c (West 2005); FLA. STAT. ANN. § 1000.05 (West 2005); IDAHO CODE § 67-5901 (2005); IND. CODE ANN. § 22-9-1-3 (West 2005); IOWA CODE § 216.9 (2005); KY. REV. STAT. ANN. § 344.555 (Baldwin 2005); ME. REV. STAT. ANN., tit. 5, § 4602 (2005); MASS. GEN. LAWS ANN. ch. 76, § 5 (West 2005); N.Y. EDUC. LAW § 3201-A (Mckinney 2005); OR. REV. STAT. § 659.850 (2005); WASH. REV. CODE §§ 28a.640.010, 28B.110.010 (2005); WIS. STAT. ANN. § 118.13 (West 2005).

10. *See, e.g.*, Cal. Const. art. I, § 31; Haw. Const. art. X, § 1; Wash. Const. art. IX, § I.

11. Some state constitutions also have their own equal protection guarantees or equal rights amendments. *See, e.g.*, Alaska Const. art. I, § 1, §3; Colo. Const. art. II, § 29; Conn. Const. art. I, § 20; Haw. Const. art. I, § 5; Ill. Const. art. I, § 18; Md. Const. decl. of rts. art. 46; Mass. Const. pt. 1, art. 1, *amended by* Mass. Const art. CVI; Mont. Const. art. II, § 4; N.H. Const. pt. 1, art. 2; N.M. Const. art. II, § 18; Pa. Const. art. I, § 28; Tex. Const. art. I §§ 3a; Utah Const. art. IV, § 1; Va. Const. art. I, § 11; Wash. Const. art. XXXI, § 1; Wyo. Const. art. VI, § 1. In these states, such provisions may serve as a further basis for challenging discriminatory practices within public education or educational programs with state involvement. *See* Newberg v. Bd. of Public Educ., 478 A.2d 1352 (Pa. Super. Ct. 1984) (a Pennsylvania case discussed later in this chapter), for a helpful example.

12. Kirstein v. Rector of Univ. of Va., 309 F. Supp. 184 (E.D. Va. 1970).

13. Alyse Reckson, *Perspectives: Girl in a "Boys" School: The Way It Was*, N.Y. Times, Apr. 24, 1983, at A76.

14. Bray v. Lee, 337 F. Supp. 934 (D. Mass. 1972).

15. Vorchheimer v. Sch. Dist. of Phila., 532 F.2d 880 (3d Cir. 1976), *rev'g* Vorchheimer v. School Dist., 400 F. Supp. 326, (E.D. Pa. 1975).

16. In a 4–4 split, the Supreme Court affirmed the decision without an opinion. Vorchheimer v. Sch. Dist. of Phila., 430 U.S. 703 (1977).

17. Newberg v. Bd. of Pub. Educ., 26 Pa. D. & C.3d 682 (Pa.Com.Pl. 1983), *appeal quashed*, 478 A.2d 1352 (Pa. Super. Ct. 1984).

18. Miss. Univ. for Women v. Hogan, 458 U.S. 718 (1982).

19. *Id.* at 728.

20. *Id.* at 729–30.

21. *Id.* at n.15.

22. United States v. Virginia, 518 U.S. 515 (1996).

23. *Id.* at 520. In order "to instill physical and mental discipline in its cadets and [to] impart to them a strong moral code," VMI used a highly confrontational "adversative method" unavailable in Virginia's other public colleges and universities.

24. *Id.* at 546–54.

25. Jones v. Bd. of Educ., 632 F. Supp. 1319, 1323 (S.D.N.Y. 1986). The board decided to make Washington Irving a coed school because it believed that as a vocational school, its single-sex admissions policy violated Title IX.

26. *Id.* at 1322.

27. *Id.* at 1323.

28. *Id.* at 1323–25.

29. Garret v. Bd. of Pub. Educ., 775 F. Supp. 1004 (E.D. Mich. 1991).

30. *Id.* at 1008 (emphasis added).

31. *Id.* at 1007 (internal citations omitted).

32. E.g., Karen Stabiner, *Boys Here, Girls There: Sure, If Equality's the Goal*, WASH. POST, May 12, 2002, at B1.

33. Nationally, there were at least 193 public schools offering some sort of single-sex education, in the form of either single-sex classrooms or single-sex schools, as of the 2004–2005 school year. *See* Nat'l Assoc'n for Single-Sex Pub. Educ., Single-Sex Public Schools in the United States, *available at* http://www.singlesexschools.org/schools-schools.htm (last visited Feb. 8, 2007).

34. Amanda Datnow et al., Is Single-Gender Schooling Viable in the Public Sector? Lessons from California's Pilot Program, Final Report (May 20, 2001), *available at* http://www.oise.utoronto.ca/depts/tps/adatnow/final.pdf.

35. *Id.* at 57–70.

36. *Virginia,* 518 U.S. at 533 (quoting Califano v. Webster, 430 U.S. 313, 320 (1977)).

37. *Id.* (quoting California Fed. Sav. & Loan Ass'n. v. Guerra, 479 U.S. 272, 289 (1987)).

38. *Id.*

39. Marcia D. Greenberger, National Women's Law Center, Statement of Marcia D. Greenberger on the Administration's Announcement to Amend Single-Sex Education Regulations (May 15, 2002), *available at* http://www.nwlc.org/details.cfm?id=1102&section=newsroom (last visited Feb. 8, 2007).

40. *Virginia,* 518 U.S. at 534 n.7.

41. 20 U.S.C.A. § 1681 (2006). Women were admitted to the United States military academies by amendment to the Defense Appropriation Authorization Act of 1976. 10 U.S.C. § 4342, notes (2005). Women must meet the same academic and other standards required of men for appointment, admission, training, graduation, and commissioning, with "minimum essential adjustments in such standards required because of physiological differences between male and female individuals."

42. *Garret,* 775 F. Supp. at 1009.

43. 34 C.F.R. § 106.34(c) (2007).

44. *Id.*

45. *Id.* § 106.34(c)(3).

46. *Id.* § 106(c)(2).

47. 20 U.S.C. §§ 1701–58.

48. United States v. Hinds County Sch. Bd., 560 F.2d 619 (5th Cir. 1977).

49. Berkelman v. S.F. Unified Sch. Dist., 501 F.2d 1264 (9th Cir. 1974).

50. *Id.* at 1269.

51. Johnson v. Bd. of Regents, 106 F. Supp. 2d 1362 (S.D. Ga. 2000), *aff'd* 263 F.3d 1234 (11th Cir. 2001).

52. 20 U.S.C. § 1681(a) (2006).

53. 34 C.F.R. § 106.34(b).

54. When reliance on a single method of measuring skill or progress in a physical

education class has an adverse effect on females (or males), the school must adopt an alternative method that doesn't have such an effect. 34 C.F.R. § 106.43 (2007).

55. 34 C.F.R. § 106.34(a).

56. *Id.* § 106.34(b).

57. 71 Fed. Reg. 62530, 62534–35 (Oct. 25, 2006).

58. 34 C.F.R. § 106.34(b).

59. 34 C.F.R. § 106.35 (2007).

60. 34 C.F.R. § 106.34(b).

61. *See, e.g.*, M. Elizabeth Tidball, *Perspective on Academic Women and Affirmative Action*, 54 EDUC. RESEARCH 130, 132 (1973); M. Elizabeth Tidball, *The Search for Talented Women*, CHANGE, 51, 51–52 (May 1974); M. Elizabeth Tidball, *Women's Colleges and Women Achievers Revisited*, 5 SIGNS 504, 508–10 (1980). *See also Miss. Univ. for Women*, 458 U.S. at 738–39 (Powell, J., dissenting).

62. Wendy Kaminer, *The Trouble with Single Sex Schools*, ATLANTIC MONTHLY, April 1998, at 22.

63. *Chestnut Hill College Goes Fully Coeducational*, CHRON. OF HIGHER EDUC., Nov. 30, 2001, at A33.

64. Michael O'Connor, *College of St. Mary Struggles for Students*, OMAHA WORLD-HERALD, July 30, 2001, at 1.

65. *Id.* (quoting the Women's College Coalition).

66. Nat'l Coalition of Girls' Schs., A Statistical Profile of NCGS Member Schools, *at* http://www.ncgs.org/type0.php?pid=51 (last visited Feb. 8, 2007).

67. *See* Am. Ass'n of Univ. Women Educ. Found., How Schools Shortchange Women: Executive Summary (1992), *available at* http://www.aauw.org/research/hssg. pdf (last visited Feb. 8, 2007).

68. AM. ASS'N OF UNIV. WOMEN EDUC. FOUND., SEPARATED BY SEX: A CRITICAL LOOK AT SINGLE-SEX EDUCATION FOR GIRLS (1998).

69. Datnow, Is Single-Gender Schooling Viable in the Public Sector?, *supra* note 34, at 74.

70. 20 U.S.C. § 1681(a)(6) (2007).

71. *Id.* §§ 1681(a)(7), 1681(a)(8).

72. 34 C.F.R. § 106.34(b).

73. 20 U.S.C. § 1686 (2006).

74. 45 C.F.R. § 86.32 (2007).

75. 34 C.F.R. § 106.37.

76. 20 U.S.C. § 1681(a)(9) (2007).

77. 34 C.F.R. § 106.37(c)(1).

78. 34 C.F.R. § 106.31(b)(6); Samuel v. Univ. of Pittsburgh, 375 F. Supp. 1119 (W.D. Pa. 1974). On appeal the court ruled that the women were entitled to restitution and that requiring each student to sue individually to recover her money imposed an undue burden.

79. 34 C.F.R. § 106.36 (2007).

80. 34 C.F.R. § 106.42 (2007).

81. 34 C.F.R. § 106.40 (2007).

82. *See, e.g.*, Cal. Educ. Code § 8911 (West 2005) (prioritizing funding for programs for pregnant and parenting teens that prevent dropouts and encourage reentry); FLA. STAT. ANN. § 232.01 (West 2005) (stating that married and/or pregnant students should not be prohibited from attending school); 410 ILL. COMP. STAT. ANN. 230/4-101 (West 2005); IOWA CODE ANN. § 216.9 (West 2005) (outlawing discrimination within educational institutions on the basis of actual or potential parental, family, or marital status); MICH. COMP. LAWS ANN. § 380.1301 (West 2005) (prohibiting exclusion or expulsion of pregnant students from public school); OR. REV. STAT. § 336.640 (2005) (stating that students may not be excluded from public schools on the basis of pregnancy or parenthood); R.I. GEN. LAWS § 40-19-2 (2005) (establishing a program for parenting and pregnant teens that will encourage them to complete school); WIS. STAT. ANN. § 118.13 (West 2005) (prohibiting discrimination against public school students on the basis of pregnancy or parental status).

83. *See, e.g.*, Perry v. Grenada Mun. Separate Sch. Dist., 300 F. Supp. 748 (N.D. Miss. 1969); Ordway v. Hargraves, 323 F. Supp. 1155 (D. Mass. 1971); Shull v. Columbus Mun. Separate Sch. Dist., 338 F. Supp. 1376 (N.D. Miss. 1972). *But cf.* Houston v. Prosser, 361 F. Supp. 295 (N.D. Ga. 1973).

84. *See, e.g.*, Eckman v. Bd. of Educ. of Hawthorn Sch. Dist., 636 F. Supp. 1214 (N.D. Ill. 1986) (affirming jury's finding that school board violated teacher's constitutional rights by discharging her on account of her decision to have and raise a child as a single parent); Street v. Cobb County Sch. Dist., 520 F. Supp. 1170 (N.D. Ga. 1981) (finding that school district violated student's constitutional rights by attempting to exclude her from day program after she began to reside with her boyfriend where district would have allowed a similarly situated married student to attend day school).

85. 34 C.F.R. § 106.40.

86. *See, e.g.*, Wort v. Vierling, 778 F.2d 1233 (7th Cir. 1985); Cazares v. Barber, No. CIV-90-0128-TUC-ACM, slip op. (D. Ariz. May 31, 1990).

87. Pfeifer v. Marion Ctr. Area Sch. Dist., 917 F.2d 779 (3d Cir. 1990).

88. Chipman v. Grant County Sch. Dist., 30 F. Supp.2d 975 (E.D. Ky. 1998). *But see* Hall v. Lee Coll., Inc., 932 F. Supp. 1027 (E.D. Tenn. 1996) (finding no violation of Title IX when religious college that forbade premarital sex suspended an unmarried pregnant student for violating that policy when no evidence was presented demonstrating the policy's disparate impact on female students and when policy applied to both male and female students).

89. Romans v. Crenshaw, 354 F. Supp. 868 (S.D. Tex. 1971).

90. Holt v. Shelton, 341 F. Supp. 821 (M.D. Tenn. 1972).

91. E.g., Davis v. Meek, 344 F. Supp. 298 (N.D. Ohio 1972); Moran v. Sch. Dist. 7, 350 F. Supp. 1180 (D. Mont. 1972); Hollon v. Mathis Ind. Sch. Dist., 358 F. Supp. 1269 (S.D. Tex. 1973), *vacated as moot*, 491 F.2d 92 (5th Cir. 1974).

92. 34 C.F.R. § 106.40(4).

93. Amer. Ass'n of Univ. Women, Hostile Hallways: The AAUW Survey on Sexual Harassment in America's Schools (1993), *available at* http://www.aauw.org/research/hostile93.cfm.

94. *Id.*

95. Amer. Ass'n of Univ. Women Educ. Found., Hostile Hallways: Bullying, Teasing, and Sexual Harassment in School (2001), *available at* http://www.aauw.org/research/upload/hostilehallways.pdf.

96. *Id.* at 31–38.

97. *Id.*

98. *Id. See also* Nat'l Women's Law Ctr., Righting the Wrongs: A Legal Guide to Understanding, Addressing, and Preventing Sexual Harassment in Schools 3–4 (1998).

99. U.S. Dep't of Educ., Office of Civil Rights, Revised Sexual Harassment Guidance: Harassment of Students by School Employees, Other Students, or Third Parties (Jan. 19, 2001), *available at* http://www.ed.gov/offices/OCR/archives/shguide/index.html.

100. 503 U.S. 60 (1992).

101. Brief for Petitioner, at 2, Franklin v. Gwinnett County Sch. Dist., 503 U.S. 60 (1992).

102. 524 U.S. 274 (1998).

103. 526 U.S. 629 (1999).

104. *See, e.g.*, Frazier v. Fairhaven Sch. Dist., 276 F.3d 52 (1st Cir. 2002); Doe v. Dallas Indep. Sch. Dist., 153 F.3d 211 (5th Cir. 1998); Montgomery v. Indep. Sch. Dist. No. 709, 109 F. Supp. 2d 1081 (D. Minn. 2000).

105. Kinman v. Omaha Pub. Sch. Dist., 94 F.3d 463, 468 (8th Cir. 1996).

106. *Montgomery*, 109 F. Supp. 2d at 1092.

107. *Id.* at 1090.

108. 92 F.3d 446 (7th Cir. 1996).

109. Nat'l Coal. for Women & Girls in Educ., Title IX at 30: Report Card on Gender Equity 15 (2002), *available at* http://www.ncwge.org/PDF/title9at30-6-11.pdf [hereinafter Title IX at 30].

110. *Id.*

111. Nat'l Women's Law Ctr., Title IX and Women's Athletic Opportunity: A Nation's Promise Yet to Be Fulfilled 2 (June 2002), *available at* http://www.nwlc.org/pdf/PromiseJune2002.pdf.

112. Title IX at 30, *supra* note 109, at 16.

113. Nat'l Women's Law Ctr., The Battle for Gender Equity in Athletics in Elementary and Secondary Schools 1 (2002), *available at* http://www.nwlc.org/pdf/Battle_June2002.pdf.

114. *Id.*

115. Title IX at 30, *supra* note 109, at 17.

116. *Id.*

117. *Id.* at 17–18.

118. 34 C.F.R. § 106.4 (2007).

119. Horner v. Ky. High Sch. Athletic Ass'n, 43 F.3d 265, 269 (6th Cir. 1994).

120. Barnett v. Tex. Wrestling Ass'n, 16 F. Supp. 2d 690 (N.D. Texas 1998).

121. Brentwood Academy v. Tenn. Secondary Sch. Athletic Ass'n, 531 U.S. 288, 294 (2001).

122. Roberts v. Colo. State Univ., 814 F. Supp. 1507, 1511 (D. Colo. 1993), *aff'd in part, rev'd in part,* 998 F.2d 824 (10th Cir. 1993).

123. Policy Interpretation: Title IX and Intercollegiate Athletics, 44 FED. REG. 71,413 *et seq.* at 71,418 (1979).

124. Cohen v. Brown Univ., 991 F.2d 888, 895 (1st Cir. 1993); *see also* Kelley v. Bd. of Trustees, 35 F.3d 265, 271 (7th Cir. 1994); Horner v. Ky. High Sch. Athletic Ass'n, 43 F.3d 265, 275 (6th Cir. 1994) (stating that this prong is least stringent benchmark in that "substantial proportionality provides a safe harbor for recipients of federal funds").

125. Dep't of Educ., Office of Civil Rights, Clarification of Intercollegiate Athletics Policy Guidance: The Three-Part Test (1996), *available at* http://www.ed.gov/about/offices/list/ocr/docs/clarific.html [hereinafter OCR Clarification].

126. *Cohen,* 991 F.2d at 895; *see also Kelley,* 35 F.3d at 271.

127. Roberts v. Colo. State Bd. of Agric., 998 F.2d at 830.

128. *Id.* at 830.

129. OCR Clarification, *supra* note 125.

130. *Id.*

131. *Cohen,* 991 F.2d at 892.

132. *Id.* at 899–900. *See also* Cohen v. Brown Univ., 101 F.3d 155, 179 (1st Cir. 1996); Pederson v. La. State Univ., 213 F.3d 858, 878 (5th Cir. 2000). In Pederson, female students at Louisiana State University sued the university and university officials to force LSU to offer women's intercollegiate varsity soccer and fast-pitch softball teams. The students claimed that LSU did not effectively accommodate female students' interests in soccer and fast-pitch softball. The court agreed and found that LSU could not rely on the low percentage of women students participating in sports as an indicator of low interest to justify its discrimination, because this low percentage was the result of the very discrimination that led LSU not to offer comparable opportunities to women athletes.

133. Dep't of Educ., Office of Civil Rights, Further Clarification of Intercollegiate Athletics Policy Guidance regarding Title IX Compliance (July 11, 2003), *available at* http://www.ed.gov/about/offices/list/ocr/title9guidanceFinal.pdf.

134. Dep't of Educ., Office of Civil Rights, Additional Clarification of Intercollegiate Athletics Policy: Three Part Test—Part Three (Mar. 17, 2005), *available at* http://www.ed.gov/about/offices/list/ocr/docs/title9guidanceadditional.html.

135. 34 C.F.R. § 106.41(c)(2)-(10) (2007).

136. *Pederson*, F.3d at 881.

137. Ridgeway v. Mont. High Sch. Ass'n, 633 F. Supp. 1564, 1572 (D. Mont. 1986) (ordering continued compliance with settlement agreements to reach gender equity in athletics).

138. 34 C.F.R. § 106.41(c).

139. ACLU of Ohio Found., Put Me In, Coach! 17 (2002).

140. 142 F. Supp. 2d 1154 (D.N.D. 2000).

141. *Id.* at 1158.

142. 34 C.F.R. § 106.41(b). The regulations define contact sports as "boxing, wrestling, rugby, ice hockey, football, basketball and other sports . . . involving bodily contact." *Id.*

143. Mercer v. Duke Univ., 181 F. Supp. 2d 525 (M.D.N.C. 2001).

144. *Id.* at 534.

145. *Id.* at 530–31.

146. *Id.* at 539 (citing Mercer v. Duke Univ., 190 F.3d 643, 647 (4th Cir. 1999)).

147. *Id.* at 552.

148. Bednar v. Neb. Sch. Activities Ass'n, 531 F.2d 922 (8th Cir. 1976) (holding that exclusion of athletically competitive girl from all-male cross-country team violated Fourteenth Amendment); Brenden v. Indep. Sch. Dist., 477 F.2d 1292 (8th Cir. 1973) (holding that prohibiting qualified girls from participating in all-male tennis, skiing, and cross-country teams violated the Fourteenth Amendment); Hoover v. Meiklejohn, 430 F. Supp. 164 (D. Colo. 1977) (holding that Colorado high school athletic association rule completely denying girls' rights to play soccer was unconstitutional); Carnes v. Tenn. Secondary Sch. Athletic Ass'n, 415 F. Supp. 569 (E.D. Tenn. 1976) (granting preliminary injunction against rule forbidding mixed participation in contact sports, including baseball, where plaintiff brought both constitutional and Title IX claims); Gilpin v. Kan. State High Sch. Activities Ass'n, Inc., 377 F. Supp. 1233 (D. Kan. 1974) (holding that state high school activities association's prohibition on boys and girls belonging to the same athletic teams violated plaintiff's constitutional rights); Reed v. Neb. Sch. Activities Ass'n, 341 F. Supp. 258 (D. Neb. 1972) (granting preliminary injunction against prohibition on girls trying out for all-male golf team).

149. Lantz v. Ambach, 620 F. Supp. 663 (S.D.N.Y. 1985).

150. *Id.* at 665–66.

151. Barnett v. Tex. Wrestling Ass'n, 16 F. Supp. 2d 690, 694 (N.D. Tex. 1998).

152. O'Connor v. Bd. of Educ., 545 F. Supp. 376 (N.D. Ill. 1982).

153. Cape v. Tenn. Secondary Sch. Athletic Ass'n, 424 F. Supp. 732 (E.D. Tenn. 1976).

154. Cape v. Tenn. Secondary Sch. Athletic Ass'n, 563 F.2d 793, 795 (6th Cir. 1977), *abrogation recognized in* Brentwood v. Tenn. Secondary Sch. Athletic Ass'n, 190 F.3d 705 (6th Cir. 1999).

155. Commonwealth v. Penn. Interscholastic Athletic Ass'n, 334 A.2d 839 (Pa. Commw. Ct. 1975).

156. Darrin v. Gould, 540 P.2d 882 (Wash. 1975); *see also* Att'y Gen. v. Mass. Interscholastic Athletic Ass'n, Inc., 393 N.E.2d 284 (Mass. 1979) (rule prohibiting boys from playing on girls' team was invalid under equal rights amendment and state statute barring sex discrimination).

157. Ridgeway v. Mont. High Sch. Ass'n, 663 F. Supp. 1564 (D. Mont. 1986).

158. *Id.* at 1581.

159. Cmties. for Equity v. Mich. High Sch. Athletic Ass'n, 26 F. Supp. 2d 1001 (W.D. Mich. 1998); Cmties. for Equity v. Mich. High Sch. Athletic Ass'n, 178 F. Supp. 2d 805 (W.D. Mich. 2001).

160. Cmties. for Equity, 178 F. Supp. 2d at 861.

161. 799 F. Supp. 513 (E.D. Pa. 1992).

162. The Williamses also sued under the Equal Protection Clause of the Fourteenth Amendment and the Equal Rights Amendment of the Pennsylvania Constitution. *Id.* at 515.

163. 34 C.F.R. § 106.41(b) ("[W]here a recipient operates or sponsors a team in a particular sport for members of one sex but operates or sponsors no such team for members of the other sex, and athletic opportunities for members of that sex have previously been limited, members of the excluded sex must be allowed to try-out for the team offered unless the sport involved is a contact sport.").

164. *Williams*, 799 F. Supp. at 515–17.

165. *Id.* at 517.

166. *Id.* at 517–18. The court described this inequity "as a consequence of th[e] plan for expanding opportunities for girls in athletics" in the 1970s when Title IX became effective.

167. Williams v. Sch. Dist. of Bethlehem, 998 F.2d 168, 175 (3rd Cir. 1993).

168. *Id.* at 175.

169. *Id.*

170. The only other successful suit by a male seeking to play on an all-women's team was Gomes v. R.I. Interscholastic League, 469 F. Supp. 659, 666 (D.R.I. 1979) (issuing a preliminary injunction against the interscholastic league rules prohibiting plaintiff from playing volleyball on the high school girls' team), *vacating as moot* 604 F.2d 733, 736 (1st Cir. 1979).

171. 695 F.2d 1126 (9th Cir. 1982), *cert. denied*, 464 U.S. 818 (1983).

172. Brief of Amici Curiae Nat'l Women's Law Ctr., at 10, Nat'l Wrestling Coaches Ass'n v. U.S. Dept. of Educ., 263 F. Supp. 2d 82 (D. D.C. 2003).

173. Nat'l Wrestling Coaches Ass'n v. U.S. Dep't. of Educ., 263 F. Supp. 2d 82 (D. D.C. 2003).

174. *Pederson*, 213 F.3d at 878.

175. *Brown*, 101 F.3d at 179. Other federal appellate courts have rejected the

quota argument. *See, e.g.*, Chalenor v. Univ. of N.D., 291 F.3d 1042, 1043 (8th Cir. 2002).

176. Nat'l Coal. for Women & Girls in Educ., Invisible Again: The Impact of Changes in Federal Funding on Vocational Programs for Women and Girls 6 (2000) *available at* http://www.ncwge.org/statements/perkins.pdf.

177. Carl D. Perkins, Vocational and Applied Technology Education Amendments of 1998, Pub. L. No. 105-332, 112 Stat. 3077 (codified as amended at 20 U.S.C. §§ 2301–2415).

178. Nat'l Women's Law Ctr., Title IX & Equal Opportunity in Vocational & Technical Educ.: A Promise Still Owed to the Nation's Young Women (2002), *available at* http://www.nwlc.org/pdf/TitleIXCareerEducationReport.pdf [hereinafter Title IX & Equal Opportunity in Vocational & Technical Educ.].

179. *Id.* at 4.

180. Am. Ass'n of Univ. Women Educ. Found., Gender Gaps: Where Schools Still Fail Our Children 88 (1998), executive summary *available at* http://www.aauw.org/research/GGES.pdf.

181. Nat'l Women's Law Ctr., Title IX & Equal Opportunity in Vocational & Technical Educ., *supra* note 178, at 5.

182. Nat'l Women's Law Ctr., Tools of the Trade: Using the Law to Address Sex Segregation in High School Career and Technical Education (2005), *available at* http://www.nwlc.org/pdf/NWLCToolsoftheTrade05.pdf [hereinafter Tools of the Trade].

183. Nat'l Women's Law Ctr., Title IX & Equal Opportunity in Vocational & Technical Educ., *supra* note 178, at 5.

184. Tools of the Trade, *supra* note 182, at 2.

185. 34 C.F.R. Pt. 100, App. B (2007).

186. 20 U.S.C. §§ 295m, 296g (2005).

187. 45 C.F.R. § 83.4 (2007).

188. *Id.* § 83.11.

189. 34 C.F.R. § 106.21(b)(2) (2007).

190. Sharif v. N.Y. State Dep't of Educ., 709 F. Supp. 345 (S.D.N.Y. 1989).

191. Press Release, The College Board, 2001 College Board Seniors are Largest, Most Diverse Group in History (Aug. 28, 2001), *available at* http://www.collegeboard.com/press/releases/10429.html.

192. 532 U.S. 275 (2001).

193. 456 U.S. 512 (1982).

194. *Id.*

195. 42 U.S.C. §§ 2000e(a)-(b) (2005).

196. *See, e.g.*, Lakoski v. James, 66 F.3d 751 (5th Cir. 1995); Gardner v. St. Bonaventure Univ., 171 F. Supp. 2d 118 (W.D.N.Y. 2001); Blalock v. Dale County Bd. of Educ., 84 F. Supp. 2d 1291 (M.D. Ala. 1999); Gibson v. Hickman, 2 F. Supp.

2d 1481 (M.D. Ga. 1998); Burrell v. City Univ. of New York, 995 F. Supp. 398 (S.D.N.Y. 1998); Cooper v. Gustavus Adolphus Coll., 957 F. Supp. 191 (D. Minn. 1997).

197. *Burrell*, 995 F. Supp. at 408.

198. *Gardner*, 171 F. Supp. 2d at 127.

199. *See, e.g.*, Cherry v. Univ. of Wisc. Sys. Bd. of Regents, 265 F.3d 541 (7th Cir. 2001); Buntin v. Breathitt County Bd. of Educ., 134 F.3d 796 (6th Cir. 1998); Bedard v. Roger Williams Univ., 989 F. Supp. 94 (D.R.I. 1997); Nelson v. Univ. of Me. Sys., 923 F. Supp. 275 (D. Me. 1996); Henschke v. N.Y. Hosp.-Med. Ctr., 821 F. Supp. 166 (S.D.N.Y. 1993).

200. *Henschke*, 821 F. Supp. at 172.

201. 441 U.S. 677 (1979).

202. Jackson v. Birmingham Bd. of Educ., 309 F.3d 1333, 1344–45 (11th Cir. 2002); Mock v. So. Dakota Bd. of Regents, 267 F. Supp. 2d 1017, 1022 (D.S.D. 2003); Atkinson v. Lafayette Coll., No. Civ.A.O1-CV-2141, 2002 WL 123449 (E.D. Pa. Jan. 9, 2002); Litman v. George Mason Univ., 156 F. Supp. 2d 579 (E.D. Va. 2001).

203. Johnson v. Galen Health Insts., Inc., 267 F. Supp. 2d 679, 689–90 (W.D. Ky. 2003); *see also* Peters v. Jenney, 327 F.3d 307, 316 (4th Cir. 2003) (finding private right of action for retaliation claim under Title VI).

204. Jackson v. Birmingham Bd. of Educ., 125 S. Ct 1497 (2005). In this case, the coach of a girls' high school basketball team complained to his supervisors that the girls' team did not receive the equal funding, access to athletic facilities, or equipment. After his complaint he began to receive negative evaluations and was eventually fired. He brought a Title IX action against the Board of Education for intentional discrimination in the form of retaliation.

205. *Id.* at 1507–8 ("If recipients were permitted to retaliate freely, individuals who witness discrimination would be loathe to report it, and all manner of Title IX violations would go unremedied as a result.").

206. *See, e.g.*, Chance v. Rice Univ., 984 F.2d 151 (5th Cir. 1993); Cannon v. Univ. of Chicago, 648 F.2d 1104, 1109 (7th Cir. 1981), *cert. denied*, 454 U.S. 1128 (1981); Fulani v. League of Women Voters Educ. Fund, 684 F. Supp. 1185, 1993 (S.D.N.Y. 1988).

207. *See, e.g.*, Roberts v. Colo. State Bd. of Agric., 998 F.2d at 833–34.

208. *See, e.g.*, 34 C.F.R. §§ 106.21(b)(2), 106.36(b)-(c), 106.52, 106.53(b), 106.54 (2007).

209. *Sharif*, 709 F. Supp. at 345.

210. 532 U.S. 275 (2001).

211. *Cannon*, 441 U.S. at 696.

212. Barrett v. Westchester Univ., 2003 WL 22803477 (E.D. Pa. Nov. 12, 2003); Weser v. Glen, 190 F. Supp. 2d 384, 395 (E.D.N.Y. 2002).

213. Brief of Amici Curiae, Nat'l Women's Law Ctr. et al., at 5–6; Litman v. George Mason Univ., 186 F.3d 544 (4th Cir.1999); North Haven Bd. of Ed. v. Bell, 456 U.S. at 521 ("There is no doubt that if we are to give [Title IX] the scope that its origins dictate, we must accord it a sweep as broad as its language.").

214. *Sandoval,* 532 U.S. at 1517.

215. Adele Kimmel et al., Feature, *The Sandoval Decision and Its Implications for Future Civil Rights Enforcement,* 76 FLA. BAR J. 24, 26 (2002).

216. 20 U.S.C. §§ 1706, 1709 (2005).

# V

# Violence against Women

Women's intimate relationships are often marked by violence. One recent study indicates that nationally, 26 percent of women, compared to 8 percent of men, report having been victimized by an intimate partner in their lifetime.[1] Indeed, when violence occurs in an intimate relationship, about 85 percent of the time a woman is the victim of that violence.[2] While violence against women occurs in every class, race, and culture, poor women are especially vulnerable to violence, because their poverty constricts their ability to escape violent relationships. It is far more difficult to separate from your abuser, for instance, when leaving the relationship means that you and your children will become homeless. Moreover, domestic violence itself tends to render women economically vulnerable. For instance, studies indicate that a large proportion of welfare recipients have been or are victims of abuse by an intimate partner.[3] Violent partners often seek to limit a woman's ability to find or keep a job, and the violence itself can pose a significant barrier to employment. Thus, violence not only hurts women physically; it is also part of a cycle that leaves them poorer and more vulnerable to further violence.

## DOMESTIC VIOLENCE

### Is domestic violence a crime?

Yes. Every state and the federal government have criminalized certain acts of domestic violence, generally physical abuse and stalking. A woman being abused by a loved one can seek police assistance, and her abuser can be arrested.[4]

**What is stalking?**

Stalking is a course of harassing conduct directed at a specific person that places her in fear for her safety. This behavior can consist of repeated phone calls, letters, surveillance, overt threats, monitoring the victim's actions, and other controlling behavior. Stalking is fairly widespread; one in twelve women will be stalked at some point in her lifetime. Paired with physical violence, stalking is also considered a high-risk indicator. Eighty-nine percent of femicide victims who had been physically abused had also been stalked in the twelve months before the murder.

Stalking is against the law in every state, though specific laws differ. Stalking across state lines or in federal territories is illegal under federal law. Women needing more information about stalking should contact the Stalking Resource Center, online at http://www.ncvc.org or by phone at 1-800-FYI-CALL or TTY 1-800-211-7996.[5]

**If a victim of domestic violence calls the police, are the police required to make an arrest?**

Sometimes. Most states have adopted some form of mandatory arrest law; however, the details of these laws differ from state to state. In general, all of them require the police to arrest an alleged abuser when there is "probable cause" to believe that he has violated a protective order. Some states even require arrest when no order of protection has been issued, if the victim has been physically injured or threatened with a weapon.[6]

States have adopted these laws to address the failure by some police to take domestic violence seriously and to enforce the laws criminalizing it. Mandatory arrest laws shield the victim of abuse from being forced to make a decision about whether her partner should be arrested when she might feel too frightened to tell the police what she wants done. Studies also suggest that abusers are less likely to abuse their victims again if they are arrested.[7] Finally, in a few states, the existence of a mandatory arrest law allows a victim of domestic violence to recover damages from the police if they fail to arrest her abuser and she is subsequently injured or her property destroyed.[8]

Despite the good intentions behind mandatory arrest policies, they are controversial among advocates for victims of domestic violence. Just as there is evidence that arrest makes an abuser less likely to abuse the victim again, there is also contradictory evidence that when an abuser is arrested, he is more likely to retaliate against his victim with violence.[9] Furthermore, mandatory arrest laws seem to increase the likelihood that the police will arrest both the abuser and his victim if both parties allege some violence, even if the victim was attempting to defend herself.[10] Some critics also point out that mandatory arrest policies remove too much control from victims. Others note that some communities, particularly communities of color and immigrant communities, may see the police as hostile in the best of circumstances. Mandatory arrest policies make it less likely that women in those communities will seek police help that would in turn risk exposing the men in their lives to the criminal justice system or possible deportation.[11]

### Can a victim of domestic violence be arrested if she calls the police?

Sometimes the police may arrest a victim of domestic violence if both she and the abuser show marks or injuries, such as scratches or bruises. This practice is often referred to as "dual arrest" or "victim arrest."[12] Many states have laws that discourage, but do not prohibit, the arrests of both people involved in a domestic disturbance.[13]

Dual arrests often occur because police officers are confused about whom to arrest when responding to domestic disturbance calls, especially where both people have injuries. To address this problem, some states have laws with "primary aggressor" language that require an officer to consider a variety of factors when making an arrest, including the relative severity of the injuries on each person, prior complaints of domestic violence, other household members' accounts of the violence, and whether one person acted in self-defense.[14] However, even with primary aggressor laws, dual arrests are more likely to occur if police officers have not received necessary domestic violence training to distinguish between a batterer and a victim acting in self-defense.[15]

### Can anything be done against police who refuse to help?

It depends on the state. In states with mandatory arrest provisions, police should automatically arrest a batterer who is violating an order of protection or assaulting his partner. Although in a recent decision,[16] the Supreme Court has apparently closed the door to a federal constitutional remedy for women injured as a result of the police's failure to arrest a batterer, this does not change the specific legal duties to arrest a batterer that police officers may have under state law. The Supreme Court decision also does not affect any remedies a woman may have under state or local law.

Victims of domestic violence wishing to hold police accountable for their actions can file complaints about a specific officer with the police department. Women can also contact local domestic violence advocacy agencies to find out if there is anything else they can do to address police responses to domestic violence. In some states with mandatory arrest laws, women or their families can sue police departments that fail to arrest a batterer as required by law. For instance in Tennessee, Oregon, and Montana, courts have held that when someone has a valid order of protection and calls the police to enforce it, the police have a legal duty to arrest the abuser, and if they fail to make the arrest, they may be held liable for any injuries or harm to the victim.[17]

Most states sharply limit a victim's right to sue negligent police under "sovereign immunity" laws that shield government officials, including police, from any liability for actions performed in the course of duty.[18] Police cannot be held legally responsible for injuries that happened because they failed to provide protection. However, there are some exceptions to these rules. For instance, in some states, police officers can be held accountable for their failure to act because they had a special duty to the victim or acted in a grossly negligent or reckless manner. These exceptions vary by state and are often difficult to prove. A woman or her family believing they may have a claim against negligent police officers should consult an attorney to discuss the options.

Victims of domestic violence who are treated unfairly by police departments may also be able to bring an equal protection claim in court under constitutional provisions prohibiting gender discrimination. If a victim can point to a policy where police regularly treat domestic violence calls differently from all other calls, she may be able to say that the overall effect of the policy hurts women or has a disparate impact on women and is therefore a form of unlawful sex discrimination. Under the federal Equal Protection Clause, such claims have been difficult to prove because of the requirement that an intent to harm or discriminate against women be a factor in the police's failure to enforce domestic violence laws. For instance, one federal court dismissed an equal protection sex discrimination claim that challenged an alleged policy of providing less police protection to victims of domestic violence than to other victims of crime because the plaintiff could not show the requisite discriminatory intent. The court emphasized that to succeed in such a claim the plaintiff must show that intentional discrimination against women was the motivating factor behind the policy.[19] Though they may recognize and possibly disapprove of the unequal treatment, most federal courts hearing similar cases have not upheld the claims because of an absence of any proof that the policy or practice at issue was adopted on the basis of gender animus.[20]

If she cannot show that intentional sex discrimination motivated the police when they failed to protect her, she can succeed if she can prove that there was no rational basis for the police to treat domestic violence differently from any other crime, but again such claims are extremely difficult to prove. In this case, courts can accept any reasonable explanation for a policy or law, so it will not be easy to prove that a bad policy is based on an irrational bias.

In spite of the difficulty of proving such cases under federal law, state constitutions may offer more protection, especially in states that have adopted an equal rights amendment or similar provision explicitly prohibiting any discrimination on the basis of sex. In these states, policies that have the effect of discriminating against women are often looked at closely and may be found unconstitutional under state law regardless of the intent with which they were adopted. Although there are no cases on record successfully arguing this theory against police departments that fail to enforce domestic violence laws, it is an area to explore with an attorney. (For more information on equal protection and disparate impact claims, see chapter 1, "Constitutional Rights: Equal Protection," and chapter 2, "Employment: Discrimination and Parenting Issues.")

### If an abuser is arrested, will he be prosecuted?

Even if an abuser is arrested, he may not be prosecuted. In some instances, this occurs because the victim does not cooperate with the prosecution. In others, it occurs because the prosecutor does not believe there is enough evidence to win the case.

A few jurisdictions have attempted to change this by adopting "no drop" policies. These policies are meant not only to prevent an abuser from avoiding prosecution by intimidating his victim into dropping the charges but also to force prosecutors' offices to take domestic violence cases seriously. In these jurisdictions, a prosecutor's discretion to decide whether or not to bring a case against an abuser is limited. In most places a victim is still free to decide whether and in what degree to cooperate. If she does not cooperate, the prosecutor will attempt to try the case without her cooperation, based on evidence such as 911 calls and police testimony.[21] In a few jurisdictions, however, a victim who changes her story or who refuses to testify at trial may be subject to contempt of court or even to prosecution herself.[22]

While no drop policies can have positive effects, they have also raised questions similar to those raised by mandatory arrest policies. Again, it is not clear whether they discourage defendants from assaulting their victims again. Some suggest that when victims are unable to drop charges against their abusers, the women are deprived of a negotiation tool they could use elsewhere to win important concessions from their abuser. Finally, no drop policies that punish the victim for refusing to cooperate with the prosecution may further victimize her and may discourage women who are abused from seeking assistance in the first place.[23]

### Other than calling the police, what legal action can a victim of domestic violence take to protect herself from her abuser?

She can go to court and request a civil protective order. Civil protective orders are available for most victims of domestic violence in every state. Each state has different rules regarding who can obtain such an order. For instance, in some states a victim of domestic violence can obtain a protective order if she is abused by someone she is dating, while in other states, she can only obtain an order if she is married to or living with her abuser, or if they have a child in common. Rules also vary as to what a petitioner must prove in order to obtain an order, but most systems are designed under the presumption that women should be able to easily seek protective orders without the assistance of a lawyer.

Civil protective orders generally order the abuser not to harm the petitioner and to stay away from the petitioner. Any violations of these orders subject abusers to possible arrest. The relief available in such an order varies from state to state, but the following types of provisions may be included:

- The abuser shall not molest, assault, harass, threaten, or physically abuse the petitioner or her children.
- The abuser must "stay away" from the petitioner and from various locations such as the petitioner's home, her place of employment, her church, her children's school, and her childcare provider. Specific addresses are included on the order only if the petitioner does not want to keep these locations secret for her own safety.
- The abuser shall not contact the petitioner in person, by telephone, in writing, or through a third party.

- The abuser must leave a home he shares with the petitioner.
- The abuser must turn over any firearms he possesses to the local police department.
- Temporary custody of minor children may be awarded to the petitioner.
- The abuser may be given visitation rights under specified conditions.
- The abuser must pay child support in a specified amount.
- The abuser must participate in and complete an offender counseling or batterer's intervention program.

More and more states give courts broad discretion to impose other conditions in individual cases, ranging from requirements that an abuser reimburse a victim for property damage to details of the methods by which decisions about a minor child will be made.

### How long do protective orders last?

Most states allow victims of domestic violence to obtain a temporary order of protection *ex parte,* which means without first notifying the abuser that she is seeking the order. These orders are issued before a court has had an opportunity to hear both sides of the story—usually on the same day that the victim fills out the necessary paperwork requesting a protective order—and last for a relatively short period of time, typically two weeks to a month, until a hearing can be scheduled where both the petitioner and the abuser can appear. After a full hearing, or when an abuser fails to appear at a hearing after receiving notice of it, courts can issue protective orders that last longer than the temporary orders, in most states from one to three years.

An individual who has received a protective order should carry a copy of it with her at all times and keep copies in her home, her car, her office, her child's school, and any other place where the abuser might contact her. She should also make sure her local police precinct has a copy. If she calls the police to alert them to a violation of the order of protection, it will be important to have proof that a valid order is in place.

### If a protective order is issued in one state, is it valid in another state?

Yes. Federal law requires that each state give "full faith and credit" to protective orders issued in another state, even temporary *ex parte* orders.[24]

This means that states must recognize and enforce protective orders issued by other states. In some states, however, an order from another state must be filed with the local court in order to be enforceable.[25]

### If a victim of domestic violence obtains a protective order, does she remain free to contact the abuser herself?

Some courts have shown a disturbing tendency to penalize a victim of domestic violence for violating a protective order if she makes contact with her abuser. A few courts have even imposed fines on victims who reinitiate contact with their abusers or have found those victims guilty of criminal contempt.[26] Domestic violence advocates worry that such penalties ignore the dynamics of domestic violence and discourage victims from seeking assistance from courts or police.[27] In any case, a victim of domestic violence will probably find it easiest to convince police to enforce her protective order and prosecutors to try a violation of the order if she does not initiate contact with the abuser herself.

### What are mutual protective orders?

Mutual protective orders are protective orders that are entered against both parties—victim and abuser. A victim of domestic violence can either agree to a protective order against her or a judge can issue one over her objection. Sometimes judges may issue mutual orders without hearing any evidence at all, or after hearing about the behavior of only one party. Laws vary from state to state about whether mutual orders of protection can be issued and under what circumstances. Generally, their use is limited, and most states curtail their use because they may be unfair and/or have the unintended results of harming the victim in future proceedings.

States with laws restricting the use of mutual protective orders generally require that such orders be issued only where there is evidence that both people are abusive.[28] For example, California has a law forbidding the use of mutual protective orders unless both people appear in court, there is evidence that both were abusive, and neither person acted in self-defense.[29] Even if a mutual protective order can be issued in one state, federal law prohibits honoring that order in another state unless both people have asked individually for civil protective orders and a court has made a finding of mutual abuse.[30]

At first glance, mutual protective orders may seem appealing to judges and lawyers. They may assume that whoever is the "real victim" will not be harmed by the order because she would want to stay away from the abuser anyway, or they may consider the mutual orders to be expedient.[31] Mutual protective orders can, however, create a number of problems for a victim of domestic abuse. They can hurt the victim in future divorce proceedings, civil proceedings on domestic violence, and criminal proceedings against the abuser because they amount to evidence that she is herself an abuser. Additionally, mutual orders confuse the police. If a batterer violates his order of protection, police may not know how to proceed because they won't know which person has the history of battering or who actually violated the order.[32] Finally, by confusing the victim with the abuser, the presence of a mutual protective order incorrectly sends a signal to both parties that the victim is partially at fault for the abuse.

### How can an individual learn more about the requirements and procedures for obtaining a protective order in a particular state?

To gain more information about the requirements for seeking a protective order in a particular state, individuals may contact their state coalition against domestic violence,[33] a local battered women's shelter, a battered women's advocacy organization, or the office of the clerk in their local courts. Victims of domestic violence can also contact the National Domestic Violence Hotline at 1-800-799-SAFE (7233) or TTY 1-800-787-3224 for referrals to local domestic violence resources.

## PARENTING

### What happens when both an abuser and a victim of domestic abuse are seeking custody of the children?

Studies show that in a divorce or separation, fathers who abuse the mothers of their children are twice as likely to seek sole custody of the children as nonabusive fathers.[34] Attempts to seek custody may be part of a batterer's efforts to control and punish a victim who is seeking to end the relationship. Consequently, policies that encourage joint custody or allow batterers to obtain custody in spite of evidence of abuse have been strongly criticized. In effect, such policies give the batterer license to continue abusing his victim, and may place the child in danger.[35]

In determining questions of custody and visitation, family court judges will generally ask what is in the best interests of the child and look at a number of factors in addition to the domestic violence, such as the child's preference, the offending parent's participation in treatment, and which parent is more likely to encourage visitation and contact with the other.[36] Different courts come to different conclusions about how domestic violence should affect this best-interests determination.

No state has adopted a firm rule that domestic violence alone will always be sufficient reason to deny custody to an abuser. However, some states require that courts presume that when there is evidence of violence, it is not in the children's best interests for abusers to have joint or sole custody, unless the batterer can prove otherwise.[37] Courts in these states may still give the batterer custody after considering a number of other factors, such as completion of an offender treatment program, whether the batterer has engaged in any more acts of domestic violence, participation in parenting classes, and the parental fitness of the mother, but it falls to the batterer to show he is the better parent. In most states, a court is required to give at least some consideration to a parent's abuse of the other in making its decision, but the laws do not specify how much weight judges should give the domestic violence.[38]

Despite these policies, many judges distrust women who allege domestic violence in custody disputes. Some believe that domestic violence survivors are inappropriately hostile and uncooperative when they refuse to come to an agreement with abusers about custody and visitation issues without court involvement. Others want to believe that abuse of the mother indicates little about the batterer's parenting capabilities, thus ignoring extensive evidence to the contrary.[39]

Problems with legal presumptions against parents who have records of domestic violence arise in localities where dual arrests and mutual protective orders are common. The court will consequently identify as batterers victims who may have been arrested after defending themselves or against whom a mutual order of protection was issued. Finally, in cases where there is evidence that both parents are perpetrators of domestic violence, courts will look to other factors to determine who should get custody. Some states even require judges to refer such cases to a child protective services agency for an investigation and report, thus creating the possibility that a child could be removed into foster care.[40]

If a domestic violence victim is in a custody dispute with her batterer, it is important she seek help from an attorney who has experience with domestic violence cases or a domestic violence advocate. These individuals can help present evidence as to why granting batterers custody would harm the children.

### Can a victim of domestic violence be found an unfit parent solely because her child was exposed to domestic violence in the home?

Acknowledging that children may suffer harm as a result of witnessing domestic violence, some states have concluded that exposure to such violence constitutes neglect, and can be the basis for placing a child in foster care. This means that in some instances, battered women have lost custody of their children because of the domestic violence they have experienced and their children have witnessed. The theory behind such removals is that these mothers have "failed to protect" their children from the harm that comes from witnessing domestic violence. In some cases, mothers also may have "failed to protect" their children from physical harm from the abuser, exposing the victim parent not only to child protective proceedings but also to possible arrest in those states with criminal "failure to protect" laws.[41]

Women whose children are removed on the basis of such charges often do not regain custody for weeks or months, during which time their children may be placed in foster care and consequently traumatized and sometimes endangered as a result. Such a policy in effect blames women for the actions of their batterers. It also, paradoxically, may reinforce the authority of the batterer, as one common threat batterers make is that if the victim tells anyone about the violence, the state will take her children because she is a bad mother. The fear of losing her children if anyone else finds out about the violence serves as an incredibly powerful incentive for a battered mother to hide and deny the violence rather than seek help.[42]

Depending on state law and the nature of the child protective intervention, such policies may implicate constitutional rights. For instance, a federal court in New York held that a New York City policy of routinely removing children from their mothers when the only charge was domestic violence against the mothers violated both mothers' and children's substantive and procedural due process rights under the Constitution.[43] On appeal, the federal court agreed that such practices could violate the constitutional rights of mothers and children, but then sent the case to state court for more guidance as to the meaning of certain neglect and removal statutes.[44] New York's highest state court held that under state law a child should not automatically be placed in foster care when the only issue was that the child had witnessed the mother's abuse by a batterer, and shortly afterwards the parties settled without any further ruling regarding the constitutional issues. To date it is unclear whether this litigation will have an effect on child protective practices and domestic violence policy in other states. (For more information on foster care, abuse, and neglect please see chapter 7, "Family Law.")

## HOUSING

### Can a landlord evict someone or otherwise discriminate against someone because she is the victim of domestic violence?

Probably not. Several recent decisions have indicated that discrimination against a person based on her status as a victim of domestic violence may be a form of impermissible sex discrimination and therefore violates the Fair Housing Act, and in many places, state law.[45] (See chapter 10, "Housing.") In most instances, federal law also specifically forbids denying individuals public housing or housing subsidized under the Section 8 program because they are victims of domestic violence.

### How do landlords discriminate against domestic violence victims?

In an effort to prevent crime, disturbances, and damage to their property, landlords may seek to exclude women who are or have been the victims of domestic violence, thus, in effect, blaming the victim for an abuser's criminal acts. For instance, landlords may refuse to accept the applications of women who have previously obtained protective orders or may evict a woman because she has been attacked in her home. Such evictions are frequently justified by reference to "zero tolerance" policies that require the eviction of everyone living in an apartment when criminal activity occurs there, regardless of whether an individual was the victim or perpetrator of the violent incident.[46] These practices can make the search for affordable housing excessively burdensome for victims of domestic violence. Discrimination and other obstacles to finding adequate housing also make it harder for women to leave their batterers and increase their risk of homelessness if they do. Indeed, according to the U.S. Conference of Mayors, 44 percent of twenty-seven major cities surveyed identified domestic violence as a primary cause of homelessness, and a 2003 survey of homeless mothers around the country found that 25 percent of the women had been physically abused in the preceding year.[47]

**What remedies are available to domestic violence victims who have been subjected to discrimination?**

Victims of domestic violence who have been subjected to discrimination may have remedies under federal and state fair housing laws. The Fair Housing Act (FHA), which addresses discrimination in housing on the basis of sex, probably prohibits discrimination against domestic violence victims.[48] When a landlord discriminates against a victim of domestic violence on the basis of gender stereotypes about battered women—e.g., battered women can always stop the violence if they want, or battered women somehow provoke or enjoy the violence against them, etc.—the landlord is discriminating on the basis of sex.[49] This would constitute unlawful sex discrimination under the FHA, as well as state fair housing laws. Furthermore, because the vast majority of domestic violence victims are women, application of "zero-tolerance" or similar policies to domestic violence victims has a disparate impact on women.[50] As a result, it is probable that such policies constitute an illegal form of sex discrimination.

In addition to the FHA and state fair housing laws, some federal, state, and local laws specifically protect the housing rights of victims and survivors of domestic violence. The Violence Against Women Act of 2005 (VAWA) prohibits public housing authorities (PHAs) from denying admission to anyone simply because she has been a victim of domestic violence, dating violence, or stalking.[51] It also requires PHAs to use leases that make clear that domestic violence, dating violence, or stalking is not good cause for evicting the victim of that violence.[52] In general, tenants in public housing can be evicted for criminal activity engaged in by their guests or people "under their control" when that activity threatens others' health, safety, or right to peaceful enjoyment of the premises.[53] Some PHAs previously relied on this lease provision to evict victims of domestic violence because of the violence of their abuser. Under VAWA, a PHA can only evict an individual because of domestic violence against her if it can prove an "actual and imminent threat" to other tenants and staff if she is not evicted.[54]

The same protections against discrimination apply in project-based Section 8 housing.[55] In addition, victims of domestic violence, dating violence, or stalking are protected from discrimination in the Section 8 housing voucher program. An individual cannot be denied a housing voucher simply because she has been a victim of domestic violence, dating violence, or stalking, and a landlord is not permitted to deny housing to a voucher holder just because she has been a victim of violence.[56] In addition, a landlord may not evict a voucher holder on the basis of the violence against her unless the landlord can show that there is an "actual and imminent threat" to other tenants or staff if she is not evicted.[57] A PHA may not terminate voucher assistance to an individual on the basis of an incident or incidents of domestic violence, dating violence, or stalking against her unless it can show an "actual and imminent threat" to other tenants or staff if assistance is not terminated.[58]

State laws provide additional protections against housing discrimination for survivors of domestic violence.[59] North Carolina, Washington, and Rhode Island prohibit discrimination against a tenant or member of a tenant's household based on the tenant's status as a victim of domestic violence, sexual assault, or stalking; entitle a victim to terminate a rental agreement upon notice to the landlord and documentation of the abuse without further obligation to the landlord; and require the landlord to change the locks if a victim requests. These states also prohibit landlords from discriminating against or evicting a tenant if she has obtained or sought a restraining order.[60] Several other states have narrower laws protecting domestic violence victims from certain types of discrimination by their landlords,[61] or are in the process of developing such laws.[62] For example, Arizona and Minnesota specifically prohibit any rental agreement provision that limits or waives the right of a tenant to call the police or other emergency assistance to respond to domestic violence. Colorado's domestic violence statute preserves the victim's right to call for emergency assistance but also ensures that a victim of domestic violence can break her lease and relocate for her own safety, provided she gives written notice and is responsible for one month's rent after she leaves.

Finally, the Constitution may prohibit some forms of discrimination against domestic violence victims by public housing authorities.[63] If the discrimination by the public housing authority is intentional—for instance, if a public housing authority evicts a female victim of violence but does not evict a male victim of violence, or punishes a battered woman on the basis of gender stereotypes about domestic violence—a woman may be able to make an equal protection claim under the Fourteenth Amendment. In contrast to the FHA, however, the Fourteenth Amendment only prohibits intentional discrimination and thus does not reach policies that have a discriminatory effect.[64]

## EMPLOYMENT

### Can an employer discriminate against a woman because she is the victim of domestic violence?

Maybe not. Illinois and New York City flatly prohibit discrimination against domestic violence victims.[65] Illinois law covers not only those who are actual victims of domestic violence but also those who have family or members of their household who are victims of domestic violence, recognizing the widespread effect of the violence on those around the victim. New York City employers cannot refuse to hire, discharge, or otherwise discriminate against any individual based on her actual or perceived status as a victim of domestic violence.[66] Both laws require employers to provide reasonable accommodations to employees who are victims of domestic violence so that they can continue to do their jobs. Domestic violence advocates hope that these laws will be models for other jurisdictions around the country.

A few other states and counties currently have laws that prevent employers from discharging or discriminating against domestic violence victims under certain circumstances.[67] Most of them prohibit discrimination against victims of domestic violence either for taking leave to address the violence, or for taking time off specifically to go to court. However, the details and terms of the laws vary. For instance, Maryland has an executive order forbidding "unfair" treatment of state employees based on their status as victims of domestic violence, while Rhode Island forbids employers from refusing to hire, firing, or otherwise discriminating against an individual solely because she seeks or obtains a protective order, or refuses to seek or obtain a protective order.

Even if a jurisdiction does not expressly prohibit discrimination against domestic violence victims, other federal or state laws may prevent an employer from discriminating on the basis of an employee's status as a victim of domestic violence. Title VII of the Civil Rights Act, the federal law banning gender discrimination in the workplace, might prohibit this sort of discrimination. Title VII forbids actions undertaken with the intention of discriminating against women, including those based on gender stereotypes. Thus, if a woman is fired or demoted because of her employer's stereotyped perception of how domestic violence victims should or might behave, she will have a claim for intentional sex discrimination.[68] Furthermore, Title VII prohibits actions or policies that have a "disparate impact" or disproportionately negative effect on women. The vast majority of victims of domestic violence are women. Therefore, an employer with a policy discriminating against domestic violence victims is probably engaging in unlawful discriminatory behavior that has a disparate impact on women, in violation of Title VII. Such theories are being tested in the courts[69] and have been fairly successful in other contexts.[70] (For more information on Title VII and employment discrimination see chapter 2, "Employment: Discrimination and Parenting Issues.")

A woman who has been fired from her job because of domestic violence may also have a claim against her employer for wrongful discharge. In most states, an employer cannot fire a worker for a reason that violates public policy. Some states have interpreted this rule to mean, for instance, that an employee cannot be fired because she missed work for jury duty or because she filed a claim for workers' compensation. It may be possible to argue that firing someone because she is a victim of domestic violence also violates public policy and constitutes a wrongful discharge. This theory is also being tested in the courts and has been used with some success in at least one case in Massachusetts.[71]

### Must an employer give a domestic violence victim leave so that she may appear in court or seek medical assistance or other assistance?

Several states have laws specifically requiring employers to give domestic violence victims unpaid leave in some circumstances.[72] For instance, California requires employers to give victims of domestic violence time off to obtain judicial relief to ensure their safety or their children's safety,[73] while Colorado law requires employers of more than fifty employees to give domestic violence victims up to three days of leave to seek a restraining order, obtain medical care or counseling, locate safe housing, make her home secure, seek legal assistance, and prepare for and attend court proceedings.[74] In states that do not have statutes explicitly providing for leave for victims of domestic violence, there may be general victim protection laws that prevent employers from firing or otherwise penalizing a victim of crime who takes time off to appear as a witness or cooperate with a criminal prosecution.[75] In addition, the federal Family and Medical Leave Act, further described in chapter 2, requires covered employers to grant employees unpaid medical leave for specified family and medical reasons, and employees should be able to take advantage of their employer's general leave policies if they exist.

**If a domestic violence victim is injured at work by her abuser, can she collect workers' compensation?**

It depends on the state. Workers' compensation is available in every state and is an insurance system that provides compensation to a worker injured on the job. The employer does not need to be at fault for the employee to collect workers' compensation, and benefits are automatic if the injury is covered. Generally, if a victim can collect workers' compensation, she will be unable to sue her employer to collect any other compensation for the same incident.

Of course, workers' compensation laws vary from state to state as to what injuries and activities are covered. Injuries are covered by workers' compensation if the injury "arises out of employment" and occurs "in the course of employment."[76] In most states, "arising out of employment" generally refers to what caused the injury and "in the course of employment" generally refers to the time and place of the injury.[77] In those states where any injury from an assault at work, regardless of who assaults the victim, is considered "an injury arising out of employment," victims of a domestic violence assault at work may be eligible for workers' compensation benefits if the conditions of employment facilitated or exacerbated the injury/assault. For example, in Wisconsin, a court held that a victim of domestic violence should receive workers' compensation for emotional injury after she was repeatedly harassed at work by her abusive ex-boyfriend's threatening phone calls, in which he stated that he knew where she lived and was going kill her.[78] The court said that taking a personal phone call was an activity incidental to employment and so the injury occurred in the course of employment. The court then said that the conditions of her employment made the injury possible because the ex-boyfriend would not have been able to harass her had the city not accidentally provided her phone number and address to him.[79] Therefore, the injury arose out of her employment.

However, except for these very limited circumstances, most courts have not expanded workers' compensation to include assault by a partner in the workplace. Courts have been reluctant to categorize injuries from domestic violence as arising out of employment. Instead, they describe the injuries as arising out of a problem or "personal animus" imported in from a private relationship. For instance, in Arizona Billie Epperson was shot at work by her husband but was denied workers' compensation benefits after an Arizona court ruled that she was ineligible because the injury did not "arise out of" her employment, nor was it made worse by the conditions of employment.[80] Similarly, other states have upheld the denial of workers' compensation claims made by women assaulted by their abusers while at work.[81]

### Can a victim of domestic violence sue her employer if her abuser assaults her at work?

Possibly. While employers are not liable for every single injury that their employees get on the job, they are liable for some. As mentioned above, if a domestic violence victim is eligible for workers' compensation benefits for an injury brought on by an attack at work, she will probably be prevented from bringing another suit against her employer for the same incident. However, if workers' compensation does not cover her claim, a victim of abuse on the job may be able to sue her employer.

If a woman's abuser is a coworker, in some circumstances she may be able to sue her employer for negligence for hiring the abuser, for not firing the abuser after the employer became aware of the abuse, for failing to warn or protect other employees, or possibly for failing to provide adequate security.[82] She may also be able to sue her employer for sexual harassment, if the employer knew about the harassment and did not take appropriate steps to stop the coworker's behavior. (For more detail, please refer to the discussion on sexual harassment at work in chapter 2, "Employment: Discrimination and Parenting Issues.")

### If a woman has to leave her job or is fired because of domestic violence, can she still collect unemployment insurance?

Maybe, if she would otherwise be eligible for unemployment benefits. Over half the states and the District of Columbia have laws that explicitly provide unemployment insurance to victims of domestic violence in these circumstances, and many other states are currently considering such legislation.[83] In most states, an individual cannot collect unemployment insurance if she left her job without "good cause" or if she was fired for "misconduct." However, those states with laws protecting victims specifically define "good cause" for leaving a job to include reasons related to domestic violence, while others have provided that conduct related to domestic violence cannot be considered "misconduct." States vary as to what documentation domestic violence victims must provide to collect the benefits. For example, in New Jersey, a domestic violence victim must provide any supporting documentation of the circumstances for leaving, while in Wisconsin, she must show that she was concerned about safety, provide a copy of a valid restraining order, and demonstrate that the order has been violated or is likely to be violated. Additionally, even if a state does not explicitly address the needs of a victim who loses her job because of the domestic violence, she may still be eligible for benefits if she can show that she left for "good cause," which might include personal safety concerns.

## WELFARE/TANF

**If a domestic violence victim receives welfare, does she have to cooperate with the state's efforts to collect child support from her abuser if she thinks child support collection will jeopardize her safety?**

Generally, no. Welfare recipients are required to cooperate with a state's child support collection efforts on behalf of their children. This means, for instance, that a recipient has to give the state the name and contact information for her child's father, if she has this information. If necessary, she must also establish paternity by submitting to blood tests or cooperating with a paternity suit. Every state, however, may grant a woman a "good cause" exemption for refusing to comply with this cooperation requirement if she believes that identifying the father of her children may jeopardize her safety.[84]

Each state decides what evidence a woman must provide to show she is a victim of domestic violence and fears for her safety. In general, a welfare recipient or applicant who fears that cooperation may endanger her should tell her caseworker about her concerns and ask for a good cause exemption. If the state welfare agency refuses to grant an exemption and punishes the woman for failing to cooperate or denies the application, she can seek a fair hearing to review the welfare agency's decision. Legal aid or legal services attorneys or domestic violence advocates may be able to provide help or representation through this process. (For more information see chapter 9, "TANF/Welfare.")

**Will a state waive other welfare program requirements for victims of domestic violence?**

Federal law permits, but does not require, states to adopt a "Family Violence Option" (FVO) that allows them to waive certain welfare program requirements for victims of domestic violence.[85] Most states have adopted either the FVO or equivalent policies, permitting welfare programs to waive certain requirements for victims of domestic violence when compliance would make it more difficult for them to escape domestic violence or the requirements would unfairly penalize victims of domestic violence.[86] Many provisions may be waived under these policies, including time limits on welfare receipt, work requirements, residency requirements, child support cooperation requirements, and child exclusion provisions.

Federal law also permits states to exempt families receiving welfare from the five-year federal time limit for welfare receipt if, among other reasons, "the family includes an individual who has been battered or subjected to extreme cruelty."[87] This provision is known as the "hardship exemption," and a state can use it to exempt up to 20 percent of its caseload from welfare time limits. Many states have adopted plans excusing battered recipients from welfare time limits under this exemption.

The details and implementation of these policies vary significantly from state to state, as does the amount of information that caseworkers give applicants and recipients regarding the availability of exemptions for victims of domestic violence. Individuals who believe that they are unable to comply with welfare program requirements because of domestic violence should ask the welfare caseworkers, local legal aid office, or a domestic violence advocate about the waivers available and how to obtain them.

## IMMIGRATION

### If a domestic violence victim is an immigrant, can she seek immigration relief without her abuser's assistance?

Yes. Generally, an immigrant married to a U.S. citizen or a lawful permanent resident is dependent on her spouse to petition for her to be granted legal immigration status. As a result, an abusive citizen or lawful permanent resident married to an undocumented immigrant can exercise control over her by refusing to file visa petitions and by threatening to have her deported. However, the Violence Against Women Act (VAWA), reauthorized in 2000, included provisions designed to address these obstacles and has created new opportunities for immigrant victims of domestic violence to obtain immigration relief through "self petitioning."[88] Under this law, an immigrant victim of domestic violence can self-petition for a visa without her abuser's cooperation or knowledge.[89] Both undocumented battered immigrants and battered immigrants with temporary visas can use this provision. Furthermore, this process can lead to the immigrant obtaining lawful permanent resident status if she is otherwise eligible, thus removing yet another obstacle to recovery and independence.

To file a self-petition, an immigrant must be married to or formerly married to a U.S. citizen or lawful permanent resident. She also must be able to demonstrate that she was subjected to violence or extreme cruelty during the marriage (or has a child who was subjected to battery or extreme cruelty), that she has good moral character, and that she married in good faith. She may include her minor children in her petition. (Victims of elder abuse by an adult U.S. citizen son or daughter may also self-petition, as may victims of child abuse or incest aged twenty-five or younger.)

The term "extreme cruelty" is very broad, including not only physical abuse or sexual abuse but also psychological abuse; therefore, it may be possible to demonstrate extreme cruelty even in the absence of physical violence. "Good moral character" is not defined in the statute, but the statute does list some behavior that shows a person is not of good moral character, such as habitual drunkenness, lying to obtain immigration benefits, prostitution, or having been convicted of certain felonies.[90] If an immigrant victim of domestic violence is divorced or if her spouse has died, she must file the petition within two years of the divorce or death. If her spouse has lost his immigration status because he was convicted of domestic violence, she may self-petition within two years of his loss of status.

Finally, to self-petition, an individual must complete and file the appropriate immigration forms with supporting documentation. Ultimately, U.S. Citizenship and Immigration Services (USCIS) will decide whether to grant the petition, but if it is granted, the applicant gains legal status and may become eligible to adjust her status to that of legal permanent resident. Because immigration law can sometimes be very tricky, an applicant should seek the assistance of an advocate or attorney.

### What can an immigrant victim of domestic violence who might otherwise be eligible to self-petition do if she is already in removal or deportation proceedings?

She can seek a "cancellation of removal" once removal (formerly called deportation) proceedings have begun.[91] An immigrant can only apply for a cancellation if she is already in removal proceedings. If the cancellation of removal is granted, she will become a lawful permanent resident. If it is denied, she will be required to leave the United States.

Under VAWA, a domestic violence victim can apply for a cancellation of removal if she is the spouse or former spouse of an abusive U.S. citizen or lawful permanent resident, or if she is the parent of a child who was abused by the child's U.S. citizen or lawful permanent resident parent. The applicant must demonstrate that she has lived in the United States for the preceding three years, that she suffered battery or extreme cruelty from her spouse while in the United States (or that her child suffered battery or extreme cruelty from his or her parent), that she is of good moral character, and that she (or her child) would suffer extreme hardship if deported. "Extreme hardship" is a key term, covering a variety of situations that a victim might face if deported. Demonstrating "extreme hardship" can include proof of the physical and psychological consequences of the violence and the lack of needed supportive services, in addition to a showing that she would have no way to support herself elsewhere. It can also be shown if there are practices in the native country that would penalize the applicant for leaving an abusive situation or place her at greater harm.[92] Given how complex applying for a cancellation can be and the seriousness of the potential outcome, an applicant should definitely seek the help of an immigration attorney or advocate.

### Are battered immigrants eligible for public welfare benefits?

In 1996, federal legislation dramatically restricted legal immigrants' eligibility for welfare benefits. However, the same legislation provided battered immigrants access to certain critical public benefits.

"Qualified" immigrants are generally eligible for federal Temporary Assistance for Needy Families (TANF) or welfare benefits, if not immediately then after a specified period of time, and some states will provide limited assistance out of state funds. "Qualified" immigrants can include victims of domestic violence (and their children) if the following four requirements are satisfied: (1) USCIS has approved a petition for permanent residency, granted cancellation of removal, *or* found that an applicant's pending application presents a case for approval; (2) the immigrant (or her child) has been subjected to battery or extreme cruelty by a U.S. resident or lawful permanent resident spouse (or parent), or by a family member of the spouse in the household; (3) there is a substantial connection between abuse and the need for benefits; and (4) the battered immigrant does not live with the abuser.[93]

If a battered immigrant is a "qualified" immigrant and is eligible for public benefits, federal law also exempts her from the "deeming" requirements otherwise applicable. Ordinarily, when an individual immigrates to the United States on the basis of a family petition, the sponsoring relative must promise to support the immigrant at an income above the poverty level. An immigrant who later applies for public benefits is assumed (or "deemed") to have full access to the income of her sponsoring relative, and thus in most cases to be ineligible for benefits. Exemption from the deeming requirements removes one barrier to immigrant victims of domestic violence accessing means-tested benefits.

**If an immigrant victim of domestic violence receives public assistance, can she be denied lawful permanent resident status because she is a public charge?**

Typically, when determining whether to grant an immigrant lawful permanent resident status, USCIS considers whether the immigrant is likely to become a public charge, and may deny lawful permanent resident status to such an individual. VAWA 2000 made clear that an immigrant victim's use of public benefits does not make her a "public charge."[94]

**Can an immigrant victim of domestic violence receive help from legal services organizations or legal aid?**

Yes. Most legal services offices receive federal Legal Services Corporation ("LSC") funding. As a condition of this federal funding, these offices generally cannot represent undocumented immigrants, as well as many legal immigrants. The law, however, makes an exception for victims of domestic violence. Legal aid offices funded with LSC money may represent battered immigrants, immigrant victims of sexual assault, and immigrant victims of trafficking in matters directly related to the domestic violence, sexual assault, or trafficking, regardless of their status.[95] Legal services offices can also represent any immigrant whose child has been battered or subjected to extreme cruelty or is the victim of sexual assault or trafficking in matters directly related to the abuse, assault, or trafficking, regardless of the immigrant's status.

**If a battered immigrant is not eligible to self-petition or to seek a cancellation of removal, is any other immigration relief available to her?**

She may be eligible for what is called a U-visa. U-visas are meant to assist undocumented victims of serious crimes who have been helpful or are likely to be helpful in a criminal investigation and/or prosecution against the batterer.[96] The criminal activity must have occurred within the United States, and a police officer, prosecutor, judge, or other government official must certify that she has been helpful in the investigation.[97] Because immigrants subject to deportation often fear reporting crimes or cooperating in their investigation, the U-visa helps to protect them and overcomes one obstacle to holding individuals accountable for crimes against noncitizens.[98]

## Rape and Sexual Assault

**What is rape?**

There is no single definition. Generally rape is defined as "forced sexual intercourse . . . [while] sexual assault includes a wide range of victimizations, [usually] distinct from rape or attempted rape."[99] Regardless of how it is defined and measured, rape is common in the United States. According to one study, one of every six women has experienced an attempted or completed rape as a child or adult.[100]

Historically, most state laws defined rape as English common law did. Under this definition, rape occurred when a man engaged in sexual intercourse with a woman not his wife, by force or threat of force, against her will and without her consent.[101] In addition, state statutes and court rules often required witness corroboration in rape cases and evidence of the "utmost" physical resistance by the woman. This definition and these rules reflected several sexist beliefs: that married women were rightfully the property of their husbands and thus could not be raped by their husbands, that women's testimony about rape could not be trusted because women falsely accuse men of rape, and that regardless of what a woman said or did, she consented to sex unless she physically resisted it.[102] Each of these presumptions made it difficult to convict men of rape. They also made it more difficult for rape victims to access the help, support, and protection they needed.

Fortunately, advocates have achieved many reforms in state and federal laws' definitions of rape in the last three decades, although stereotypes about rape and rape victims persist. All states, for example, have expanded the definition of rape to include sexual assault occurring within a marriage, though different laws and penalties still sometimes apply to marital rape.[103] States have largely abandoned the "utmost resistance" requirement, recognizing the injustice of refusing to acknowledge that a rape had occurred unless a woman risked her life trying to resist. In addition, states' criminal laws now punish various sorts of sexual assault, including not only vaginal penetration but also oral and anal penetration and other sorts of sexual contact.[104] A few states, in attempts to counteract stereotypes and prejudices associated with the word "rape" and to shift the focus to the violent aspect of the crime, have even tried changing the terminology from rape to "sexual assault," "sexual battery," or "criminal sexual conduct."[105] Some laws are gender neutral, recognizing that men as well as women can be raped.

These changes reflect a more comprehensive view of what constitutes sexual violence. However, state legislatures and courts have not uniformly adopted the reforms, nor have societal attitudes and prejudices regarding rape and sexual assault necessarily changed as rapidly as the laws themselves. Therefore, these crimes remain underreported to authorities, and some of the most difficult to prove in court.

### May a husband be convicted of raping his wife?

Yes. All states have expanded the definition of rape to include assault within marriage.

Historically, the law did not protect married women against rape by their husbands. Married women were presumed to consent to all marital sex, and therefore, in theory, they could not be raped. Defenders of this rule argued that it would be harmful to the marital relationship if women were allowed to prosecute their husbands.[106] These theories ignored reality and in effect sanctioned rape.

Some differences in the treatment of rape within and outside of marriage remain, in spite of the progress of the last three decades. Many people still do not recognize spousal rape as rape,[107] and barriers remain to its prosecution. Most states simply removed the marital rape exemption in their laws, treating rape within marriage the same as any other crime. Others explicitly eliminated the marriage defense to rape allegations, and a few designated a separate crime of spousal or marital abuse. However, some states define rape within a marriage at a lower level of criminality, or only criminalize certain kinds of marital rape—for example, where the parties have formally separated. Other states have attached more stringent time requirements to reporting, thus barring charges after a certain period of time has passed. Finally, several states require a higher degree of force for marital rape cases than others. As a result, although every state has criminalized at least some forms of rape within marriage, reform in this area is still necessary.[108]

### If a woman does not physically resist, can her attacker be convicted of rape?

It depends on a particular state's law, but generally, yes. Historically, courts used to require "utmost resistance" or strenuous physical resistance to convict someone of rape. In other words, the victim had to increase the risk to her own life in order to establish that she was raped. To counter the harms caused by this "resistance" requirement, reformists worked to shift the law's focus from her resistance to the rapist's use of force and her lack of consent. As a result, many states have either eliminated the resistance requirement completely or replaced the utmost resistance standard with a requirement of "reasonable resistance."[109]

Nevertheless, a key aspect of proving rape is showing the victim's lack of consent to intercourse. Generally, physical resistance is not supposed to be an issue in determining consent.[110] Yet it remains extremely difficult to successfully prosecute rapists when the victim did not resist physically because of factors such as the attacker's larger size, fear based on previous beatings from him, his greater age or authority, his threatening appearance and manner, the isolation of the location of the rape, or the attacker's threats that he might harm her. In such situations, even if her explicit "no" makes it clear that the victim did not consent, the law or the jury hearing the facts has sometimes found the rapist not guilty and inappropriately converted her lack of physical resistance into "consent" to sex.[111]

### Must a woman have corroborating evidence for a successful prosecution of her attacker?

Generally, no. Prosecution of rape can, in theory, rest on the word of the victim, as with other crimes.

Historically, courts required that a rape victim's testimony be "corroborated" by physical injuries, witness testimony, or other supporting evidence. Today, because of legal reform, only three states have specific corroboration requirements for adult victims, and even these have been limited.[112] New York requires corroboration only when the victim could not consent due to "mental defect or mental incapacity."[113] Ohio requires corroboration for the offense of "sexual imposition," which is a lesser offense than rape.[114] Finally, Texas requires corroboration only if the first complaint of rape or assault is made more than one year after the rape. The first complaint can have been made to "any person, other than the defendant."[115] The other states will allow rape convictions based on the victim's uncorroborated testimony.[116]

Nevertheless, many prosecutors may be hesitant to bring a case without some corroborating evidence, because they believe that juries will not convict. Although the statistics say otherwise, popular belief remains that "real rape" causes physical injury, and many still believe that women lie about rape.[117] Again, although the law has changed, society is only slowly following.[118]

**What are cautionary instructions?**

Courts may sometimes provide juries with what are called "cautionary instructions." These instructions warn that rape is a charge easily made by the victim, that rape is a difficult charge to disprove, and that the testimony of the victim requires more careful scrutiny by the jury than does the testimony of the other witnesses in the trial.[119]

Cautionary instructions are prohibited by statute or caselaw in thirty-seven states and the District of Columbia.[120] In the thirteen states where cautionary instructions are not expressly prohibited, they are also not required and judges have considerable discretion whether to issue them.

These instructions are based on the assumption "that jurors are ordinarily biased in favor of an alleged rape victim and so should be cautioned against this natural inclination,"[121] and that victims regularly lie about rape. They are prejudicial and obsolete and should be eliminated where they are still used. Due process safeguards, such as the right to present witnesses, the right to counsel, and the presumption of innocence should ensure that the defendant receives a fair trial, making such instructions unnecessary.[122]

**Must a victim immediately report a rape for her attacker to be prosecuted?**

No. For many years the law required victims to report an attack to the police immediately. Otherwise, a rapist could not be criminally prosecuted. The requirement reflected the view that "a willing participant in sexual relations [may become] a vindictive complainant [at a later date]."[123] This immediate complaint requirement has never been imposed for other crimes. All but three states no longer require victims to file a report within a specified period of time.[124]

Most states will also allow the defense to introduce evidence of the time it took for the victim to make the complaint as a factor that a jury may consider in judging her credibility.[125] Courts will generally allow the prosecution to introduce evidence of the victim's complaint, if the victim did complain promptly, in order to rebut any assumption a juror might make that an individual who failed to complain promptly was not really raped.[126]

### What is rape trauma syndrome?

Some women who have been raped suffer emotional and psychological harm that leads them to act in ways that lead others to doubt the truthfulness of their charge. Typical behavior may include delayed reporting of an offense, reluctance to discuss the rape, recantations of allegations of abuse, continued contact with the assailant, or a lack of emotion in describing the rape.[127]

Prosecutors have sometimes sought to have psychological experts testify in court to explain these behaviors as typical of rape trauma syndrome, a psychological condition that is a stress response to rape or attempted rape.[128] This testimony may be useful to rebut jurors' misconceptions about a rape victim's behavior. For example, an expert might clarify that it is typical of rape trauma syndrome for a victim to deny being raped to her friends or to ask the assailant not to tell anyone. The expert could also describe the clinical symptoms that victims of rape trauma syndrome display and compare these symptoms to those displayed by the victim.[129] Many courts will permit this form of expert evidence to be introduced,[130] though a few will not.[131] However, experts are generally not allowed to testify about whether they believe the victim was in fact raped. They may only testify that the victim's behavior is consistent with that of individuals with rape trauma syndrome.[132]

### Can a defendant put forward evidence about a woman's sexual history as part of his defense?

Sometimes, but important legal reforms have limited this practice. Courts used to view women's past sexual history as relevant to the issue of whether a woman had consented to sex. The myth was that if a woman was "unchaste," i.e., had previously consented to intercourse with a man not her husband, she would consent to intercourse with any man. "Unchaste" women were also believed to be more likely to lie. These myths often resulted in the admission of a victim's past sexual history in rape prosecutions, which protected women who had little, if any, prior sexual experience but punished those who did. The admission at trial of evidence of past sexual history humiliated many victims, violated their right to privacy, and led juries not to convict in situations where the woman *had* been raped but had previously had consensual sex with other men.

Almost all states and the federal government have now enacted rape shield laws, which prohibit using evidence about a victim's past sexual history in a rape trial unless a defendant can show that the evidence is relevant and meets other strict standards. The details of these laws vary from state to state.[133] While most evidence of a victim's prior sexual conduct will be kept out of the trial, the judge can admit such evidence if, for instance, the defendant is using it to show that another man was the source of semen or injuries to the victim that have been introduced as evidence that a rape occurred.[134] Similarly, the alleged rapist can usually try to prove that the victim previously engaged in consensual intercourse with him and thereby attempt to prove that she consented this time.[135] This second exception often makes it more difficult to prove rape when the victim had a prior sexual relationship with the accused. Evidence of a victim's past sexual history is also permitted in some jurisdictions to demonstrate that she had a pattern of consenting to the particular sort of activity alleged in the case.[136]

Because of these exceptions, the effectiveness of rape shield laws varies from state to state and case to case. Given the prevalence of many rape myths and the continued belief that "bad girls" ask to be raped, more advocacy is needed to ensure that rape shield laws really do protect victims from being put on trial when the rapist is the one who should be under scrutiny by a court.

### Is date rape a crime too?

Yes. Date rape is a form of acquaintance or nonstranger rape. The term "date rape" refers specifically to rape by someone who is on a date with the victim or dating the victim. Regardless of the relationship between attacker and victim, date rape is still forced sexual intercourse without the victim's consent.

Acquaintance rape, which includes date rape, is a broader term referring to rape by anyone whom the victim may know, such as a friend, coworker, or other associate. Acquaintance rape is widespread. In fact, the majority of rapes and sexual assaults are committed by someone the victim knows. Approximately 70 percent of female rape victims knew their assailant.[137]

Acquaintance rape is also a crime. Except in some cases of marital rape, the relationship between victim and attacker is legally irrelevant. In practice, however, it is more difficult to prove acquaintance rape. As discussed above, many people still believe common rape myths such as that "real rape" is stranger rape and that women lie about rape.[138] Attackers in acquaintance rape tend to use less physical force, so it can be more difficult to overcome the jurors' potential assumption that there must be physical resistance. Furthermore, because evidence of prior consensual sex may sometimes be used by the attacker to prove that the victim consented on the date in question, it may be more difficult to prove rape when the victim had a prior sexual relationship with or was dating the attacker.

**Is it illegal for prison officials to assault female prisoners?**

Yes, it is illegal. It is important to note the especially vulnerable situation that female prisoners face when alleging rape. Rape is illegal and the rape laws should apply to an incarcerated woman as to any other woman. There should be no requirement of physical resistance, no requirement that her story be corroborated, and no requirement of physical injury. However, especially for female prisoners, corroboration is often an "unofficial" requirement for effective prosecution of prison officials who sexually abuse or rape them. As a general rule, however, if a rape case against a prison official depends on her word versus his word, courts and juries will believe the official. Congress has begun to examine the plight of inmates by passing the Prison Rape Elimination Act,[139] but its provisions are limited and focus more on monitoring the extent of the problem. (For a more in-depth discussion about the rights of female prisoners and the issues they face see chapter 8, "The Criminal Justice System.")

# Notes

1. Patricia Tjaden and Nancy Thoennes, Dep't of Justice, NCJ 181867, Extent, Nature, and Consequences of Intimate Partner Violence: Findings from the National Violence Against Women Survey 9 (2000), *available at* http://www.ncjrs.gov/pdffiles1/nij/181867.pdf.

2. Matthew R. Durose, Caroline W. Harlow, Patrick A. Langan, et al., Dep't of Justice, NCJ 207846, *Family Violence Statistics* 1 (2005), *available at* http://www.ojp.usdoj.gov/bjs/pub/pdf/fvs.pdf (last visited Feb. 8, 2007); Callie Marie Rennison and Sarah Welchans, Dep't of Justice, NCJ 178247, *Intimate Partner Violence* 1 (2000), *available at* http://www.ojp.usdoj.gov/bjs/pub/pdf/ipv.pdf.

3. Rennison and Welchans, *Intimate Partner Violence, supra* note 2, at 3.

4. Not all victims of domestic violence are women, just as not all abusers are men. However, for convenience and reflecting this guide's focus on the rights of women, in this chapter, victims will generally be referred to in the feminine ("women"/"she"/"her") while abusers will be referred to in the masculine ("men"/"he"/"him").

5. All information about stalking obtained from the Stalking Resource Center

of the National Center for Victims of Crime, http://www.ncvc.org/ (last visited Feb. 8, 2007).

6. *See* Alaska Stat. § 18.65.530 (2004); Ariz. Rev. Stat. Ann. § 13-3601(B) (2005); Cal. Penal Code § 836(c) (West 2005); Colo. Rev. Stat. Ann. § 18-6-803.6(1) (West 2005); Conn. Gen. Stat. § 46b-38b(a) (2005); Del. Code Ann. tit. 10 § 1046 (2005); D.C. Code Ann. § 16-1031(a) (2001); Iowa Code § 236.12 (2005); Kan. Stat. Ann. § 22-2307 (2004); Ky. Rev. Stat. Ann. § 403.760(2) (Baldwin 2005); La. Rev. Stat. Ann. § 46:2140 (West 2005); Me. Rev. Stat. Ann. tit. 19-A, § 4012(5)-§ 4012(6) (2005); Md. Code Ann., Fam. Law § 4-509(b) (West 2005); Mass. Gen. Laws Ann. ch. 209A, § 6(7) (2005); Minn. Stat. Ann. § 518B.01, subd. 14(e) (West 2005); Miss. Code Ann. § 99-3-7(3) (West 2005); Mo. Ann. Stat. § 455.085 (Vernon 2005); Neb. Rev. Stat. § 42-928 (2005); Nev. Rev. Stat. Ann. § 171.137 (West 2004); N.H. Rev. Stat. Ann. § 173-B:9 (2005); N.J. Stat. Ann. § 2C:25-21 (2005); N.M. Stat. Ann. § 40-13-6(C) (West 2005); N.Y. Crim. Proc. Law § 140.10(4) (McKinney 2005); N.C. Gen. Stat. § 50B-4.1(b) (West 2005); N.D. Cent. Code § 14-07.1-11 (2005); Ohio Rev. Code Ann. § 2935.032(A)(1) (Baldwin 2005); Or. Rev. Stat. § 133.055(2) (West 2003); Pa. Con. Stat. Ann. Tit. 23 § 6113 (Purdon 2005); R.I. Gen. Laws § 12-29-3 (2004); S.C. Code Ann. § 16-25-70(B) (2004); S.D. Codified Laws § 23A-3-2.1 (2005); Tenn. Code Ann. § 36-3-611 (West 2005); Tex. Code Crim. Proc. Ann. art. 14.03(b) (Vernon 2005); Utah Code Ann. § 77-36-2.4(1) (West 2005); Va. Code Ann. § 19.2-81.3(B) (West 2005); Wash. Rev. Code Ann. § 10.31.100(2) (West 2005); W. Va. Code Ann. § 48-27-1001(a) (West 2005); Wis. Stat. Ann. § 968.075 (West 2005).

7. Deborah Epstein, *Procedural Justice: Tempering the State's Response to Domestic Violence*, 43 Wm. & Mary L. Rev. 1843, 1851–56 (2002) [hereinafter Epstein, *Procedural Justice*].

8. *See, e.g.,* Matthews v. Pickett County, 996 S.W.2d 162 (Tenn. 1999); Nearing v. Weaver, 670 P.2d 137 (Or. 1983). *But see,* Latiolais v. Guillory, 747 So.2d 675 (La. Ct. App. 1999); Ford v. Town of Grafton, 693 N.E.2d 1047 (Mass. App. Ct. 1998).

9. Donna M. Welch, *Mandatory Arrest of Domestic Abusers: Panacea or Perpetuation of the Problem of Abuse?*, 43 DePaul L. Rev. 1133, 1150–56 (1994) (discussing different studies regarding effect of arrest on recidivism in domestic violence cases).

10. *Id.* at 1159; *see generally* Catherine Popham Durant, *When to Arrest: What Influences Police Determination to Arrest When There Is a Report of Domestic Violence?*, 12 S. Cal. Rev. L. & Women's Stud. 301, 309–13 (2003); Sandy Chesnut, *The Practice of Dual Arrests in Domestic Violence Situations*, 70 Miss. L.J. 971, 976–78 (2000).

11. *See, e.g.,* Linda G. Mills, *Killing Her Softly: Intimate Abuse and the Violence of State Intervention*, 113 Harv. L. Rev. 550 (1999); Miriam H. Ruttenberg, *A Feminist Critique of Mandatory Arrest: An Analysis of Race and Gender in Domestic Violence Policy*, 2 Am. U. J. Gender Soc. Pol'y & L. 171 (1994).

12. Michael T. Morley et al., *Developments in Law and Policy: Emerging Issues in Family Law*, 21 Yale L. & Pol'y Rev. 169, 212 (2003) [hereinafter Morley, *Emerging Issues in Family Law*]; Susan R. Buel, *Effective Assistance of Counsel for Battered Women Defendants: A Normative Construct*, 26 Harv. Women's L.J. 217 (2003).

13. *See, e.g.*, Ala. Code § 13A-6-134 (2005); Alaska Stat. § 18.65.530 (2004); Ariz. Rev. Stat. Ann. § 13-3601(B) (2005); Cal. Penal Code § 836(c) (West 2005); Colo. Rev. Stat. Ann. § 18-6-803.6(1) (West 2005); La. Rev. Stat. Ann. § 46:2140 (West 2005); Miss. Code Ann. § 99-3-7(3) (West 2005); Mo. Ann. Stat. § 455.085 (Vernon 2005); N.J. Stat. Ann. § 2C:25-21 (2005); S.C. Code Ann. § 16-25-70(B) (2004).

14. *See, e.g.*, Ala. Code § 13A-6-134 (2005); Miss. Code Ann. §§ 99-3-7(3) (b), (c) (West 2005); S.C. Code Ann. § 16-25-70(D) (2004).

15. Morley, *Emerging Issues in Family Law*, *supra* note 12, at 212–13.

16. Castle Rock v. Gonzales, 545 U.S. 748 (2005) (finding no federal constitutionally protected right to police enforcement of a restraining order).

17. *See, e.g.*, Matthews v. Pickett County, 996 S.W.2d 162 (Tenn. 1999); Nearing v. Weaver, 670 P.2d 137 (Or. 1983); Massee v. Thompson, 90 P.3d 394 (Mt. 2004). *But see, e.g.*, Latiolais v. Guillory, 747 So.2d 675 (La. Ct. App. 1999); Ford v. Grafton, 693 N.E.2d 1047 (Mass. App. Ct. 1998).

18. *See, e.g.*, Zelig v. County of Los Angeles, 45 P.3d 1171 (Cal. 2002).

19. Watson v. City of Kansas City, 857 F.2d 690, 696–97 (10th Cir. 1988); *see generally* Emily Martin and Caroline Bettinger-Lopez, *Castle Rock v. Gonzalez and the Future of Police Protection for Victims of Domestic Violence*, 11 Domestic Violence Report (Oct./Nov. 2005), at 13.

20. *See, e.g.*, Soto v. Flores, 103 F.3d 1056 (1st Cir. 1997); Navarro v. Block, 72 F.3d 712, 716 (9th Cir. 1995); Eagleston v. Guido, 41 F.3d 865, 878–79 (2d Cir. 1994), *cert. denied*, 516 U.S. 808 (1995); Ricketts v. City of Columbia, 36 F.3d 775, 775–82 (8th Cir. 1994), *cert. denied*, 514 U.S. 1103 (1995); McKee v. City of Rockwall, 877 F.2d 409 (5th Cir.1989), *cert. denied*, 493 U.S. 1023 (1990); Hynson ex. rel Hynson v. Chester Legal Dept., 864 F.2d 1026 (3rd Cir. 1988).

21. The common prosecutorial practice of relying on police testimony regarding the victim's statements has recently become more difficult, as the result of the Supreme Court's decision in Davis v. Washington, 547 U.S. 813 (2006). This domestic violence case addressed whether the Constitution allows prosecution based on an alleged victim's statements made shortly after an alleged crime, when the person who made those statement does not testify and the criminal defendant thus has no opportunity to cross-examine her. The Supreme Court found that the Constitution permitted a prosecutor to rely on statements made to 911 immediately after the assault that identified the defendant as the assailant, but excluded statements made by a victim to police investigating an alleged assault.

22. Cheryl Hanna, *No Right to Choose: Mandated Victim Participation in Domestic Violence Prosecutions*, 109 Harv. L. Rev. 1849 (1996); Morley, *Emerging Issues in*

*Family Law, supra* note 12, at 213–18; Epstein, *Procedural Justice, supra* note 7, at 1866–67.

23. Epstein, *Procedural Justice, supra* note 7, at 1869–70.

24. 18 U.S.C.A. § 2265, 2266 (2005).

25. *See* Office for Victims of Crime, Dept. of Justice, Enforcement of Protective Orders, Legal Series Bulletin #4, 3–4 (January 2002), *available at* http://www.ojp.usdoj.gov/ovc/publications/bulletins/legalseries/bulletin4/welcome.html.

26. *See* Morley, *Emerging Issues in Family Law, supra* note 12, at 218–19.

27. *Id.* at 219.

28. MD. CODE. ANN., FAM. LAW § 4-506 (2003) (mutual protective orders only upon finding of mutual abuse and mutual self-defense); KY. REV. STAT. ANN. § 403.735 (2003) (mutual protective orders legal only if both parties petition for them and mutual abuse is demonstrated); UTAH CODE ANN. § 30-6-4.5 (2002) (mutual protective orders issued only if there is a hearing, both parties petition, and there was no self-defense by one party).

29. CAL. FAMILY CODE § 2047 (2003).

30. 18 U.S.C.A. § 2265(c)(1)(2) (2005).

31. *See generally* Emily Sack, *Battered Women and the State: The Struggle for the Future of Domestic Violence Policy,* 2004 WIS. L. REV. 1657, 1683 (2004); Jennifer Paige Hanft, *What's Really the Problem with Mutual Protective Orders?,* 22 OCT WYO. LAW 22 (1999).

32. Elizabeth Topliffe, *Why Civil Protective Orders Are Effective Remedies for Domestic Violence but Mutual Protective Orders Are Not,* 67 IND. L.J. 1039, 1063 (1992).

33. A list of state coalitions can be found on the website of the National Coalition against Domestic Violence, http://www.ncadv.org.

34. Caitlin Glass et al., *Custody and Visitation: Considerations for Every Attorney Retained by a Survivor of Domestic Violence,* 36 CLEARINGHOUSE REV. 529, 529 (2003).

35. Laurel A. Kent, *Addressing the Impact of Domestic Violence on Children: Alternatives to Laws Criminalizing the Commission of Domestic Violence in the Presence of a Child,* 2001 WIS. L. REV. 1337 (2001).

36. *See, e.g.,* PA. STAT. ANN. 23 § 5303(a) (2005).

37. These states include Alabama, Arizona, Arkansas, California, Delaware, District of Columbia, Florida, Hawaii, Idaho, Iowa, Louisiana, Massachusetts, Minnesota, Nevada, North Dakota, Oklahoma, Oregon, South Dakota, Texas, and Wisconsin. *See* Nancy Lemon, *Statutes Creating Rebuttable Presumptions against Custody to Batterers: How Effective Are They?,* 28 WM. MITCHELL L. REV. 601, 611–12 n.50 (2001).

38. Kristina C. Evans, *Can a Leopard Change His Spots? Child Custody and Batterer's Intervention,* 11 DUKE J. GENDER L. & POL'Y 121, 123–26, nn. 35–39 (2004).

39. *See* Joan S. Meier, *Domestic Violence, Child Custody, and Child Protection:*

*Understanding Judicial Resistance and Imagining the Solutions*, 11 Am. U.J. Gender Soc. Pol'y & L. 657, 672–75, 700–707 (2003); Lundy Bancroft and Jay G. Silverman, The Batterer as Parent: Addressing the Impact of Domestic Violence on Family Dynamics (2002).

40. *See, e.g.,* Del. Code. Ann. 13 § 705A(d) (2005).

41. *See generally* Melissa A. Trepiccione, *At the Crossroads of Law and Social Science: Is Charging a Battered Mother with Failure to Protect Her Child an Acceptable Solution When Her Child Witnesses Domestic Violence?*, 69 Fordham L. Rev. 1487, 1489–1501 (2001); Jeanne A. Fugate, *Who's Failing Whom? A Critical Look at Failure-to-Protect Laws*, 76 N.Y.U. L. Rev. 272, 274 (2001) (discussing civil and criminal "failure to protect" laws in the fifty states); Lois A. Weithorn, *Protecting Children from Exposure to Domestic Violence: The Use and Abuse of Child Maltreatment Statutes*, 53 Hastings L.J. 1, 92–94 (2001) [hereinafter Weithorn, *Protecting Children from Exposure to Domestic Violence*].

42. *See generally* Weithorn, *Protecting Children from Exposure to Domestic Violence, supra* note 41, at 124–30.

43. Nicholson v. Williams, 203 F. Supp. 2d 153 (E.D.N.Y. 2002) ("A mother must be treated equally under the Fourth, Ninth, Thirteenth, Fourteenth, and Nineteenth Amendments. Separating her from her children merely because she has been abused—a characteristic irrelevant to her right to keep her children—treats her unequally from other parents who are not abused.").

44. Nicholson v. Scoppetta, 344 F.3d 154 (2d Cir. 2003).

45. *See, e.g.,* Bouley v. Young-Sabourin, 2005 WL 950632 (D. Vt.); United States v. CBM Group, HUDALJ 10-99-0538-8 (Apr. 13, 2001) (Determination of Reasonable Cause) [hereinafter Alvera] *available at* http://www.legalmomentum.org/issues/vio/alveradeterm.pdf.

46. *See, e.g.,* Alvera, *supra* note 45.

47. National Coalition for the Homeless, NCH Fact Sheet #7: Domestic Violence and Homelessness (June 2005) (internal cites omitted) *available at* http://www.nationalhomeless.org/publications/facts/domestic.pdf.

48. Bouley v. Young-Sabourin (plaintiff demonstrated a prima facie case of sex discrimination under the FHA when she showed an attempt to evict immediately after she was battered by her husband).

49. *Id.*

50. *See, e.g.,* Alvera, *supra* note 45; Press Release, ACLU, In First Settlement of Its Kind, Michigan Domestic Violence Victims Will No Longer Face Eviction (Dec. 10, 2003) *available at* http://www.aclu.org/womensrights/violence/13130prs20031210.html.

51. Violence Against Women Act and Department of Justice Reauthorization Act of 2005, Pub. L. No. 109-162, §§ 606, 607 (2006); 42 U.S.C. 1437d(l)(5) (2006).

52. 42 U.S.C. § 1437d(l)(5) (2006).

53. 42 U.S.C. § 1437d(l) (2006); *see* Dep't of Housing & Urban Dev. v. Rucker, 535 U.S. 125 (2002).

54. 42 U.S.C. § 1437d(l)(6) (2006).

55. 42 U.S.C. §§ 1437f(c)(9), 1437f(d)(1) (2006).

56. 42 U.SC. §§ 1437f(o)(6)(B), 1437f(o)(20)(A) (2006).

57. 42 U.S.C. § 1437f(o)(7)(C) (2006).

58. 42 U.S.C. §§ 1437f(o)(20)(B), (C), (D) (2006).

59. For a listing of current state and local laws, *see* Legal Momentum, Housing Laws Protecting Victims of Domestic Violence and Sexual Assault, *available at* http://www.legalmomentum.org/issues/vio/housing.pdf (last visited Mar. 1, 2007).

60. North Carolina (S.B. 1029, Gen. Ass. Sess. 2005 (N.C. 2005) to be codified at N.C. Gen. Stat. §§ 42-42.1, 42-42.2 and 42-45.1); Rhode Island (2002 R.I. Pub. Laws 118); Washington (WASH. REV. CODE ANN. § 59.18.352, WASH. REV. CODE ANN. § 59.18.130(8)(b)(ii)).

61. ARIZ. REV. STAT. ANN § 33-1315; MINN. STAT. § 504B.205; *see also* California (CAL. HEALTH & SAFETY CODE § 34328.1); Colorado (COLO. REV. STAT. ANN. § 38-12-401; § 38-12-402; § 13-40-104(4); § 13-40-107.5(5)(b)); Iowa (IOWA CODE §§ 562A.27A & §§ 562B.25A93) (2003); Louisiana (LA. REV. STAT. ANN. 46.213(a) (2) & 40:506(d)); New Mexico (N.M. STAT. ANN. § 47-8-33(J)); Oregon (2003 ORE. H.B. 2765); Texas (TEX. PROP. CODE ANN. § 92.015, S.B. 1186/H.B. 211, 79th Leg. (Tex. 2005), to be codified at TEX. PROP. CODE § 92.016)); Utah (UTAH CODE ANN. § 57-22-5.1); Virginia (VA. CODE. ANN. § 55-225.5 and § 55-248.18:1); and Wisconsin (WIS. STAT. ANN. § 106.50 (5m)(d)).

62. States with proposals for laws protecting victims of domestic violence from housing discrimination include Hawaii (H.B. 2021 22nd Leg. (Haw. 2004)); Iowa (S.F.208, H.F. 361, H.F. 444, H.F. 554, 81st Gen. Ass. (Iowa 2005)); Kansas (H.B. 2864, 80th Leg. (Kan. 2004)); Massachusetts (S.B. 793, 184th Gen. Ct. (Mass. 2005)); New York (S.BV. 4112, A.B. 6282, 228th Ann. Leg. Sess. (N.Y. 2005)); Oregon (H.B. 3290, 72nd Leg. Ass. (Ore. 2003)); and Washington (S.B. 5553, 58th Leg. (Wash. 2003), H.B. 2144, 58th Leg. (Wash. 2003)). New York City has also proposed legislation (New York City (Intro. 305 of 2004 (New York City Council 2004))). *Information as seen at* Legal Momentum website, at http://www.legal momentum.org/issues/vio/FactsheetPage.shtml.

63. Lenora M. Lapidus, *Doubly Victimized: Housing Discrimination against Victims of Domestic Violence,* 11 AM. U. J. GENDER, SOC. POLICY, & LAW 377, 382 (2003) [hereinafter Lapidus, *Doubly Victimized*].

64. *Id.* at 383. In some situations, the First Amendment may provide the basis for a constitutional claim as well. The First Amendment protects the right of individuals to seek help from the government. It is possible to argue that because "zero tolerance" policies have the effect of discouraging women from reporting violence

and seeking a restraining order, they effectively chill protected speech. Courts have held that the First Amendment protects the right to seek aid from law enforcement. *See* Forro Precision, Inc. v. IBM, 673 F. 2d 1045 (9th Cir. 1982). Further, the Supreme Court has said that the right to petition includes access to the courts. *See* Cal. Motor Transp. v. Trucking Unlimited, 404 U.S. 508 (1972). If a woman is evicted after having sought aid from law enforcement officers, the argument can be made that she was punished for exercising her First Amendment rights. Lapidus, *Doubly Victimized, supra* note 63.

65. 820 ILL. COMP. STAT. 180/30 (West 2005) (Illinois employers with fifty or more employees, state and local agencies, and school districts are prohibited from refusing to hire, firing, harassing, or otherwise discriminating or retaliating against any individual who is or is perceived to be a victim of domestic or sexual violence or who has a family or household member who is, or is perceived to be, a victim of domestic or sexual violence.).

66. N.Y.C. CODE § 8-107.1 (2005).

67. ANN. CAL. LAB. CODE § 230(c) (West 2005); COLO. REV. STAT. § 24-34-402.7 (West 2005); CONN. GEN. STAT. § 54-85b; MIAMI-DADE CTY. FLA. CODE § 11A-61; HAW. REV. STAT. § 378-72 (2005); ME. REV. STAT. Tit 26 § 850 (2005); Md. Exec. Order No. 01.01.1998.25; N.Y. PENAL LAW § 215.14 (McKinney 2005); N.C. GEN. STAT § 95-241 (West 2005); R.I. GEN. LAWS § 12-28-10 (2004). For a list of current state and local laws and descriptions, *see* Legal Momentum, State Law Guide: Employment Discrimination against Victims of Domestic and Sexual Violence, last updated Jan. 2006, *available at* http://www.legalmomentum.org/issues/vio/discrim.pdf (last visited Mar. 1, 2007).

68. Price Waterhouse v. Hopkins, 490 U.S. 228, 250 (1989).

69. *See, e.g.,* Greer v. Beck's Pub & Grill, No. C03-2070 LRR (N.D. Iowa, Jan. 4, 2006) (alleging disparate impact discrimination and disparate treatment discrimination under Title VII after a victim of domestic violence was fired after she obtained a protective order). For a description of the case, *see* Wendy Weiser and Deborah Widiss, *Employment Protection for Domestic Violence Victims*, CLEARINGHOUSE REV. J. OF POVERTY LAW & POL'Y 3, 6 (May-June 2004).

70. *See generally* Julie Goldscheid, *The Civil Rights Remedy of the 1994 Violence Against Women Act: Struck Down but Not Ruled Out*, 39 FAM. L. Q. 157, 175–79 (2005).

71. *See, e.g.,* Apessos v. Memorial Press Group, 15 MASS. L. RPTR. 322, 2002 WL 31324115, (Mass. Super. 2002) ("A victim should not have to seek physical safety at the cost of her employment.").

72. For a list of current legislation *see* Legal Momentum, *State Law Guide: Time Off from Work for Victims of Domestic or Sexual Violence*, last updated Jan. 2006, *available at* http://www.legalmomentum.org/issues/vio/timeoff.pdf (last visited Mar. 1, 2007).

73. Ann. Cal. Lab. Code § 230 & § 230.1 (West 2005).

74. Colo. Rev. Stat. § 24-34-402.7. Before taking this leave, the employee must exhaust all applicable annual leave, vacation leave, personal leave, and sick leave.

75. *See, e.g.,* N.Y. Penal Law § 215.14 (2005); Conn. Gen. Stat. § 54-85b (2005).

76. Legal Momentum, Know Your Rights: Domestic Violence or Sexual Assault at Work (reformatted 2005) [hereinafter Legal Momentum, Know Your Rights]; *see, e.g.,* Royall v. Indus. Comm'n, 476 P.2d 156, 159 (Ariz. 1970).

77. Epperson v. Indus. Comm'n of Ariz., 549 P.2d 247, 249 (Ariz. 1976).

78. Weiss v. City of Milwaukee, 559 N.W.2d 588 (Wis. 1997).

79. "When an attack occurs during the course of employment and arises from personal animus imported from a private relationship, the incident arises out of the claimant's employment if employment conditions have contributed to or facilitated the attack." *Id.* at 595.

80. Epperson v. Indus. Comm'n of Ariz., 549 P.2d at 250 (categorizing the attack at work as "an assault of a purely private origin").

81. *See, e.g.,* Gutierrez v. Artesia Pub. Schools, 583 P.2d 476 (N.M. 1978); Johnson v. Drummond, Woodsum, Plimpton & MacMahon, P.A., 490 A.2d 676 (Me. 1985); Guillory v. Interstate Gas Station, 653 So.2d 1152 (La. 1995); Fair v. People's Sav. Bank, 542 A.2d 1118 (Conn. 1988); Peavler v. Mitchell & Scott Mach. Co., 638 N.E.2d 879 (Ind. Ct. App. 1994); In re Colas v. Watermain, 744 N.Y.S.2d 229 (N.Y. App. Div. 2002).

82. Legal Momentum, Know Your Rights: Domestic Violence or Sexual Assault at Work, *supra* note 76.

83. Ariz. Rev. Stat Ann. § 23-771 (2005); Cal. Unemp. Ins. Code §§ 1030, 1032, 1256; Colo. Rev. Stat. Ann. § 8-73-108(4)(r); Conn. Gen. Stat. § 31-236(a) (2)(A(iv)); Del. Code Ann. tit. 19, § 3314(1); D.C. Code § 51-131 (2005); Ill. Comp. Stat. Ann. chap 820 § 405/601((B)(6)(a) (West 2005); Ind. Code Ann. § 22-4-15-1(c)(8) (West 2005); Kan. Stat. Ann. § 44-706(a)(12) (2004); Me. Rev. Stat. Ann. tit. 26, § 1043(23)(B)(3) (2005); Mass. Gen. Laws ch. 151A, §§ 1(g 1/2), 25(e); Minn. Stat. § 268.095(1)(8) (2005); Mont. Code Ann. § 39-51-2111; Neb. Rev. Stat. Ann. § 48-624(7)(1) (effective 1/1/2006); N.H. Rev. Stat. Ann. tit. 23, § 282-A:32(I)(a)(3) (2005); N.J. Rev. Stat. § 43:21-5(j) (2005); N.M. Stat. Ann. § 51-1-7(A)(1)(b) (West 2005); N.Y. Lab. Law § 593(1)(a) (McKinney 2005); N.C. Gen. Stat. § 96-14(1f) (West 2005); Okla. Stat. Ann. tit. 40, §§ 2-405(5), 3-106(G)(8) (2005); Or. Rev. Stat. § 657.176(12) (West 2005); R.I. Gen. Laws § 28-44-17.1 (2005); 2005 S.C. Laws Act 50 (H.B. 3682) to be codified at S.C. Cod. Ann. § 41-31-125, 41-35-130; S.D. Codified Laws § 61-6-13.1; Tex. Lab. Code Ann. §§ 207.045, §§ 207.046 (Vernon 2005); 2005 Vt. Acts & Resolves 49, Bill S.0041, to be codified at 21 Vt. Stat. Ann. ch. 16A, as seen at http://www.leg.

state.vt.us/; WASH. REV. CODE §§ 50.20.050, 50.20.100, 50.20.240, and 50.29.020 (West 2005); WIS. STAT. § 108.04(7)(s) (West 2005); WYO. STAT. § 27-3-311(a)(i) (C) (2005). For a list of state laws and pending legislation, *see* Legal Momentum, *State Law Guide: Unemployment Insurance Benefits* (July 2006), *available at* http://www.legalmomentum.org/issues/vio/ui.pdf.

84. 45 C.F.R. § 260.55 (2005).

85. 42 U.S.C. § 602(a)(7); 45 C.F.R. § 260.50 *et seq.* (2005).

86. GAO-05-701 TANF, TANF: State Approaches to Screening for Domestic Violence Could Benefit from HHS Guidance 11 (Aug. 2005) *available at* http://www.gao.gov/new.items/d05701.pdf (last visited Mar. 1, 2007).

87. 42 U.S.C. § 608(a)(7)(C)(iii) (2005).

88. 8 U.S.C. § 1154(a)(1)(A)(iii) (2005).

89. 8 U.S.C. § 1367 (2005). Confidentiality provisions in federal law bar the INS and Justice Department from releasing any information about a VAWA self-petition, including the existence of a petition, to anyone, including the abuser.

90. 8 U.S.C.A. § 1101 (2005).

91. 8 U.S.C. § 1229b(2) (2005).

92. 8 C.F.R. § 240.20(c) and § 240.58(c) (2005).

93. 8 U.S.C. § 1641(c) (2005).

94. VAWA 2000 § 1505(f).

95. Pub. L. No. 104-208, § 502, 110 Stat. 3009, 3009–59 (1996).

96. 8 U.S.C. § 1184 (2005).

97. *Id.*

98. For more information on the rights of immigrants, see the ACLU's most recent edition of the Rights of Immigrants, http://www.aclu.org/immigrants/gen/11713pub20000908.html (last visited Mar. 1, 2007). This is only an overview of a few relevant provisions of immigration law and doesn't begin to detail the many provisions and technicalities that may come into play in any individual situation.

99. Rape, Abuse, and Incest National Network (RAINN), What Is Rape? What Is Sexual Abuse?, *available at* http://www.rainn.org/statistics/definitions.html. It is important to note that in some states the term "rape" has been eliminated from some criminal statutes. Instead, legislators adopted terms such as "sexual assault in the first degree," etc., the elements of which mirror the above definition of rape. For purposes of this section, the above definitions will apply.

100. National Task Force to End Sexual and Domestic Violence against Women, Violence Against Women Act 2005, Sexual Assault Services Act, *available at* http://www.vawa2005.org/sasa.pdf (citing the National Violence Against Women Survey, "Prevalence, Incidence, and Consequences of Violence against Women," November 1998); *see generally* Dean Kilpatrick and Kenneth J. Reggiero, *Making Sense of Rape in America: Where Do the Numbers Come From and What Do They Mean?* 2 (National Crime Victims Research and Treatment Center).

101. Susan Estrich, Real Rape 8 (Harvard Univ. Press 1987); Cassia C. Spohn, *The Rape Reform Movement: The Traditional Common Law and Rape Law Reforms*, 39 Jurimetrics J. 119, 122 (1999) [hereinafter Spohn, *The Rape Reform Movement*].

102. Estrich, Real Rape, *supra* note 101, at 8.

103. National Center for Victims of Crime, Spousal Rape Laws 1 (2000) *available at* http://www.vawnet.org/SexualViolence/PublicPolicy/SpousalRape.php.

104. *See, e.g.,* Ill. Comp. Stat. Ann. ch. 720 5/12–13; Mich. Comp. Laws Ann. § 750.520a. (2005); Minn. Stat. Ann. § 609.341, § 609.342, § 609.343; § 609.344, § 609.345 (2005); *see generally* Spohn, *The Rape Reform Movement, supra* note 101, at 122; Andrea A. Curcio, *The Georgia Roundtable Discussion Model: Another Way to Approach Reforming Rape Laws,* 20 Ga. St. U. L. Rev. 565, 573 (2004) [hereinafter Curcio, *Another Way to Approach Reforming Rape Laws*].

105. Curcio, *Another Way to Approach Reforming Rape Laws, supra* note 104.

106. Robin West, *Equality Theory, Marital Rape, and the Promise of the Fourteenth Amendment,* 42 Fla. L. Rev. 45, 64 (1990).

107. National Center for Victims of Crime, *Spousal Rape Laws, supra* note 103.

108. Michelle J. Anderson, *Marital Immunity, Intimate Relationships, and Improper Inferences: A New Law on Sexual Offenses by Intimates,* 54 Hastings L.J. 1465 (2003) (analyzing the law on marital immunity in state sexual offense statutes).

109. Curcio, *Another Way to Approach Reforming Rape Laws, supra* note 104, at 575.

110. *See generally* Victoria Nourse, *The "Normal" Successes and Failures of Feminism and the Criminal Law,* 75 Chi.-Kent L. Rev. 951, 953–61 (2000).

111. Scholars have pointed out that in spite of reform, juries still believe many rape myths, some of the most common being that real rape victims always have serious injuries, that if a women doesn't fight back she really wanted it, and that women lie about being raped to get even with men. *See generally* Curcio, *Another Way to Approach Reforming Rape Laws, supra* note 104, at 586–87.

112. *See generally* Michelle J. Anderson, *The Legacy of the Prompt Complaint Requirement, Corroboration Requirement, and Cautionary Instructions on Campus Sexual Assault,* 84 B.U. L. Rev. 945, 966–73 (2004) [hereinafter *Legacy*].

113. N.Y. Penal Law § 130.16 (McKinney 2005).

114. Ohio Rev. Code Ann. § 2907.06(B) (West 2005) (Sexual imposition is essentially offensive or inappropriate sexual contact of another person without that person's consent. The statute states that "[n]o person shall be convicted of a violation of this section solely upon the victim's testimony unsupported by other evidence.").

115. Tex. Crim. Proc. Code Ann. § 38.07(a) (Vernon 2005). ("A conviction . . . is supportable on the uncorroborated testimony of the victim of the sexual offense if the victim informed any person, other than the defendant, of the alleged offense within one year after the date on which the offense is alleged to have occurred.") The corroboration requirement is waived if the victim is under seventeen,

is over sixty-five, or has diminished capacity to care for herself. *See also Legacy, supra* note 112, at nn. 121–22.

116. *Legacy, supra* note 112, at 970–73.

117. *Id.* at 979–81.

118. Estrich, Real Rape, *supra* note 101, at 43 (citing Note, *Corroborating Charges of Rape*, 67 Colum. L. Rev. 1137, 1137–38 [1967]).

119. A. Thomas Morris, *The Empirical, Historical, and Legal Case against the Cautionary Instruction: A Call for Legislative Reform*, 1988 Duke L. J. 154, 157 and n.20 (1988).

120. *Legacy, supra* note 112, at 973–77, 980–87.

121. *Id.* at 980.

122. People v. Rincon-Pineda, 14 Cal. 3d 864, 878, 538 P.2d 247 (Cal. 1975).

123. Dawn M. Dubois, *A Matter of Time: Evidence of a Victim's Prompt Complaint in New York*, 53 Brook. L. Rev. 1087, 1101 (1988).

124. These states are California, which requires that a complaint of spousal rape be made within a year or corroborated by physical evidence, Cal. Penal Code § 262-(5)(b); Illinois, which requires a complaint of spousal rape within thirty days, unless there is good cause, 720 Ill. Comp. Stat. Ann. 5/12-18(c) (West 2004); and South Carolina, which requires that a complaint of spousal rape be made within thirty days of the offense and has no good cause exceptions, S.C. Code Ann. § 16-3-615(B). None of these states has a prompt complaint requirement for rape outside of marriage.

125. *See, e.g.,* State v. Troupe, 677 A.2d 917, 929 (Conn. 1996); Pa. Cons. Stat. § 3105.

126. E.g., *Troupe*, 677 A.2d at 927–28; State v. Hill, 578 A.2d 370, 377 (N.J. 1990); *see generally* Kathryn M. Stanchi, *The Paradox of the Fresh Complaint Rule*, 37 B.C.L. Rev. 441 (1996); *cf.* People v. Brown, 35 Cal. Rptr. 2d 407, 415–18 (Cal. 1994) (finding such evidence admissible to establish fact that victim complained, regardless of whether complaint was prompt).

127. Karla Fischer, *Defining the Boundaries of Admissible Expert Psychological Testimony on Rape Trauma Syndrome*, 1989 U. Ill. Law Rev. 691, 712 (1989) [hereinafter Fischer, *Defining the Boundaries*]; *see also* Katherine M. Davis, *Rape, Resurrection, and the Quest for Truth: The Law and Science of Rape Trauma Syndrome in Constitutional Balance with the Rights of the Accused*, 49 Hastings L.J. 1511 (1998).

128. Arthur H. Garrison, *Rape Trauma Syndrome: A Review of a Behavioral Science Theory and Its Admissibility in Criminal Trials*, 23 Am. J. Trial Advoc. 591, 630–32 (2000) (rape trauma symptom goes beyond determining that the victim has suffered a traumatic experience and explains how that traumatic experience is manifested based on various factors. RTS puts observed behavior in the context of an incident of rape.).

129. Fischer, *Defining the Boundaries, supra* note 127, at 715.

130. *See* Kenneth Winchester Gaines, *Rape Trauma Syndrome: Toward Proper Use in the Criminal Trial Context*, 20 AM. J. TRIAL ADVOC. 227, 235–41 (Winter 1996–1997) [hereinafter Gaines, *Rape Trauma Syndrome*] (setting out jurisdictions in which such testimony has been ruled admissible and the purposes for which this evidence has been admitted).

131. Commonwealth v. Gallagher, 547 A.2d 355 (Pa. 1988); State v. Black, 745 P.2d 12, 16–19 (Wash. 1987); State v. Saldana, 324 N.W.2d 227, 229 (Minn. 1982).

132. Gaines, *Rape Trauma Syndrome, supra* note 130, at 232.

133. *See, e.g.*, Michelle J. Anderson, *Time to Reform Rape Shield Laws*, 19 CRIM. JUST. 14, 15–16 (Summer 2004) (describing varieties of rape shield laws and the jurisdictions in which each variety has been adopted).

134. *See, e.g.*, Fed. R. Evid. § 412(b)(1)(A); *see generally* K. Winters, *Federal Rape-Shield Statute*, 43 U. OF MIAMI L. REV. 947 (1989).

135. *See, e.g.*, Fed. R. Evid. 412(b)(1)(B). *See generally* Winters, *supra* note 134, at 959–60.

136. Michelle J. Anderson, *From Chastity Requirement to Sexuality License: Sexual Consent and a New Rape Shield Law*, 70 GEO. WASH. L. REV. 51, 98–103 (2002); *see also* Anderson, *Time to Reform Rape Shield Laws, supra* note 133.

137. Shannon Catalano, U.S. Dep't of Justice, 2004 National Crime Victimization Survey, 9 (September 2005), *available at* http://www.ojp.usdoj.gov/bjs/cvict_c.htm#violent.

138. National Sexual Assault Hotline, http://www.rainn.org/statistics/punishing-rapists.html; Dana Vetterhoffer, Comment, *No Means No: Weakening Sexism in Rape Law by Legitimizing Post-Penetration Rape*, 49 ST. LOUIS U. L. J. 1229, 1248–59 (2005) (discussing rape myths in analysis of law); Kara M. DelTufo, Book Review, *Resisting "Utmost Resistance": Using Rape Trauma Syndrome to Combat Underlying Rape Myths Influencing Acquaintance Rape Trials*, 22 B.C. THIRD WORLD L.J. 419, 424 (2002) (reviewing SUSAN EHRLICH, REPRESENTING RAPE: LANGUAGE AND SEXUAL CONSENT (2001)).

139. Prison Rape Elimination Act of 2003, Pub. L. No. 108-79, 117 Stat. 972 (2003), codified at 42 U.S.C. § 15601 *et seq.* (2005).

# VI

# Reproductive Freedom

Reproductive freedom, if fully realized, allows women and men to make important life decisions—free from government interference —about when and whether to become a parent. It ensures meaningful access to reproductive health care (including abortion, contraception, and prenatal care) and supports programs that provide the information we all need to lead healthy lives. Being able to decide whether and when to have a child is critical to women and their families. As the U.S. Supreme Court has observed, "The ability of women to participate in the economic and social life of the Nation has been facilitated by their ability to control their reproductive lives."[1] Reproductive freedom, in other words, is the cornerstone of women's equality and the foundation for building healthy families.

Unfortunately, we are far from achieving full reproductive freedom. Many women, for example, lack meaningful access to contraception, to pregnancy care, and to abortion. In recent years, restrictions on abortion have increased, as has vocal opposition to contraception. At the same time, support for women having children remains limited, and the government continues to pour millions of dollars a year into programs that deprive teens of the sexuality education they need to make healthy and responsible life decisions.

This chapter will discuss the main issues surrounding reproductive freedom, including the right to abortion and restrictions on that right, access to contraception, the right to bear children, sterilization, and comprehensive sexuality education.

### What are reproductive rights?

Reproductive rights, if fully realized, allow women and men to make informed, meaningful decisions about whether and when to become parents, free from intrusion by the government. Reproductive rights protect access to

198

the full spectrum of reproductive health care, from sexuality education and birth control to prenatal care and childbearing assistance to adoption information and assistance to abortion counseling and services.

### What have reproductive rights meant for women and their families?

Being able to decide whether and when to have a child has made a critical difference to women at all stages of life, as well as to their families, their partners, their children, and others. Although people have always sought to control whether and when to bear children, contraception has only become safe, effective, and readily available in the last forty years. The birth control pill became available for the first time in the early 1960s,[2] but, as explained later in this chapter, it was not until 1965 that the U.S. Supreme Court struck down laws prohibiting contraceptive use for married people.[3] Only in 1972 did the Court extend that ruling to unmarried people.[4]

Reproductive rights have dramatically improved the health of women and their children in the United States. The number of unintended births has declined dramatically. For example, from 1961 to 1965, 20 percent of births to married women were unwanted; that proportion dropped to 9 percent by 2002.[5] This reduction in unintended births has significantly improved women's health, as the medical risks of pregnancy and childbirth are greatest when women have unplanned or closely spaced pregnancies.[6] Only about half of women with unplanned pregnancies receive early prenatal care, while almost three-fourths of women with planned pregnancies receive such care.[7] The ability to plan the timing, number, and spacing of births thus increases the likelihood of positive health outcomes for women and their families.[8]

Access to safe and legal abortion has also improved the health and lives of women and their families. Estimates of the number of illegal abortions in the 1950s and 1960s range from two hundred thousand to 1.2 million annually.[9] Many women died from those procedures. In 1965, for example, illegal abortions were the cause of nearly 17 percent of deaths relating to pregnancy and childbirth.[10] Thousands of other women suffered severe consequences short of death, including perforations of the uterus, cervical wounds, serious bleeding, infections, poisoning, shock, and gangrene.[11] In 1969, before New York legalized abortion, abortion complications resulted in 23 percent of all pregnancy-related admissions to city hospitals in New York City.[12] After the legalization of abortion, morbidity and mortality as a result of abortions radically declined. Today, abortion is one of the safest and most commonly performed clinical procedures.[13] The risk of death is 0.6 deaths per one hundred thousand legal abortions,[14] and abortion is safer than carrying a pregnancy to term.[15]

Reproductive rights also protect the freedom to bear children. In the first half of the twentieth century, involuntary sterilization was permitted in thirty states, and tens of thousands of individuals were sterilized against their will. People who were institutionalized were particularly vulnerable, as were the poor and people of color.[16] Fortunately, sterilization subsequently fell out of favor, and in 1942 the U.S. Supreme Court declared the right to bear children a fundamental right.[17] (Even so, women who were receiving Medicaid were sometimes sterilized without their knowledge and consent, as recently as the 1960s.)[18]

**What have reproductive rights meant for women's equality?**

Reproductive rights have also furthered women's equality. As one court explained, "Since time immemorial, women's biology and ability to bear children have been used as a basis for discrimination against them. . . . This discrimination has had a devastating effect upon women."[19] Moreover, unplanned pregnancies "undermine women's abilities by precluding [them] from participating fully in the 'marketplace and the world of ideas.'"[20] Reproductive rights have enabled women to remedy these inequities. As the Supreme Court observed in 1992, "The ability of women to participate in the economic and social life of the Nation has been facilitated by their ability to control their reproductive lives."[21]

**Does the U.S. Constitution protect reproductive rights?**

Yes. In 1965, the U.S. Supreme Court—this country's highest judicial authority—held that the right of privacy is a fundamental right guaranteed by the U.S. Constitution and that this right protects the use of contraception. In that case, *Griswold v. Connecticut*, the Supreme Court heard a challenge to a Connecticut statute that made the use of contraceptives a crime, even for married people.[22] The Supreme Court held that such a restriction on birth control for married people violated the right to privacy protected by the Constitution.[23] In 1972, in *Eisenstadt v. Baird*, the Supreme Court extended that right to all people, married or single, when it struck down a Massachusetts statute that criminalized the use of contraceptives for unmarried people.[24] The Court explained that "if the right to privacy means anything, it is the right of the individual, married or single, to be free from unwanted governmental intrusion into matters so fundamentally affecting a person as the decision whether to bear or beget a child."[25] These decisions provided the constitutional foundation for *Roe v. Wade*, which held that the right of privacy includes the right to end a pregnancy.[26] That case is discussed later in this chapter.

### Are reproductive rights in jeopardy?

Yes. As of this writing in 2008, the U.S. Supreme Court has two new justices, appointed by President George W. Bush. The Court as newly constituted recently upheld an unprecedented federal law that criminalizes abortion procedures that doctors say are the safest for some women.[27] This ban is very similar to a law that the Supreme Court—with different justices —struck down just seven years prior.[28] This decision is the first Supreme Court decision to uphold an abortion restriction that lacks protection for women's health. Indeed, the decision goes so far as to put an interest in fetal life above the interest in women's health.[29] Its language invites politicians to pass additional restrictions on abortion. Further changes on the Supreme Court could put reproductive rights in even greater jeopardy.

Recently, several state legislatures have considered outright bans on abortion, and in 2006, one state—South Dakota—tried to enact such a blatantly unconstitutional ban. (In a November 2006 referendum, the voters rejected this measure.)[30] Regulations short of outright bans have also increased in the last decade, making abortion more difficult to obtain and even effectively unavailable for many women.

More than access to abortion is at stake. Opponents of reproductive rights increasingly seek to limit access to contraception and to promote programs in schools that advocate abstinence until marriage, without providing any information about how to protect against unintended pregnancy and sexually transmitted disease for those teens who decide to have sex. Federal funding for abstinence-only-until-marriage programs has totaled more than a billion dollars since 1996.[31]

At the same time, efforts are also underway to discourage women from exercising their right to have children. For example, under the guise of welfare reform, many states have enacted punitive "child exclusion" policies. These policies discourage women who receive state assistance from having children by depriving them of increases in benefits if they bear an additional child while receiving public assistance.[32]

## ABORTION

### What did the Supreme Court decide in *Roe v. Wade*?

The U.S. Supreme Court established the right to an abortion in its 1973 decision, *Roe v. Wade*. Prior to *Roe*, abortion was illegal in most states except to save a woman's life or where the pregnancy threatened the women's health or resulted from rape or incest.[33] In *Roe*, the Supreme Court considered the constitutionality of a Texas law that made it a crime to perform an abortion unless the woman's life was in danger.[34] The case was filed by "Jane Roe," an unmarried woman who wanted to end her pregnancy.

The Supreme Court struck down the Texas law. Relying on its previous decisions declaring the right of privacy in *Griswold* and *Eisenstadt*, the Court concluded that the right of privacy protected "a woman's decision whether or not to terminate her pregnancy."[35] The Court characterized this right as "fundamental" to a woman's "life and future," and like all "fundamental" rights, it was accorded the highest level of constitutional protection: the government could not prohibit or interfere with abortion without a "compelling" reason to do so. After viability (that is, the point when the fetus is potentially able to survive outside the woman—currently around twenty-four weeks of pregnancy),[36] a state may ban abortion, except where it is necessary for the preservation of the life or health of the woman.[37] *Roe* rendered state laws outlawing abortion unconstitutional, making abortion services safer and more accessible to women throughout the country.[38]

### What was the status of the right to abortion during the 1970s and 1980s?

In the face of *Roe*, many states and cities passed new restrictions on abortion. Over the following two decades, the Supreme Court struck down many of those restrictions. For example, following *Roe*, the Supreme Court invalidated requirements that a woman obtain the consent of her spouse prior to an abortion;[39] that any abortion after the first trimester of pregnancy be performed in a hospital (given that abortions could be safely performed in other clinical settings);[40] and that a woman receive information designed to discourage abortion and then be prevented from having the abortion for at least twenty-four hours after receiving the information.[41] At the same time, however, as is discussed in greater detail later in this chapter, the Supreme Court upheld bans on government funding of abortion for poor women,[42] as well as requirements that teens involve a parent or go to court prior to an abortion.[43]

### What is the significance of the Supreme Court's 1992 decision, *Planned Parenthood v. Casey*?

In 1992, in *Planned Parenthood of Southeastern Pennsylvania v. Casey*, the U.S. Supreme Court considered the constitutionality of several Pennsylvania abortion restrictions.[44] Changes in the makeup of the Supreme Court led many to believe that the Court might overturn *Roe* when it decided that case.

In *Casey*, the Court did not overrule *Roe*. Indeed, the Court reaffirmed that a woman has a constitutional right to choose abortion before viability; after viability, the Court reiterated, a state may ban abortion, provided there is an exception if the woman's life or health is at stake.[45]

At the same time, the Court significantly scaled back the constitutional protection for abortion and made it more difficult for women to succeed in challenging laws restricting access to it. In particular, the Court abandoned the highest level of protection set forth in *Roe*—protection given fundamental rights—in favor of a new test that permits many abortion restrictions to survive constitutional review.[46] Under this new test, state regulations of abortions prior to viability are constitutional unless they constitute an "undue burden" on abortion. A law that regulates abortion survives the "undue burden" test unless it has the "purpose or effect" of placing a "substantial obstacle in the path of a woman seeking an abortion of a nonviable fetus."[47]

This change had significant and immediate consequences. Applying the new test, the Court reversed several previous decisions.[48] In particular, the Court upheld Pennsylvania's law compelling doctors to provide information designed to discourage abortion, holding that the law does not constitute an "undue burden" as long as the information is truthful and not misleading.[49] In addition, the Court upheld a restriction that prevented a doctor from performing an abortion for twenty-four hours after the woman first received the information mandated by the state.[50] The Court reasoned that regulations "which do no more than create a structural mechanism by which the State . . . may express profound respect for the life of the unborn are permitted, if they are not a substantial obstacle to the woman's exercise of the right to choose."[51] It upheld the requirement despite evidence that it increased costs and delays for women seeking abortion, particularly those with the fewest financial resources and those who needed to travel long distances for care.[52] Prior to *Casey*, such restrictions had been held unconstitutional.[53]

The Court struck down only one provision of the Pennsylvania law: that a woman must notify her spouse before obtaining an abortion. As will be explained in further detail later in this chapter, the Court concluded that this requirement posed an "undue burden," particularly for women who could not notify their spouses because of abuse.[54] (It is worth noting that now Supreme Court Justice Samuel Alito, while a judge on the U.S. Court of Appeals for the Third Circuit [which considered the Pennsylvania regulations before the Supreme Court reviewed them], maintained that the requirement was constitutional.)[55]

At the same time, even while chipping away at the right to abortion, the Supreme Court in *Casey* set forth its most forceful articulation of the importance of the right to abortion to women's lives. The Court recognized that "[t]he ability of women to participate in the economic and social life of the Nation has been facilitated by their ability to control their reproductive lives."[56] The right to abortion has enabled women to "organize intimate relationships and ma[ke] choices that define their views of themselves and their places in society."[57]

### What did the Court decide in its 2000 decision, *Stenberg v. Carhart*?

In the *Stenberg* decision, the Supreme Court held unconstitutional Nebraska's so-called "partial-birth abortion" ban, a ban similar to those passed in more than two dozen states in the 1990s.[58] In a 5–4 decision, the Court struck Nebraska's law for two reasons: the ban's failure to include a health exception impermissibly threatened women's health, and the ban prohibited the most common methods of second-trimester abortion, thereby placing an undue burden on a woman's right to an abortion.[59] The decision was a great victory for women and their physicians.

The Court's reasoning was significant. First, the Court held the ban unconstitutional because it lacked an exception to protect women's health.[60] In so doing, the Court reaffirmed that the government may not act to endanger women's health. It also emphasized that, as long as sound medical opinion supports the safety of a particular procedure (and regardless of whether there are dissenting voices in the medical community), the treating physician must retain the discretion to choose the method most appropriate for the patient's health.[61] The Court recognized that the American College of Obstetricians and Gynecologists (ACOG), which represents more than 90 percent of all physicians specializing in obstetrics and gynecology in the United States, opposed the ban.[62]

Second, looking to evidence in the case, the Court concluded that the ban did not, as its proponents claimed, target any single, discrete abortion procedure but instead encompassed an array of safe and common methods.

Indeed, the Court found that the ban would prohibit the procedures by which more than 95 percent of the abortions between twelve and twenty weeks of pregnancy are performed.[63] The Court concluded that the ban placed an unconstitutional obstacle in the path of women seeking abortions before fetal viability.[64]

Advocates for reproductive rights had hoped this case would put to rest legislative efforts to ban certain abortion methods. Unfortunately, as discussed below, the U.S. Congress enacted a federal ban, and the challenge to that ban ended up in the Supreme Court—with dramatically different results—just seven years later.

### What did the Supreme Court hold in its 2007 decision addressing abortion, *Gonzales v. Carhart*?

In *Gonzales v. Carhart*, the Supreme Court upheld the so-called "Partial-Birth Abortion Ban Act of 2003"—the first ever federal ban on abortion methods.[65] Congress passed the law in response to the Supreme Court's 2000 decision in *Stenberg v. Carhart*, discussed above, in which the Court struck down Nebraska's ban on so-called "partial-birth abortion."[66] Congress's ban, like Nebraska's, lacked an exception to protect women's health.[67]

This time, however, the Court's composition—and its decision—were different. In *Gonzales*, the Court—with two new Justices—upheld the ban.[68] Considering the lack of a health exception, the Court reasoned that, in the face of medical uncertainty whether a banned method was necessary to protect women's health, Congress could constitutionally omit a health exception.[69] In this way, the Court overruled one of its holdings in *Stenberg v. Carhart*—all the while not acknowledging it was doing so. The Court also held that the ban did not constitute an undue burden because it prohibited only one abortion method.

*Gonzales* was the first decision in which the Court upheld an abortion restriction lacking protection for women's health. It thus undermined a core principle of thirty years of abortion jurisprudence that women's health must remain paramount. And the Court went so far as to rule that the "[s]tate's interest in promoting respect for human life at all stages in the pregnancy" could outweigh a woman's interest in protecting her own health.[70]

In an impassioned dissent, Justice Ginsburg attacked the majority for placing women's health in danger and for undermining women's struggle for equality. She wrote that women's "ability to realize their full potential . . . is intimately connected to 'their ability to control their reproductive lives.'"[71]

She further wrote that the Court's reasoning "reflects ancient notions about women's place in the family and under the Constitution—ideas that have long since been discredited."[72] She concluded that "the Act, and the Court's defense of it, cannot be understood as anything other than an effort to chip away at a right declared again and again by the Court—and with increasing comprehension of its centrality to women's lives."[73]

**What are the implications of the *Gonzales* decision?**

As a result of the *Gonzales* decision, the federal ban is in effect and can be enforced in all fifty states. While the Supreme Court decision suggests that the ban prohibits only one abortion method, it provides doctors with scant guidance about what might subject them to criminal and civil liability under the ban. The decision puts medical decisions in the hands of politicians, not doctors.

The decision will also spark more abortion restrictions. A fundraising letter from Americans United for Life, for example, characterizes the decision as having opened "the door to more aggressive regulation of abortion."[74] It goes on to say that, in light of the decision, "We're confident that most of the cases in the lower federal courts will now be resolved in favor of the state legislation, and we are planning new model bills for the next legislative sessions to take full advantage of this new opportunity. We expect to be very busy."[75] The response to the decision by Leslee Unruh, one of the proponents of the attempt to ban abortion in South Dakota in 2006, is also telling: "It's like someone gave me $1 million and told me 'Leslee, go shopping.' We're brainstorming and we're having fun."[76] There will no doubt be great challenges ahead to protect access to abortion.

**Why is federal constitutional protection for abortion important? What would be the status of the right to an abortion if *Roe v. Wade* were overturned?**

If *Roe v. Wade* were reversed and the federal Constitution no longer protected abortion, states could decide whether to ban or otherwise restrict abortion. The consequences for women would be great. In some states, abortion bans remain on the books even though they cannot now be enforced; were *Roe* reversed, prosecutors could attempt to revive and enforce those bans immediately.[77] In other states, old abortion bans have been enjoined by the courts, but state officials could ask the courts to lift those injunctions.[78] In still other states, opponents of reproductive rights would seek to enact new bans and would probably succeed in many states.[79] In fact, women in more than half the country would be vulnerable to abortion bans if *Roe* were overturned.[80]

## What rights does a teen have to an abortion?

The Supreme Court has held that laws restricting teenagers' access to abortion by requiring them to involve a parent in their abortion decision (either by notifying a parent or obtaining consent from a parent prior to the procedure) are constitutional as long as a confidential and expeditious alternative is available.[81] In most states, that alternative takes the form of a court proceeding, known as a judicial bypass. In that proceeding, a teen may obtain an abortion without involving her parents if she goes to court and proves to a judge that she is either "(1) . . . mature enough and well enough informed to make her abortion decision, in consultation with her physician, independently of her parents' wishes; or (2) that even if she is not able to make this decision independently, the desired abortion would be in her best interests."[82] The law must also ensure that the judicial bypass proceeding is resolved quickly and that the anonymity of the teen is protected.[83]

## What are the harms of state laws restricting teens' access to abortion?

As of this writing, more than thirty states currently enforce laws that require minors to involve a parent (or obtain a judicial bypass) before they can obtain an abortion.[84] These laws put teens' health and safety at risk, without increasing communication between teens and their parents. Even in the absence of any legal requirements, most teens who are pregnant and seeking an abortion involve a parent in the decision.[85] The younger the teen, the more likely her parents are to know about her decision: 90 percent of teens under fifteen report that at least one parent knew of their decision.[86] And those teens who cannot involve their parents have many valid reasons for not doing so. For instance, one-third of teens who do not tell their parents about a pregnancy have already been the victims of family violence and fear it will recur.[87] Long-term studies of abusive and dysfunctional families reveal that the incidence of violence escalates when a wife or teenage daughter becomes pregnant.[88] Anecdotal evidence bears out those studies: after a law requiring parental notification went into effect in Colorado, one teen called a clinic to reschedule her appointment because "when [her mother] received the notification, . . . she went ballistic, kicked her out of the house, stole the money she had saved for the procedure, told her if she went through the procedure, she would disown her."[89] In another case, a father murdered his daughter upon learning of her intended abortion.[90]

For those teens who do not involve their parents in their abortion decision, the alternative of going to court for a judicial bypass is often daunting or logistically impossible. Many teens are too scared to go before a judge to make this a real option. As the Supreme Court of California has recognized, "[M]inors frequently may be too embarrassed or frightened to seek judicial authorization and may endanger their health or forfeit their right of choice rather than venture into an unfamiliar and intimidating court setting."[91] The U.S. Supreme Court has also acknowledged that "[t]he court experience produce[s] fear, tension, anxiety, and shame among minors."[92] Some teens, particularly in small towns, fear that despite legal guarantees of anonymity, their confidentiality will be compromised. One court cited a case in which "a girl discovered that her bypass hearing would be conducted by her former Sunday school teacher."[93] Another court noted that "one teenager's parents received an anonymous letter informing them that their daughter had been seen in the courthouse seeking a judicial bypass."[94] In addition, for those teens who choose to proceed, going to court inevitably delays the abortion, which "means a first trimester abortion can become a more difficult and more costly second trimester abortion, or even, if it is far enough into the gestation period, that an abortion will no longer be available."[95] For these reasons, several major medical organizations, including the American Academy of Pediatrics and the American College of Obstetricians and Gynecologists, oppose laws requiring teens seeking abortions to involve a parent or go to court.[96]

In those states where such laws are in effect, the ACLU and other organizations often work to ensure that teens who need to go to court for permission for an abortion are connected quickly with a lawyer trained and willing to help them through the court process.

### Can laws that require teens to involve their parents in the decision whether to have an abortion be challenged in court?

These laws can sometimes be challenged, under either a state or the federal constitution. Advocates—including the ACLU—have prevailed in several cases by making legal claims through state constitutions, which often provide more rights than the federal Constitution. For example, in a case brought by the ACLU, the New Jersey Supreme Court struck down the state's law restricting teenagers' abortions.[97] Prior to this ruling, teens had the right to consent on their own to all health care necessary to continue a pregnancy to term, but could not consent on their own to an abortion. The court concluded that the state failed to produce sufficient justification "for distinguishing between minors seeking an abortion and minors seeking medical and surgical care relating to their pregnancies."[98] Thus, the law was unconstitutional because it did not treat all pregnant teens the same.[99]

Some teen abortion restrictions are also susceptible to challenge under the U.S. Constitution. Courts strike such laws under the federal Constitution most often because of flaws in the judicial bypass process. For example, in 1999, the U.S. Court of Appeals for the Ninth Circuit struck down an Arizona parental consent law because it did not have sufficient guarantees to ensure that the bypass would be expeditious.[100]

**Does the Constitution protect poor women's access to abortion?**

The federal Constitution protects the right to abortion for all women. That being said, in reality, the reproductive rights of the poorest women have been burdened for decades. Abortion has been severely restricted within the federal Medicaid program, which pays for comprehensive health care services for low-income people. If a woman eligible for Medicaid decides to carry a pregnancy to term, Medicaid pays for the costs associated with the pregnancy and childbirth. If the woman instead decides to end her pregnancy, Medicaid will not pay for her abortion even if continuing the pregnancy will harm her health.[101]

That discriminatory treatment is the result of a federal measure, first passed in 1976, commonly known as the "Hyde Amendment." The language of the amendment has varied over time. Initially, it prohibited federal Medicaid coverage for all but life-saving abortions. Currently, federal funds cannot be used for any Medicaid abortion unless the pregnancy is life-threatening or results from rape or incest.[102]

The Hyde Amendment was challenged in court as violating poor women's reproductive rights. In 1980, the Supreme Court upheld the amendment, stating that the U.S. Constitution permits the government to withhold Medicaid funds for virtually all abortions, while continuing to fund all other medically necessary services, including prenatal care and childbirth.[103] The Court reasoned that the discrimination was permissible because the Hyde Amendment placed no government obstacle in the path of a woman seeking an abortion: "The financial constraints that restrict an indigent woman's ability to enjoy the full range of constitutionally protected freedom of choice are the product not of governmental restrictions on access to abortions, but rather of her own indigency."[104] Moreover, the Court stated that the government can constitutionally encourage childbirth over abortion by funding one but not the other.

### Have there been efforts to restore the right to an abortion for poor women?

Most states have followed the federal government's lead and restricted state funding for abortion. The ACLU and other legal advocates have successfully challenged these restrictions in many states. Because of these legal challenges, in thirteen states,[105] courts have ordered nondiscriminatory public funding of abortion.[106] For example, in a case brought by the ACLU, Alaska's Supreme Court concluded that it was discriminatory for the state to prohibit funding for medically necessary abortions, while funding all other medically necessary pregnancy care:

Alone among Medicaid-eligible Alaskans, women whose health is endangered by pregnancy are denied health care based solely on political disapproval of the medically necessary procedure. This selective denial of medical benefits violates Alaska's constitutional guarantee of equal protection. Once the State undertakes to fund medically necessary services for poor Alaskans, it may not selectively exclude from that program women who medically require abortions.[107]

Four other states provide funding voluntarily—Hawaii, Maryland, New York, and Washington.[108] Thus, as of this writing, seventeen states currently use state dollars to fund abortions for poor women on the same or similar terms as other pregnancy-related and general health services.[109]

### What are the consequences of bans on public funding for abortion?

Bans on public funding for abortion rob low-income women of their reproductive rights by depriving them of the means to exercise those rights. The restrictions leave many women on Medicaid little choice but to use money they need for food, rent, clothing, or other necessities to pay for an abortion. One study showed that nearly 60 percent of women on Medicaid were forced to divert money that would otherwise be used to pay their daily and monthly expenses, such as rent, utility bills, food, and clothing for themselves and their children.[110] Court filings in a Georgia case showed that women sell their cars, leaving them without transportation for work and necessities; they sacrifice payment for utilities; and some arrive at the clinic with no money even for food and no place to sleep overnight except their car.[111] Many poor women must also delay their abortions, increasing their medical risks, while they scrape funds together.

In addition, studies estimate that where public funding is unavailable, between 18 and 35 percent of Medicaid-eligible women who would have had abortions instead continue their pregnancies.[112] For example, one woman in Georgia managed to gather the funds for an abortion and a bus ticket to Atlanta for the procedure, but she was forced to carry her pregnancy to term because she was unable to raise the additional funds necessary to travel to the bus station.[113]

These bans also jeopardize women's health as women with cancer, diabetes, or heart conditions, or other health conditions easily exacerbated by pregnancy are denied coverage for abortions. For example, in one case, a doctor described a patient who suffered from hyperemesis gravidarum, a syndrome accompanied by vomiting so severe that she was admitted to the hospital (care covered by Medicaid): "She had to stay in the hospital for four weeks, in pain and hooked up to feeding tubes, while she struggled to gather the money" for the abortion.[114] In the majority of states, Medicaid leaves these women without coverage for an abortion—but will help them if they continue the pregnancy.

### May the government attempt to discourage a woman from having an abortion?

Yes. As of this writing more than twenty states enforce laws that require doctors to give women information intended to discourage them from having an abortion ("biased counseling" laws), and then prohibit the abortion for a specified period of time—generally at least twenty-four hours—after the woman receives the information ("mandatory delay" laws).[115] Some states will only allow counseling to be given in person—rather than over the phone or the Internet—which requires women to make two trips to the provider: the first to receive the state-mandated information and the second, at least twenty-four hours later, to obtain the abortion.[116] A handful of states require state-mandated counseling but do not mandate a delay before the abortion procedure.[117]

The Supreme Court upheld such laws in *Planned Parenthood v. Casey*. In that case, the Court found that the 24-hour waiting period, despite increasing the costs and delays for women seeking abortions, did not pose a substantial obstacle to abortion.[118] The Court also held that compelled provision of information designed to discourage abortion is permissible, so long as the information is truthful and not misleading.[119] Since *Casey*, court challenges to similar laws have been largely unsuccessful in both state and federal court.[120]

### What are the consequences of laws that require delays before abortions?

Mandatory delay laws make obtaining an abortion more difficult and costly for many women. The harm of such restrictions is felt most by those who have the fewest resources—poor women, teens, rural women, working women without insurance or sick leave, and battered women. Making a second trip to an abortion provider is extremely difficult, if not impossible, for many women as 87 percent of U.S. counties have no abortion providers.[121] As a result, many women—particularly those in rural areas—must travel significant distances to reach a clinic.[122] The second trip results in added costs for women, who must take extra time off from work, find childcare, and arrange for the necessary travel. Together with the cost of the abortion itself, these costs can prevent women from obtaining abortions.[123] Indeed, data from Mississippi showed that requiring women to make two trips to the clinic prevents between 10 and 13 percent of women from getting the abortions they seek.[124]

Mandatory delay laws also force women to seek later abortions. For example, after a law requiring women to make two trips to the clinic took effect in Mississippi, the proportion of abortions performed after the first trimester increased by 40 percent.[125] While abortion is one of the safest medical procedures performed today, risks of complications increase as the weeks progress.[126] Delay also increases the costs associated with the abortion because second-trimester abortions are more expensive and most abortion clinics do not perform second-trimester abortions at all, forcing women to travel even greater distances.[127]

Nor do biased counseling requirements serve any health purpose. State laws—as well as standards of the medical profession—already require that health care practitioners provide women with information about their health care options while obtaining consent to medical procedures.

### May the government require a woman to obtain her husband's consent or give him notice before an abortion?

No. The U.S. Supreme Court has held that states may not require a woman to notify, or obtain the consent of, her husband before obtaining an abortion.[128] In *Casey*, the Supreme Court struck down a Pennsylvania law that required a woman to notify her husband before obtaining an abortion. As the Court recognized, the vast majority of women consult their husbands before obtaining an abortion.[129] But as the Court also noted, "there are millions of women in this country who are the victims of regular physical and psychological abuse at the hands of their husbands. Should these women become pregnant, they may have very good reasons for not wishing to inform their husbands of their decision to obtain an abortion."[130] Moreover, the Court emphasized that the Pennsylvania statute improperly "enables the husband to wield an effective veto over his wife's decision."[131] As the Court observed, "We must not blind ourselves to the fact that the significant number of women who fear for their safety and the safety of their children are likely to be deterred from procuring an abortion as surely as if the Commonwealth had outlawed abortion in all cases."[132] The Court therefore held that the spousal notification requirement was likely to prevent a significant number of women from obtaining an abortion, and invalidated the provision as constituting an "undue burden" on the right to choose abortion. In addition, the Court emphasized, such a requirement would give a husband "a troubling degree of authority over his wife"—a degree that would reflect antiquated notions of marriage and women's status. As the Court succinctly stated, "A State may not give to a man the kind of dominion over his wife that parents exercise over their children."[133]

### What about women in the military? Can they access abortions, particularly if they are overseas?

Current federal law prohibits military personnel and their dependents from obtaining abortion services at U.S. military hospitals, even if they pay for those services with their own funds. (The only exception is if the woman's life is threatened by the pregnancy.)

For military women and dependents stationed overseas, this ban poses grave health risks. Local, overseas medical facilities are often inadequate, unsafe, or entirely unavailable. Traveling to a safe facility can result in delays that may substantially increase the risks of the abortion procedure. Travel to another country, moreover, may be difficult if not impossible for a woman who is stationed in a country with active hostilities, as during the Iraq war. Not only may the trip be too dangerous to take, but the woman must seek and obtain leave from her superior officers, which may require her to disclose her pregnancy and decision to seek an abortion to those officers. Sadly, moreover, there is a growing need for abortion care among women in the military, given the incidence of sexual assault.[134]

**Does the federal government restrict access to abortion for other women as well?**

Yes. In addition to the bans on abortion funding for poor women and for those in the military, Congress has also denied abortion coverage to most federal employees and their dependents, federal prisoners, Peace Corps volunteers, and Native American women.[135]

**What actions has the government taken against violence directed at abortion clinics?**

Throughout the 1980s and 1990s, clinics and their employees faced increased physical violence, including threats, blockades, arsons, shootings, and even murders. In response, in 1994, Congress passed the Freedom of Access to Clinic Entrances Act (FACE). The statute prohibits the use of force, threats of force, physical obstruction, and property damage intended to interfere with people obtaining or providing reproductive health services. FACE does not apply to peaceful praying, picketing, or other free speech by antichoice demonstrators—provided these activities do not obstruct physical access to clinics or involve threats.[136]

While FACE has been a valuable tool, it has not stopped antichoice violence. In 1998, a bomb detonated at an Alabama clinic, killing a security guard and gravely injuring a nurse. That same year, a New York doctor who provided abortions was shot to death while standing in his kitchen.[137]

**How available are abortion services?**

Currently, 87 percent of U.S. counties have no known abortion provider. Moreover, the number of abortion providers has steadily decreased since 1992.[138] This trend has accelerated because many hospitals no longer permit abortions. Mergers between religiously affiliated hospitals and nonsectarian hospitals have exacerbated this problem. In 1999, 18 percent of hospital beds were in religiously affiliated institutions.[139] Moreover, significant consolidation within the Catholic health care system has given it dominance in certain geographic areas. By 1998, ninety-one Catholic hospitals in twenty-seven states were the only hospitals in their counties.[140]

The consequences for reproductive health care are significant, as Catholic hospitals are prohibited by church doctrine from providing not only abortion but also a variety of reproductive health care services, including sterilization, contraceptive services (including emergency contraception), AIDS prevention services, and many types of infertility treatments.[141]

## CONTRACEPTION

### Is there a legal right to obtain and use contraceptives?

Yes. The Supreme Court has recognized that the ability to obtain and use contraception is central to reproductive freedom. In the *Griswold* case in 1965, the Supreme Court declared that the constitutional right of privacy includes the right to use and make decisions relating to contraception.[142] In the *Eisenstadt* case in 1972, the Supreme Court made clear that this right extended to unmarried persons.[143] The Supreme Court further expanded these rulings in *Carey v. Population Services* in 1977, when it struck down a restriction on the distribution of contraceptives to minors. Under these rulings, the government may not restrict the use, sale, or distribution of contraceptives without a "compelling" reason for doing so.[144]

### How is contraception important to women's reproductive health and freedom?

Contraception is a basic health need for virtually all women at some point in their lives. Contraception helps women and families time and space births and avoid unintended pregnancies. While 85 percent of sexually active women not using birth control become pregnant in any given year, only 8 percent of women taking birth control pills (the most common method of contraception) become pregnant.[145]

### Do teens have a right to obtain and use contraceptives without their parents' consent?

Yes, although this right is often under attack.[146] In *Carey*, discussed above, the Supreme Court ruled that the federal Constitution protects teens' rights to obtain nonprescription contraceptives. The Court concluded that the "right to privacy in connection with decisions affecting procreation extends to minors as well as adults," and struck down a New York law that prohibited the sale of nonprescription contraceptives (such as condoms, foams, and spermicidal jellies) to anyone under the age of sixteen.[147] Following the principles articulated in *Carey*, courts that have considered the issue have rejected as unconstitutional requirements that a teen involve a parent before getting contraception.[148]

Teens' access to contraception, however, is often at risk. Proposals to require parental consent for contraceptive services for minors are repeatedly debated in the state legislatures. In addition, while two of the most important sources of family planning funds in the nation—Title X of the Public Health Service Act[149] and the federal Medicaid program[150]—currently require confidentiality for teens seeking contraceptive services in those programs, there are frequent attempts in the U.S. Congress either to require or to permit parental involvement.

If such proposals were to pass, they would have significant consequences for teens' reproductive health, as guarantees of confidentiality are critical to teens' seeking vital health services. Indeed, one study found that 47 percent of sexually active teenage girls said that they would stop using *all* reproductive health care services if they could not obtain contraceptives without telling their parents, and another 12 percent said they would stop using some reproductive health care services or would delay testing or treatment for HIV or other STDs. Of those teens who would stop or delay accessing reproductive health care, 99 percent said that they would continue to have sex.[151] For this reason, leading medical organizations, including the American Medical Association, the American Academy of Pediatrics, and the Society for Adolescent Medicine, among others, oppose laws that would require teens to involve a parent before they access contraception.[152]

### Does the government provide contraceptive services as part of its health programs?

Yes, at least in some programs. Primarily through two major programs —Medicaid and Title X—family planning services are available for low-income women.

Family planning services are not available for all who need them, however. Title X of the Public Service Health Act is a critical source of funds for family planning services, but it is unable to serve everyone in need. Funding for Title X has not kept pace with inflation—between 1980 and 2004, funding decreased by nearly 60 percent in real dollars.[153] (Funding has decreased even though studies have shown that every dollar spent on publicly funded family planning services can save state and federal governments more than five dollars in medical care, income support, and social services from unintended pregnancies over five years.)[154]

Medicaid also provides family planning services, but many who need assistance in obtaining family planning services do not qualify for Medicaid. Moreover, even those who qualify for Medicaid may not be able to obtain coverage. Under the Deficit Reduction Act of 2005, U.S. citizens seeking treatment under Medicaid must show proof of citizenship, such as a birth certificate or a passport, to receive benefits. Studies show that this requirement could jeopardize the Medicaid coverage—or delay needed medical care—for millions of low-income American citizens (in particular, African-Americans, senior citizens, and rural residents) who lack the necessary documentation.[155]

Many immigrant women face special burdens in obtaining contraception and other family planning services, among other health and social services. Most legal immigrants who arrived in the country after August 1996 are denied federal Medicaid for the first five years of residency, except in emergency situations.[156] These women not only have no access to Medicaid family planning services, but they are denied coverage for prenatal care, postpartum care, and treatment for breast and cervical cancer (except in emergency circumstances).[157]

### What is "contraceptive equity," and how does it affect a woman's access to contraception?

Many women rely on employer-based private health insurance to cover their health care expenses. However, these plans historically have not covered prescription contraceptives to the same extent as other prescription drugs.[158] Lack of insurance coverage forces many women to choose less expensive and less reliable methods of contraception, increasing the likelihood of unintended pregnancy.

"Contraceptive equity" measures require employer-based insurance policies that already cover prescription drugs and devices to also cover prescription contraceptive drugs and related medical services. As of this writing, the measures have been passed in more than twenty states and are being debated in many other states and in Congress.[159] In addition to addressing a basic issue of fairness, contraceptive equity provisions serve significant public health goals. By eliminating the financial barriers to effective contraception, contraceptive equity will reduce the number of unintended pregnancies.

In addition, the Equal Employment Opportunity Commission (EEOC) (the federal agency charged with enforcing federal civil rights laws) has issued an opinion stating that this inequity—where health insurance covers prescription drugs but not prescription contraception—constitutes sex discrimination in employment under Title VII of the Civil Rights Act of 1964.[160] The first courts to consider this issue agreed and held that employers may not discriminate by offering prescription drug coverage while excluding coverage for contraception.[161] Unfortunately, a later decision by a Court of Appeals held the opposite, further highlighting the importance of state contraceptive equity measures.[162]

Partly as a result of this activity, coverage of prescription contraceptives has increased substantially in recent years.[163] Nevertheless, more work remains to ensure that women can afford prescription contraceptives: more than half of all women of reproductive age live in states without contraceptive equity measures. Moreover, the state measures cannot protect the significant number of women who receive their insurance through employer self-insured plans, which are governed by federal law. For these women, action by Congress is necessary. Unfortunately, Congress has so far failed to enact a contraceptive equity measure.[164]

### What about employers and insurers with religious objections to contraception? Do they have to comply with contraceptive equity laws?

Based on analysis of the Constitution, and religious and reproductive rights, the ACLU believes that religiously affiliated institutions that employ and serve people of many faiths and provide secular services, such as hospitals, charities, and social service organizations, should be bound by "contraceptive equity" mandates, on the ground that employers who engage in secular functions should not be permitted to impose their religious beliefs on their employees, who may not share those beliefs.[165] The ACLU believes that only employers whose primary purpose is to promote religion and who serve and hire primarily people of the faith—such as churches, temples, and mosques—should be exempted. The ACLU and others have therefore advocated for contraceptive equity laws that include exemptions only for such entities. To date, laws that include such exemptions have been upheld against challenge by religiously affiliated organizations.[166]

### What is emergency contraception ("EC" or the "Morning after Pill")?

Emergency contraception ("EC," also known as the "morning after pill") is a high dose of hormonal contraceptives—the same hormones found in ordinary birth control pills. It reduces the risk of pregnancy if taken within

72 to 120 hours of unprotected sexual intercourse or contraceptive failure. The sooner that treatment begins, the more effective it is.

### How can women obtain EC, and what is being done to make it more widely available?

In August 2006, in a significant development for women, the FDA approved the sale of EC without a prescription for women aged eighteen and over (who present a government-issued proof of age).[167] Young women under eighteen, women who lack acceptable identification, and women who need a prescription to obtain financial assistance under Medicaid must still obtain a prescription for EC. These women may, therefore, face challenges getting the drug quickly, particularly if they seek it over the weekend, when doctor's offices are closed. Given the narrow window of time in which EC is effective, these delays can deprive women of needed medical care.

Efforts are underway to make EC more available to these women. As of this writing, for example, in nine states policies allow pharmacists to dispense EC to all women (including minors) without a physician's advance prescription.[168]

### Is EC readily available for survivors of sexual assault?

The American College of Obstetricians and Gynecologists, the American Public Health Association, and other major medical groups consider counseling about EC and providing it upon request the standard of care for rape survivors.[169] Nevertheless, EC is not always readily available to women who have been sexually assaulted, and the government has often failed to ensure needed access. The U.S. Department of Justice's first national guidelines for treating sexual assault survivors failed to mention EC, even though the guidelines addressed pregnancy risk evaluation and care.[170]

Moreover, many hospital emergency rooms fail to provide sexual assault survivors with EC, and some even fail to inform those women that this treatment is available. Surveys of emergency care facilities show that, in eight of the eleven states studied, fewer than 40 percent of facilities dispense EC on-site to sexual assault survivors.[171] A survey of Catholic hospitals in 2002 found that only 23 percent provided EC to victims of sexual assault.[172]

Reproductive health and sexual assault advocates are working together to ensure greater availability of EC for survivors. For example, in Pennsylvania, the Clara Bell Duvall Reproductive Freedom Project of the ACLU of Pennsylvania, along with the Pennsylvania Coalition Against Rape, surveyed hospitals and sent letters to every hospital in Pennsylvania, thanking those with good policies and urging others to change their policies to better meet the needs of sexual assault patients. The Pennsylvania advocates also held training sessions for health care professionals, law enforcement, advocates, and legal professionals to help ensure that sexual assault patients received appropriate care. After these efforts, the number of Pennsylvania hospitals providing EC to assault survivors increased by 64 percent.[173]

Advocates are also working for the passage of legislation that requires emergency care facilities to dispense EC upon request to women who have been sexually assaulted. As of this writing, eight states have enacted such laws;[174] Congress and other states are considering similar measures.[175] However, as with contraceptive equity measures,[176] "EC in the ER" legislation is threatened by efforts to include "refusal clauses" that allow emergency care facilities to claim a religious or moral objection to EC and opt out of the mandate. Emergency care facilities, however, treat and employ people of many faiths. They accordingly should not be allowed to impose one set of religious beliefs on the people of diverse backgrounds who provide and seek their care.[177] If an emergency care facility is unwilling to dispense EC, it is not equipped to treat rape victims.

Unfortunately, even in states with "EC in the ER" laws, additional work is needed to ensure compliance. A 2006 survey of Catholic hospitals in four states with laws on the books revealed that, despite the law and in some cases hospital policy, those answering the phones at 35 percent of hospitals reported that EC was not available at the hospital.[178]

### What barriers do women face in their pharmacies when purchasing contraception, including EC?

Unfortunately, women can face hurdles finding a pharmacist or pharmacy willing to sell EC or other methods of contraception. No one knows for sure how many such refusals have occurred, but there is ample anecdotal evidence of pharmacist and pharmacy refusal to fill prescriptions for birth control, including EC, with incidents documented in more than eighteen states.[179] There are also cases of pharmacists even refusing to transfer prescriptions to another pharmacy, or to return the prescription to the woman to be filled elsewhere.[180] Even though EC is now available without a prescription for women eighteen and over, refusals continue to be a problem, because under FDA conditions, EC is kept behind the counter, and thus women must still request it.[181]

The ACLU believes that a pharmacy has the obligation to satisfy any lawful and appropriate request to purchase contraception—either with a prescription order or from behind the counter—without added delay. If an individual pharmacist has a religious objection to selling contraceptives, the pharmacy should honor the objection, provided the pharmacy ensures that patients receive their contraceptives in a timely manner at the same pharmacy.[182]

Advocates, including the ACLU, are working to secure laws and company policies ensuring that women can obtain contraception at their local pharmacies. For example, in 2005, the governor of Illinois issued an emergency rule that received federal approval, requiring pharmacies to fill all valid prescriptions for contraceptives without delay.[183] Similarly, in 2007, the Washington State Board of Pharmacy adopted new rules requiring pharmacies to fill all lawful prescriptions.[184]

## Childbearing and Sterilization

### Is there a right to bear children?

Yes. The Supreme Court has held that procreation is a fundamental right. In *Skinner v. Oklahoma*, in 1942, the Court reasoned that the "right to have offspring" is a "right which is basic to the perpetuation of the race."[185]

### Has that right been limited?

Yes. During the early 1900s, laws authorizing compulsory eugenic sterilization were authorized in thirty states, in the guise of social reform. These laws generally authorized certain institutions or legal authorities to sterilize people (including the mentally disabled, the mentally ill, the deaf, blind, and epileptic, the homeless, orphans, and homosexuals) against their will in order to prevent future procreation.[186] In 1927, in *Buck v. Bell*, the U.S. Supreme Court upheld Virginia's compulsory sterilization law. In that decision, Justice Oliver Wendell Holmes made the infamous statement, "It is better for all the world, if instead of waiting to execute degenerate offspring for crime, or to let them starve for their imbecility, society can prevent those who are manifestly unfit from continuing their kind. . . . Three generations of imbeciles are enough."[187]

The eugenics movement subsequently fell out of favor. Although *Buck v. Bell* was never explicitly overruled, in 1942, the U.S. Supreme Court examined and struck down as unconstitutional an Oklahoma law that permitted the sterilization of thrice-convicted felons. The Court noted that "[t]his case touches a sensitive and important area of human rights. Oklahoma deprives certain individuals of a right which is basic to the perpetuation of the race—the right to have offspring."[188]

Nevertheless, despite the Supreme Court ruling, involuntary sterilizations continued. For example, as recently as the 1960s, women who received Medicaid were sometimes sterilized without their knowledge and consent.[189]

### What other restrictions have been imposed on the right to bear children?

Welfare reform has posed new threats to the right to bear children. Reform measures often include punitive "child exclusion" policies. Under these policies, the government attempts to deter childbearing by depriving welfare recipients of increases in benefits if they bear an additional child while receiving public assistance. The ACLU has opposed "child exclusions" at both the federal and state levels, and helped to stop Congress from mandating that the states implement such policies as part of the restructuring of the welfare system in 1996. Unfortunately, as of this writing, more than twenty states have voluntarily implemented such programs.[190] Instead of providing necessary services and benefits to poor families, child exclusion policies deny benefit increases that are needed to raise additional children. Moreover, one study in New Jersey found that the child exclusion did reduce birth rates of women on welfare, but only because so many more of them chose to have abortions.[191] (For a more detailed discussion of current welfare law, see chapter 9, "TANF/Welfare.")

### Can the state monitor and punish pregnant women for their conduct during pregnancy?

No. Pregnant women have the same constitutional right of reproductive freedom as other free adults. Women do not forfeit those rights just because they are pregnant. Unfortunately, in recent years, some government officials have sought to control the conduct of pregnant women. For example, pregnant women have been forced, sometimes against their religious beliefs, to undergo cesarean sections; ordered to have their cervixes sewn up to prevent miscarriage; or incarcerated for consuming drugs or alcohol. In many of these cases, the invasive state actions were rescinded by higher officials or reversed by the courts, but those decisions often came too late as the women had already suffered and been deprived of their rights.[192]

For example, in one case, government officials in South Carolina surreptitiously drug tested pregnant women who met certain criteria (e.g., minimal or no prenatal care, unexplained preterm labor, birth defects, or poor fetal growth) and then reported positive cocaine tests to the police. In the early months of the program, women were arrested immediately after they or their newborns tested positive for cocaine. An "amnesty" program was later added that allowed women to opt for drug treatment to avoid arrest, but if they failed to follow through with treatment or if they tested positive a second time, they were arrested. Government officials dropped the program after the U.S. Department of Health and Human Services began to investigate for civil rights violations, but not before thirty women (twenty-nine of whom were African-American) were arrested.[193] A challenge to the program landed in the U.S. Supreme Court, which held that the program violated the Fourth Amendment protection against unreasonable search and seizure if the women did not consent to the searches.[194] A subsequent federal court ruling confirmed that no such consent was obtained, and the program was deemed unconstitutional.[195]

These government actions are harmful as well as unconstitutional, as they drive women away from health care, to the detriment of their health and that of their babies.[196] For example, the South Carolina policy discussed above appears to have driven drug-using women out of the health care system in that region, isolating them in their drug use rather than helping them have healthy pregnancies and babies.[197] For this reason, numerous medical and public health organizations, including the American Medical Association, the American Academy of Pediatrics, the American Public Health Association, the American College of Obstetricians and Gynecologists, and many other prominent groups, have denounced the practice of punishing women for their conduct during their pregnancies and instead advocate services to promote women's health.[198]

### Do women have a right to be sterilized?

Yes. The right to be sterilized is part of the constitutional right of privacy in matters related to childbearing, and voluntary sterilization is legal in all fifty states. It has, however, become more difficult for women to obtain this service. As explained previously in this chapter, the growing number of hospital mergers between sectarian and nonsectarian hospitals has curtailed reproductive services, including sterilization.[199] For example, women who seek to have their tubes tied immediately after childbirth—when the sterilization procedure is safest and easiest—are sometimes denied the service.[200]

These women must then face a separate surgery at another hospital after they recover from childbirth, if another hospital is available at all.

## COMPREHENSIVE SEXUALITY EDUCATION

### What is comprehensive sex education?

Comprehensive sexuality education teaches young people how to make healthy and responsible decisions about sexuality. Comprehensive sexuality education stresses the importance of having sex only when you are emotionally ready and physically prepared, and it provides accurate and complete information about how to use contraceptives effectively to prevent unintended pregnancy and STDs.

Such information is necessary to protect teen health. Studies show that by the age of nineteen, more than two-thirds of all U.S. teens have had sexual intercourse, and that approximately 750,000 teens between the ages of fifteen and nineteen become pregnant each year.[201] Furthermore, over nine million people between the ages of fifteen and twenty-four are infected with sexually transmitted diseases each year, and approximately one-half of all new HIV infections occur among people under age twenty-five.[202]

Programs that include information about both postponing sexual activity and effective use of contraception have been shown to "delay the onset of sex, reduce the frequency of sex, reduce the number of sexual partners among teens, or increase the use of condoms and other forms of contraception" among sexually active teens.[203] In addition, contrary to claims by proponents of abstinence-only-until-marriage programs (discussed below), comprehensive sexuality education does not increase sexual activity.[204]

The majority of American parents believe that their children should receive comprehensive sex education. A 2004 study found that an overwhelming majority of parents want sex education curricula to cover topics such as birth control options and their proper use, abortion, and sexual orientation.[205] Teachers agree. A 1999 study of seventh- through twelfth-grade teachers in the specialties most often responsible for sex education found that, again, an overwhelming majority believed that, by twelfth grade, sex education courses should cover birth control methods (93.4 percent), factual information about abortion (89 percent), where to go for birth control (88.8 percent), the correct way to use a condom (82 percent), and sexual orientation (77.8 percent), among other topics.[206] Major medical organizations, including the American Medical Association, the American Academy of Pediatrics, the American College of Obstetricians and Gynecologists, and the Society for Adolescent Medicine, similarly support comprehensive sex education.[207]

### What are abstinence-only-until-marriage programs, and what threat do they pose to teens?

Abstinence-only-until-marriage programs focus on abstaining from sex until marriage and censor other information that can help young people make responsible, healthy, and safe decisions in the event they are sexually active. Such programs are devastating for gay and lesbian youth, who are often denied the right ever to marry; they are also stigmatizing for teens whose parents are gay or lesbian or who are not married.

There is no credible evidence that abstinence-only-until-marriage programs reduce sexual activity or risk-taking behaviors among teens.[208] In fact, a recent study commissioned by Congress concluded that teens in abstinence-only programs "were no more likely . . . to have abstained from sex and, among those who had reported having sex, they had similar numbers of sexual partners and had initiated sex at the same mean age" as other teens.[209] Similarly, another study found that while virginity-pledge programs —which encourage students to make a pledge to abstain from sex until marriage—have demonstrated limited success in delaying first intercourse, virginity pledgers are less likely than nonpledgers to use contraception at first intercourse.[210]

Despite this research, these programs have federal support. Since 1996, the U.S. Congress has allocated more than a billion dollars to abstinence-only-until-marriage programs. By contrast, there are no federal programs devoted to supporting comprehensive sexuality education. The federal dollars for abstinence programs come with harmful conditions. As a condition of federal funding, grantees must offer curricula that have as their "exclusive purpose" teaching the benefits of abstinence and that teach that sexual activity outside of marriage is "likely to have harmful psychological and physical effects."[211] Programs must also censor critical information that teens who are or become sexually active need to protect themselves from STDs and pregnancy.[212] Recipients of the funding may not advocate contraceptive use or teach contraceptive methods except to emphasize their failure rates.[213]

To the extent that the programs include information about contraception, it is often inaccurate and/or incomplete.[214] For example, a 2004 study released by California Congressman Henry Waxman found that the curricula used by many government-funded abstinence-only-until-marriage programs contain misleading or inaccurate information about abortion, contraception, and sexually transmitted infections.[215]

Unfortunately, abstinence-only-until-marriage programs are increasingly prevalent in high schools. In 1999, 23 percent of secondary sexuality education teachers taught abstinence as the only way of avoiding STDs and pregnancy, up from 2 percent in 1988.[216] As of 2002, 35 percent of public school districts required abstinence to be taught as the only option for unmarried people and either prohibited the discussion of contraception or limited discussion to its ineffectiveness.[217]

### What is being done to protect teens' health and provide them with accurate information?

The ACLU and other advocates for comprehensive sexuality education are working to reverse the gains made by abstinence-only-until-marriage programs and to ensure that teens receive the information they need to stay healthy. In addition to working on the state and local fronts to prevent the use of these programs in schools, advocates are working at the federal level to reduce funding for abstinence-only programs and to ensure that inaccuracies about contraception are corrected. For example, the ACLU has sent letters to the U.S. Department of Health and Human Services (HHS) alerting it to medical inaccuracies in several curricula receiving federal funding and asking it to remedy the problem.[218] The ACLU has also successfully challenged the misuse of taxpayer dollars in abstinence-only-until-marriage programs that unlawfully promote religion. For example, the ACLU filed a lawsuit in 2005 challenging the Silver Ring Thing, a program that describes its mission as to "saturate the United States with a generation of young people who have taken a vow of sexual abstinence until marriage. . . . This mission can only be achieved by offering a personal relationship with Jesus Christ as the best way to live a sexually pure life."[219] As a result of the lawsuit, HHS suspended the Silver Ring Thing's funding and ultimately, the parties reached a settlement in which HHS agreed that any future funding would be contingent on the program's compliance with federal law.[220] Advocates also seek to convince Congress to end funding for abstinence-only-until-marriage programs and to enact the Responsible Education About Life Act, which would be the first federal program devoted to funding comprehensive sex education.

**What can you do to help protect reproductive freedom and build the world we want?**

The decision when and whether to become a parent is one of the most private a person can make and one that has a profound effect on all aspects of our lives. To participate fully in society, women and men must have the resources, health care, and education they need to build and maintain healthy lives and healthy families. To achieve this world, we must continue to strive for reproductive freedom for everyone. Help us build this world.

- *In the world we want*, all women—rich or poor—have meaningful access to birth control and are able to obtain reproductive health care, including prenatal care and abortion, when needed. Reproductive health care is basic health care.
- *In the world we want*, sexuality education gives teens the information they need to make healthy and responsible life decisions.
- *In the world we want*, teenagers can get confidential reproductive health care, including birth control, emergency contraception, and abortion care, when they need it.

## NOTES

1. Planned Parenthood v. Casey, 505 U.S. 833, 856 (1992).

2. Planned Parenthood Federation of America, Inc., Fact Sheet, A History of Birth Control Methods 9 (Nov. 1, 2006), *available at* http://www.plannedparenthood.org/files/PPFA/fact-bc-history.pdf.

3. Griswold v. Connecticut, 381 U.S. 479 (1965); *see infra* text accompanying notes 23–26.

4. Eisenstadt v. Baird, 405 U.S. 438 (1972).

5. Planned Parenthood Federation of America, Inc., Fact Sheet, *Griswold v. Connecticut:* The Impact of Legal Birth Control and the Challenges that Remain 2 (Jun. 1, 2005), *available at* http://www.plannedparenthood.org/files/PPFA/fact-griswold.pdf.

6. Rachel Benson Gold, *Rekindling Efforts to Prevent Unplanned Pregnancy: A Matter of "Equity and Common Sense,"* 9 GUTTMACHER POL'Y REV. 2, 2 (2006), *available at* http://www.guttmacher.org/pubs/gpr/09/3/gpr090302.pdf.

7. University of California San Francisco, Center for Reproductive Health Research & Policy, Fact Sheet on Benefits of Family Planning (2005), *available at* http://crhrp.ucsf.edu/publications/files/BenefitsofFPPlanning.pdf.

8. *Women and Societies Benefit When Childbearing Is Planned,* Issues in Brief (Guttmacher Inst., New York, NY), Aug. 2002, *available at* http://www.guttmacher. org/pubs/ib_3-02.html; Adam Sonfield, *Preventing Unintended Pregnancy: The Need and the Means,* 6 Guttmacher Rep. on Pub. Pol'y 7 (2003), *available at* http://www.guttmacher.org/pubs/tgr/06/5/gr060507.pdf.

9. Rachel Benson Gold, *Lessons from before Roe: Will Past Be Prologue?,* 6 Guttmacher Rep. on Pub. Pol'y 8, 8 (2003), *available at* http://www.guttmacher.org/pubs/tgr/06/1/gr060108.pdf.

10. *Id.*

11. American Civil Liberties Union, Position Paper, The Right to Choose: A Fundamental Liberty 1 (Fall 2000), *available at* http://www.aclu.org/FilesPDFs/ACFF1D.pdf.

12. Planned Parenthood Federation of America, Inc., Fact Sheet, Medical and Social Health Benefits since Abortion Was Made Legal in the U.S. 1 (Dec. 29, 2006), *available at* http://www.plannedparenthood.org/files/PPFA/fact-health-benefits.pdf.

13. *Facts on Induced Abortion in the United States,* In Brief (Guttmacher Inst., New York, NY), May 2006, *available at* http://www.guttmacher.org/pubs/fb_induced_abortion.pdf.

14. Stanley K. Henshaw, *Unintended Pregnancy and Abortion: A Public Health Perspective, in* A Clinician's Guide to Medical and Surgical Abortion 11, 19 (Maureen Paul et al. eds., 1999).

15. *Facts on Induced Abortion in the United States, supra* note 13, at 2.

16. In re Romero, 790 P.2d 819, 821 (Colo. 1990); Janet Simmonds, Note, *Coercion in California: Eugenics Reconstituted in Welfare Reform, the Contracting of Reproductive Capacity, and Terms of Probation,* 17 Hastings Women's L.J. 269, 271–76 (2006); Michael G. Silver, Note, *Eugenics and Compulsory Sterilization Laws: Providing Redress for the Victims of a Shameful Era in United States History,* 72 Geo. Wash. L. Rev. 862, 862–69 (2004).

17. Skinner v. Oklahoma, 316 U.S. 535, 541 (1942).

18. Relf v. Weinberger, 372 F. Supp. 1196, 1199 (D.D.C. 1974), *vacated,* 565 F.2d 722 (D.C. Cir. 1977).

19. Doe v. Maher, 515 A.2d 134, 159 (Conn. Super. Ct. 1986).

20. Sylvia A. Law, *Sex Discrimination and Insurance for Contraception,* 73 Wash. L. Rev. 363, 367 (1998).

21. Planned Parenthood v. Casey, 505 U.S. 833, 856 (1992).

22. 381 U.S. 479, 480, 486 (1965).

23. *Id.* at 485–86.

24. 405 U.S. 438, 453 (1972).

25. *Id.*

26. 410 U.S. 113, 154 (1973).

27. Gonzales v. Carhart, 127 S. Ct. 1610, 1615 (2007).

28. Stenberg v. Carhart, 530 U.S. 914, 921 (2000).

29. *Gonzales*, 127 S. Ct. at 1636–37.

30. Press Release, American Civil Liberties Union, ACLU Celebrates Victory for Women's Health as South Dakotans Defeat Extreme Abortion Ban (Nov. 8, 2006), *available at* http://www.aclu.org/reproductiverights/abortionbans/27314prs20061108. html.

31. *See infra* text accompanying notes 149–57, 179–81, 208–17.

32. *See infra* text accompanying notes 190–91.

33. Gold, *supra* note 9, at 8, 9.

34. Roe v. Wade, 410 U.S. 113, 117–18 (1973).

35. *Id.* at 153.

36. *Id.* at 152, 155.

37. *Id.* at 163–64. Forty states and the District of Columbia prohibit abortions after viability. Less than one-half of 1 percent of all abortions are performed after twenty-four weeks of pregnancy. Planned Parenthood Federation of America, Inc., Frequently Asked Questions: The Federal Abortion Ban (Mar. 13, 2007), *available at* http://www.plannedparenthood.org/news-articles-press/politics-policy-issues/courts-judiciary/fab-faq-13438.htm.

38. *See* Gold, *supra* note 9, at 11.

39. Planned Parenthood of Cent. Mo. v. Danforth, 428 U.S. 52, 65–66 (1976).

40. City of Akron v. Akron Ctr. for Reprod. Health, 462 U.S. 416, 431–33 (1983).

41. Thornburgh v. Am. Coll. of Obstetricians & Gynecologists, 476 U.S. 747, 760 (1986); *Akron*, 462 U.S. at 449–50.

42. *See infra* text accompanying notes 101–4.

43. *See infra* text accompanying notes 81–83.

44. 505 U.S. 833 (1992).

45. *Id.* at 846.

46. *Id.* at 874.

47. *Id.* at 878.

48. City of Akron v. Akron Ctr. for Reprod. Health, 462 U.S. 416 (1983); Thornburgh v. Am. Coll. of Obstetricians & Gynecologists, 476 U.S. 747 (1986).

49. *Casey*, 505 U.S. at 882.

50. *Id.* at 886–87.

51. *Id.* at 877.

52. *Id.* at 885–86.

53. *See supra* text accompanying note 41.

54. *Casey*, 505 U.S. at 892–97; *see infra* text accompanying notes 128–33.

55. Planned Parenthood v. Casey, 947 F.2d 682, 719 (3d Cir. 1991) (Alito, J., dissenting), *aff'd in part, rev'd in part*, 505 U.S. 833 (1992).

56. *Casey*, 505 U.S. at 852.

57. *Id.*

58. Stenberg v. Carhart, 530 U.S. 914, 921 (2000).

59. *Id.* at 930.

60. *Id.* at 930–38.

61. *Id.* at 937.

62. *Id.* at 932, 935–37; *see also* American College of Obstetricians & Gynecologists, Statement of Policy, Abortion Policy (Sept. 2000); American College of Obstetricians & Gynecologists on the Subject of "Partial-Birth Abortion" Bans (July 2002). Other medical organizations agree. American Medical Women's Association, Statement on H.R. 1122 (May 1997); Letter from Georges C. Benjamin, Executive Dir., Am. Pub. Health Ass'n, to Members of the U.S. House of Representatives (Mar. 2003), *available at* http://www.apha.org/advocacy/activities/actionissues/legiationactionopposingpartial.htm.

63. *Stenberg*, 530 U.S. at 924, 938–39.

64. *Id.* at 946.

65. Gonzales v. Carhart, 127 S. Ct. 1610, 1627, 1629 (2007); Partial-Birth Abortion Ban Act of 2003, 18 U.S.C. § 1531 (2006).

66. *Stenberg*, 530 U.S. at 946; *see supra* text accompanying notes 58–64.

67. *Gonzales*, 127 S. Ct. at 1633.

68. *Id.* at 1639.

69. *Id.* at 1635–37.

70. *Id.* at 1636.

71. *Id.* at 1641 (Ginsburg, J., dissenting) (quoting Planned Parenthood v. Casey, 505 U.S. 833, 856 (1992)).

72. *Id.* at 1649 (Ginsburg, J., dissenting).

73. *Id.* at 1653 (Ginsburg, J., dissenting).

74. Letter from Clark D. Forsythe, President, Americans United for Life, A New Dawn: Gonzales v. Carhart Begins a New Day in Abortion Law (May 1, 2007), *available at* http://www.unitedforlife.org/articles/a_new_dawn_2007-05.htm.

75. *Id.*

76. Stephanie Simon, *Joyous Abortion Foes to Push for New Limits*, L.A. TIMES, Apr. 19, 2007, at A25.

77. CENTER FOR REPRODUCTIVE RIGHTS, WHAT IF ROE FELL? THE STATE-BY-STATE CONSEQUENCES OF OVERTURNING ROE V. WADE 1, 8 (2004), *available at* http://www.reproductiverights.org/pdf/bo_whatifroefell.pdf.

78. *Id.* at 1, 10.

79. *Id.* at 10–11.

80. *Id.* at 7–8.

81. Belloti v. Baird, 443 U.S. 622, 643–44 (1979); *see also* City of Akron v. Akron Ctr. for Reprod. Health, 462 U.S. 416, 439–40 (1983); Planned Parenthood v. Ashcroft, 462 U.S. 476, 491 (1983); Ohio v. Akron Ctr. for Reprod. Health,

497 U.S. 502, 511–12 (1990); Hodgson v. Minnesota, 497 U.S. 417, 461, 497–501 (1990); Planned Parenthood v. Casey, 505 U.S. 833, 899 (1992).

82. *Id.*

83. *Id.*

84. *Parental Involvement in Minors' Abortions*, STATE POLICIES IN BRIEF 1 (Guttmacher Inst., New York, NY), Aug. 1, 2007, *available at* http://www.guttmacher.org/statecenter/spibs/spib_PIMA.pdf.

85. Stanley K. Henshaw and Kathryn Kost, *Parental Involvement in Minors' Abortion Decisions*, 24 FAM. PLAN. PERSP. 196, 196 (Sept. 1992). This national survey showed that 61 percent of teens discussed their decision to have an abortion with at least one parent. A majority of teens who did not talk to a parent turned to another trusted adult.

86. *Id.* at 200 & Table 3.

87. American Academy of Pediatrics, *The Adolescent's Right to Confidential Care When Considering Abortion*, 97 PEDIATRICS 746, 748 (1996), *available at* http://aappolicy.aappublications.org/cgi/reprint/pediatrics;97/5/746.pdf; *see generally* Henshaw & Kost, *supra* note 85, at 203–4.

88. *See* Council on Ethical and Judicial Affairs, AMA, *Mandatory Parental Consent to Abortion*, 269 J. AM. MED. ASS'N 82 (1993).

89. Memorandum of Law in Support of Plaintiffs' Motion for Summary Judgment at 36, Planned Parenthood v. Owens, 107 F. Supp. 2d 1271 (D. Colo. 2000) (No. 99-WM-60) (quoting testimony of Charisse Tuma-Meiers at 48–49).

90. *See* Planned Parenthood of Blue Ridge v. Camblos, 155 F.3d 352, 390 n.3 (4th Cir. 1998) (Michael, J., concurring); *see also* Planned Parenthood v. Miller, 63 F.3d 1452, 1462 (8th Cir. 1995) (discussing case of father who assaulted clinic staff and forced his daughter to leave the clinic upon learning that she planned to have an abortion); Planned Parenthood v. Farmer, 762 A.2d 620, 634 (N.J. 2000) ("Many minor women will encounter interference from their parents after the state-imposed notification. In addition to parental disappointment and disapproval, the minor may confront physical or emotional abuse, withdrawal of financial support, or actual obstruction of the abortion decision."); Am. Acad. of Pediatrics v. Lungren, 940 P.2d 797, 829 (Cal. 1997) (discussing evidence establishing that "many minors who do not voluntarily consult their parents have good reason to fear that informing their parents will result in physical or psychological abuse to the minor often because of previous abuse conduct or because the pregnancy is the result of intrafamily sexual activity").

91. *Lungren*, 940 P.2d at 831.

92. Hodgson v. Minnesota, 497 U.S. 417, 441 (1990).

93. Memphis Planned Parenthood v. Sundquist, 2 F. Supp. 2d 997, 1001 (M.D. Tenn. 1997), *rev'd on other grounds*, 175 F.3d 456 (6th Cir. 1999).

94. *Farmer*, 762 A.2d at 636.

95. *Id.* at 637.

96. *See* Cynthia Dailard and Chinue Turner Richardson, *Teenagers' Access to Confidential Reproductive Health Services*, 8 GUTTMACHER REP. ON PUB. POL'Y 6, 10 (2005), *available at* http://www.guttmacher.org/pubs/tgr/08/4/gr080406.pdf (citing positions of various medical organizations).

97. *Farmer*, 762 A.2d 620.

98. *Id.* at 638.

99. *Id.*; *see also* N. Fla. Women's Health & Counseling Servs. v. Florida, 866 So.2d 612 (Fla. 2003).

100. Planned Parenthood of S. Ariz. v. LaWall, 180 F.3d 1022 (9th Cir. 1999). Arizona subsequently amended its parental consent law, and in 2002, the Ninth Circuit upheld that amended law in Planned Parenthood of Southern Arizona v. LaWall, 307 F.3d 783 (9th Cir. 2002).

101. *See* Harris v. McRae, 448 U.S. 297 (1980).

102. *See* Heather D. Boonstra, *The Heart of the Matter: Public Funding of Abortion for Poor Women in the United States*, 10 GUTTMACHER POL'Y REV. 12 (2007), *available at* http://www.guttmacher.org/pubs/gpr/10/1/gpr100112.pdf; American Civil Liberties Union, Fact Sheet, Access Denied: Origins of the Hyde Amendment and Other Restrictions on Public Funding for Abortions (Dec. 1, 1994), *available at* http://www.aclu.org/reproductiverights/abortion/16396res19941201.html.

103. *McRae*, 448 U.S. at 314–18.

104. *Id.* at 316.

105. Arkansas, Arizona, California, Connecticut, Illinois, Massachusetts, Minnesota, Montana, New Jersey, New Mexico, Oregon, Vermont, and West Virginia.

106. *See* Alaska v. Planned Parenthood, 28 P.3d 904 (Alaska 2001); Simat Corp. v. Ariz. Health Care Cost Containment Sys., 203 Ariz. 454 (2002); Committee to Defend Reprod. Rights v. Myers, 625 P.2d 779 (Cal. 1981); Doe v. Maher, 515 A.2d 134 (Conn. Super. Ct. 1986); Doe v. Wright, No. 91 CH 1958 (Ill. Cir. Ct. Dec. 2, 1994); Moe v. Sec'y of Admin. & Fin., 417 N.E.2d 387 (Mass. 1981); Women of Minn. v. Gomez, 542 N.W.2d 17 (Minn. 1995); Jeannette R. v. Ellery, No. BDV-94-811 (Mont. Dist. Ct. May 22, 1995); Right to Choose v. Byrne, 450 A.2d 925 (N.J. 1982); N.M. Right to Choose/NARAL v. Johnson, 975 P.2d 841 (N.M. 1998); Planned Parenthood Ass'n v. Dep't of Human Res., 663 P.2d 1247 (Or. Ct. App. 1983), *aff'd on statutory grounds,* 687 P.2d 785 (Or. 1984); Doe v. Celani, No. S81-84CnC (Vt. Super. Ct. May 26, 1986); Women's Health Ctr. v. Panepinto, 446 S.E.2d 658 (W. Va. 1993).

107. *Alaska v. Planned Parenthood,* 28 P.3d at 905.

108. *State Funding of Abortion under Medicaid,* STATE POLICIES IN BRIEF (Guttmacher Inst., New York, NY), Aug. 1, 2007, at 1–2, *available at* http://www.guttmacher.org/statecenter/spibs/spib_SFAM.pdf.

109. *Id.*

110. Heather Boonstra and Adam Sonfield, *Rights without Access: Revisiting Pub-*

*lic Funding of Abortion for Poor Women*, 3 GUTTMACHER REP. ON PUB. POL'Y 8, 10 (2000), *available at* http://www.guttmacher.org/pubs/tgr/03/2/gr030208.pdf.

111. Memorandum of Law in Support of Plaintiffs' Motion for a Temporary Restraining Order & Preliminary Injunction at 13, Feminist Women's Health Center v. Burgess. FILE NO. 2003-CV-78487 (Ga. Super. Ct. filed Dec. 12, 2006).

112. Stanley K. Henshaw and Lawrence B. Finer, *The Accessibility of Abortion Services in the United States, 2001,* 35 PERSP. ON SEXUAL & REPROD. HEALTH 16, 23 (2003), *available at* http://www.guttmacher.org/pubs/psrh/full/3501603.pdf.

113. Memorandum of Law, *supra* note 111, at 12 (quoting Declaration of Helen Swanson ¶ 9) ("It sounds unbelievable, but because she lacked $40 she was forced to continue a pregnancy and have a baby she didn't want. That wouldn't have happened if Medicaid had covered the abortion, or even just the transportation.").

114. *Id.* at 8 (quoting Declaration of Tyrone Malloy, M.D. ¶ 26).

115. *Mandatory Counseling and Waiting Periods for Abortions,* STATE POLICIES IN BRIEF (Guttmacher Inst., New York, NY), Aug. 7, 2007, at 1, *available at* http://www.guttmacher.org/statecenter/spibs/spib_MWPA.pdf.

116. *Id.*

117. *Id.*

118. Planned Parenthood v. Casey, 505 U.S. 833, 886–87 (1992).

119. *Id.* at 882.

120. E.g., Woman's Choice—East Side Women's Clinic v. Newman, 305 F.3d 684 (7th Cir. 2002); Clinic for Women, Inc. v. Brizzi, 837 N.E.2d 973 (Ind. 2005); Barnes v. Moore, 970 F.2d 12 (5th Cir. 1992); Pro-Choice Miss. v. Fordice, 716 So. 2d 645 (Miss. 1998); *but see, e.g.,* Planned Parenthood of Middle Tenn. v. Sundquist, 38 S.W.3d 1 (Tenn. 2000) (striking down mandatory delay and biased counseling provisions as a violation of state constitution).

121. Lawrence B. Finer and Stanley K. Henshaw, *Abortion Incidence and Services in the United States in 2000,* 35 PERSP. ON SEXUAL & REPROD. HEALTH 6, 10 (2003), *available at* http://www.guttmacher.org/pubs/psrh/full/3500603.pdf.

122. Henshaw and Finer, *supra* note 112, at 18 ("Survey Respondents estimated that 8% of women having abortions in nonhospital facilities travel more than 100 miles to obtain this service, and that an additional 16% travel 50–100 miles. . . . [P]roviders [have] also reported that 24% of clients traveled at least 50 miles, including 8% and 7%, respectively, who traveled more than 100 miles.").

123. American Civil Liberties Union, Fact Sheet, Government-Mandated Delays before Abortion (Jan. 15, 2003), *available at* http://www.aclu.org/reproductiverights/abortion/16397res20030115.html.

124. Woman's Choice—East Side Women's Clinic v. Newman, 132 F. Supp. 2d 1150, 1151 (S.D. Ind. 2001), *rev'd,* 305 F.3d 684 (7th Cir. 2002); *see also* Ted Joyce et al., *The Impact of Mississippi's Mandatory Delay Law on Abortions and Births,* 278 J. AM. MED. ASS'N 653, 653–58 (1997).

125. Joyce et al., *supra* note 124.

126. Henshaw, *supra* note 14, at 20.

127. Stanley K. Henshaw, *Factors Hindering Access to Abortion Services*, 27 Fam. Plan. Persp. 54, 57–58 (1995).

128. Planned Parenthood of Cent. Mo. v. Danforth, 428 U.S. 52, 69 (1976) (spousal consent); Planned Parenthood v. Casey, 505 U.S. 833, 897 (1992) (spousal notification).

129. 505 U.S. at 888, 892.

130. *Id.* at 893.

131. *Id.* at 896–97.

132. *Id.* at 894.

133. *Id.* at 898.

134. Letter from American Civil Liberties Union to the House Armed Services Committee Strongly Supporting the Davis Amendment to the FY 2007 National Defense Authorization Act (May 2, 2006), *available at* http://www.aclu.org/reproductiverights/gen/25410leg20060502.html; Letter from American Civil Liberties Union to Senate Supporting Women's Health and Reproductive Rights in the Defense Authorization Bill (July 25, 2005), *available at* http://www.aclu.org/reproductiverights/abortion/19887leg20050725.html; Coalition Letter to U.S. House of Representatives in Support of Rep. Shays' Amendment to the Defense Authorization Bill (May 17, 2005), *available at* http://www.aclu.org/reproductiverights/abortion/12628leg20050517.html.

135. Boonstra, *supra* note 102, at 14–15.

136. Freedom of Access to Clinic Entrances Act, 18 U.S.C. § 248 (1994); *see also* Brief of *Amicus Curiae* American Civil Liberties Union in Support of Defendants-Appellees, Cheffer v. Reno, 55 F.3d 1517 (11th Cir. 2005) (No. 94-2976).

137. National Abortion Federation, History of Violence: Murders and Shootings, *available at* http://www.prochoice.org/about_abortion/violence/murders.asp (last visited July 16, 2007).

138. Finer and Henshaw, *supra* note 121, at 10.

139. ACLU Reproductive Freedom Project, Religious Refusals and Reproductive Rights 1 (2002), *available at* http://www.aclu.org/FilesPDFs/ACF911.pdf; Lois Utley and Ronnie Pawelko, MergerWatch Project, Educ. Fund of Family Planning Advocates of N.Y.S., No Strings Attached: Public Funding of Religiously Sponsored Hospitals in the United States 9–11 (2002), *available at* http://www.mergerwatch.org/pdfs/bp_no_strings.pdf.

140. Catholics for a Free Choice, You Can't Always Get What You Need: A Woman's Guide to Catholic Health Care 12 (2003), *available at* http://www.catholicsforchoice.org/topics/healthcare/documents/2003youcantalwaysgetwhatyouneed.pdf; Liz Bucar, Catholics for a Free Choice, Caution: Catholic Health Restrictions May Be Hazardous to Your Health 5 (1999), *available at* http://www.catholicsforchoice.org/topics/healthcare/documents/1998caution

catholichealthrestrictions.pdf; ACLU Reproductive Freedom Project, *supra* note 139, at 1.

141. Bucar, *supra* note 140, at 4; American Civil Liberties Union, Fact Sheet, Hospital Mergers: The Threat to Reproductive Health Services (Dec. 31, 1995), *available at* http://www.aclu.org/reproductiverights/religion/16525res19951231.html.

142. Griswold v. Connecticut, 381 U.S. 479 (1965).

143. Eisenstadt v. Baird, 405 U.S. 438, 453 (1972).

144. Carey v. Population Servs. Int'l, 431 U.S. 678, 688 (1977).

145. Cynthia Dailard, *U.S. Policy Can Reduce Cost Barriers to Contraception*, Issues in Brief (Guttmacher Inst., New York, NY), July 1999, *available at* http://www.guttmacher.org/pubs/ib_0799.html.

146. American Civil Liberties Union, Fact Sheet, Preventing Teenagers from Getting Contraceptives Unless They Tell a Parent Puts Teens at Risk (July 18, 2003), *available at* http://www.aclu.org/reproductiverights/contraception/16389res20030718.html; Heather Boonstra and Elizabeth Nash, *Minors and the Right to Consent to Health Care*, 3 Guttmacher Rep. 4, 4 (2000), *available at* http://www.guttmacher.org/pubs/tgr/03/4/gr030404.pdf.

147. *Carey*, 431 U.S. at 693.

148. Planned Parenthood Ass'n v. Matheson, 582 F. Supp. 1001, 1008, 1009 (D. Utah 1983); *see also* Parents United for Better Schs., Inc. v. Sch. Dist. of Phila. Bd. of Educ., 978 F. Supp. 197, 209–10 (E.D. Pa. 1997).

149. Public Health Service Act, 42 U.S.C. § 300a (1976).

150. Medicaid Act, 42 U.S.C. § 1396 (1984).

151. Diane M. Reddy et al., *Effect of Mandatory Parental Notification on Adolescent Girls' Use of Sexual Health Care Services*, 288 J. Am. Med. Ass'n 710, 712–13 (2002).

152. *See* Center for Adolescent Health and the Law, Policy Compendium on Confidential Health Services for Adolescents 31 (2d ed. 2005).

153. Adam Sonfield et al., Cost Pressures on Title X Family Planning Grantees, FY 2001–2004, at 2 (2006), *available at* http://www.guttmacher.org/pubs/2006/08/01/CPTX.pdf.

154. University of California San Francisco, Center for Reproductive Health Research & Policy, Fact Sheet on Family PACT: An Overview (2006), *available at* http://crhrp.ucsf.edu/publications/files/FPACT_FS_2006_Overview.pdf.

155. Adam Sonfield, *The Impact of Anti-Immigrant Policy on Publicly Subsidized Reproductive Health Care*, 10 Guttmacher Pol'y Rev. 7, 9 (2007), *available at* http://www.guttmacher.org/pubs/gpr/10/1/gpr100107.pdf; Leighton Ku et al., Center for Budget and Policy Priorities, New Survey Finds 3 to 5 Million Citizens' Medicaid Coverage Jeopardized by Budget Reconciliation Bill (Jan. 21, 2006), *available at* http://www.cbpp.org/1-26-06health.pdf.

156. Rachel Benson Gold, *Immigrants and Medicaid after Welfare Reform*, 6

Guttmacher Rep. on Pub. Pol'y 6, 6 (2003), *available at* http://www.guttmacher. org/pubs/tgr/06/2/gr060206.pdf. States have the option of using their own funds to assist legal immigrants, and several states have chosen to do so. *Id.*

157. *Id.* at 8.

158. For example, in 1993, although 97 percent of traditional fee-for-service health insurance plans covered prescription drugs, half of those plans did not cover any contraceptive method, only one-third covered oral contraceptives, and only 15 percent covered all five of the leading FDA-approved reversible contraceptives (the pill, IUD, diaphragm, implant, and injectable). HMOs offered more comprehensive coverage, but only 39 percent of HMOs covered all five prescription methods, and 7 percent covered no prescription contraceptives at all. *See* Dailard, *supra* note 145; American Civil Liberties Union, Fact Sheet, Promoting Access to Contraception and Opposing Threats to Its Availability at Home and Abroad (July 1, 1998), *available at* http://www.aclu.org/reproductiverights/contraception/16527res19980701.html.

159. *Insurance Coverage of Contraceptives*, State Policies in Brief (Guttmacher Inst., New York, NY), Aug. 1, 2007, at 1, *available at* http://www.guttmacher.org/ statecenter/spibs/spib_ICC.pdf.

160. U.S. Equal Employment Opportunity Comm'n, Decision on Coverage of Contraception (Dec. 14, 2000), *available at* http://www.eeoc.gov/policy/docs/ decision-contraception.html.

161. Erickson v. Bartell Drug Co., 141 F. Supp. 2d 1266 (W.D. Wash. 2001); *see also* Cynthia Dailard, *Contraceptive Coverage: A 10-Year Retrospective*, 7 Guttmacher Rep. on Pub. Pol'y 6, 8 (2004), *available at* http://www.guttmacher.org/ pubs/tgr/07/2/gr070206.pdf.

162. In re Union Pacific R.R. Employment Practices Litig., 479 F.3d 936 (8th Cir. 2007).

163. Adam Sonfield et al., *U.S. Insurance Coverage of Contraceptives and the Impact of Contraceptive Coverage Mandates*, 36 Persp. on Sexual & Reprod. Health 72 (2004), *available at* http://www.guttmacher.org/pubs/psrh/full/3607204.pdf.

164. Dailard, *supra* note 161, at 9.

165. American Civil Liberties Union, *supra* note 158; ACLU Reproductive Freedom Project, *supra* note 139.

166. Catholic Charities of Sacramento v. Super. Ct., 85 P.3d 67 (Cal. 2004); Catholic Charities of the Diocese of Albany v. Serio, 859 N.E.2d 459 (N.Y. 2006).

167. *See* Letter from Steven Galson, Director, Ctr. for Drug Evaluation & Research, Food & Drug Admin., to Joseph A. Carrodo, Vice President, Duramend Research, Inc., *available at* http://www.fda.gov/cder/foi/appletter/2006/021045s011ltr. pdf; Memorandum from Steven Galson, Director, Ctr. for Drug Evaluation & Research, Food & Drug Admin. to NDA 21-045, S-011 (Aug. 24, 2006), *available at* http://www.fda.gov/cder/drug/infopage/planB/memo.pdf.

168. *Emergency Contraception*, State Policies in Brief (Guttmacher Inst., New

York, NY), Aug. 1, 2007, at 1, *available at* http://www.guttmacher.org/statecenter/ spibs/spib_EC.pdf; Jane Hutchings et al., *When the Morning After Is Sunday: Pharmacist Prescribing of Emergency Contraceptive Pills*, 53 J. AM. MED. WOMEN'S ASS'N 230 (1998); Jacqueline S. Gardner et al., *Increasing Access to Emergency Contraception through Community Pharmacies: Lessons from Washington State*, 33 FAMILY PLANNING PERSP. 172 (2001), *available at* http://www.guttmacher.org/pubs/journals/3317201. pdf.

169. American Civil Liberties Union, Fact Sheet, Ensuring Access to Emergency Contraception after Rape (Feb. 13, 2007), *available at* http://www.aclu.org/ reproductiverights/contraception/16425res20070213.html.

170. Press Release, American Civil Liberties Union, Broad Coalition of Advocates Implores U.S. Department of Justice to Add Pregnancy Prevention to National Protocol for Treating Rape Survivors (Jan. 6, 2005), *available at* http://www.aclu. org/reproductiverights/contraception/12742prs20050106.html.

171. American Civil Liberties Union, *supra* note 169.

172. CATHOLICS FOR A FREE CHOICE, COMPLYING WITH THE LAW: HOW CATHOLIC HOSPITALS RESPOND TO STATE LAWS MANDATING THE PROVISION OF EMERGENCY CONTRACEPTION TO SEXUAL ASSAULT PATIENTS 10 (2006), *available at* http:// www.catholicsforchoice.org/topics/healthcare/documents/2006complyingwiththe law.pdf.

173. American Civil Liberties Union, Reproductive Freedom Project Briefing Paper, Preventing Pregnancy after Rape: Emergency Care Facilities Put Women at Risk 3 (Dec. 2004), *available at* http://www.aclu.org/reproductiverights/gen/ 12748pub20041215.html.

174. Three states require emergency care facilities to provide information about EC to women who have been sexually assaulted. Because the needs of rape survivors are so acute and the window to prevent pregnancy through EC so brief, the ACLU believes that legislation that does less than impose a blanket requirement on hospitals to offer rape survivors EC is unacceptable. American Civil Liberties Union, *supra* note 169.

175. Heather Boonstra, *Emergency Contraception: Steps Being Taken to Improve Access*, 5 GUTTMACHER REP. ON PUB. POL'Y 10, 10–11 (2002), *available at* http:// www.guttmacher.org/pubs/tgr/05/5/gr050510.pdf.

176. *See supra* text accompanying notes 165–66.

177. American Civil Liberties Union, *supra* note 169.

178. CATHOLICS FOR A FREE CHOICE, *supra* note 172, at 7.

179. ACLU REPRODUCTIVE FREEDOM PROJECT, RELIGIOUS REFUSALS AND REPRODUCTIVE RIGHTS: ACCESSING BIRTH CONTROL AT THE PHARMACY 4 (2007), *available at* http://www.aclu.org/images/asset_upload_file576_29402.pdf; National Women's Law Center, Fact Sheet, Pharmacy Refusals 101 (July 2007), *available at* http:// www.nwlc.org/pdf/PharmacyRefusals101July2007.pdf; Boonstra, *supra* note 175, at

11; Planned Parenthood Federation of America, Inc., Fact Sheet, Refusal Clauses: A Threat to Reproductive Rights (Dec. 17, 2004) (citing newspaper accounts), *available at* http://www.plannedparenthood.org/files/PPFA/fact-refusal-clauses.pdf; Cynthia Dailard, *Beyond the Issue of Pharmacist Refusals: Pharmacies That Won't Sell Emergency Contraception*, 8 GUTTMACHER REP. ON PUB. POL'Y 10, 10 (2005), *available at* http://www.guttmacher.org/pubs/tgr/08/3/gr080310.pdf.

180. Dailard, *supra* note 179, at 10.

181. National Women's Law Center, *supra* note 179.

182. ACLU REPRODUCTIVE FREEDOM PROJECT, *supra* note 179, at 2.

183. ILL. ADMIN. CODE tit. 68, § 1330.91 (j)(i) (2006).

184. WASH. ADMIN. CODE 246-869-010 (2007); *see also* WASH. ADMIN. CODE 246-863-095 (2007) (rule applicable to pharmacists).

185. Skinner v. Oklahoma, 316 U.S. 535, 536 (1942).

186. In re Romero, 790 P.2d 819, 821 (Colo. 1990); Janet Simmonds, Note, *Coercion in California: Eugenics Reconstituted in Welfare Reform, the Contracting of Reproductive Capacity, and Terms of Probation*, 17 HASTINGS WOMEN'S L.J. 269, 271–76 (2006); Michael G. Silver, Note, *Eugenics and Compulsory Sterilization Laws: Providing Redress for the Victims of a Shameful Era in United States History*, 72 GEO. WASH. L. REV. 862, 862–69 (2004).

187. Buck v. Bell, 274 U.S. 200, 207 (1927).

188. *Skinner*, 316 U.S. at 536.

189. Relf v. Weinberger, 372 F. Supp. 1196, 1199 (D.D.C. 1974), *vacated*, 565 F.2d 722 (D.C. Cir. 1977).

190. National Conference of State Legislatures, Family Cap Policies (2007), *available at* http://www.ncsl.org/statefed/welfare/familycap05.htm.

191. Press Release, American Civil Liberties Union, In Legal First, NJ Supreme Court to Consider Law Denying Aid to Children of Families on Welfare (Jan. 21, 2003), *available at* http://www.aclu.org/womensrights/povertywelfare/ 13169prs20030121.html; Rutgers University, *Report on the Impact of New Jersey's Family Development Program: Results from a Pre-Post Analysis of AFDC Case Heads from 1990–1996* (Dec. 1997). The study found that the policy resulted in approximately 240 more abortions per year among women on welfare than would have been expected without the policy.

192. American Civil Liberties Union, *supra* note 11, at 3; American Civil Liberties Union, Fact Sheet, Ferguson v. City of Charleston: Social and Legal Contexts (Sept. 25, 2000), *available at* http://www.aclu.org/reproductiverights/lowincome/ 12511res20001101.html; American Civil Liberties Union, Fact Sheet, Coercive and Punitive Governmental Responses to Women's Conduct during Pregnancy (Sept. 30, 1997), *available at* http://www.aclu.org/reproductiverights/gen/16529res19970930. html.

193. American Civil Liberties Union, Fact Sheet, Ferguson v. City of Charleston, *supra* note 192.

194. Ferguson v. City of Charleston, 532 U.S. 67 (2001).

195. Ferguson v. City of Charleston, 308 F.3d 380 (4th Cir. 2002).

196. National Advocates for Pregnant Women, What's Wrong with Making It a Crime to Be Pregnant and to Have a Drug Problem? (Mar. 9, 2006), *available at* http://advocatesforpregnantwomen.org/main/publications/fact_sheets/whats_wrong _with_making_it_a_crime_to_be_pregnant_and_to_have_a_drug_problem.php.

197. American Civil Liberties Union, Fact Sheet, Ferguson v. City of Charleston, *supra* note 192.

198. *Id.*; National Advocates for Pregnant Women, *supra* note 196.

199. ACLU Reproductive Freedom Project, *supra* note 139, at 1; *see supra* text accompanying note 139–41.

200. ACLU Reproductive Freedom Project, *supra* note 139, at 2; F. Gary Cunningham et al., Williams Obstetrics 1556 (21st ed. 2001).

201. *Facts on American Teens' Sexual and Reproductive Health*, In Brief (Guttmacher Inst., New York, NY), Sept. 2006, at 1, 2, *available at* http://www.guttmacher.org/pubs/fb_ATSRH.pdf.

202. *Id.*; Centers for Disease Control & Prevention, HIV Prevention Strategic Plan through 2005 18 (2001), *available at* http://www.cdc.gov/hiv/resources/reports/psp/pdf/prev-strat-plan.pdf.

203. Douglas Kirby, The National Campaign to Prevent Teen Pregnancy, Emerging Answers: Research Findings on Programs to Reduce Teen Pregnancy, Summary 16 (2001), *available at* http://www.teenpregnancy.org/resources/data/pdf/emeranswsum.pdf.

204. *Id.* at 18.

205. Kaiser Family Foundation et al., Sex Education in America: General Public/Parents Survey 5, 9 (2004), *available at* http://www.kff.org/newsmedia/upload/Sex-Education-in-America-General-Public-Parents-Survey-Toplines.pdf.

206. Jacqueline E. Darroch et al., *Changing Emphases in Sexuality Education in U.S. Public Secondary Schools 1988–1999*, 32 Fam. Plan. Persp. 204, 206 (2000), *available at* http://www.guttmacher.org/pubs/journals/3220400.pdf.

207. Advocates for Youth and SIECUS, Toward a Sexually Healthy America: Roadblocks Imposed by the Federal Government's Abstinence-only-until-Marriage Education Program 22–24 (2001), *available at* http://www.advocatesforyouth.org/publications/abstinenceonly.pdf.

208. American Civil Liberties Union, Fact Sheet, Abstinence-Only-Until-Marriage Programs Censor Vital Health Care Information (Aug. 22, 2007), *available at* http://www.aclu.org/reproductiverights/sexed/12670res20070822.html.

209. Impacts of Four Title V, Section 510 Abstinence Education Programs xvii (2007), *available at* http://aspe.hhs.gov/hsp/abstinence07/report.pdf; *see also* American Civil Liberties Union, *supra* note 208; Barbara Devaney et al., The Evaluation of Abstinence Education Programs Funded under Title V Section 510: Interim Report 1 (2002) (concluding that there was no "definitive

research" linking abstinence education funding with the downward trend in teens reporting they have had sex).

210. PETER S. BEARMAN AND HANNAH BRUCKNER, PROMISING THE FUTURE: VIRGINITY PLEDGES AS THEY AFFECT TRANSITION TO FIRST INTERCOURSE 35 (2000), *available at* http://www.siecus.org/media/pdf/Bearman2001.pdf.

211. 42 U.S.C. § 710(b)(2)(A), (E) (2003).

212. American Civil Liberties Union, *supra* note 208.

213. *Id.*

214. *Id.*

215. UNITED STATES HOUSE OF REPRESENTATIVES COMMITTEE ON GOVERNMENT REFORM—MINORITY STAFF SPECIAL INVESTIGATIONS DIVISION, THE CONTENT OF FEDERALLY FUNDED ABSTINENCE-ONLY EDUCATION PROGRAMS (2004).

216. Darroch et al., *supra* note 206, at 209.

217. *Sexuality Education*, FACTS IN BRIEF (Guttmacher Inst., New York, NY), Aug. 2002, *available at* http://www.guttmacher.org/pubs/fb_sex_ed02.pdf.

218. *See, e.g.*, Press Release, American Civil Liberties Union, ACLU Announces Multi-State Action Calling on Government to Fix Medical Inaccuracies in Federally Funded Abstinence-Only-Until-Marriage Curricula (May 9, 2007), *available at* http://www.aclu.org/reproductive rights/sexed/29641prs20070509.html.

219. American Civil Liberties Union, *supra* note 208.

220. *Id.*

# VII

## Family Law

In the past twenty years the definition of family has been changing drastically to include families headed by gay and lesbian couples, foster and adoptive families, extended families, stepfamilies, and other "new families." Court decisions and laws, however, still often reflect a narrow conception of what constitutes a family. Individual challenges to traditional notions of the nuclear two-parent family consisting of husband, wife, and children have forced the law around nontraditional families to grow and adapt, but that development has been piecemeal at best. Given how diverse society is today, it is perhaps not surprising, then, that the law governing nonnuclear families is often contradictory from state to state, even county to county. As society continues to redefine its notions of family, we can hope that the law will follow and the rights of nontraditional families will be recognized as equal to those of traditional families.

This chapter provides a brief overview of several issues in family law that are important to women today. For more detail on these and other topics, please see *The Rights of Families*, the authoritative ACLU guide on the law of the family, and *The Rights of Lesbians, Gay Men, Bisexuals, and Transgender People*, fourth edition, which discusses the challenges facing same-sex couples.

### CREATING LEGALLY RECOGNIZED, LONG-TERM RELATIONSHIPS

Individuals in intimate relationships often want to create legal ties that bind them to each other, either through marriage or through other formal partnerships. Couples who do not or cannot marry can take steps to ensure that

241

in the absence of marriage they, their loved ones, and their property are protected under law.

**What is a marriage?**

There is no short answer to this question. Ideas of who can marry and what constitutes a marriage continue to be subject to debate. However, in the United States marriage is generally seen as a civil contract between two people and is associated with a number of rights, obligations, and entitlements, including federal benefits, insurance coverage, inheritance rights, and certain property rights. Recent controversies have focused on the extension or denial of the right to marry to same-sex couples. Even the federal government, which generally leaves the intricacies of family law to the individual states, has become involved in the debate surrounding same-sex marriages, passing the 1996 Defense of Marriage Act (DOMA), which defines marriage as the legally sanctioned union between a man and a woman.[1] Several states followed with their own mini-DOMAs, similar legislation in the form of laws and/or state constitutional amendments explicitly limiting marriage to heterosexual unions.[2] On the other hand, Massachusetts, California, and Connecticut have formally extended marriage licenses to same-sex couples,[3] and Vermont, while defining marriage as the union between a man and woman, simultaneously passed legislation permitting civil unions for same-sex couples that provide all the rights and responsibilities associated with marriage under state law.[4] Additionally, New York recognizes the marriages of same-sex couples performed in other states.[5]

**What are the rights and responsibilities that accompany marriage?**

Over one thousand rights and responsibilities are automatically conferred to couples based on marital status, in part due to the societal and governmental assumption that married individuals will be mutually dependent and support one another throughout their time together. Laws reinforce these obligations. According to one federal survey there are 1,138 federal laws in which marriage is a factor in determining or receiving benefits, rights, and privileges,[6] and there are countless other state and local laws and practices that attach to marital status.

Generally at the federal, state, and local levels, there is an assumption that married individuals will support each other both financially and emotionally during the marriage. The laws governing divorce and alimony when a marriage is dissolved, as well as inheritance rights and survivors benefits upon the death of one's spouse, reflect these beliefs. Married couples are also often responsible for the "necessary" debts of each other, and governments, banks, and other financial institutions will often consider both spouses' incomes and debts in such matters as taxes (thus the right to file jointly and claim some exemptions) credit, loans, and public assistance. Though it is impossible to list all the different rights here, other privileges associated with marriage include the right to visit one's spouse in the hospital and to make medical decisions for him or her in an emergency; eligibility for family health insurance, life insurance, and disability insurance; the right to seek compensation in the event of a spouse's wrongful death or serious accident; the right to Social Security survivors' benefits and military benefits; the right to file joint petitions to immigrate to the United States or to sponsor a spouse's immigration application or visa; and in criminal law the protection of most domestic violence laws, as well as (in some states) the marital privilege not to testify against one's spouse.

Some of these rights and responsibilities can be reproduced through private contracts and agreements, wills, and powers of attorney. But many others cannot. For instance, an unmarried woman cannot contract to be able to sue for the wrongful death of her partner, nor can she contract to receive workers' compensation dependency benefits or survivors' benefits. Much of the debate around same-sex marriage focuses on allowing couples to access all these legal rights and protections, as well as the formal recognition of their long-term commitment to each other.

### Can gay and lesbian couples marry?

As of this writing, gay couples may only marry in the state of Massachusetts,[7] and there is no guarantee that these marriages will be recognized in other states. In 2003 the Massachusetts Supreme Court found that under the state constitution the ability to marry could not be limited to couples of the opposite sex.[8] Once married, gay and lesbian couples receive the same benefits and protections under state law as opposite-sex married couples.

In contrast, the federal government through its Defense of Marriage Act defines marriage as only the union between a man and a woman, denies same-sex couples the corresponding federal benefits provided spouses, and gives the states the option not to recognize same-sex marriages performed elsewhere. Forty states have laws or constitutional amendments explicitly defining marriage as between a man and a woman, and denying recognition of same-sex marriages performed in other jurisdictions.[9]

In many places, legal and political battles over marriage rights are ongoing. Cases have been filed in several state courts seeking the right to marry for same-sex couples, and activists on both sides of the issue continue to push for legislation expanding or limiting the right to marriage.[10]

### Can transsexuals or transgendered persons marry someone of the opposite gender but same biological sex?

In those states where marriage is restricted to a union between a man and a woman, transgender and transsexual persons face unique challenges with regard to marriage. Whether that individual is allowed to marry a person of the same biological sex depends on state law. When litigated, courts generally have two legal approaches to this issue.[11] Some courts validate marriages that involve postoperative transsexuals, finding that their sex operations deserve consideration when determining the person's sex for the purposes of marriage.[12] Other courts invalidate marriages that involve postoperative transsexuals, arguing that the individual has been born into and will remain a particular gender and sex.[13]

### What is common law marriage?

A common law marriage is a marriage between a man and a woman that is entered into without a license or ceremony. A couple can enter into a common law marriage by agreeing to be married, presenting themselves as married in their dealings with others, living together for a significant period of time (not generally defined and varying by state), and assuming mutual obligations to each other.[14] However, only ten states[15] and the District of Columbia allow marriages to be contracted in this way. All states will recognize the validity of common law marriages entered into in the states that still allow them.

### Do women and men have the right to use any name they choose if they marry?

Yes. Despite the social custom of wives taking their husbands' names, the legal system has long recognized the right, under common law, of any person, whether married or unmarried, to use any name she likes, as long as she is not doing so for a fraudulent purpose such as avoiding criminal prosecution or cheating one's creditors.

In most states, to change one's name, one simply begins using a new name and notifies friends, associates, and creditors. It is a good idea to use the new name consistently and to change relevant legal documents, such as checkbooks, voter registration, driver's license and car registration, Social Security identification, credit cards, and tax returns. Additionally, many states have laws requiring people to notify authorities—e.g., those concerned with voter registration, driver's licenses, car registration, and certificates of title—when their name changes "by marriage or otherwise." In addition, most states have established formal procedures by which a person may change his or her name, resulting in a court order and public record of the name change.

### What is a civil union?

A civil union is a legal status for same-sex couples that is equivalent to legal marriage under state law.[16] Civil unions are permitted in Vermont and Connecticut. In both states, same-sex couples may enter into civil unions, no matter where they reside, and these spouses will enjoy the same protection as married couples under Vermont and Connecticut law.[17] However, civil unions do not provide access to federal benefits afforded married couples, and whether governments, institutions, and employers outside these two states will recognize these civil unions is a contested issue.

### What is domestic partnership?

"Domestic partnership" is a general term used to describe a committed relationship between an unmarried same-sex or opposite-sex couple. Some states, municipalities, and employers seeking to confer rights and privileges on unmarried couples in committed relationships use this term. The rights, benefits, and obligations associated with domestic partnership vary among jurisdictions and employers.

### Which states recognize domestic partnerships?

California, Maine, and New Jersey offer domestic partnership registries, while Hawaii and Vermont recognize such relationships but call them "reciprocal beneficiary relationships."[18] Hawaii, Vermont, California, New Jersey, and Maine provide the broadest state recognition to domestic partnerships. Washington, Oregon, New Mexico, Connecticut, New York, Rhode Island, and Massachusetts also recognize domestic partnerships but do not provide as many benefits.[19]

The definitions of "domestic partner" and the rights to which a domestic partner is entitled vary from state to state. For instance, California allows opposite-sex couples where at least one partner is over sixty-two and all same-sex couples to register as domestic partners. Its law grants domestic partners almost every right and responsibility granted married persons under state law, including, but not limited to, rights to financial support during and after the relationship, eligibility for workers' compensation benefits, and rights to make certain health care decisions for one's partner.[20] In comparison, Hawaii allows both single-sex and opposite-sex couples to enter into reciprocal beneficiary relationships and thus gain access to most marriage rights under state law, except access to family court rights (such as alimony) or health insurance benefits.[21] Other states offer much more limited domestic partner benefits. For example, Iowa and New York offer domestic partner health and dental benefits to state employees.[22]

**What benefits do employers provide for domestic partners?**

It depends on the employer. According to the Human Rights Campaign, in 2005, eleven states, 129 municipalities, 280 colleges and universities, and over half of Fortune 500 companies offered some sort of domestic partner benefit to employees.[23] These benefits may include health, dental, and vision insurance, sick leave and bereavement leave, accident and life insurance, death benefits, parental leave (for a child parented by domestic partners), housing rights and tuition reduction (at universities and colleges), and the use of recreational facilities.[24]

**Do all employers provide benefits to domestic partners?**

No. Although many states, municipalities, private companies, and institutions of higher education have begun to grant economic and noneconomic benefits to the domestic partners of employees, other employers will only provide benefits to married spouses and dependent children of their employees. Their policies tend to exclude unmarried couples, domestic partners, and other "nontraditional" family members. The federal government, which is the nation's largest employer, provides no benefits to partners in unmarried couples.

**What are some of the legal limitations of civil unions or domestic partnerships?**

Because civil unions and domestic partnerships are not recognized by every state or by every employer, legal rights will not necessarily move with a couple if they relocate to a different state or change jobs. Couples may also face obstacles in formally dissolving their civil unions or domestic partnerships in a state that does not recognize these arrangements. As mentioned above, civil unions and domestic partnerships do not allow couples to gain access to the federal benefits available to married persons, such as the right under the Family and Medical Leave Act to take time off to care for a family member, the right to sponsor a spouse for immigration, and the right to receive Social Security survivors' benefits upon the death of a spouse.

### Should unmarried couples prepare a will?

Yes, an unmarried couple should absolutely prepare a will if each wants property to go to the other. The inheritance laws in most states (with some exceptions in states that recognize civil unions or domestic partnerships) do not permit property to be given to an unmarried surviving partner without a will.[25] Generally, if a person dies without a will, her property is distributed according to the state laws of intestate succession. Laws of intestate succession generally require the deceased's property to be distributed in certain percentages among various defined survivors, such as spouses, children, parents, brothers, and sisters.[26]

### Can an unmarried person make decisions about health care for her partner if her partner is incapacitated?

Generally, no. Such decisions will usually fall to next of kin, and most states will not recognize an unmarried partner, regardless of the degree of the commitment or nature of the relationship, as next of kin. If the couple has entered a domestic partnership or civil union, in a state recognizing such unions, then an unmarried person can make some decisions, usually outlined by law, for the incapacitated partner.

An unmarried couple can anticipate crises by executing a medical power of attorney, which specifically gives one individual authority to make medical decisions for another if he or she is incapacitated. Unmarried partners can also create durable powers of attorney for finances, giving one partner the right to make financial decisions for the other if he or she becomes incapacitated. The power of attorney can be limited to one type of act, such as selling a home, or can grant more generalized decision-making power. Unmarried partners can also complete hospital visitation authorization forms, instructing a hospital to give first priority in visitation to the partner in the event of an emergency. These documents together can give each partner the rights that usually go to next of kin in a crisis.

### How else can unmarried couples make legal arrangements in recognition of their relationship?

Unmarried couples can do a number of things to establish their legal rights and obligations toward each other.[27] Partners can co-own property to ensure they both have legal rights to ownership should an emergency occur or the relationship end. They can keep records of each person's contribution to the couple's expenses to aid property distribution in case of a breakup and (ideally with the assistance of an attorney) can enter into cohabitation agreements explaining how property will be divided in that event.

If they are raising a child together, and only one person is a legal parent, that parent can complete a document authorizing the partner to consent to emergency medical treatment for the child. The legal parent can also create a document nominating the partner as guardian for the child in the event the legal parent dies or becomes incapacitated; however, this document will not override the rights of another living parent.

## DISSOLVING LEGAL TIES: ENDING MARRIAGES, CIVIL UNIONS, AND DOMESTIC PARTNERSHIPS

### What is the difference between a divorce and an annulment?

A divorce is the legal dissolution or ending of a valid marriage. An annulment declares that a marriage was invalid when it took place or, essentially, that a legal marriage never really existed. The general grounds for annulment are different from the grounds for divorce, and vary by state.[28]

### What is a legal separation?

A legal separation is usually a preliminary step to divorce. Some people, for religious, economic, or personal reasons, will file for a legal separation and never seek a divorce. Generally, the couple must file papers in court asking to be declared legally separated and may also enter into a separation agreement. These agreements address issues such as financial support for the dependent spouse, custody, visitation, and child support, and responsibility for paying debts. Where there is no agreement, couples can always ask the court to order spousal or child support.

### Are there any legal requirements to end a domestic partnership or civil union?

While state and local laws vary, there are some general requirements for ending a domestic partnership. A domestic partnership usually ends (1) upon the death of a partner; (2) when one partner marries; or (3) when the partners cease to live together. Usually, when the partnership ends, partners must submit notification to employers and/or the court, depending on the state.

In both Connecticut and Vermont, ending civil unions is a process parallel to divorce and the states' respective divorce and separation laws apply.[29] It is unclear whether civil unions from these states can be dissolved in other jurisdictions that recognize them. For more detailed information please refer to *The Rights of Lesbians, Gay Men, Bisexuals, and Transgender People,* fourth edition.

### How does a divorce change a woman's legal status?

The purpose of divorce is to divide the former couple's property, to establish any continuing obligations between them, and to determine their rights and responsibilities towards any children they might have.[30] One obvious change in legal status is that a woman may marry again after a divorce. In addition, a woman's legal rights to her children, the couple's joint property, and her assets may change depending on the outcome of the divorce.

### What are grounds for divorce?

Grounds for divorce vary from state to state. There has been a widespread adoption of "no-fault" grounds for divorce; that is, a couple is allowed to divorce without a showing that one party is at fault. No-fault grounds for divorce include irretrievable breakdown of the marriage, irreconcilable differences, incompatibility, and separation (that is, living apart for a certain length of time, generally more than six months, and in some states two or three years). Some states allow one spouse to seek and obtain a no-fault divorce without the other spouse's agreement. Other states require the court to grant a divorce if both spouses seek it; still others require the court to make case-by-case determinations in deciding whether to grant the divorce.

Depending on the state, it may also be possible to obtain a divorce based on traditional fault grounds such as adultery, desertion, extreme cruelty, drug or alcohol addiction, imprisonment, and deviant sexual conduct.[31]

### Is it necessary to hire a lawyer?

Not always. If there are no children and no property, marital couples may be able to handle their own divorce without lawyers. This is called appearing *pro se* ("for oneself"). In some areas, the clerk's office in the court may have forms or otherwise be willing to help in handling the paperwork. Although this alternative is much less costly than hiring a lawyer, it can be confusing. Anyone who has children, property, or other complex issues should seek the advice of a lawyer.

**Does the lawyer a woman hires need to be someone other than her spouse's lawyer?**

Yes. No matter how amicable the relationship with her spouse, once a woman is seriously considering a divorce she has interests separate from her spouse's and should be represented separately to avoid a conflict of interests. *This is vital.* Even if she decides eventually not to retain a lawyer to represent her, she should consult with a lawyer of her own at least once to get impartial advice on her situation.

**What is mediation?**

Mediation is a voluntary process in which a neutral third party, a mediator, helps the couple reach a mutually acceptable agreement about each partner's respective rights and responsibilities after divorce. It is less formal than court proceedings, and even if each party has legal representation, the lawyers should not actively participate in the mediation. The goal of mediation is to help the parties reach an agreement. The mediator does not have authority to impose a decision on the parties, although some mediators do pressure parties to agree to a settlement.

**Are there any situations in which mediation should not be used?**

Yes. Generally, survivors of domestic violence or other forms of physical, sexual, or emotional abuse by their partner should not use mediation. The effectiveness of mediation relies on good faith bargaining between parties who possess equal power, which usually does not exist in an abuser/victim situation. For example, despite a woman's expectations, she may be too fearful of retaliation to speak up forcefully for her own interests, or the abuser may use the informality of the mediation process to intimidate and harass the victim.

**Is mediation ever mandatory?**

Yes, mediation is mandatory in a small minority of states, such as California.[32] In some states mediation is required on certain issues, such as custody and/or visitation. In other states mediation is strongly encouraged but not required. Most states that mandate mediation exempt victims of domestic violence from the requirement, except California.[33]

**Do women who changed their surname upon marriage and want to change it back to their maiden name upon dissolution have to take any special steps?**

Generally, divorced women have the same common law right as others to use any name they like and need merely begin using the name of their choice. However, some states may require women to change their name either through the divorce process or through a formal name-change procedure. In addition, many states have laws permitting women to obtain a name change as part of a divorce decree, which is probably the quickest way to effect the change.

**What property is subject to division in a divorce?**

All physical and financial possessions that have been acquired in the family after marriage and up to the time of divorce—including cash, houses, furnishings, cars, boats, land, stocks and bonds, businesses, or business interests—are property that can be divided in a divorce depending on state law. Pension rights are usually included, as is the value of a professional education or practice in some states.

**How is property divided?**

At the time of divorce, property is divided between the husband and wife by separation agreement, by property settlement agreement, or by court order. The principles used to decide how to divide property vary widely from state to state. Generally, property division is a one-time event and the arrangements are settled at the close of the divorce case, even if some property still needs to be transferred or payments made. It is usually not possible to return to court and request a change in the property division agreement or order, unless there has been fraud, coercion, or a misrepresentation of assets.

**How is property divided in a community-property state?**

In the nine community-property states[34]—Arizona, California, Idaho, Louisiana, Nevada, New Mexico, Texas, Washington, and Wisconsin—property is classified as separate or community. Separate property generally includes property that a spouse owned prior to the marriage, the property a spouse acquired during the marriage by gift or inheritance, and property acquired during the marriage that can be traced back to property included in one of the two former categories. Community property consists of all other property acquired during the marriage.

At the time of divorce, community property is usually divided in two equal shares. However, the rules vary from state to state. In a few states, some "equitable principles" are also applied in determining how to divide the property. For example, according to these principles, the family home is automatically awarded to whichever parent has custody of the children.

### How is property divided in a separate-property state or common-law state?

In the remaining states and the District of Columbia, property is classified as either separate or marital property.[35] Similar to principles used in community property states, marital property generally includes all the property acquired during the marriage except inheritances and gifts. However, common-law states differ in that marital property is not automatically assumed to belong to both parties at the time of acquisition.

In most common-law states, marital property must be "equitably divided" at the time of divorce. "Equitable division" can work differently depending on the state. Basically there are two methods: (1) division of only marital property and (2) division of both marital and separate property. The majority of states exclude gifts and inheritances from consideration for either of these methods, but some do not.

Most equitable distribution laws provide a list of factors the divorce court should weigh in deciding how to divide property fairly. These often include length of marriage; age, health, and earning ability of husband and wife; contributions of each to homemaking and care of the children; contributions of each in acquiring or developing the property being considered; and who will have custody of the children. Under these laws, marital "fault," such as adultery, desertion, or cruelty, is often officially eliminated or diminished in importance in dividing the marital property.[36]

### What is alimony?

Alimony, also called "maintenance" or "spousal support," is financial support for an economically dependent former spouse provided through regular payments by the husband or wife after the marriage has ended. Traditionally, alimony is ordered by a court on the basis of one spouse's need or entitlement and the other spouse's ability to pay,[37] and may be ordered temporarily (rehabilitative or short-term alimony) or until the person receiving alimony remarries or dies (permanent alimony). A few states have mandated time limits on alimony, except in specified circumstances, and most states limit the availability of alimony depending on a variety of factors.

Alimony may also be awarded as a fixed sum payable either all at once or in a series of payments as part of or in lieu of a property settlement, as repayment of a debt, or as repayment of expenses incurred by the receiving spouse during the marriage.[38] It is possible for spouses to return to court later to request lower payments or more alimony if circumstances change. Finally, contrary to popular perception, both men and women can be ordered to pay alimony.[39]

**What factors are considered in awarding alimony?**

As with most of family law, each state has different factors that courts consider in deciding whether to award alimony, how much to award, and how long to award it.[40] Generally, however, courts will consider at least some of the following factors: the financial resources of the person requesting alimony; the time necessary for that person to acquire education or training for employment; the standard of living during the marriage; the length of the marriage; the age, physical fitness, and emotional condition of the person requesting support; and the ability of the other partner to meet his or her own needs and still contribute to the former spouse's support. Other considerations may include earning capacity of each spouse, whether children live in the home, the contributions of the spouse seeking support to the other spouse's education or career, and any premarital agreements.

Finally, many states continue to use the fault principle in determining alimony awards, despite the widespread adoption of "no-fault" grounds for divorce. While marital fault has been explicitly excluded as a factor in awarding alimony in at least twenty states, it is a bar to alimony in a minority of states.[41]

**How can an alimony award be enforced?**

An unpaid alimony award can be enforced through legal action. Courts have a number of remedies available to them to force payment of alimony. For instance, the court can order that the alimony payments be automatically deducted from the paying spouse's salary. If the court finds the nonpaying spouse in contempt of court, it can place that spouse in jail or impose a fine.[42] To enforce an alimony award, a woman may consult an attorney. If she is also owed child support payments by her ex-spouse, a woman may also be able to use the services of the state or local child support enforcement agency. (See below for more information on child support enforcement.)

## CHILD SUPPORT

**What is child support?**

Children are entitled to financial support from both parents. Regardless of income, any parent or guardian who is caring full-time for a child in his or her custody is eligible to apply for and receive child support from a non-custodial parent.[43] The noncustodial parent is obligated to pay regular child support payments to help care for the child. This is true even if the parent with custody is working or receiving public assistance.

Unpaid child support remains an urgent national problem. The federal government has passed a number of laws designed to address the issue, including the Federal Child Support Enforcement Amendments of 1984,[44] the Family Support Act of 1988,[45] and the Child Support Recovery Act of 1992.[46] Finally, the Personal Responsibility and Work Opportunity Reconciliation Act (PRWORA) of 1996,[47] which focused on welfare reform, included numerous provisions to improve child support collection in hopes of alleviating some of the economic cost of providing benefits for poor children. "Study after study has documented . . . dramatic declines in children's standards of living after their parents separate,"[48] and the most recent census data show that fewer than 45 percent of custodial parents owed child support payments received the full amount they were due.[49]

**Do child support laws apply to children born to unmarried parents?**

Yes. Parents are obligated to support their children, regardless of whether they were ever married. Thus, for example, federal law explicitly requires child support enforcement agencies to provide services to establish paternity and assist in the collection of child support for all children. In addition, federal law requires all states to have procedures to permit the establishment of paternity at any time prior to a child's eighteenth birthday in order to facilitate collection and enforcement. (See below for more information on paternity establishment.)

**What should be provided for in a child support award?**

The basic child support award, established according to a formula set out in law, is theoretically considered to be sufficient to cover the essentials of childrearing, such as food, clothing, and shelter. Where economically feasible and appropriate, child support awards can also include provisions for continued health insurance coverage, medical support when there are high medical expenses not covered by insurance, the cost of long distance calls and travel, costs of higher education, and other extras.

**What guidelines have been established to determine the proper amounts of child support?**

The federal Child Support Enforcement Amendments of 1984 mandated that all states set guidelines for support orders, and all states have now done so. The 1988 Family Support Act requires states to follow the support guidelines in all cases, except when a court explicitly finds that applying the guidelines would be unjust or inappropriate. Within the parameters set by federal law, all states have developed their own child support legislation.

**Can child support be increased to compensate for increased cost of living?**

Yes. The Family Support Act requires periodic review and adjustment of individual support awards. In addition, a separation agreement or court order can provide for both an automatic cost-of-living adjustment and increased payments as children grow older and have higher expenses. If an agreement or order does not cover this, it is often possible to return to court to ask for higher payments to keep up with inflation or increased expenses.

**What are the options for enforcing child support orders?**

Federal law requires that all states have a system developed for automatic wage withholding for all child support awards in order to minimize costs and delays in collecting such awards. Withholding is probably the most effective and easiest enforcement technique because child support is simply deducted from a noncustodial parent's paycheck. Unfortunately, it is of limited use if the person required to pay is unemployed, self-employed, or paid under the table.

With an attorney's help, a woman can also bring an enforcement action against the noncustodial parent, but this may be very costly. She can also go to her local or state child support enforcement agency (sometimes referred to as support collection units or IV-D agencies). They are usually part of a social services department, family court, probation office, or the state attorney general's office. These agencies are publicly funded and serve all clients wishing to use their services, even if the individuals do not receive any public assistance.

The Family Support Act established specific time limits that apply to child support enforcement agencies in taking applications for assistance, locating the paying parent, establishing paternity, and obtaining and enforcing support orders, so that there is some hope that the back payments will be recovered relatively quickly. Remedies that these agencies use to collect delinquent child support payments include imposing liens, intercepting tax refunds, and reporting the past due unpaid child support to credit bureaus. If the noncustodial parent is also behind in alimony payments, the agency can collect those in addition to the child support award.

**What can a woman do if the nonpaying parent lives out of state?**

The usual difficulties of collecting child support are exacerbated when the noncustodial parent lives out of state. All states have enacted the Uniform Interstate Family Support Act (UIFSA),[50] which makes it easier for a custodial parent or child support collection agency to collect past due payments from an out-of-state parent.[51] UIFSA not only applies to child support orders from different states but also requires states to recognize and enforce child support orders from outside the United States. It makes clear that the court in the state where the custodial parent and child reside can hold a hearing regarding child support and can issue orders against the out-of-state parent, eliminating the need for two or more courts to become involved in simply hearing a case. UIFSA also facilitates the out-of-state parent's participation in the proceeding by authorizing him or her and out-of-state witnesses to testify or be deposed by telephone or videoconference and by allowing the out-of-state parent to submit documents to the court by fax. Once a support order is issued, UIFSA states that the custodial parent can bypass the courts and child support collection agencies in the other state and mail a withholding order[52] directly to the nonpaying parent's employer, thus triggering wage withholding without the necessity of a hearing. In the alternative, the child support order can be registered and enforced by the courts or child support enforcement agency in the second state, without modification. With UIFSA and the myriad enforcement remedies that already exist, custodial parents have a greater chance of receiving back payments on child support orders, even when the noncustodial parent lives out of state.

Again, however, when enforcing interstate child support orders it is often helpful to consult with an attorney and/or child support enforcement agency. In spite of the many attempts to simplify and streamline the process, the laws and mechanisms of enforcement can often be very technical and somewhat confusing.

## Paternity Establishment and Disestablishment

### What is paternity?

Paternity is legal fatherhood. For unmarried women, establishing the paternity of their children can often be the key to securing child support and other benefits, emotional and financial, for the child. For unmarried fathers, paternity establishment creates a right to petition for custody and visitation of the child and provides a legal basis for building a father-child relationship, while legally obligating the father, regardless of involvement, to financially support that child.

Recently, because of the availability of genetic testing, it has become more common for a father to challenge his paternity after it has been established. Paternity disestablishment severs any legal parental obligation a man once thought to be the father might have to the child, and in some cases may subject a mother to criminal or civil actions due to fraud. Though federal law provides guidelines for states to establish paternity, it is relatively silent regarding disestablishment. In the face of a challenge to paternity, some states provide little or no guidance at all, while other states have detailed procedures in place.[53]

### How is a child's paternity established?

Every state has different rules for the establishment of paternity, but there are several common approaches.[54] All states presume that when a child is born to a married couple, the husband is the father of the child.[55] When a child is born to unmarried parents, the child's paternity can be established through the father's voluntary acknowledgment of paternity or through a paternity suit, both of which may include genetic testing. Finally, a man's behavior toward a child can create a legal presumption that he is the father.[56] In some states, paternity is established when a man lives with the child, usually before a certain age and/or for a specified period of time, and openly holds the child out as his natural child.[57] Unless this presumption is challenged, the man will be considered the child's legal father.

### Why establish paternity?

Certain benefits and entitlements flow directly from a legal determination that a man is a child's father. A child's paternity must be established before a court can order a father to pay child support. That child also gains inheritance rights if the father dies without a will, as well as access to Social

Security survivors' benefits upon the father's death or disability, veteran's benefits, workers' compensation, and health insurance, if the father is eligible for such benefits.

A father *may* also gain rights to visitation and custody if paternity is established, though both are subject to court determinations of what is in the best interests of the child.

### How does a voluntary paternity acknowledgment work?

The easiest way to legally establish the paternity of a child born to unmarried parents is for the parents to sign an acknowledgment stating the father's identity. Hospitals and state birth record agencies offer this service. By federal law, parties to a voluntary acknowledgment have sixty days after signing to withdraw their consent. After sixty days, the voluntary acknowledgment conclusively establishes that the man named is the father of the child, and this can only be changed by court order.[58]

### What is a paternity suit?

A paternity suit is a court proceeding to determine whether a particular man is the father of a child. The mother, the alleged father, or a state agency, such as a child support agency, can bring a paternity suit while the child is a minor and present evidence of that man's paternity. If any party requests DNA tests, a court must order genetic testing.

If the genetic test or other evidence demonstrates that the man is the father, the court will issue an order of paternity. A court may also issue a judgment establishing paternity when an alleged father fails to appear in court after being properly notified of the suit, with or without a DNA test.[59]

### How does one challenge paternity?

The process for paternity disestablishment varies by state. In the case of voluntary paternity acknowledgment, the father or mother must go to court and prove that the acknowledgment was based on fraud (e.g., the mother lied to the alleged father about his parenthood), duress (e.g., the mother was threatened with violence if she did not identify the man as the father), or mistake (e.g., the alleged father honestly, but incorrectly, believed that he was the father when he signed the acknowledgment).[60] Usually if a man acknowledged paternity knowing that he was not the biological father, he will not be able to contest the acknowledgment.

Most states have created procedures for challenging paternity that have been established by court order. New evidence, usually DNA test results, will sometimes show that the legally recognized father is not the biological father.[61] However, again there is a great variety in state law and because there is no coherent national framework to address this issue, those wishing to bring a case disestablishing paternity or to defend against such a case should consult a lawyer.

## Custody, Visitation, and Guardianship

### What is custody?

Child custody refers to the parental rights, privileges, duties, and powers associated with child rearing.[62] These rights include the right to direct a child's activities and education; the right to make decisions regarding the child's care, health, and religion; and the obligation to care for, shelter, and clothe the child.[63] More generally, custody of a child means that the parent or individual raises the child, lives with him or her, and has the authority to make everyday decisions about the child's well-being and upbringing.

No standard terminology exists that precisely describes all the possible custody arrangements. Therefore, each custody determination may have unique characteristics, and ideally will lead to an arrangement that is in the best interests of the child concerned.

### Who decides where the children will live and who will care for them?

Usually, the parents decide. If the parents cannot agree, then a judge decides. In most cases, couples work out their custody arrangements by agreement. Sometimes, a mediator or an attorney helps parents reach an agreement.

Custody litigation can occur if the parents are unmarried or if they are in the middle of divorce. In either case, the judge hearing the case will issue custody orders that take into account the best interests of the child. If the parents come to an agreement on their own or through mediation, a court technically retains the power to review the arrangement to make sure that it is in the child's best interests. However a court will commonly accept such agreements.[64]

### What types of custody arrangements are permissible?

**Joint custody** is an arrangement in which the parents generally share legal rights and responsibilities as well as, to varying degrees, the physical custody and control of the child, depending on the terms of a parenting or custodial agreement or a court order. Joint custody is also known as shared custody, shared parenting, cocustody, coparenting, concurrent custody, divided custody, and joint managing conservatorship.[65]

**Sole custody** grants nearly absolute custody and control of the child to one parent (or another individual), except for visitation rights that may be granted to the noncustodial parent.[66]

In recent decades, joint custody has become increasingly common. Theoretically, joint custody means that the children spend approximately equal amounts of time in the care of each parent, though in practice it may be little different than sole custody, except when it comes to making major decisions. In several states, joint or split custody can be done only by agreement of the parties; in many other states it cannot be done at all. In still other states there is a legal presumption in favor of joint custody.

It is not clear whether it is generally better for children to have a single, continuous primary caretaker who makes the final decisions on important questions such as medical treatment and schools, or whether it is more important for children to have equal access to and nurturing from both parents. Therefore, custody orders should be designed to fit the specific needs of each family and each child, with a focus on the child's best interests.

### Are unmarried mothers guaranteed custody of their children?

No. Although in the absence of court involvement, unmarried mothers will often in practice exercise custody without a court order, unmarried mothers and fathers whose paternity has been established have equal rights to custody of their children. To legally establish custody, a single mother can go to court for a custody order. However, going to court requires naming the father in the court papers and notifying him of the case, which could cause him to ask for visitation rights or custody, something he may not have considered previously.

### Does a woman need a court order for temporary custody before the actual divorce if her husband agrees to leave the children with her?

Until there is a court order, both parents are equally entitled to custody of their children. Therefore, without that order it is perfectly legal for one parent to take the children even if he or she has an understanding or signed a written agreement to leave them with the other parent. The police will not intervene in this case, and the parent who has lost the children will have to start a separate court process from the beginning to regain custody.

If, during a divorce, there is the slightest suspicion that one's spouse may take the children, no matter how amicable the relationship, it is always best to obtain a temporary custody order while a divorce is pending. This may be critical if there has been a threat to take the children out of the state or country.

### What factors do courts take into account in custody determinations?

In all jurisdictions, courts determine which parent will be awarded custody by a standard known as the "best interests of the child."[67] The factors that contribute to a judge's determination of a child's best interests include, but are not limited to, the age, gender, and mental and physical health of the child and parents; the parents' lifestyles; emotional ties between parent and child; the parents' financial status; the child's established living pattern; the quality of the child's schools; the child's preference (taking this factor into account may be mandatory, depending on the age of the child and the state); and the parents' ability and willingness to communicate with the child and with each other.[68]

The primary caretaker, the parent upon whom the child has relied to satisfy his or her basic physical and psychological needs, usually has a significant advantage in gaining custody,[69] but there is no guarantee that a primary caretaker will be awarded custody. However, the noncustodial parent will almost always have the right to reasonable visitation and contact with his or her children, unless the court finds that such contact is contrary to the child's best interests (such as cases in which there has been serious abuse, etc.).

### Can final orders of custody be changed?

Yes, but only in certain circumstances or on the agreement of the parents. Generally, either parent can petition the court and ask for an order of custody to be modified if there has been a significant or substantial change in circumstances.[70] What constitutes such a change in circumstances varies by state. But if a court finds that a given change is significant, it can then reevaluate a custody decision in light of the change and, as always, determine what arrangement would be in the best interests of the child.[71]

### Can a court restrict a custodial parent's right to move?

Yes. Most states will allow noncustodial parents to go to court and contest a decision by the custodial parent to move to another state with the child. Such proceedings address the ability of a custodial parent to move with the minor children to a different state, away from the noncustodial parent. Some states explicitly limit the right of a parent to relocate,[72] but usually the issue must be litigated if the parents cannot come to some agreement outside of court. Each state and each court views relocations differently, with some favoring relocation and continued care with the custodial parent and others viewing such moves negatively because of the effect on the children's relationship with the noncustodial parent.[73]

### Does the noncustodial parent have rights to information about his or her child?

Generally, yes. Even if there is no formal agreement or court order, noncustodial parents in many jurisdictions have the right to access their children's medical and educational records. A custody agreement or order may expand this right and require each parent to provide certain types of information to the other, such as immediate notification in case the child is injured, hospitalized, or incarcerated and notification of any changes of address or of any trips planned for the child.[74]

### Do grandparents have any rights to visitation with their grandchildren?

Every state has now passed legislation that gives grandparents the right to ask a court to grant them visitation of their grandchildren in certain circumstances, for example, if the child's parents have divorced or one parent has died.[75] In *Troxel v. Granville*, however, the U.S. Supreme Court reaffirmed that parents have a fundamental constitutional right to raise their children as they see fit and therefore, in considering whether to grant visitation rights to grandparents, a court must give heavy weight to a parent's preferences.[76] Because of this decision, the parent's wishes will usually trump any grandparent objections to or wishes regarding visitation, especially when the parents have not completely denied all visitation to the grandparents but have simply provided less time than the grandparents want.

### Have courts upheld the rights of lesbian women and bisexual, transgender, and transsexual people to be granted custody of their children after a divorce?

The law is mixed. As of this writing, six states allow, but do not require, denial of custody based solely on a parent's sexual orientation.[77] In recent years there has been a growing focus on the bond between a child and his or her parent, regardless of sexual orientation or gender identity,[78] though some courts and judges still discriminate against lesbian, gay, bisexual, transgender, and transsexual parents in custody disputes. However, all custody decisions are decided on a case-by-case basis according to the court's determination of the child's best interests, and it is impossible to predict how each judge will make a custody determination. Many jurisdictions will not consider sexual orientation or gender identity as a factor in a custody evaluation, unless it is shown to adversely affect the child; a few states have caselaw or statutes declaring that sexual orientation in custody determinations is irrelevant.[79] As a practical matter, however, lesbian and gay parents—even in those states —may be denied custody or visitation. Judges may be directed by their own or community prejudices when considering the best interests of the child, and may find reasons other than the parent's sexual orientation or gender identity to deny custody or visitation.

A divorced lesbian, bisexual, transgender, or transsexual parent whose custody rights are challenged should obtain the help of a sympathetic lawyer.

### Can a same-sex partner obtain custody or visitation rights with respect to a biological child of her partner that she has helped to raise?

Again, the law on this is very mixed and continues to develop. If that coparent has been able to adopt the child, and is in a jurisdiction where that adoption is honored, he or she should have the same rights and obligations as any other legal parent to custody and visitation. In those states recognizing civil unions and same-sex marriages, the law regarding custody and visitation rights for same-sex couples should follow that of the law applying to heterosexual couples. However, where the coparent has been unable to adopt the child and the child already has a second legal parent, it is unlikely that courts will even grant that partner the opportunity to request visitation and/or custody. For purposes of the law, she is technically a legal stranger. On the other hand, some courts have been willing to permit an award of custody or visitation rights to the nonbiological parent. These courts may use concepts of "*de facto* parent" or "psychological parent" to describe the relationship between the child and the coparent and find that a continued relationship of some sort is in the child's best interests.[80]

Finally, in situations where there is only one legal parent, documents, such as coparenting agreements, custody agreements, and visitation agreements, etc., can be drafted to try to protect the relationship between the partner and the child. However, there is no guarantee that the courts will enforce such private arrangements.

**What is guardianship?**

Legal guardianship is similar to legal custody. It establishes a legal relationship between a child and adult. The guardian will be expected to meet the child's basic needs, care for the child, and make decisions about the child's life, health, education, etc. The most important aspect of guardianship is that it does not completely sever the legal relationship between the biological parents and the child. There are many different variations on guardianship, depending on each state's law, but in general, "guardianships can be used to appoint a legal representative for a child, as an alternative to adoption or as a temporary means of caring for a child when a parent is unable to do so."[81]

**How can parents provide a guardian for their children in case of an emergency?**

Parents can provide a guardian for their children in case of an emergency by executing a testamentary guardianship or by nominating a stand-by or temporary guardian. A "testamentary guardianship" exists where parents designate an adult guardian for their children in case of death. In order to establish a guardianship, a living parent must name a guardian in writing and usually have that document witnessed pursuant to state law.[82] In this document, the parents should set out specific instructions on what should happen with the child in the event of a tragedy.

Many states either allow parents to appoint a stand-by guardian or have enacted a provision for limited, emergency, or temporary guardianships.[83] A stand-by guardian is a person other than a minor child's natural parent who cares for the child when that parent is ill or seriously injured.[84] Designations of stand-by guardians must be in writing and usually must be witnessed; however, a stand-by guardianship is probably not valid if the minor has another living parent whose whereabouts are known and who is willing and able to care for the child.[85]

## ADOPTION

**How are children placed for adoption?**

Adoption is the legal process by which a parent-child relationship is formed between a child and an adult who is not the child's biological parent.[86] A child can be adopted either after his or her biological parents have died, after the biological parents have relinquished their parental rights, or after those rights have been involuntarily terminated by a court.

A child may be placed for adoption in several ways. The most recent national statistics show that approximately 40 percent of all adoptions involve children who were placed by a government agency through foster care. Another 15 percent were international adoptions usually arranged through a private agency. Other children were adopted by a relative, usually a stepparent, or were placed for adoption either by privately run, state-licensed adoption agencies or through private-placement adoptions, where the birth parent selects the adoptive parent with or without the assistance of an intermediary.[87]

**Who must consent to the adoption?**

Parents have a fundamental constitutional right to raise their children and guide their upbringing.[88] In light of this, if the child's biological parents are alive, the child cannot be adopted unless those parents have consented to the adoption or unless a court has terminated parental rights.[89] If the child was born to married parents, the consent of both the mother and the father is required, even if the parents have since separated or divorced.[90] When the child is born to unmarried parents, the consent of the mother is required. State law determines when the father's consent will be required. In general, when a father has had a "substantial relationship" with the child, as determined by considering factors such as the degree of the father's commitment, the formal acknowledgement of paternity, financial support (including offers of support regardless of whether they were accepted), attempts to bond with the child, and evidence of neglect or abuse, the law will require the father's consent to adoption. Otherwise he may very well have little or no say in whether or not the child is adopted.[91]

**May a minor consent to the adoption of his or her child?**

Yes. In most states, the fact that either or both birth parents are minors does not affect their ability to consent to their child's adoption. However, eight states and territories require the additional approval of an unmarried minor's parent or legal guardian.[92]

**Does an unmarried father have the right to be notified that adoption proceedings are pending?**

Generally yes, but it depends on the state. In most states, an unmarried biological father, or putative father, has the right to formal notice and hearing if an adoption of his child is pending.[93] However, the Supreme Court, while affirming that the relationship between an unwed father and his child deserves some protection under the Constitution, has held that this protection only extends to those fathers who have demonstrated a commitment to parenting the child or who have developed a "substantial relationship" with the child.[94] Most states have enacted laws that require notice to a father who is known by the mother, has acknowledged the child, or, where applicable, has registered in the state's putative father registry (a list that an alleged father of a child born outside marriage can sign stating that he is or may be the father of that child).

## Do grandparents have the right to be notified when their grandchild is put up for adoption?

In most cases, grandparents do not have the right to be notified of a child's adoption unless they are his or her legal guardians.[95] However, as mentioned previously, in some states and territories, if a parent consenting to the adoption is a minor, grandparents may also have to consent to the adoption.

## What qualifications must prospective parents have in order to adopt a child?

Any adult determined to be a fit parent can adopt a child who has been freed for adoption. However, each state uses different factors and regulations to determine parental fitness, and private agencies may be even more selective than required by statute.[96] Most agencies will require certain documentation from prospective parents, such as a marriage license (where applicable), birth certificates, medical reports, criminal checks and child abuse clearances, and character references. Applicants must often be interviewed and participate in a homestudy, which is a series of meetings with a social worker who assesses the prospective home and family.

## Can single people adopt?

Yes, single adults can adopt in all states, provided they are deemed fit parents. However, some agencies strongly prefer married couples to unmarried persons as adoptive parents, and may be reluctant to deem a single person a fit parent. Finally, one state, Utah, prohibits adoption by anyone "cohabiting with someone outside of a valid legal marriage,"[97] so an unmarried woman living with someone, male or female, in a committed romantic relationship will not be able to adopt in that state.

## Can gay men and lesbians adopt?

Yes, but not everywhere. As mentioned above, in most states, an unmarried adult, regardless of sexual orientation, may adopt a child as a single parent, provided he or she is deemed fit. However, at the time of this writing, Florida has a statute banning gay and lesbian persons from adopting under any circumstances.[98] Mississippi explicitly prohibits same-sex couples from adopting,[99] and Utah forbids adoption by anyone cohabiting outside of a valid legal marriage, which has the effect of barring gay and lesbian couples or individuals living with their partners from adopting. Oklahoma will not recognize any adoption by more than one person of the same sex, even if that adoption is valid in a different state.[100] Additionally, while most states do not have explicit bans, gays and lesbians may face problems at the local level, where most adoption decisions are made,[101] and to date there is no clear constitutional prohibition on an agency or court taking into account sexual orientation when determining whether adoption by a particular individual or couple is in the child's best interests.

Whether gay and lesbian couples can adopt a child together varies from state to state. Four states—California, Massachusetts, New Jersey, and Vermont—and the District of Columbia explicitly permit joint adoption by gay and lesbian couples,[102] and in a few states that do not have a statute or court decision explicitly addressing the issue, joint adoption by gay couples is routine.[103] In other places, a person will adopt a child individually and then his or her partner will ask the court to allow him or her to also adopt the child through a second adoption proceeding, generally known as "second-parent adoption." It is important to note, however, that outcomes in adoption cases are very case specific. Where some state courts will regularly recognize second-parent and joint adoptions, others will routinely deny them. Still others make such individualized determinations regarding families that it is even more difficult to ascertain any patterns.

## What is second-parent adoption?

Second-parent or coparent adoption is the process by which a gay or lesbian individual can adopt his or her partner's biological (or adopted) child. Traditionally, a "stepparent exception" has existed in adoption statutes, so that upon marriage a man or woman could adopt his or her spouse's child without terminating the spouse's parental rights. Provided all required consents are in place, particularly that of the noncustodial parent if needed, the process for stepparent adoptions is fairly straightforward in most states.[104]

However, for gay and lesbian couples, who cannot marry, such adoptions remain a newer development and are still the subject of controversy. Courts are split as to whether the stepparent exception applies to unmarried same-sex couples, although the number of states that have permitted this kind of adoption has been growing in recent years. As of this writing, nine states—California, Connecticut, Illinois, Indiana, Massachusetts, New Jersey, New York, Pennsylvania, and Vermont—and the District of Columbia have either caselaw or statutes expressly permitting second-parent adoption regardless of sexual orientation.[105] Trial courts in at least fifteen other states have granted second-parent adoptions on a case-by-case basis by determining that such an adoption is in the child's best interests.[106] However, as mentioned above, adoption by gay men and lesbians is restricted or barred in some places, and two states—Mississippi and Oklahoma—currently will not recognize adoptions by same-sex couples. Four states have higher court decisions holding that second-parent adoptions are not permissible under their adoption statutes.[107]

Most advocates agree that the benefits for a child of having two legal parents are significant. A child with two legal parents has two sources of support and inheritance rights. Furthermore, second-parent adoption is the only way to protect the parent-child relationship in the event of separation or incapacity of the legal parent. Continued advocacy is necessary to ensure that all courts look objectively at the best interests of the child and the importance of the parent-child relationship at issue, without regard to the petitioning parent's sexual orientation.

### What can partners who seek to be jointly recognized as parents do if second-parent adoption or joint adoption is not available to them?

If second-parent adoption is not available, the partners can prepare a written coparenting or custody agreement declaring that they and their child are a family. Coparenting agreements state that both partners consider themselves coparents with shared rights and responsibilities for their child, while custody agreements describe in detail how custody of a child will be established in the event of a separation. The legal parent may also nominate her partner as guardian of the child in her will and/or fill out an authorization for emergency consent allowing the partner to consent for emergency medical treatment for the child. It is important to note, however, that none of these options creates a legally recognized parental relationship and a court will have considerable discretion in choosing whether to enforce them if challenged.

## FOSTER CARE, CHILD ABUSE, AND NEGLECT

**What is foster care?**

Foster care is a government-run system providing care to children who cannot live with their parents, usually because of problems in the family. It includes placements with individual families, in group homes, and in residential treatment centers or institutions.

**Why do children enter foster care?**

Most often, children enter foster care when there are allegations of neglect or abuse in the home or when a child has been abandoned. In these cases a judge usually orders the child to be removed. Sometimes, a parent will ask the state to take the children into foster care temporarily because he or she is temporarily unable to meet the child's needs.

**Are all children who are found to be abused or neglected placed in foster care?**

No. Federal law and state law require state agencies to make "reasonable efforts," except in specified cases where those efforts are excused, to prevent unnecessary foster care placements. These efforts should be designed to keep children at home or to expedite their return home by providing services to their families to address the underlying problems.[108] In theory, but not always in practice, children should only be placed in care if it is the best alternative.

**Is there a difference between child abuse and neglect?**

In theory, abuse is supposed to be more serious than neglect, resulting in more acute injury or harm to the child. However, no two states have laws that define child abuse and child neglect in exactly the same way, and some avoid the issue by referring to "child maltreatment."

Generally, abuse is the infliction of serious physical injury or sexual abuse upon a child by a parent or guardian. State laws sometimes define abuse broadly, so a parent may be found to have abused a child by creating the *risk* of serious harm or injury. Neglect is generally a lapse of care on the part of the parent or the creation of a risk of harm to the child. For example, most states consider the parents' failure to provide their children with adequate food, shelter, clothing, medical care, supervision, or education to be child neglect.[109] However, it is important to note that the line between abuse and neglect is often very hazy in practice. More importantly, the power of the government to intervene is generally the same regardless of the charge.

### What happens when someone has reason to believe a child is being maltreated?

Every state has laws that create a mechanism, usually a central agency, registry, or hotline that takes calls, for people to report suspicions of child abuse and neglect. Anyone can report his or her suspicions of child abuse or neglect; it is up to the agency to determine whether the report is founded. Furthermore, most states also have "mandated reporter" statutes, meaning that certain professionals, such as doctors, nurses, hospital staff, social workers, police officers, welfare workers, and teachers, are required to report any suspicions of child abuse or neglect.[110]

### What happens if a person required to report child abuse or neglect fails to report?

Most state laws provide that a mandated reporter who fails to report suspicions of abuse or neglect may be criminally prosecuted. However, such prosecutions are very rare.[111] Nonetheless, violations of mandatory reporting laws can lead to loss of one's job and, in some states, possible civil liability for negligence, meaning the child can sue that individual for damages if his or her failure to report contributed to an injury of the child.

### Does a parent have a right to a hearing regarding whether his or her child is placed in foster care?

Yes. Even when a parent has agreed to place his or her child in foster care, federal law requires that a hearing be held within 180 days of the placement to determine whether it is in the best interests of the child.[112] When a child has been removed from the home without the parent's consent because the child welfare agency believes the child is in danger, the parent is entitled to a hearing reviewing the agency's emergency removal within a very short time, generally a few days or less.[113] Finally, if there is no emergency, the parent is entitled to a hearing *before* the child is removed from the home. Many state laws (but not federal) entitle parents who cannot afford to hire counsel to a court-appointed lawyer for these hearings.[114]

### Can children be taken from their parents without a hearing?

Yes, but only under certain circumstances and only by certain people. Every state authorizes police officers, doctors, or social-welfare agencies to remove a child from his or her home over parental objection, if that person reasonably believes that the child would die or be seriously injured if not removed.

However, in all states, parents are entitled to a court hearing shortly thereafter to review the necessity of the emergency removal. Furthermore, every effort must be made to locate the parents of a child removed under emergency conditions.[115] The time between removal and the hearing varies from state to state. For example, in New York, the hearing must be held "as soon as practicable" or no later than three days after a parent or child's lawyer files an application for a hearing.[116]

### Can a parent be found to have abused a child even if there is no direct evidence that he or she inflicted the child's injuries?

Yes. Many acts of child abuse occur in the home without any other witnesses. To make it easier to protect children, most states require that the government agency show that a parent abused or neglected a child by a "preponderance of the evidence" or by "clear and convincing evidence," both lower standards than the "beyond a reasonable doubt" standard in criminal cases. In other words, the state must show that more likely than not a parent harmed the child. The burden is on the parent to explain a child's injuries to the court's satisfaction, and if the parent is unable to provide a reasonable, credible explanation, the court can conclude that the parent caused the injuries.

### Can evidence of the maltreatment of one child result in a finding of neglect or abuse of another?

Yes. Evidence of parental neglect or abuse of one child may result in the finding of abuse or neglect of other children in the same household.[117]

### Who decides what happens to a child after he or she is placed in foster care?

Generally, the child welfare agency that has placed the child in foster care is in charge of planning for the child, meaning that it must develop an individualized service plan in consultation with the child, if he or she is old enough, and the child's parents, if they are capable. A caseworker is then assigned to monitor the case and make sure the child's needs are met while in foster care. Foster parents provide the daily care of the child. Federal law requires that a local court or administrative panel periodically review these plans to determine whether placement is still necessary, whether the placements and plans are appropriate and meet the child's needs, and whether the agency has been making efforts to help achieve a stable permanent home for the child.[118]

**Do children in foster care have the right to contact with their biological family members?**

Yes. Parents have the right to reasonable visitation with their children in foster care and children in foster care have the right to visit their parents, unless a showing can be made that such visitation presents a risk to the child's safety and well-being.[119] Of course, reasonable visitation varies depending on the case and the state.

Additionally, children have a right to associate with their brothers and sisters. Therefore, agencies should make every effort to place siblings together, and where that is not possible there should be regular visitation. However, the state does not need to provide a certain number of visits between siblings.[120]

## Termination of Parental Rights

**What is termination of parental rights?**

Termination of parental rights occurs when the state permanently ends a parent's legal relationship with his or her child. In other words, a parent's legal right to make any decisions about his or her child's education, well-being, and upbringing is permanently severed.[121]

**In what situations can a state terminate a person's parental rights?**

A parent's constitutional right to raise his or her children is well established, and the Supreme Court has recognized that there are few situations so grave as to require breaking a parent's bond with his or her children.[122] Therefore, a state cannot deprive a parent of his or her parental right without an individualized determination that he or she is unfit to raise his or her children.[123] This includes a hearing before a judge, where the state must prove its allegations against the parent by clear and convincing evidence.[124]

A common reason for the termination of parental rights is evidence of serious abuse or gross and longstanding neglect of the child. Rights can also be terminated if a parent has abandoned the child, usually meaning that the parent has disappeared for an extended period of time, without reason, and with no efforts to contact or make plans for the child. Finally, according to the federal Adoption and Safe Families Act of 1997 (ASFA), except in certain situations, if a child has been in foster care for fifteen out of the past twenty-two months, a state agency must file a petition to terminate the parental rights of that child's parents.[125] (See chapter 8, "The Criminal Justice System," for more information about ASFA and its effect on parental rights.)

### Do parents have the right to be notified before the state seeks to terminate their rights?

Yes. The constitutional guarantee of due process of law requires that parents be notified before a hearing in which their parental rights might be terminated.[126] Therefore, they have the right to written notice of the hearing that includes the allegations against them, so that they know what they are being accused of and can prepare a defense.

### Do parents have the right to a lawyer at these termination hearings?

There is no constitutional right to a lawyer at these hearings, but most states nevertheless provide court-appointed counsel for parents who cannot afford a lawyer.[127]

## NOTES

1. U.S.C. § 7 (2000).

2. *An Analysis of the Law Regarding Same-Sex Marriage, Civil Unions, and Domestic Partnerships: A White Paper*, 2005 A.B.A. SEC. FAM. L., 9 [hereinafter *White Paper*], *available at* http://www.abanet.org/family/reports/WhitePaper.pdf.

3. Goodridge v. Dep't. of Pub. Health, 798 N.E.2d 941 (Mass. 2003); *In re* Marriage Cases, 43 Cal. 4th 757 (Cal. 2008); Kerrigan v. Comm'r of Pub. Health, No. SC 17716 (Conn. Oct. 28, 2008).

4. VT. STAT. ANN. tit. 15, § 8 (2005) (marriage is the legally recognized union between one man and one woman); *id.* § 1204 (establishing civil unions).

5. Martinez v. County of Monroe, 850 N.Y.S.2d 740, 50 A.D.3d, 189 (App. Div. 2008).

6. U.S. GEN. ACCOUNTING OFFICE, DEFENSE OF MARRIAGE ACT: UPDATE TO PRIOR REPORT 04-353R (Jan. 4, 2004), *available at* http://www.gao.gov/new.items/d04353r.pdf; U.S. GEN. ACCOUNTING OFFICE, DEFENSE OF MARRIAGE ACT, 97-16 (Jan. 31, 1997), *available at* http://www.gao.gov/archive/1997/og97016.pdf; *see also*

Sean Cahill and Samuel Slater, *Marriage: Legal Protections for Families and Children*, NAT'L GAY & LESBIAN TASK FORCE POL'Y INST. (2004), *available at* http://www. soros.org/resources/articles_publications/publications/marriage_20040324/ngltf_marriage_brief.pdf.

7. Same-sex couples can also marry in Canada, Spain, and several other countries outside the United States. *See White Paper, supra* note 2, at 41.

8. *Id.*

9. *Id.*

10. *See, e.g.,* City & County of San Francisco v. State, 27 Cal.Rptr.3d 722 (Cal. Ct. App. 2005); Kerrigan v. Comm'r of Pub. Health, 904 A.2d 137 (Conn. 2006); Deane v. Conaway, 2006 WL 148145 (Md.Cir.Ct. 2006); Lewis v. Harris, 908 A.2d 196 (N.J 2006); Samuels v. N.Y. State Dep't of Health, 850 N.E.2d 24 (N.Y. 2006); Hernandez v. Robles, 855 N.E.2d 1 (N.Y. 2006); Li v. Oregon, 110 P.3d 91 (Or. 2005); Anderson v. King County, 138 P.3d 963 (Wash. 2006). For more information, *see* NAN D. HUNTER, COURTNEY G. JOSLIN, AND SHARON M. McGOWAN, THE RIGHTS OF LESBIANS, GAY MEN, BISEXUALS, AND TRANSGENDER PEOPLE (NYU Press, 4th ed. 2004); *see also* ACLU Get Equal, http://www.aclu.org/getequal/caseprofiles. htm (describing current case profiles); Lambda Legal List of Case Summaries, http://www.lambdalegal.org/cgi-bin/iowa/cases/summary.html; Human Rights Campaign website, http://www.hrc.org.

11. *See generally* John A. Fisher, *Sex Determination for Federal Purposes: Is Transsexual Immigration via Marriage Permissible under the Defense of Marriage Act?*, 10 MICH. J. GENDER & L. 237, 245–56 (2004).

12. *Id.*; *see* M.T. v. J.T., 355 A.2d 204 (N.J. Super. Ct. App. Div. 1976) (holding that a male-to-female postoperative transsexual's marriage to a male was valid).

13. *See* Fisher, *supra* note 11, at 256; *In re* Estate of Gardiner, 42 P.3d 120, 135 (Kan. 2002) (holding that a male-to-female transsexual does not fit the definition of female and is therefore male for marital purposes); Anonymous v. Anonymous, 325 N.Y.S.2d 499, 500 (N.Y. Sup. Ct. 1971) (holding that postmarital male-to-female operation may have changed sex but the client was not a true female); *In re* Ladrach, 513 N.E.2d 828 (Ohio Prob. Ct. 1987) (holding that postoperative male-to-female transsexual was legally male and therefore could not be issued a marriage license to marry another male); Littleton v. Prange, 9 S.W.3d 223, 224 (Tex. App. 1999) (holding that a doctor cannot change the gender of a person, and so a postoperative transsexual is legally the preoperative sex).

14. BLACK'S LAW DICTIONARY 439 (2d ed. 1996); *see also* Facts of Law, Common Law Marriage Facts, http://www.factsoflaw.com/marriage_civil_union/common_law_marriage.htm (last visited Mar. 6, 2007); Alternatives to Marriage Project, Common Law Marriage Fact Sheet, http://www.unmarried.org/common.html (last visited Mar. 6, 2007).

15. These states are Alabama, Colorado, Iowa, Kansas, Montana, Oklahoma,

Rhode Island, South Carolina, Texas, and Utah. New Hampshire recognizes common law marriages entered into in their state for inheritance purposes only. Five additional states only recognize common law marriages if they were entered into before specified dates—Georgia (before 1/1/1997), Idaho (1/1/1996), Indiana (1/1/1958), Ohio (10/10/1991), and Pennsylvania (9/2003)—because statutes abolishing common law marriage were only enacted recently. *See also* Legal Information Institute, http://www.law.cornell.edu/topics/Table_Marriage.htm (last visited Mar. 6, 2007) (providing a detailed table of states' recognition of common law marriage).

16. *White Paper, supra* note 2, at 23–32.

17. Vt. Stat. Ann. tit. 15, § 1204; S.B. No. 963, Gen. Assem., Reg. Sess. (Conn. 2005).

18. *White Paper, supra* note 2, at 9.

19. For more detailed information summarizing state benefits and law regarding same-sex couples in each state, *see White Paper, supra* note 2, at 23–32.

20. Assembly Bill 205 of 2003(Ch. 421, Cal. Stats. of 2003); *White Paper, supra* note 2, at 24–25.

21. Haw. Rev. Stat. § 572C-1 *et seq.*; *White Paper, supra* note 2, at 25–26.

22. *White Paper, supra* note 2, at 27, 30.

23. Human Rights Campaign Found., Domestic Partner Health Benefits, http://www.hrc.org/Template.cfm?Section=The_Issues&Template=/TaggedPage/TaggedPageDisplay.cfm&TPLID=26&ContentID=31366 (last visited Mar. 6, 2007) [hereinafter Domestic Partner Health Benefits].

24. Human Rights Campaign Found., The State of the Family: Laws & Legislation Affecting Gay, Lesbian, Bisexual & Transgender Families (2002), http://www.hrc.org/documents/SoTF.pdf; *see also* Domestic Partner Health Benefits, *supra* note 23.

25. California's law of intestate succession changed on July 1, 2003. Under the new law, if a domestic partner dies without a will, trust, or estate plan, the surviving domestic partner will inherit the deceased partner's separate property in the same manner as a surviving spouse. CAL. FAM. CODE § 297.5(c) (2003). The state of New Hampshire recognizes civil unions for purposes of inheritance only.

26. *See, e.g.,* Van Dyck v. Van Dyck, 425 S.E.2d 853, 855 (Ga. 1993); Nat'l Coalition on Lesbian Rights, *available at* http://www.nclrights.org/projects/insuring relationships.htm.

27. Katherine C. Gordon, *The Necessity and Enforcement of Cohabitation Agreements: When Strings Will Attach and How to Prevent Them—A State Survey,* 37 BRANDEIS L.J. 245, 253 (1998).

28. Grounds for annulment can include bigamy; that one party was under the age of consent at the time of the marriage; that one party had an incurable physical incapacity at the time of marriage that would prevent the couple from having sexual relations; or that one party had a severe mental incapacity at the time of the

marriage that prevented him or her from understanding the nature of the marriage relationship.

29. Vermont Civil Union FAQs, http://www.vermontcivilunion.com/union/faq. html (last visited Mar. 6, 2007); Love Makes a Family of Connecticut, http://www. lmfct.org/splashpage.html (last visited Mar. 6, 2007).

30. Barbara Stark, *Divorce Law, Feminism, and Psychoanalysis: In Dreams Begin Responsibilities*, 38 UCLA L. REV. 1483, 1439 (1991).

31. *See generally* A.B.A. FAM. L.Q., Family Law in the Fifty States, http://www. abanet.org/family/flq/tables.html (last visited Mar. 6, 2007).

32. Alana Dunnigan, Comment, *Restoring Power to the Powerless: The Need to Reform California's Mandatory Mediation for Victims of Domestic Violence*, 37 U.S.F.L. REV. 1031, 1064 n.3 (2003) ("California is one of only eleven states that mandate mediation. *See* CAL. FAM. CODE § 3170 (West 1994 & Supp. 2002); DEL. CODE ANN. tit. 13, § 711A (1999); DEL. FAM. CT. C.P.R. 16; FLA. STAT. ANN. § 44.102 (West 1998); HAW. REV. STAT. § 580-41.5 (Supp. 2001); HAW. FAM. CT. R. 94(a); IDAHO CIV. P.R. 16(j); KY. CT. R. 1 & 509; ME. REV. STAT. ANN. tit. 19-A § 25 (1998); NEV. REV. STAT. ANN. § 3.475 (1998); N.C. GEN. STAT. § 50-13.1(b)–(c) (2001); OKLA. STAT. tit. 43, § 107.3 (2001); S.D. CODIFIED LAWS § 25-4-56 (1999); W. VA. CODE ANN. § 48-9- 202(3)(b) (West 2001).").

33. *See supra* note 32 and accompanying text.

34. In Alaska, spouses can sign an agreement designating certain assets as community property.

35. Traditionally, in those states, property had been classified according to who had purchased it or whose name it was in. This distinction led to vast inequalities as men were much more likely than women to acquire and hold title to property. As a result, advocates helped create the distinct concepts of separate and marital property, which led, in turn, to the application of equitable principles in dividing that property.

36. Of course, the rules surrounding equitable distribution do not take into account judicial biases. Thus, a judge may take into account his or her personal interpretations of marital fault under the guise of equity and fairness when making a ruling regarding property division.

37. Brenda L. Storey, *Surveying the Alimony Landscape: Origin, Evolution, and Extinction*, 25 FAM. ADVOC. 10 (2003); *See also* MARTIN GUGGENHEIM ET AL., THE RIGHTS OF FAMILIES: THE BASIC ACLU GUIDE TO THE RIGHTS OF TODAY'S FAMILY MEMBERS 72 (S. Ill. Univ. Press 1996); AMERICAN BAR ASSOCIATION LEGAL GUIDES, *Alimony/Maintenance*, A.B.A. GUIDE TO FAMILY LAW ch. 10, http://www.abanet.org/ publiced/practical/books/family/home.html (last visited Mar. 6, 2007) [hereinafter *Alimony/Maintenance*].

38. *Alimony/Maintenance, supra* note 37, at 4–6.

39. Orr v. Orr, 440 U.S. 268 (1979).

40. Storey, *supra* note 37, at 11–13; *Alimony/Maintenance, supra* note 37.

41. *Alimony/Maintenance, supra* note 37; *see, e.g.,* DEL. CODE ANN. tit. 13, § 1512(c) (2005); 750 ILL. COMP. STAT. ANN. 5/503(d) (West 2005); MINN. STAT. § 518.58 (2005); VA. CODE ANN. § 20-107.1(B) (2006) (Evidence of marital fault is a bar to permanent alimony "unless the court determines from clear and convincing evidence, that a denial of support and maintenance would constitute a manifest injustice, based upon the respective decrees of fault during the marriage and relative economic circumstances of the parties."); GA. CODE ANN. § 19-6-1(b) (2006) (A party shall not be entitled to alimony if it is established by a preponderance of the evidence that the separation between the parties was caused by that party's adultery or desertion.).

42. Other remedies available to courts include garnishment, attachment, and liens. Garnishment is the process by which property or money owed to the nonpaying spouse by someone else is paid or transferred to the dependent spouse. Attachment is the act of seizing property to secure or satisfy a debt, usually authorized by court order. A lien is a claim on property so that when a property is sold or transferred the person to whom support is owed is reimbursed from the proceeds of the sale.

43. *See* BASIC FACTS ON CHILD SUPPORT 2005, CHILDREN'S DEFENSE FUND (2005).

44. Pub. L. No. 98-378, 98 Stat. 1305 (1984).

45. Pub. L. No. 100-485, 102 Stat. 2343 (1988).

46. Pub. L. No. 102-521, 106 Stat. 9403 (1992) (codified as amended at 18 U.S.C. § 228 (2005)).

47. Pub. L. No. 104-193, 110 Stat. 2105 (codified as amended in various sections of 42 U.S.C.).

48. GUGGENHEIM ET AL., *supra* note 37, at 31.

49. U.S. CENSUS BUREAU, U.S. DEP'T. OF COM., CURRENT POPULATION REPORTS: CUSTODIAL MOTHERS AND FATHERS AND THEIR CHILD SUPPORT: 2001 (October 2003), http://www.census.gov/prod/2003pubs/p60-225.pdf (last visited Mar. 12, 2007).

50. John J. Sampson and Barry J. Brooks, *Uniform Interstate Family Support Act (2001) with Prefatory Note and Comments with Still More Unofficial Annotations),* 36 FAM. L.Q. 329 (2002).

51. As part of welfare reform, the 1996 PRWORA mandated that all state enact UIFSA, with amendments, by January 1, 1998, as a condition of state eligibility for the federal funding of child support enforcement. 42 U.S.C.A. § 666(f).

52. Wage withholding, as mentioned above, occurs when the child support payment is deducted directly from the noncustodial parent's salary.

53. *See* Paula Roberts, *Truth and Consequences: Part 1—Disestablishing the Paternity on Non-Marital Children,* 37 FAM. L.Q. 35 (2003).

54. *See* 42 U.S.C. § 666(a)(5) (Supp. IV 1982). Federal law makes federal child support enforcement funding contingent on states adopting paternity-establishment procedures consistent with the requirements set out in this provision, and all states have done so. Roberts, *supra* note 53, at 1–2.

55. *See generally* Niccol D. Kording, *Little White Lies That Destroy Children's Lives: Recreating Paternity Fraud Laws to Protect Children's Interests*, 6 J.L. & FAM. STUD. 237, 239–49 (2004) (outlining how paternity determinations are made throughout the United States). *See also* Roberts, *supra* note 53 (listing states with marital presumption of paternity).

56. Kording, *supra* note 55, at 244.

57. In some states, the requirement for cohabitation has been lifted, such that the main consideration for the presumption of paternity based on a father's conduct is the parent-child relationship. *See, e.g.,* ALA. CODE § 26-17-5(a) (2005); PA. CONS. STAT. ANN. § 5102(b)(2) (West 2005).

58. 42 U.S.C. § 666(a)(5)(C) (federal guidelines for establishment of paternity via voluntary acknowledgment of paternity).

59. 42 U.S.C. § 666(a)(5) (2000).

60. *Id.* § 666(a)(5)(D)(iii).

61. Roberts, *supra* note 53, at 11–12.

62. 3–32 LINDA HENRY ELROD ET AL., FAMILY LAW AND PRACTICE § 32.01 (Matthew Bender 2004) [hereinafter FAMILY LAW AND PRACTICE].

63. *Id.*

64. GUGGENHEIM ET AL., *supra* note 37, at 4.

65. FAMILY LAW AND PRACTICE, *supra* note 62, at § 32.08 (1).

66. Sole custody is also known as sole managing conservatorship, with the visitation rights of the other parent referred to as possessory conservatorship. *Id.*

67. FAMILY LAW AND PRACTICE, *supra* note 62, at § 32.06 (1).

68. Joan B. Kelly, *The Determination of Child Custody, in* 4(1) THE FUTURE OF CHILDREN 121, 128–31 (Spring 1994), *available at* http://www.futureofchildren.org/usr_doc/vol4no1ART8.pdf; A.B.A. LEGAL GUIDES, *Custody and Visitation*, A.B.A. GUIDE TO FAMILY LAW ch. 12 [hereinafter *Custody and Visitation*], *available at* http://www.abanet.org /publiced/practical/books/family/home.html.

69. FAMILY LAW AND PRACTICE, *supra* note 62, at § 32.06.

70. *Custody and Visitation*, *supra* note 68, at 13.

71. *Id.*

72. *See, e.g.,* MICH. COMP. LAWS ANN. § 722.31 (2005) ("[E]xcept as otherwise provided in this section, a parent of a child whose custody is governed by court order shall not change a legal residence of the child to a location that is more than 100 miles from the child's legal residence. . . ."); TENN. CODE ANN. § 36-6-108 (2005) ("If a parent who is spending intervals of time with a child desires to relocate outside the state or more than one hundred (100) miles from the other parent within

the state, the relocating parent shall send a notice to the other parent . . . the other parent may, within thirty (30) days of receipt of notice, file a petition in opposition to removal of the child.").

73. Lance Cagle, Comment, *Have Kids, Might Travel: The Need for a New Road-map in Illinois Relocation Cases*, 25 N. Ill. U. L. Rev. 255 (2005).

74. *Id.*

75. Michael Varela, *All for the Love of a Child: The Current State of Califor-nia's Grandparent Visitation Statute in Light of Troxel v. Granville*, 44 Santa Clara L. Rev. 595, 619 n.3 (2004); *see, e.g.,* Ala. Code § 30-3-4 (1983); Alaska Stat. § 25.24.150 (1983), Ariz. Rev. Stat. Ann. § 25-337.01 (Supp. 1984); Ark. Code Ann. § 9-18-103 (1993); Cal. Fam. Code § 3103 (Deering 1994); Colo. Rev. Stat. § 19-1-117 (1994); Fla. Stat. Ann. § 752.01(1) (1993); Ga. Code. Ann. § 19-7-3 (1994); Haw. Rev. Stat. § 571-46.3 (1994); 750 ILCS 5/607 (Ill. 1994); Iowa Code Ann. § 589.35 (1993); Ky. Rev. Stat. Ann. § 405.021 (Baldwin 1994).

76. Troxel v. Granville, 530 U.S. 57 (2000).

77. Human Rights Campaign Found., Custody and Visitation Laws, http://www.hrc.org/Template.cfm?Section=Custody_Visitation&CONTENTID=20488&TEMPLATE=/TaggedPage/TaggedPageDisplay.cfm&TPLID=66 (last visited Mar. 12, 2007) (naming Alabama, Kentucky, Mississippi, Utah, North Carolina, and Virginia as the six states that use a parent's sexual orientation to deny or restrict custody).

78. *See, e.g.,* Kantaras v. Kantaras, 884 So. 2d 155 (Fla. Dist. Ct. App. 2004); *see also* Matt Bean, *Florida Transsexual Granted Custody of Children*, Court TV Online, Feb. 21, 2003, http://news.findlaw.com/court_tv/s/20030221/21feb2003173926.html.

79. *See, e.g.,* S.N.E. v. R.L.B., 699 P.2d 875 (Alaska 1985) (a parent's sexual orientation and status as a partner in a same-sex relationship were insufficient bases upon which to deny custody to a parent); D.C. Code § 16-914 (a)(1)(A) (2001) (in custody proceeding, "the race, color, national origin, political affiliation, sex, or sexual orientation of a party, in and of itself, shall not be a conclusive consider-ation").

80. Robin Cheryl Miller, Annotation, *Child Custody and Visitation Rights Arising from Same-Sex Relationship*, 80 A.L.R.5th 1 (2005). *See generally* V.C. v. M.J.B., 748 A.2d 539 (N.J. 2000) (denying joint custody to biological mother's same-sex former domestic partner in spite of fact that she was the psychological parent of the chil-dren but granting visitation rights based on best interests of the children).

81. Peter Mosanyi, II, Comment, *Survey of State Guardianship Statutes: One Concept, Many Applications,* 18 J. Am. Acad. Matrimonial Law 253 (2003).

82. Joyce E. McConnell, *Securing the Care of Children in Diverse Families: Build-ing on Trends in Guardianship Reform,* 10 Yale J. L. & Feminism 29, 36 (1998).

83. Mosanyi, *supra* note 81.

84. *Id.*

85. *See, e.g.,* 23 Pa. Cons. Stat. Ann. § 5611(a) (West 2001).

86. Guggenhiem et al., *supra* note 37, at 205.

87. Child Welfare Information Gateway, U.S. Dep't of Health & Human Servs., How Many Children Were Adopted in 2000 and 2001? (2004), *available at* http://www.childwelfare.gov/pubs/s_adopted/index.cfm.

88. *See generally* Guggenhiem et al., *supra* note 37, at 87–93 (discussing constitutional rights of families).

89. 2 Am. Jur. 2d *Adoption* § 67 (2004).

90. Guggenhiem et al., *supra* note 37, at 209.

91. Ardis L. Campbell, Annotation, *Rights of Unwed Father to Obstruct Adoption of His Child by Withholding Consent,* 61 A.L.R.5th 151 (2005). The Supreme Court has acknowledged differences in types of fathers. *See* Stanley v. Illinois, 405 U.S. 645 (1972); Quilloin v. Walcott, 434 U.S. 246 (1978); Caban v. Mohammed, 441 U.S. 380 (1979); Lehr v. Robertson, 463 U.S. 248 (1983). For a general review of the rights of fathers and putative fathers, *see* Child Welfare Information Gateway, U.S. Dep't of Health & Human Servs., Consent to Adoption: Summary of State Laws (2004), *available at* http://www.childwelfare.gov/systemwide/laws_policies/statutes/consentall.pdf; Child Welfare Information Gateway, U.S. Dep't of Health & Human Servs., The Rights of Presumed (Putative) Fathers (2004), *available at* http://www.childwelfare.gov/systemwide/laws_policies/statutes/putativeall.pdf.

92. Indiana: Ind. Code § 31-19-9-1 (minor parent under age eighteen may consent without concurrence of individual's parent or guardian unless "court, in the court's discretion, determines that it is in the best interest of the child to be adopted to require the concurrence"); Michigan: Mich. Comp. Laws Ann. § 710.43 (4) ("If the parent of the child to be adopted is an unemancipated minor, that parent's consent is not valid unless a parent, guardian, or guardian ad litem of that minor parent has also executed the consent."); Minnesota: Minn. Stat. Ann § 259.24(2) (2006) and Adoption Procedure Rule 31.02; New Hampshire: N.H. Rev. Stat. Ann. § 170-B:5 (2004) (if the parent is under eighteen years old, the court may require the assent of his or her parent or guardian); Oklahoma: 10 Okla. Stat. Ann. tit. 10, § 7503-2.1(B)(2) (2007) (referring to minors only under the age of sixteen); Rhode Island: R.I. Gen. Laws §§ 15-7-5, 15-7-10 (1956); Guam: Guam Code Ann. tit. 19, § 4206(a) (2006); and Puerto Rico: P.R. Laws Ann. tit. 31, § 535 (2006).

93. Campbell, *supra* note 91, at § 14(a); *see also Stanley,* 405 U.S. 645.

94. Alison S. Pally, *Father by Newspaper Ad: The Impact of In Re the Adoption of a Minor Child on the Definition of Fatherhood,* 13 Colum. J. Gender & L. 169 (2004); *see Stanley,* 405 U.S. 645; *Quilloin,* 434 U.S. 246; *Caban,* 441 U.S. 380; *Lehr,* 463 U.S. 248.

95. Ellis v. Hamilton, 669 F.2d 510, 514 (7th Cir. 1982); Gordon v. Lowell, 95 F. Supp. 264 (E.D. Pa. 2000).

96. For a summary of current state laws regarding who may adopt, *see* CHILD WELFARE INFORMATION GATEWAY, U.S. DEP'T OF HEALTH & HUMAN SERVS., WHO MAY ADOPT, BE ADOPTED, OR PLACE A CHILD FOR ADOPTION? SUMMARY OF STATE LAWS (2006), *available at* http://www.childwelfare.gov/systemwide/laws_policies/statutes/partiesall.pdf.

97. UTAH CODE ANN. § 78-30-1(3)(b) (2000) ("A child may not be adopted by a person who is cohabitating in a relationship that is not a legally valid and binding marriage under the laws of this state. . . . For purposes of this Subsection (3) (b), 'cohabitating' means residing with another person and being involved in a sexual relationship with that person."). *Id.*

98. FLA. STAT. ANN. § 63.042(3) (West 2003).

99. MISS. CODE ANN. § 93-17-3(2) (2006) (prohibiting adoption by couples of the same gender).

100. OKLA. STAT. ANN. tit. 10, § 7502-1.4 (West 2004) (Oklahoma does not recognize an adoption by more than one individual of the same sex from any other state.).

101. ERIC FERRERO ET AL., ACLU LESBIAN & GAY RIGHTS PROJECT, TOO HIGH A PRICE: THE CASE AGAINST RESTRICTING GAY PARENTING (2002) [hereinafter TOO HIGH A PRICE].

102. *Id.* at 18.

103. *Id.*

104. GUGGENHEIM ET AL., *supra* note 37, at 227–28.

105. *See White Paper, supra* note 2, at 14; CAL. FAM. CODE § 9000(b) (West 2004); CONN. GEN. STAT. ANN. § 45a-724(3) (West 2004); *In re* M.M.D, 662 A.2d 837 (D.C. 1995); Petition of K.M., 653 N.E.2d 888 (Ill. App. Ct. 1995); *In re* Adoption of M.M.G.C., 785 N.E.2d 267 (Ind. Ct. App. 2003); Adoption of Tammy, 619 N.E.2d 315 (Mass. 1993); *In re* Adoption of Two Children by H.N.R., 666 A.2d 535 (N.J. Super. Ct. App. Div. 1995); *In re* Jacob, 660 N.E.2d 397 (N.Y. 1995); *In re* Adoption of R.B.F., 803 A.2d 1195 (Pa. 2002); *In re* Adoption of B.L.V.B., 628 A.2d 1271 (Vt. 1993); VT. STAT. ANN. tit. 15A , § 1ñ102(b) (2005).

106. TOO HIGH A PRICE, *supra* note 101, at 19.

107. *See In re* Adoption of T.K.J., 931 P.2d 488 (Colo. Ct. App. 1996); *In re* Adoption of Luke, 640 N.W.2d 374 (Neb. 2002); *In re* Adoption of Doe, 719 N.E.2d 1071 (Ohio Ct. App. 1998); In the Interest of Angel Lace M., 516 N.W.2d 678 (Wis. 1994).

108. *See* GUGGENHEIM ET AL., *supra* note 37, at 150 & n.34 (1996); 42 U.S.C. § 671(a)(15) (2006); CAL. WELF. & INST. CODE §§ 16000, 16500.5, 16501 (West 1991 & Supp. 1994); COLO. REV. STAT. ANN. § 19-3-100.5 *et seq.* (West 1994); N.Y. SOC. SERV. LAW §§ 409, 409-(e)(1)(d) (McKinney 1992).

109. GUGGENHEIM ET AL., *supra* note 37.

110. *See, e.g.,* N.Y. SOC. SERV. LAW § 413 (McKinney 2005); MASS. GEN. LAWS

Ann. ch. 119 § 51A (West 1993); Minn. Stat. Ann. § 626.5562(2) (West 1983 & Supp. 1994); Okla. Stat. Ann. tit. 21, § 846(A)(2) (West 1983 & Supp. 1995).

111. *See, e.g.,* People v. Dossinger, 472 N.Y.S. 2d 808, 812 (N.Y. Sup. Ct. 1983), *aff'd as modified,* 106 A.D.2d 661 (N.Y. App. Div. 1984).

112. Guggenheim et al., *supra* note 37, at 151; 42 U.S.C. § 672(e) (2006).

113. *See, e.g.,* N.Y. Fam. Ct. Act §§ 1026, 1027 (McKinney 2005).

114. *See, e.g., id.* § 262(a)(i); Cal. Welf. & Inst. Code § 317 (West 2005); D.C. Code Ann. § 16-2304 (2005); Mass. Gen. Ann. Laws ch. 119, § 29 (West 2005). *But see,* Lassiter v. Dep't of Soc. Servs., 452 U.S. 18 (1981).

115. *See* Guggenheim et al., *supra* note 37, at 127; Sims v. State Dep't of Public Welfare, 438 F. Supp. 1179, 1193 (S.D. Tex. 1977), *rev'd on other grounds sub nom;* Moore v. Sims, 442 U.S. 415 (1979).

116. N.Y. Fam. Ct. Act §§ 1027(a), 1028(a) (McKinney 2006); Duchesne v. Sugarman, 566 F.2d 817, 829 (2d Cir. 1977).

117. Custody of Michel, 549 N.E.2d 440 (Mass. App. Ct. 1990); *In re* Appeal in Pima County Juvenile Dependency Action, 785 P.2d 121 (Ariz. Ct. App. 1990).

118. 42 U.S.C. § 675(6) (2006).

119. Guggenheim et al., *supra* note 37, at 164. *But see* Winston v. Children & Youth Servs. of Delaware Cty., 748 F. Supp. 1128 (E.D. Pa. 1990), *aff'd* 948 F.2d 1380 (3d Cir. 1991) (holding there is no enforceable right of visitation under the 1980 Adoption Assistance and Child Welfare Act).

120. Guggenheim et al., *supra* note 37, at 164; Aristotle P. v. Johnson, 721 F. Supp. 1002 (N.D. Ill. 1989); B.H. v. Johnson, 715 F. Supp. 1387 (N.D. Ill. 1989).

121. *See* Santosky v. Kramer, 455 U.S. 745, 748 (1982).

122. Troxel v. Granville, 530 U.S. 57 (2000); M.L.B. v. S.L.J., 519 U.S. 102, 119 (1996) (citing *Santosky,* 455 U.S. at 787 (Rehnquist, J. dissenting)); Pierce v. Society of Sisters, 268 U.S. 510 (1925).

123. *See* Catherine J. Ross, *The Tyranny of Time: Vulnerable Children, "Bad" Mothers, and Statutory Deadlines in Parental Termination Proceedings,* 11 Va. J. Soc. Pol'y & L. 176, 182 (2004); *Santosky,* 455 U.S. at 759.

124. *Santosky,* 455 U.S. at 768.

125. Adoption and Safe Families Act, 42 U.S.C.§ 675(5)(E)(i)-(iii).

126. Alsager v. Dist. Court of Polk County, 406 F. Supp. 10, 24–25 (S.D. Iowa 1975), *aff'd by* 545 F.2d 1137 (8th Cir. 1976). Notice requirements outlined in *In re* Gault, 387 U.S. 1 (1967) were applied to parental termination hearings in Alsager.

127. Lassiter v. Dep't of Soc. Servs., N.C., 452 U.S. 18 (1981); Brown v. Division of Family Services, 803 A.2d 948, 956 (Del. 2002) (stating that since *Lassiter* was decided in 1981, Delaware is one of only five states that has not "established a right for indigent parents to be represented by counsel at state expense for termination hearings").

# VIII

## The Criminal Justice System

The United States has the highest incarceration rate in the world.[1] As of 2004, the number of people behind bars surpassed two million, and, although the vast majority of prisoners are still men, the number of women prisoners has grown nearly 53 percent in the last twenty years.[2] At the end of 2003, considering all forms of correctional supervision —probation, parole, jail, and state and federal prison[3]—more than one million women were behind bars or under the control of the criminal justice system.[4]

Women of color, particularly African-American and Hispanic women, are incarcerated at disproportionately higher rates than their white counterparts. For instance, African-American women's incarceration rates have increased by 800 percent since 1986, compared to an increase of 400 percent for women of all races.[5] In 2003, African-American women were more than twice as likely as Hispanic women, and nearly five times more likely than white women, to be incarcerated.[6]

In addition, the rate of detention for girls in the juvenile justice system has increased significantly in recent years. The patterns leading to girls' incarceration often differ from those of boys, as do their needs once incarcerated. However the juvenile justice system has been built around the profile of the young male offender, and, as a result, girls' specific needs often are not met when they enter the system and its institutions, and again post-incarceration when they attempt to reenter their communities.[7]

This chapter addresses the legal rights of women and girls involved in the criminal and juvenile justice systems.

## WOMEN IN PRISON

### Who are the women in prison and why are their numbers increasing?

Most women in prison in the United States are between the ages of twenty-five and forty-four, are mothers, and have no college education. Women of color make up nearly two-thirds of the female prison population.[8] Furthermore, women in prison are disproportionately poor: nearly 37 percent of them had an earned income of less than $600/month prior to their incarceration, and almost 60 percent were not employed full-time prior to their incarceration.[9]

Most women in prison have committed nonviolent crimes. In fact, as of 2000 approximately 60 percent of women were serving time for nonviolent crimes, such as prostitution, fraud, or drug offenses,[10] and women represent less than 20 percent of those arrested for violent crime.[11] Finally, many women enter the criminal justice system due to their attempts to survive victimization. In one study of women under criminal supervision, nearly 60 percent of state inmates, 50 percent of federal inmates, 47 percent of jailed women, and 40 percent of probationers reported having suffered physical and/or sexual abuse in their childhoods and immediate pasts.[12] Not surprisingly, given that advocates have long agreed that many victims of abuse use drugs as a means of coping with or masking the abuse, almost 89 percent of the women in prison who reported having been abused also stated that they had used drugs regularly before their incarceration.[13] A significant number of women in prison suffer from mental illness and/or have substance abuse problems.[14]

### How have drug laws and policies affected women's incarceration rates?

The "war on drugs"—laws, policies, and practices that prohibit and harshly punish the use, possession, and/or sale of illegal drugs or controlled substances—has had a devastating and disparate impact on women, as well as on their children and families. The explosion of the female prison population in the past twenty years is due in large part to drug conspiracy laws and mandatory minimum sentencing laws for drug offenses. With the adoption of the Federal Sentencing Guidelines and other mandatory sentencing schemes, gender, family, and childcare responsibilities were eliminated as permissible factors for a judge to consider in deciding whether and for how long to sentence a convicted person to probation or imprisonment. These "gender-neutral" policies, combined with heightened penalties for drug-related violations, have had a much greater impact on women than on men because women are more likely than men to have lived with and had primary caretaking responsibility for dependent children.

As a result of expanded liability for drug offenses and increases in mandatory minimum sentencing schemes, the number of women incarcerated in the United States has spiraled upward in the last twenty-five years.[15] From 1985 to 1996, drug arrests of women increased by 95 percent while drug arrests of men increased by 55 percent. Between 1980 and 2004, the number of women in state and federal prisons increased from 12,300 to more than 105,000;[16] from 1986 to 1996 alone the number of women incarcerated for drug offenses in state prisons rose by 888 percent in contrast to a rise of 129 percent for all other nondrug offenses.[17] In 2002, 31.5 percent of the women in state prisons were serving time for drug offenses,[18] and in 2003, 58 percent of all women in federal prison had been convicted of drug offenses.[19]

Women of color and poor women have been most harshly impacted by these trends. In 2003, over half (about 58 percent) of all criminally sentenced women were minorities,[20] and approximately 37 percent of incarcerated women had monthly incomes of less than $600 prior to their arrest.[21] In 1997, 44 percent of Hispanic women and 39 percent of African-American women incarcerated in state prisons were convicted of drug offenses, compared to 23 percent of white women.[22]

Several lawsuits decided recently by the U.S. Supreme Court have generated uncertainty with respect to the constitutionality of certain sentencing schemes. In *Apprendi v. New Jersey*[23] and *Blakely v. Washington*,[24] the Court held that state sentencing guidelines are unconstitutional when they require judges, rather than juries, to impose specific and generally longer sentences than those imposed by juries based on additional judicial findings relating to the crime made after the jury has returned a guilty verdict. The Supreme Court reasoned that under the Sixth Amendment to the U.S. Constitution guaranteeing a right to a jury trial, any facts that are relied upon to impose an increased sentence in a state court must be found beyond a reasonable doubt by the jury, not by a judge. In 2005, in *United States v. Booker*,[25] the Court applied these rules to the Federal Sentencing Guidelines and found that those guidelines also violated the Sixth Amendment by requiring judges to increase defendants' sentences on the basis of facts (such as drug quantity) determined by the judges during sentencing proceedings rather than by juries during the trial. As a consequence, the Court struck down those provisions that made the Federal Sentencing Guidelines mandatory, and instead ruled them merely advisory.

**Do women retain any rights when they are incarcerated?**

Yes. Courts have held that prisoners do not lose all of their rights because of their conviction and incarceration. The Eighth Amendment to the U.S. Constitution protects against cruel and unusual punishment and has been used to challenge harmful conditions of confinement,[26] including the absence of adequate medical care,[27] sexual assault while in prison,[28] brutality by guards,[29] and other dangerous conditions of confinement.[30]

Courts have not, however, interpreted the Fourth Amendment to the U.S. Constitution, which protects against unreasonable searches and seizures, to provide much protection to prisoners. For example, random searches of cells and living quarters are permissible.[31] Prisoners can generally be strip-searched after visits or for other reasons.[32] More intrusive body-cavity searches require greater justification, such as suspicion that the prisoner is concealing drugs or other contraband.[33]

The Due Process Clause of the Fourteenth Amendment to the U.S. Constitution provides some guarantees of procedural fairness in prison discipline,[34] but it applies only if the discipline results in an "atypical and significant hardship" compared to the ordinary incidents of prison life.[35] Generally there is no constitutional protection against transfer from one prison to another, even if the second prison is in another state.[36] Prison officials may limit correspondence and impose other restricted First Amendment rights as long as the restrictions are "reasonably related to legitimate penological interests."[37] However, the Religious Land Use and Institutionalized Persons Act, passed in 2000, provides some additional protection for prisoners' religious rights.[38]

**Can male prison guards be employed in prisons in which women are incarcerated?**

Yes, but not necessarily in all positions. Title VII of the Civil Rights Act of 1964 provides that all persons must receive equal consideration for employment regardless of their sex.[39] (See chapter 2, "Employment: Discrimination and Parenting Issues," for more information.) Following the passage of Title VII, the U.S. Supreme Court held that men's prisons could not exclude women from employment as guards because of their sex.[40] Since that ruling, some courts have held that men may be barred from working in certain positions in women's prisons, while other courts have reached the opposite result.[41]

In many cases courts have found that certain practices violated the constitutional rights of women prisoners and have limited women prisoners' exposure to male guards. For example, in 1993, the U.S. Court of Appeals for the Ninth Circuit found that clothed body searches by male guards violated women prisoners' Eighth Amendment right to be free from cruel and unusual punishment.[42] In addition, in 1980, the U.S. Court of Appeals for the Second Circuit held that women prisoners were entitled to privacy from the view of male guards while they undressed.[43] In other cases, courts have suggested that prisons could protect women prisoners' privacy by allowing them nonmonitored private time, providing appropriate sleepwear, or adjusting male guards' work assignments.[44]

Yet, as 70 percent of the correctional officers in women's prisons currently are men, many male guards watch women in the shower or using the toilet.[45] Furthermore, only Florida, Michigan, South Dakota, and the Federal Bureau of Prisons currently prohibit pat-down searches by guards of the opposite sex.[46] Over the past several years, reports of male guards' systemic sexual abuse of female prisoners, including sexual harassment, assault, and rape, have been documented by the U.S. Department of Justice, the United Nations Human Rights Commission, Amnesty International, and Human Rights Watch. These reports document that corrections officers not only use actual or threatened physical force but also use their authority to provide or deny goods and privileges to female prisoners to compel them to have sex with the guards or, in other cases, to reward them for having done so. Male officers also use mandatory pat-frisks to grope women's breasts, buttocks, and vaginal areas. In addition, male corrections officers and staff also engage in verbal abuse and harassment of female prisoners, creating a sexualized and hostile environment for female prisoners.[47] Several factors, such as age, sexual orientation, and race, play significant roles in determining which women are targeted for sexual assault by prison officials. First-time, young, mentally ill, lesbian, or transgender prisoners often suffer more sexual abuse.[48]

As of 2000, fourteen states had no law prohibiting sexual relations between prisoners and correctional staff.[49] By May 2006, all states had passed such a law; however, no state has a statute that ensures full protection from custodial sexual misconduct of all persons in custody, including felony penalties for custodial sexual misconduct and bans on corrections officers' assertions of prisoner consent to a sexual act as a defense.[50]

The ACLU generally opposes blanket bans on employing correctional personnel of one sex in a prison for members of the opposite sex because such policies often deny jobs to women, constitute sex discrimination, and violate the civil rights and civil liberties of employees. However, the ACLU supports the personal privacy rights of prisoners, who should not be forced to display their bodies to, or be subjected to pat downs, strip searches or body-cavity searches by correctional personnel of the opposite sex. Thus, in 2001, the ACLU submitted a friend-of-the-court brief in *Everson v. State of Michigan Dept. of Corrections*[51] in support of a policy challenged by male and female corrections officers. The policy assigned only female corrections officers to housing units and transportation duties at three correctional facilities housing female prisoners. The ACLU argued that female-only assignments did not violate Title VII of the Civil Rights Act, which prohibits employers from discriminating on the basis of sex (see chapter 2: "Employment: Discrimination and Parenting Issues"), because the policy was necessary to protect the female prisoners' physical safety, rehabilitation, and privacy and did not affect the corrections officers' pay, seniority, or opportunities for promotion. This policy was a necessary response to a history of sexual abuse at the Michigan prison. Because this history might not exist in all prisons, not all gender-specific assignments would be justified.

Prison officials can, and should, develop policies and practices that accommodate the rights of both employees and prisoners.[52] Examples include using privacy curtains for prisoners to change behind; installing cameras in common and housing units while ensuring that officials do not use cameras to spy on undressed prisoners; not assigning correctional personnel of the opposite sex to patrol the shower and bathroom areas; and requiring that all pat downs, strip searches and body-cavity searches be conducted by personnel of the same sex.

## PARENTING BEHIND BARS

### Is maintaining contact and custody of children a major concern for women prisoners?

Yes. Most women in prison are mothers and most were the primary caretakers of their children prior to their incarceration. An estimated eighty thousand incarcerated mothers are parents to approximately two hundred thousand children under age eighteen.[53]

Given such statistics, the impact of women's incarceration on families is particularly severe, even though the vast majority of incarcerated parents are men. One study found that nine in ten fathers in state prison reported that their children lived with the other parent, but only about one in four mothers in prison said her child's father was the current caregiver, and one in three mothers lived alone with her children in the month prior to arrest.[54] As a result, when mothers are incarcerated, children are more likely to go into substitute kinship care with relatives or into foster care.

The incarceration of a parent is dramatically disruptive to a family. The child of an incarcerated mother will typically live with at least two different caretakers while his or her mother is in prison; 11 percent of these children will have three or more different caretakers. The majority of these children live apart from siblings.[55] For children in foster care, the state agencies in charge of their well-being frequently fail to inform incarcerated mothers of the children's whereabouts or to involve them in the process of reunification of the family unit once the mothers are released.

Among the impediments to maintaining family ties during incarceration are prison officials' refusal to notify families when a prisoner has been moved; delayed correspondence between an incarcerated parent and her child due to transfer of the prisoner from one facility to another; and restrictions on prisoners' ability to make phone calls, including a requirement that all calls be made collect, which many foster care agencies do not accept[56] and many families cannot afford. Because many states have only one prison for women, contact is also hindered by geographical distance.[57] Over 60 percent of mothers in prison are incarcerated more than one hundred miles from their children, making visitation difficult, financially prohibitive, and often impossible.[58] Fewer than half of imprisoned mothers report a personal visit with their children after entering state prison.[59]

Studies have demonstrated the importance of maintaining contact between incarcerated mothers and their children. A 1993 Congressional report found that the separation of children from their parents due to parental incarceration in prisons and jails may cause harm to the children's psychological well-being and hinder their growth and development.[60] Another study found that for parents, maintaining family ties during incarceration decreased the likelihood of repeated offenses and provided a powerful incentive to participate in rehabilitative programs.[61]

### Are there any programs in place that allow incarcerated mothers to maintain contact with their children?

Pioneering programs in some states have addressed the importance of mother-child relationships and the particular needs of incarcerated mothers and their children. Women lucky enough to be sentenced to such programs may keep their children in prison nurseries, may reside in community residences with their children, or may benefit from enhanced visitation and counseling programs that focus on the preservation and development of a parent-child bond.[62]

Residential mother-child correctional programs are programs that (1) house women prisoners and their children together; (2) operate under the supervision of correctional authorities; and (3) provide services to mothers and their children for extended periods of time during the first five years of the children's lives. Most advocates for prisoners with families agree that such programs are safe alternatives to traditional incarceration for mothers.[63] Unfortunately, in spite of their positive outcomes, such programs are very limited and only a small minority of incarcerated mothers are able to benefit from them.

In California, for example, the Mother-Infant Care Program allows low-security-risk women prisoners with children under six years of age to serve their sentences in one of seven halfway houses statewide. Mothers receive parenting courses, counseling, vocational training, and college classes.[64] The Federal Bureau of Prisons program, Mothers and Infants Together (MINT), allows low-security-risk pregnant women to be placed in a community-based program two months before expected delivery and to remain there with their babies up to three months after delivery in order to facilitate positive mother-child bonding. Women in the program receive prenatal and postnatal care, as well as counseling related to chemical dependencies, physical and sexual abuse, budgeting, and employment.[65]

Enhanced visiting programs have also proven useful in preserving the mother-child relationship, where contact is deemed in the best interests of the child. For instance, the Girl Scouts Beyond Bars program operates in a few cities to unite mothers in prison or jail with their daughters for two Saturdays each month. Mothers spend supervised time working on troop projects with their daughters and discuss issues such as avoiding drugs, coping with family conflict, and preventing teenage pregnancy. New York's Bedford Hills Correctional Facility operates a play room open to children every day of the year and teaches women parenting and life skills by permitting them to visit with their children as often as possible. Only 10 percent of women who complete the program return to prison, in contrast to a recidivism rate of 52 percent for prisoners overall.[66]

### Is imprisonment a ground for termination of parental rights?

When a parent's rights are terminated, the legal parent-child relationship is severed. As a general rule this can only happen after a court hearing in which a judge declares a parent unfit or a danger to his or her child. A court should not and technically cannot presume that a mother is unfit to raise her child simply because she is incarcerated.

However, in many states incarceration may be considered grounds for termination because it falls into the larger definition of abandonment or permanent neglect. Furthermore, given the Adoption and Safe Families Act (ASFA) timeline of fifteen out of twenty-two months (see below), women who are serving long prison sentences and whose children are in foster care are at a very high risk of having their parental rights terminated. (For more information on termination of parental rights proceedings, see chapter 7, "Family Law.")

**What is the Adoption and Safe Families Act?**

The Adoption and Safe Families Act (ASFA), enacted by Congress in 1997, exposes incarcerated mothers to a high risk of permanently losing their parental rights. With the goal of promoting stability and permanency for children, one of ASFA's provisions requires that a state file a petition to terminate parental rights when a child has been in foster care for fifteen of the preceding twenty-two months so that the child can be freed for adoption. If an incarcerated mother does not have consistent contact with her child for a significant period of time, the state or agency can initiate termination of parental rights proceedings for "failure to plan" or "abandonment." Because many women are sentenced to prison terms for longer than fifteen months or face significant obstacles to maintaining contact with their children while incarcerated, ASFA can have the effect of making reunification with children impossible.[67] ASFA also allows states to file a petition for termination of parental rights even if it is determined that the state did not make reasonable efforts, or any efforts at all, to preserve the family unit.[68]

By the end of 1999, every state and the District of Columbia amended their laws to comply with ASFA in order to remain qualified to receive federal matching funds for their foster care systems.[69] States vary in the ways in which they have implemented the federal statute; thus it is difficult to measure precisely the impact of ASFA on incarcerated parents.[70]

Some states, such as Illinois and South Carolina, have passed statutes that define the placement of a child in foster care for fifteen out of the most recent twenty-two months as proof in itself of parental unfitness and thus an independent ground for termination. While the Illinois Supreme

Court overturned the Illinois statute,[71] the South Carolina statute remains in force.[72]

Many other states have passed implementing statutes that severely curtail the rights of incarcerated parents and impede their ability to reunify with their children upon release from prison. For example, while ASFA sets out circumstances under which a state is exempt from making "reasonable efforts" to reunite parents and children,[73] at least five states—Alaska, Kentucky, North Dakota, South Dakota, and Tennessee—have gone beyond ASFA to define parental incarceration as one such circumstance.[74] These states allow child welfare authorities to refrain from providing supportive or reunification services to incarcerated mothers and their children simply because of the mother's incarceration. Thirteen states—Arizona, Colorado, Florida, Idaho, Illinois, Iowa, Louisiana, Michigan, Ohio, Rhode Island, Tennessee, Texas, and Wyoming—have statutorily added repeated or long-term incarceration as a ground for involuntary termination of parental rights.[75] As a result, if an incarcerated mother is unable to place her child with a relative or friend prior to her incarceration,[76] child welfare authorities in these states can remove her child and proceed towards the termination of her parental rights almost immediately, depending on the terms of the statute.[77]

In contrast, other states have taken more flexible approaches by embracing the limited exceptions presented by ASFA to the fifteen out of twenty-two month rule for initiating termination proceedings and/or offering limited protections for incarcerated parents. For instance, Minnesota law requires judges who are overseeing termination proceedings to make findings regarding the length of time a child has been in foster care, the parent's efforts to rehabilitate and maintain contact with the child, and the extent to which the state offered services to the parent. The second and third factors direct the court's attention to parental behavior while the child was in foster care rather than simply to the passage of time.[78] Similarly, Oregon allows child welfare authorities to refrain from filing termination proceedings if the child is being cared for by a relative, the child welfare office has not provided reasonable efforts as required, or "compelling reasons" suggest that filing a petition to terminate parental rights is not in the child's best interests.[79]

In Utah, incarcerated parents are entitled to "reasonable services" for reunification with their children, unless a judge determines that such services would be detrimental to the child.[80] Similarly, New York's statute specifies that a "parent" includes an incarcerated parent unless indicated otherwise, and as a result the requirement that the state agency exercise "diligent efforts" to assist the parent and child to develop a meaningful relationship applies to incarcerated parents as well.[81]

Finally, many states offer limited protection to the rights of some incarcerated parents, depending primarily on the severity of the crime for which the parent was convicted. For example, while California child welfare agencies are required by statute to offer and provide reunification services to incarcerated parents,[82] they are excused from such "reasonable efforts" toward reunification if the parent has been convicted of a violent felony.[83]

### What rights do incarcerated parents have in proceedings to terminate their parental rights?

Like any parents, incarcerated parents have the right to be notified if the state seeks to terminate their parental rights, and they have a right to a hearing. The court must provide an incarcerated parent with transportation to court if the parent wants to appear. However, if a parent fails to appear in court, the judge may assume that all of the allegations against her are true and enter a finding against her that would ultimately result in the termination of her parental rights.

## HEALTH CARE FOR WOMEN IN PRISON

### Is health care a concern for women prisoners?

Yes. Lack of health care is a major problem for most, if not all, women in prison, and indeed for men in prison as well. Women's unique needs, however, are generally less well addressed than those of men. Many women are pregnant when they are arrested, need routine gynecological care, have alcohol- or drug-dependency problems, and/or suffer from depression, poor nutrition, or sexually transmitted diseases. Furthermore, substantial numbers of women enter prison with significant health problems because the majority, due to poverty, had limited or no access to health care before incarceration.[84] Nearly 23 percent of women inmates nationwide are identified as mentally ill, compared to nearly 16 percent of men.[85] Many women report having been abused prior to incarceration. Additionally, HIV infection has hit this population particularly hard. In 2003, 2.8 percent of all female state prisoners were HIV positive, compared to 1.9 percent of males.[86] Finally, once incarcerated, women prisoners are at risk of sexual or physical abuse by corrections officers or other prisoners.

Despite these serious medical concerns, prison facilities generally do not provide adequate services or treatment to women prisoners. Barriers to care for women in prison include a shortage of qualified medical professionals; the use of nonmedical personnel to provide healthcare; a copayment system that requires prisoners to pay for medical services; frequent and long delays in medication refills, diagnostic testing, and follow-up treatment; and a failure to provide preventive care.[87]

Pregnant prisoners, in particular, face severe hardships. Correctional systems rarely have adequate prenatal protocols, staff, equipment, or resident obstetricians or obstetrical services.[88] In addition, the treatment of pregnant women in prison is often inhumane. For example, pregnant women in prison are routinely transported to and from facilities and hospitals in restraints. Women in all stages of labor, including during delivery, are frequently shackled by the ankle to their hospital beds.[89] Furthermore, infants born to women in prison are often separated from their mothers shortly after birth or once their mothers are discharged from the hospital, causing trauma to mothers and their children.[90] Finally, prisons often deprive pregnant prisoners of adequate nutrition and exercise. The failure to provide appropriate prenatal and childbirth services has resulted in infant deaths, late-term miscarriages, stillbirths, and emotional trauma resulting from the inability to secure medical care.[91]

### Have there been any advances in health care for women prisoners?

Not nearly enough. As legislators, policymakers, and the public become aware of the gross inadequacy of medical care provided to women in prison, conditions could improve. Medical services for women prisoners could be improved by requiring that prison medical facilities be adequately staffed with certified and licensed professionals, conducting appropriate screening for mental illness, substance addiction, and trauma, and expanding the provision of drug treatment and therapeutic programs.[92]

Other possible improvements in health care for incarcerated women include

• improved and humane pregnancy care that would at a minimum include instituting a nationwide ban on shackling women prisoners during labor, allowing women to remain with their newborn infants for a minimum of seventy-two hours, and permitting women to nurse their newborn infants when possible or to provide expressed milk;

- creating adequate counseling programs for women who have been victims of domestic violence, sexual abuse, and/or physical abuse; who suffer from depression and other mental illnesses; or who have suffered miscarriages or the death of an infant;
- instituting routine gynecological care, including mammograms, yearly pap smears, and their necessary medical treatment.

## EDUCATION FOR INCARCERATED WOMEN

**Do women prisoners face problems with education, vocational training, and work opportunities?**

Yes. Access to educational and vocational training opportunities are extremely limited in women's prisons. Researchers have identified numerous disparities in programs and services available to incarcerated women and girls as compared to men and boys. Women and girls have less access than men and boys to educational and vocational training and work-release programs. These services are essential to rehabilitation. Without access to education and skills training, women and girls are less equipped to succeed in reentering their communities after being released from prison or detention facilities and thus are more likely to reoffend.

Constitutional equal protection challenges to these disparities in educational and vocational training,[93] recreational programs,[94] and employment opportunities[95] have been brought with limited success.[96] In recent years, however, in spite of the evidence of persistent inequality in educational opportunities for incarcerated women, the trend has been for courts to refuse to compare programs and services available to male and female prisoners, reasoning that the two groups are not "similarly situated" for purposes of equal protection analysis or finding "sufficient parity" between the services available to each group despite evidence to the contrary. Generally such a finding means that equal protection challenges to the limited access and lower quality of programs by women prisoners are unsuccessful.

Thus, for example, a 1979 Michigan case alleging sex discrimination at the Huron Valley Women's Facility was successful[97] and resulted in a court order that Michigan take comprehensive action to upgrade the women's postsecondary education program, vocational training and apprenticeship programs, and work-pass programs until they were "substantially equivalent" to those programs available to male prisoners. However, upon revisiting the issue after twenty years of court supervision and after female prisoners cited continued sex-based disparities between the programs,[98] the court found that there was sufficient equality in the educational, vocational, apprenticeship, and work-pass programs afforded to male and female prisoners to satisfy the requirements of the Equal Protection Clause.[99] Women prisoners have also brought claims of sex discrimination in educational and vocational programming under Title IX of the Education Amendments of 1972 (20 U.S.C. §§ 1681–1688), which bans sex discrimination in federally funded educational programs, again with limited success.[100] (See chapter 4, "Education," for more information.)

In 1994, women prisoners in Nebraska brought a lawsuit alleging that prison officials violated their rights under Title IX and the Equal Protection Clause by failing to provide equal educational and vocational opportunities for male and female prisoners in Nebraska.[101] The U.S. Court of Appeals for the Eighth Circuit, in its analysis of the women prisoners' claims, concluded that male and female prisoners were not similarly situated for purposes of prison programs and services and therefore such services could not be compared.[102] The court held that any differences in the programs offered to male and female prisoners were the result of the different characteristics and the different circumstances surrounding their incarceration.[103]

Similarly, in a case decided by the U.S. Court of Appeals for the D.C. Circuit in 1996, female prisoners at three correctional facilities raised Title IX and equal protection claims, alleging that they were discriminated against in access to academic, vocational, work, and recreational programs on the basis of their sex.[104] These female prisoners asserted that their male counterparts had access to extensive programs, including carpentry, bricklaying, electrical and mechanical work, and welding, whereas they were relegated to work details in stereotypically female fields, such as clerical, housekeeping, and culinary assignments.[105] The U.S. Court of Appeals for the D.C. Circuit found that equal protection and Title IX analyses were not applicable because the male and female prisoners were not similarly situated.[106]

## LEGAL REMEDIES AND REFORM

### How can conditions for women in prison be improved?

There are many strategies that women prisoners and advocates can employ to improve conditions for women in prison. Litigation is one strategy that has enabled many women to enforce their rights. For example, in 1977 a lawsuit on behalf of women in prison was filed in New York,[107] alleging that the prison's medical and record-keeping procedures caused substantial delays in medical care, that the methods of screening medical complaints were grossly inadequate, and that plaintiffs were denied adequate access to medical staff. The U.S. District Court for the Southern District of New York held that these practices violated the Constitution and ordered remedial measures.

More recently, pregnant women have filed lawsuits seeking to improve prenatal and postpartum care. Legal Services for Prisoners with Children brought three suits in five years against California's largest women's prison and two California county jails.[108] One lawsuit, *Harris v. McCarthy*,[109] led to the creation of a pregnancy-related health care team, implementation of protocols for normal and high-risk pregnancies, and identification of an obstetrics managing physician who would establish a general plan of care for every pregnant women in prison.[110]

In another lawsuit, *Rios v. Rowland*,[111] plaintiffs charged the California Department of Corrections (CDC) with failing to implement the Mother-Infant Care Program. The parties resolved the case through a settlement agreement. Under the terms of the settlement agreement, the CDC is now required, among other things, to notify women of the program within one week after they are taken into custody, to allow pregnant women to submit applications prior to delivery, and to maintain regional waiting lists of eligible prisoners. In a third case, *West v. Manson*,[112] prison officials agreed to provide pregnant prisoners with extra milk and bran, other special dietary supplements, prenatal vitamins, and access to prenatal classes. Prison officials also agreed not to impose physical restraints, such as the use of leg irons, without medical approval.

### What legal remedies are available to women prisoners who have suffered custodial sexual abuse?

In the early 1990s, the abuse of female prisoners in state and federal prisons around the country came under investigation by the U.S. Department of Justice, Human Rights Watch, Amnesty International, and the United Nations, resulting in documentation reports and litigation.[113] Between 1994 and 1996, Human Rights Watch conducted a two and a half year study of women's prisons in the United States, involving five states and the District of Columbia. Human Rights Watch found significant abuses of women prisoners in the Michigan system, including rape, sexual harassment, impregnation, and retaliation. The Justice Department's investigations confirmed these findings.[114]

Custodial sexual misconduct that involves unwanted touching will almost always constitute an assault or similar tort under state law. The law varies from state to state with regard to how and under what circumstances women prisoners can recover for such misconduct.

Women seeking civil redress for custodial sexual misconduct often file claims under the Eighth Amendment to the Constitution. An Eighth Amendment violation occurs when two requirements are met. First, the alleged injury must be objectively serious. Most courts will hold that sexual assault or unwanted sexual touching satisfies this requirement; verbal abuse may not suffice.

Second, the prison official being sued must have a sufficiently culpable state of mind. In other words, if a woman seeks to hold supervisory officials responsible for the misconduct of their subordinates, she must show that they acted with "deliberate indifference"—that is, that they knew the risk of harm but disregarded it.[115] If a prisoner is suing the officer who sexually assaulted her, she must show that he acted "maliciously and sadistically for the very purpose of causing harm"[116]—in other words, that he meant to hurt her. However, one court has held that sexual abuse or rape of a prisoner by staff is, by definition, "malicious and sadistic."[117]

In such litigation, the Prison Litigation Reform Act (PLRA) of 1996 poses significant obstacles to lawsuits brought by prisoners. First, the PLRA requires that prior to filing a lawsuit in federal court, a prisoner must exhaust the prison's grievance procedure—that is, she must file a complaint with the grievance system and appeal through all available levels of appeal.[118] Some courts have ruled that prisoners who fail to file a timely grievance are permanently barred from later suing in federal court.[119] Other courts have ruled that a prisoner may sue as long as she completes the grievance process, even if her grievance was untimely under the grievance rules.[120]

The PLRA also provides that a prisoner cannot recover money damages in federal court for "mental or emotional injury" unless she has previously suffered a physical injury.[121] This provision essentially bars any monetary relief to prisoners who have been subjected to emotional abuse by prison officials and suffer injuries that are exclusively psychological or emotional in nature.[122] This legislation was passed despite congressional testimony indicating that it may leave women subjected to custodial sexual abuse without legal remedies.[123] Thus, some courts have held that prisoners subjected to abusive body-cavity searches may not recover damages because they have suffered no physical injury.[124] However, one court has held that sexual assault is by definition a physical injury,[125] and most courts have held that the "mental or emotional injury" provision does not prevent a plaintiff from recovering punitive damages in appropriate cases.[126] Finally, the PLRA does not apply to lawsuits brought by a former prisoner challenging actions that occurred while she was incarcerated.[127]

The restrictive requirements of the PLRA and other laws have made it more difficult for prisoners to file lawsuits in federal court and thus have reduced significantly protections against custodial sexual abuse. International human rights law, however, provides another potential source of protection.[128] The International Covenant on Civil and Political Rights and the International Convention Against Torture and Other Cruel, Inhuman and Degrading Treatment or Punishment require states to prohibit torture, which includes sexual abuse, and to investigate and punish any abuse. In addition, the United Nations Standard Minimum Rules for the Treatment of Prisoners (UN Rules) require that governments prohibit sexual abuse within prisons, provide methods for prisoners to report such abuse, and punish abusive conduct.[129] Because U.S. advocates have only recently begun to use international human rights law in domestic lawsuits, not all judges accept this source of law as controlling.

## CAPITAL PUNISHMENT

### How many women have received the death penalty?

Since the U.S. Supreme Court reinstated capital punishment in 1976, 155 women have been sentenced to death. As of January 1, 2004, there are fifty-five women on death row, comprising 1.5 percent of the total death row population and 0.1 percent of the total population of women prisoners in the United States.[130] These women range in age from twenty-one to seventy-three years old and have been on death row for periods ranging from a few weeks to nearly twenty years.[131]

Women account for one in ten murder arrests, one in fifty death sentences imposed at trial, and one in ninety actual executions.[132] Since 1976, only eleven women have been executed,[133] and of the 155 women sentenced to death since 1976, seventy-nine (approximately 50 percent) have left death row as a result of judicial reversal or executive commutation of their sentence.[134] Research remains to be done on why women leave death row at higher rates than men. It may be that it is more unusual to have women on death row and thus their cases receive closer scrutiny, or that judges and governors are more likely to intervene in cases where women are death-eligible out of concern for political popularity and support.[135]

Only a small percentage of the offenses for which women are convicted are eligible for capital punishment.[136] The majority of women who kill, kill family members or loved ones. Generally, unless blatantly predatory or resulting in multiple deaths, these crimes do not result in death sentences, regardless of whether the killer is a man or a woman.[137] However, a recent national survey of women on death row by the ACLU found that many women are sentenced for crimes that usually do not result in a death sentence for men. Thus, thirteen women who killed their husbands or boyfriends, ten women who killed their children, and two who killed both their husbands and their children are currently on death row.[138]

### What are the unique issues facing women on death row?

Women's experiences on death row mirror many of the problems that have been documented in the cases of men condemned to death, such as inadequate defense counsel, official misconduct on the part of the prosecutor, poverty, alcoholism, drug abuse, mental retardation, and mental illness. However, in addition to these problems, the majority of women on death row have also suffered abuse and domestic violence. Moreover, once incarcerated, women face unique challenges living on death row, including mistreatment and lack of access to necessary services that are generally available to their male counterparts. Most significantly, many women sentenced to death live in virtual isolation, which often leads to psychosis or exacerbates existing mental illnesses.

The death penalty, as presently administered in our country, results in discrimination against the poor, the uneducated, and members of minority communities. Men and women end up on death row for primarily the same three reasons: poverty, race, and geography. First, poor people are more likely to be sentenced to death simply because they cannot afford to retain counsel and so must be represented by lawyers who are compensated by the state. These lawyers, despite their best intentions, often cannot provide clients with the same range and depth of service provided by lawyers who are paid by their clients or have greater financial resources available to mount a defense. Second, it is indisputable that the race of the accused and the race of the victim matter when it comes to capital punishment.[139] While African-Americans make up about 12 percent of the national population, African-American men and women account for more than 40 percent of the inmates on death row, and approximately one-third of those executed since 1977.[140] Lastly, the capital punishment system is inconsistent throughout the country. Some states employ the death penalty and others do not.[141] Such differences in state law lead to widespread discrepancies in the sentences imposed for similar crimes.

However, in recent years the Supreme Court has struck down the death penalty for individuals who are mentally retarded and for those who were juveniles at the time of the offense. In 2002, in *Atkins v. Virginia*,[142] the Court held that it is a violation of the Eighth Amendment ban on cruel and unusual punishment to execute death row inmates who are mentally retarded. In 2005, the Court in *Roper v. Simmons*[143] held that the Eighth and Fourteenth Amendments forbid the execution of individuals who were under the age of eighteen when they committed their crimes.

One case that highlights concerns common to many women on death row is that of Wanda Jean Allen. On January 11, 2001, Allen became the first woman executed in Oklahoma. Race, class, sexual orientation, and mental capacity were all factors in her trial and execution. Wanda Jean, an African-American woman, shot her lover, Gloria Leathers, after a domestic dispute in 1988. On April 19, 1989, jurors rejected Allen's claim of self-defense and found her guilty of first-degree murder. Subsequently, jurors took only two hours to decide that Allen should be sentenced to death.

Poverty undoubtedly played a role in Wanda Jean's sentencing. She had secured an attorney for $800, but the attorney later requested that the judge release him from representing Wanda Jean because he had never tried a capital case. The judge refused either to release the attorney or to provide Wanda Jean with a public defender. The attorney, operating with little experience and few resources, did not have Wanda Jean undergo psychological testing, and so no evidence of her mental retardation ever came up at trial.[144] Homophobia also influenced her trial and sentencing. At trial, the prosecution characterized Wanda Jean as "the man" in her lesbian relationship, playing upon stereotypes and distorting the facts.[145] Unfortunately, the story of Wanda Jean is illustrative of typical death penalty cases and thus sheds light upon the inequities and biases inherent in our system of capital punishment.

## GIRLS IN THE JUVENILE JUSTICE SYSTEM

**What are the demographics of girls in the juvenile justice system?**

Just as the rate of women's incarceration has soared in recent years, the number of girls entering the juvenile justice system has also risen. The nature and causes of girls' delinquency often differ from those of boys.[146] In 1998, over 2.6 million youth under age eighteen were arrested; 27 percent of these youth were female (697,000).[147] In 1998, girls accounted for 22 percent of all aggravated assaults, 30 percent of curfew and loitering violations, 31 percent of simple assaults, and 58 percent of all runaways.[148] Three trends are evident in female juvenile arrests: (1) female youth arrest rates are increasing;[149] (2) arrests have increased more for girls than for boys in several categories;[150] and (3) arrests have increased for female violent crimes.[151]

For girls, risk factors contributing to their entry into the juvenile justice system include physical and sexual abuse, pregnancy, and emotional issues such as depression, post-traumatic stress disorder, negative body image, and eating disorders.[152] Many girls entering the juvenile justice system are likely to have experienced extreme trauma prior to arrest, or are arrested because of that victimization or their efforts to survive it. Girls are three times more likely than boys to have been sexually abused prior to arrest.[153] The majority of young women entering the juvenile justice system typically do so for status offenses, which are behaviors that are in violation of the law only when juveniles, not adults, commit them, such as running away or underage drinking.[154] Girls also enter the juvenile justice system for committing crimes that are either gender-based or considered a "rite of passage," including prostitution and shoplifting.[155]

While the majority of girls' violations are nonviolent, the rising arrest rates indicate that prevention efforts are either not succeeding or not being conducted with sufficient frequency.

**What are the needs of girls in the juvenile justice system?**

Historically, the juvenile justice system has not focused on girls' needs because the system was designed around the paradigm of the young male juvenile offender.[156] However, with more girls entering the system, researchers and policy makers now acknowledge that girls' needs must be considered when services are improved and new programs are implemented. According to researchers, girls in the juvenile justice system identify their most urgent needs as those for housing, jobs, financial assistance, childcare, and medical services for themselves and often their children.[157]

Researchers have suggested that programs for girls should include the following: sexual and physical abuse intervention; counseling on safe sexual practices; birth control or prenatal care for those who are pregnant; counseling for drug and alcohol dependency; parenting skills and visitation with children; stress management workshops; and the development of a sense of empowerment.[158] It is also important for juvenile justice programs to recognize that girls' mental health needs differ significantly from those of boys, due in part to their histories of abuse. Studies show that "girls overwhelmingly have childhood histories of trauma and abuse, mental health disorders, and family separation . . . [and suffer from] higher rates of depression, Post-Traumatic Stress Disorder (PTSD) and other diagnosable mental health disorders than boys. These disorders cause significant distress and contribute to behavioral problems in custody."[159]

In 1974, Congress passed the Juvenile Justice and Delinquency Prevention Act (JJDPA), which provides federal support and assistance to state and local governments and to the private sector in order to assist youth in the juvenile justice system. The legislation called for states to meet two requirements: remove all status offenders from secure confinement and eliminate contact between juvenile and adult offenders.[160] While the JJDPA was not specifically designed to assist girls, its focus on the needs of status offenders impacted many girls in the juvenile justice system. However, one amendment to the JJDPA allows judges to reclassify juveniles who disobey court orders—e.g., run away from a nonsecure placement, miss school, etc.—as delinquents, resulting in incarceration for status offenders who violated their probation terms or otherwise disobeyed a court order.[161] When Congress reauthorized the JJDPA in 1992, new language was added requiring states to evaluate the services their juvenile justice systems provided to girls, which has prompted a few states to attempt to improve planning for girls in the system.[162]

### What do model programs for girls in the juvenile justice system look like?

Effective programming and assistance for female juvenile offenders recognize the unique needs of girls, address the risk factors that increase girls' likelihood of delinquent behaviors, include a continuum of options ranging from prevention and intervention to aftercare, and are developmentally appropriate.[163] The Office of Juvenile Justice and Delinquency Prevention defines gender-specific services as "those that are designed to meet the unique needs of female offenders, that value female perspectives, that celebrate and honor the female experience, that respect and take into account female development and that empower young women to reach their full potential."[164]

Many experts in gender-specific and gender-sensitive programming within the juvenile justice system consider the Female Intervention Team in Baltimore, Maryland, and the Harriet Tubman Residential Center in Syracuse, New York, to be model programs. The Female Intervention Team is a community-based program for female juvenile offenders whose mission is "to restore hope to young women who have lost their direction and focus." The program provides girls with a variety of services, including academics, health referrals, counseling, computer training, pregnancy prevention, teen parenting classes, and conflict resolution workshops.[165] The Harriet Tubman Residential Center houses twenty-five girls between the ages of fourteen and seventeen. The center's curriculum highlights the strengths, achievements, and diversity of women throughout the history of New York, with the expectation that by learning about the accomplishments of these women, girls will come to understand that they also have opportunities and potential to set and reach their goals. The center provides a mix of education and therapy focusing on the development of girls' internal-control and problem-solving skills. As girls prepare to leave the center, the staff assists them in locating community resources to provide follow-up support and services.[166]

The juvenile justice system remains far from meeting the unique needs of female juvenile offenders. To accomplish its aim of rehabilitating girls who have been adjudicated delinquent, the system must develop gender-specific programming and strive to connect this programming to issues faced by girls in society at large.


## DISCRIMINATORY LAW ENFORCEMENT: PROSTITUTION

**Who are sex workers?**

The terms "sex work" and "sex worker" have been adopted by sex workers themselves in an effort to redefine commercial sex as a legitimate form of employment. Approaching sex work from an employment perspective allows it to be understood as integral to mainstream debates on human rights, women's rights, and workers' rights. Furthermore, the word "prostitute" has been used to denounce and degrade women. This book avoids using the terms "prostitute" or "prostitution," except when discussing criminal laws or prosecution.[167] Although significant numbers of men provide commercial sex to other men and sometimes to women, men are rarely prosecuted for prostitution,[168] and this section focuses on women sex workers.

The majority of sex workers—80–90 percent—work in brothels, massage parlors, escort services, or as independent "call girls."[169] The remaining 10–20 percent of sex workers solicit on the streets. Street sex workers, primarily poor women and women of color, are disproportionately targeted for police harassment and arrest, while women working off the streets, who are generally more financially stable and white, are treated less harshly.[170] Consequently, while women of color comprise 40 percent of street sex workers, they account for 55 percent of those arrested for prostitution and 85 percent of those sentenced to jail.[171] Thus, the burden of antiprostitution policy falls most heavily upon poor women and women of color.

### Are statutes that outlaw prostitution constitutional?

Yes, courts generally have held various aspects of antiprostitution statutes constitutional. For example, statutes outlawing prostitution or solicitation of sex workers have been held not to violate constitutional rights to privacy.[172] Courts have found that engaging in sexual activity for hire with a consenting adult in a private home without a preceding public solicitation is not a fundamental right protected by the state or federal guarantees of privacy.[173] Courts have also held that antiprostitution laws do not necessarily violate the equal protection or due process provisions of the Fourteenth Amendment.[174] One court has found that a statute that prohibits sexual acts between persons not married to each other in exchange for money but does not prohibit the same act between married couples did not violate equal protection or due process.[175] The court reasoned that the privacy interest of married couples, as well as public health concerns associated with commercial sex, justified such differential treatment.[176] A court has also held that statutes outlawing prostitution, even when understood as prohibiting a contract to perform sexual services for hire, do not intrude on free speech.[177] In addition, a court has held that a statute may prohibit an offer to perform sexual services for money as much as it may prohibit the actual act of performing those services.[178] Such statutes have also been held constitutional on the ground that legislatures may outlaw the entrance into an agreement to perform an illegal act in addition to outlawing the illegal act itself.[179]

**Do different laws apply to sex workers than to their patrons?**

In some states, yes. Female sex workers can be sent to jail because they have had sex with male customers; their male sexual partners generally are not subject to any penalty for the very same sex acts for which the women are incarcerated. The disparity results both from unequal laws and from unequal or selective enforcement of the laws. Some states have laws that make criminal only the act of having sex in return for the *receipt* of money. They do not make criminal the act of having sex in return for *giving* money.[180]

Other states have laws making the act of giving money for sex a crime, albeit a lesser crime than receiving money for sex.[181] But most officials who administer the criminal justice system are male, and male police, lawyers, and judges usually do not arrest, prosecute, or convict men for the crimes of "patronizing a prostitute" or "aiding and abetting." When enforcement is attempted against male customers, there is often a strong public outcry against the unfairness of harming their reputations.[182]

**Can unequal prostitution laws be challenged as violating constitutional principles?**

Yes. Because most sex workers in the United States are female, discriminatory prostitution laws can be challenged on the ground that they deny women their constitutional rights to equal protection, due process, and privacy. Female sex workers have been successful in their efforts to amend laws that punish only women for engaging in commercial sex. By comparing the treatment of the female sex worker to that of the male sex worker through litigation and advocacy, female sex workers have brought attention to these unequal laws or enforcement of laws. However, the result of these efforts has been to increase the prosecutions of male sex workers rather than to decrease the prosecutions of female sex workers. For example, an Alaska court used Alaska's equal rights amendment to strike the word "female" from the state prostitution law, thus expanding the scope of the law to include both men and women. Similarly, a Massachusetts court interpreted a facially discriminatory state law as reaching both male and female sex workers to avoid the equal protection problem that would have existed had the statute continued to apply only to women.[183]

Female sex workers have also argued that laws that prohibit women from engaging in prostitution but do not prohibit men from patronizing a sex worker are unconstitutional under both state and federal constitutions.[184] Such arguments have largely been unsuccessful, generally on the theory that it is permissible to target sellers of an illicit service more heavily that buyers.[185] However, despite the unwillingness of courts to overturn laws that penalize sex workers to the exclusion of their patrons, most state legislatures have enacted statutes that provide some punishment of patrons.[186]

**Can the selective enforcement against women of prostitution laws that apply to both men and women be challenged?**

Yes. However, the success of challenges on constitutional grounds to selective enforcement has been mixed. On average, prostitution arrests include 70 percent female sex workers, 20 percent male sex workers, and 10 percent customers.[187] There have been cases in which female sex workers have successfully challenged a police department's "selective enforcement" of prostitution laws, that is, the practice of arresting female sex workers and not arresting male customers where the law is broad enough to allow arrest of both seller and buyer.[188] In one case, police testimony indicated that it was department policy not to arrest male customers of sex workers, and the court ruled that this violated the state equal rights amendment.[189] At least one judge has acted independently and used her court to stem the discriminatory practices of police departments by instituting a policy not to hear cases against sex workers unless the customer was also arrested.[190]

Others courts, however, have condoned discriminatory enforcement. For example, in remarkably similar cases, California and New York courts refused to find sex discrimination where a pattern of enforcing the prostitution law primarily against female sex workers and not against male customers was demonstrated. The courts upheld the police department practices on the theory that it was permissible to concentrate on the " 'profiteer,' rather than the customer, of a commercial vice."[191] Other courts have affirmed law enforcement practices of arresting accused sex workers while giving citations or warnings to patrons as not being sex discrimination on the ground that sex workers and patrons are not similarly situated under the law.

Many local governments have responded to the disparity in treatment of solicitors and sex workers by creating new programs targeted at solicitors. These programs range from revocation of convicted solicitors' driver's licenses to publication of the names of convicted solicitors in various media. Other local governments have required convicted solicitors to attend educational programs aimed at deterring them from soliciting sex workers in the future.[192]

**Can police officers engage in sexual acts with sex workers before arresting them or is that entrapment?**

The laws of most states allow law enforcement officers to engage in sexual acts with sex workers to facilitate catching the sex workers in the process of breaking the law. For example, a police officer can initiate sexual activity with a woman, remove her clothes, touch her breasts, and place his face close to her vagina while urging her on and then arrest her.[193] This behavior does not meet the legal standard for entrapment.

Entrapment occurs when a person is induced or persuaded by law enforcement agents to commit a crime that she had no previous intent to commit.[194] The general policy behind entrapment is that the government should not be able to acquire damaging evidence leading to a possible conviction by inducing an innocent person to commit a crime. However, a police officer can engage in lies and strategic maneuvers without entrapping someone; he could pretend to be someone else and to offer, either directly or indirectly, to engage in an illegal activity with the person.[195] As a general rule entrapment is a very difficult defense to prove.

To demonstrate that entrapment occurred, a defendant must provide some evidence that the police officer induced her to commit the crime. If the police officer simply presented an opportunity to commit a crime, then it is unlikely that the entrapment defense will succeed.[196] Courts differ on how much inducement or suggestion the police can offer before the entrapment defense becomes viable.[197] However, courts tend to focus on whether the police officer's actions would be likely to cause an innocent person to commit the crime.[198]

**Can police officers arrest sex workers for standing and/or walking around in public areas?**

It depends. Statutes criminalizing "loitering for the purposes of committing prostitution" or "loitering with the intent to commit prostitution" exist in many states.[199] Although these statutes are gender neutral, law enforcement agents often use them as a basis for issuing citations or arresting women who are in public places and exhibit behavior that the officers believe indicates a desire to commit prostitution. Courts in various states are divided on whether these statutes are constitutional because the Supreme Court has invalidated criminal statutes that are overly vague.[200] Some courts have held that such statutes are void on similar grounds because despite making certain behavior illegal, the statutes also prohibit legal behavior, discourage the exercise of First Amendment rights, or do not provide adequate notice of the prohibited behavior.[201] These courts have recognized that a legislature's unwillingness to narrowly tailor a law allows an arresting officer broad discretion in pursuing alleged violators of the law.

Even where a jurisdiction has laws in place that constrain the movement of women for purposes of prostitution, there are limits to the behavior that can be considered criminal under such laws. To sustain a conviction under these laws, the state must demonstrate beyond a reasonable doubt that a woman had a specific intent to engage in prostitution. In *City of Portland v. Miller*, the court addressed the subjective, but critical, subtleties of this issue. In *Miller*, a police officer observed a woman waving and smiling at people in approaching cars, some of which slowed down but did not stop. An officer in an unmarked car drove by her but she did not wave at him. She also went in and out of a restaurant-bar nearby. She did this for approximately thirty to forty minutes and then went into the restaurant-bar to have a drink. She was seated at the bar when the police officers entered and asked her to step outside; they questioned her and she told them she had not been outside at all. At this point, the officers arrested her for violating a Portland city ordinance that outlawed loitering with intent to commit prostitution. After the court reviewed the evidence, it found that nothing in the woman's behavior met the legal standard for criminal behavior. The court dismissed the charges, finding that the state had not proven the elements beyond a reasonable doubt because it was "not a violation of the law merely to look like a prostitute might."[202]

### What alternatives are there to criminal penalties for prostitution?

Criminalization of prostitution promotes social control over women's sexuality and bodies through the penalization and stigmatization of women who engage in sex work. Enforcing antiprostitution laws is costly and, more importantly, encourages police harassment of poor women and women of color.[203] Moreover, there is no evidence that criminalization has decreased the rate of prostitution. As one author noted, "The laws and general strategy of repression seem to have had remarkably little effect on the prostitution economy."[204]

One alternative to criminalization is legalization, which can carry its own set of burdens stigmatizing and controlling women. The legalization of prostitution entails the removal of restrictions against prostitution and the implementation of regulatory systems, including licensing, registration, and health testing. Nevada presently has a system of legalized prostitution in place in some of its counties. In 1971, Nevada state law was amended to provide that "[i]n a county whose population is 250,000 or more, the license board shall not grant any license to a petitioner for the purpose of operating a house of ill fame or repute or any other business employing any person for the purpose of prostitution."[205] The Nevada Supreme Court held that this language implicitly allowed counties with smaller populations to license brothels.[206] Prostitution remains illegal in Nevada outside of the licensed brothels in the less populated counties.[207] Of the less populous counties, four counties prohibit prostitution, six ban it in the unincorporated areas of the county, and seven permit it throughout the county.[208] In 1999 nearly a thousand women worked in thirty-three licensed brothels in Nevada.[209] However, the Nevada system serves the interests of men and brothel keepers. Brothel owners charge women for their rooms, and some also charge for food. In addition, owners often take 50 percent of the women's gross earnings. Furthermore, brothel owners typically do not provide women with health insurance, workers' compensation, unemployment insurance, vacation pay, or retirement benefits.[210] Arguably, then, legalization of prostitution is paternalistic and stigmatizes sex workers as a group of women who must be regulated and controlled.[211] While Nevada is presently the only state to legalize sex work, regulated prostitution has been permitted for years in certain European countries, with no noticeable harmful effect.[212]

The best alternative to criminalization of prostitution is decriminalization without the institution of a broad regulatory system. Decriminalization calls for the removal of all laws and regulations applicable to voluntary sex work between consenting adults but does not impose a regulatory scheme in place of the criminal system. Instead, sex work would be governed by the same civil, business, and professional codes of conduct currently governing all legal businesses. Decriminalization would ensure that sex workers have access to fair wages, health care, and safe work environments. Unfortunately, sex work has not yet been decriminalized without being replaced by a regulatory scheme anywhere in the United States.[213]

### Are there laws that protect sex workers from abuse by their customers or pimps?

Although sex workers are afforded the same legal protection as the general population, the reality is that the violence and abuse they suffer is commonly ignored. As a result, the justice system fails those who need its assistance the most. Statistics indicate that sex workers are often violated or abused by their customers. One study showed that 70 percent of sex workers have experienced rape or abuse by a customer. Sex workers were subjected to these violations on average 31.3 times. The sex workers surveyed also reported being attacked or beaten by a customer 4.3 times. The study also revealed that 73 percent of the sex workers had experienced rapes *unrelated* to their work.[214] Recent studies have also compared the dynamic that exists between many pimps and the women who work for them as equivalent to the dynamic that exists in relationships marked by domestic violence.

Sex workers are often unwilling and afraid to report the abuse they have suffered to the same police officers who are also often their harassers. Sex workers are also reluctant to report abuse for the same reasons that other victims of sexual assault are reluctant: they may fear being stigmatized and having their stories of abuse doubted. The justice system, itself, also poses a significant obstacle to sex workers reporting abuse. The fears of sex workers that they will not be believed are often proved reasonable when their credibility is challenged in rape cases.[215] The fact that trial courts will allow a victim's history of prostitution to be presented at trial creates a forum for a sex worker to suffer public humiliation.[216]

Fortunately, at least one jurisdiction has provided sex workers with a legal remedy against some of their abusers. The Florida legislature enacted a statute in 1992 that allows sex workers to file lawsuits against their pimps for coercing them into prostitution. The statute allows sex workers to recover compensatory and punitive damages from their pimps.[217] Some local governments have implemented innovative programs to better meet the needs of sex workers, even while it remains difficult to prosecute the abusers. Essex County, New Jersey, for example, created a task force on crimes against sex workers and allocated resources to developing relationships with sex workers in order to gain information necessary to address their needs. The San Francisco Task Force on Prostitution urged local prosecutors to adopt a policy refusing to prosecute individuals engaged in sex work and to redirect resources toward increased enforcement of laws addressing expressed neighborhood concerns, such as noise and littering.[218]

### Should sex workers be subjected to mandatory testing for venereal diseases, such as syphilis, gonorrhea, or HIV, when solicitors are not subject to such testing?

No. Such mandatory testing is unsound public health policy. The U.S. Department of Health reports that only 3–5 percent of the sexually transmitted diseases in this country are related to sex work.[219] Studies have shown no correlation between sex with sex workers and positive HIV status. Indeed, it has been found that sex workers are more likely than other people to use condoms and engage in safer sex practices to prevent the transmission of disease.[220] Additionally, testing only one partner in a sexual transaction obviously does little to halt the spread of a disease.

Mandatory testing of sex workers may be vulnerable to legal challenge on equal protection and Fourth Amendment grounds.[221] Courts, however, have held that requiring sex workers to submit to HIV testing constitutes neither an unreasonable search and seizure in violation of the Fourth Amendment to the U.S. Constitution nor a violation of equal protection guaranteed under the Fourteenth Amendment.[222]

As a practical matter, targeting sex workers for forced testing simply will not work as a public health prevention strategy. If there is any group that will be driven underground by such a policy, it is sex workers. An alternative to mandatory testing of sex workers would be a program requiring venereal disease counseling (which would offer testing on a voluntary basis) for both sex workers and their customers, similar to the programs required of persons convicted of driving while intoxicated. As with any counseling and testing program, confidentiality and antidiscrimination protections should be enforced.[223]

# Notes

1. Gail Russell Chaddock, *U.S. Notches World's Highest Incarceration Rate*, CHRISTIAN SCIENCE MONITOR, Aug. 18, 2003.

2. Paige M. Harrison and Allen J. Beck, *Prisoners in 2004*, BUREAU JUST. STAT. BULL. 1–2, 4 (Oct. 2005).

3. Usually, women sentenced to terms of a year or more are sent to prison; those incarcerated for less than a year and those awaiting adjudication or arraignment are sent to jail.

4. WOMEN IN PRISON PROJECT, CORRECTIONAL ASS'N OF N.Y., WOMEN IN PRISON FACT SHEET (2005), *available at* http://www.correctionalassociation.org/WIPP/publications/Women_in_Prison_Fact_Sheet_2005.pdf [hereinafter WOMEN IN PRISON FACT SHEET].

5. SUSAN BOYD, FROM WITCHES TO CRACK MOMS: WOMEN, DRUG LAW, AND POLICY (Carolina Academic Press 2004).

6. Myrna S. Raeder, *A Primer on Gender-Related Issues That Affect Female Offenders*, 20 CRIM. JUST. 4, 4 (2005) [hereinafter Raeder, *A Primer*] (*citing* Paige M.

Harrison and Allen J. Beck, *Prisoners in 2003*, BUREAU JUST. STAT. BULL., 10 (Nov. 2004)).

7. Marsha Levick and Francine T. Sherman, *When Individual Differences Demand Equal Treatment: An Equal Rights Approach to the Special Needs of Girls in the Juvenile Justice System*, 18 WIS. WOMEN'S L.J. 9, 9 (2003).

8. WOMEN IN PRISON FACT SHEET, *supra* note 4.

9. *Id.*

10. JOHN IRWIN, VINCENT SCHIRALDI, AND JASON ZIEDENBERG, JUSTICE POLICY INSTITUTE, AMERICA'S ONE MILLION NONVIOLENT PRISONERS 6 (Mar. 1999), *available at* http://www.justicepolicy.org/downloads/onemillionnonviolentoffenders.pdf.

11. Raeder, *A Primer, supra* note 6, at 6.

12. *Id.* (*citing* Caroline Wolf Harlow, *Prior Abuse Reported by Inmates and Probationers*, BUREAU JUST. STAT. BULL., 2 (Apr. 1999)); *see also* LEGAL SERVICES FOR PRISONERS WITH CHILDREN, FACT SHEET ON WOMEN PRISONERS, http://prisoners withchildren.org/pubs/womgen.pdf (last visited Mar. 20, 2007) [hereinafter FACT SHEET ON WOMEN PRISONERS].

13. Raeder, *A Primer, supra* note 6, at 7; WOMEN IN PRISON PROJECT, CORRECTIONAL ASSOCIATION OF NEW YORK, SURVIVORS OF ABUSE IN PRISON FACT SHEET (Mar. 2005), *available at* http://www.correctionalassociation.org/WIPP/publications/Suvivors_of_Abuse_Fact_Sheet_2005.pdf.

14. Raeder, *A Primer, supra* note 6, at 6–7.

15. Michelle S. Jacobs, *Piercing the Prison Uniform of Invisibility for Black Female Inmates,* 94 J. CRIM. L. & CRIMINOLOGY 795, 795–96 (2004); *see also* Myrna S. Raeder, *Gender and Sentencing: Single Moms, Battered Women, and Other Sex-Based Anomalies in the Gender-Free World of the Federal Sentencing Guidelines*, 20 PEPP. L. REV. 905 (1993).

16. THE SENTENCING PROJECT, FACT SHEET: WOMEN IN PRISON (Oct. 2005), *available at* http://www.sentencingproject.org/pdfs/1032.pdf [hereinafter SENTENCING PROJECT FACT SHEET].

17. MARC MAUER, CATHY POTLER, AND RICHARD WOLF, THE SENTENCING PROJECT, GENDER AND JUSTICE: WOMEN, DRUGS, AND SENTENCING POLICY 4 (Nov. 1999), *available at* http://www.sentencingproject.org/tmp/File/Drug%20Policy/dp_genderandjustice.pdf.

18. Harrison and Beck, *Prisoners in 2004, supra* note 2, at 4.

19. ACLU, CAUGHT IN THE NET: THE IMPACT OF DRUG POLICIES ON WOMEN AND FAMILIES 1–2 (Mar. 2005) [hereinafter CAUGHT IN THE NET].

20. Raeder, *A Primer, supra* note 6, at 2.

21. SENTENCING PROJECT FACT SHEET, *supra* note 16.

22. *Id.*

23. Apprendi v. New Jersey, 530 U.S. 466 (2000).

24. Blakely v. Washington, 542 U.S. 296 (2004).

25. United States v. Booker, 543 U.S. 220 (2005).

26. Rhodes v. Chapman, 452 U.S. 337 (1981).

27. Estelle v. Gamble, 429 U.S. 97 (1976), *reh'g denied,* 429 U.S. 1066 (1977).

28. Farmer v. Brennan, 511 U.S. 825 (1994).

29. Hudson v. McMillian, 503 U.S. 1 (1992); Hope v. Pelzer, 536 U.S. 730 (2002).

30. Helling v. Ms Kinney, 509 U.S. 25 (1993).

31. Hudson v. Palmer, 468 U.S. 517 (1984).

32. Bell v. Wolfish, 441 U.S. 520 (1979).

33. Vaughan v. Ricketts, 950 F.2d 1464 (9th Cir. 1991).

34. Wolff v. McDonnell, 418 U.S. 539 (1974).

35. Sandin v. Conner, 515 U.S. 472 (1995).

36. Meachum v. Fano, 427 U.S. 215 (1976) (intrastate transfers); Olim v. Wakinekona, 461 U.S. 238 (1983) (interstate transfers).

37. Turner v. Safley, 482 U.S. 78 (1987).

38. Religious Land Use and Institutionalized Persons Act of 2000, 42 U.S.C. § 2000cc-1(a)(1)-(2) (2000) ("No government shall impose a substantial burden on the religious exercise of a person residing in or confined to an institution," unless the burden furthers "a compelling governmental interest" and does so by "the least restrictive means."); Cutter v. Wilkinson, 544 U.S. 709 (2005) (holding that RLUIPA in increasing level of protection of prisoners' and other incarcerated persons' religious rights did not violate U.S. Constitution).

39. 42 U.S.C. § 2000e-2 (1976).

40. Dothard v. Rawlinson, 433 U.S. 321 (1977) (where female plaintiff sued to reverse discriminatory height and weight requirements for prison guards).

41. *Compare* Everson v. Mich. Dep't of Corr., 391 F.3d 737 (6th Cir. 2004) (prison system may bar men from certain positions in women's prison), *and* Robino v. Iranon, 145 F.3d 1109 (9th Cir. 1998) (prison system may bar men from certain positions in women's prison), *with* Torres v. Wis. Dep't. of Health & Soc. Servs., 838 F.2d 944 (7th Cir. 1988) (men may not be barred from working in women's prison), *and* Forts v. Ward, 621 F.2d 1210 (2d Cir. 1980) (men may not be barred from working in women's prison).

42. Jordan v. Gardner, 986 F.2d 1521, 1526 (9th Cir. 1993) (en banc).

43. Forts v. Ward, 621 F.2d 1210 (1980).

44. Tharp v. Iowa Dep't. of Corr., 68 F.3d 223 (8th Cir. 1995) (adjusting male guards' work assignments did not violate Title VII because male plaintiffs were not harmed); *Torres,* 838 F.2d 944 (suggesting that to protect women prisoners' privacy, prisons could provide them with appropriate sleepwear and allow them to cover windows while dressing or using toilet); Everson v. Mich. Dep't of Corr., 222 F. Supp. 2d 864 (E.D. Mich. 2002) (suggesting that department of corrections could allow for gender-specific assignment for certain tasks), *rev'd on other grounds,* 391 F.3d 737 (6th Cir. 2004).

45. Delisa Springfield, *Sisters in Misery: Utilizing International Law to Protect United States Female Prisoners from Sexual Abuse*, 10 IND. INT'L & COMP. L. REV. 457, 464 (2000).

46. AMNESTY INTERNATIONAL USA, ABUSE OF WOMEN IN CUSTODY: SEXUAL MISCONDUCT AND SHACKLING OF PREGNANT WOMEN 6 (2001) [hereinafter ABUSE OF WOMEN IN CUSTODY 2001].

47. Martin A. Greer, *Human Rights and Wrongs in Our Own Backyard: Incorporating International Human Rights Protections under Domestic Civil Rights Law—A Case Study of Women in United States Prisons*, 31 HARV. HUM. RTS. J. 71, 81 (2000).

48. Springfield, *supra* note 45.

49. ABUSE OF WOMEN IN CUSTODY 2001, *supra* note 46, at 6.

50. The recommendations are (1) statutes should not allow for making the prisoner criminally liable for engaging in sexual conduct (Arizona, California, Delaware, and Nevada currently make this possible); (2) statutes should penalize custodial sexual misconduct as a felony (five states and the U.S. Bureau of Prisons do not treat it as such); (3) statutes should cover all forms of sexual abuse (this is not so in seventeen states); (4) statutes should not allow an officer to claim a prisoner consented to the sexual act(s) in order to avoid prosecution (this defense is permitted in Colorado, Missouri, and New Hampshire); (5) statutes should cover all staff and custodians (twenty-eight states and the U.S. Bureau of Prisons do not cover all staff and custodians); and (6) statutes should cover all correctional facilities and locations (this is not the case in fourteen states and the U.S. Bureau of Prisons). AMNESTY INTERNATIONAL USA, ABUSE OF WOMEN IN CUSTODY: SEXUAL MISCONDUCT AND SHACKLING OF PREGNANT WOMEN—UPDATE (2006), *available at* http://www.amnestyusa.org/women/custody/keyfindings_legislation.html.

51. Everson v. Mich. Dep't of Corr., 222 F. Supp. 2d 864, 895 (E.D. Mich. 2002).

52. For more information on this subject, *see* Rebecca Jurado, *The Essence of Her Womanhood: Defining the Privacy Rights of Women Prisoners and the Employment Rights of Women Guards*, 7 AM. U.J. GENDER SOC. POL'Y & L. 1 (1999).

53. FACT SHEET ON WOMEN PRISONERS, *supra* note 12.

54. WOMEN IN PRISON PROJECT, CORRECTIONAL ASSOCIATION OF NEW YORK, IMPRISONMENT AND FAMILIES FACT SHEET (2005), *available at* http://correctionalassociation.org/WIPP/publications/Families%20Fact%20Sheet%202007.pdf [hereinafter IMPRISONMENT AND FAMILIES FACT SHEET].

55. *Id.*

56. *Id.*

57. Jeremy Travis, *Families and Children*, 69 J. FED. PROBATION 31, 36 (2005); *see also* Pitts v. Meese, 684 F. Supp. 303 (D.D.C. 1987); Pitts v. Thornburgh, 866 F.2d 1450 (D.C. Cir. 1989).

58. IMPRISONMENT AND FAMILIES FACT SHEET, *supra* note 54.

59. *Id.*

60. Family Unity Demonstration Project Act, Durenberger (and Simon) Amendment No. 1176, S1607, 103rd Cong. 1st Sess. (Nov. 2, 1993) in 139 Cong. Rec. S15624 (Nov. 10, 1993).

61. ABUSE OF WOMEN IN CUSTODY 2001, *supra* note 46 at 25.

62. Examples of such programs include the following: in New York, the Children's Center at Bedford Hills Correctional Facility, which has a prison nursery in which mothers in prison may keep their children up to one year after birth, as well as extensive visitation and family support programs; in California, the Family Foundations Program (FFP), which is an alternative sentencing program where inmates serve exactly twelve months in this program regardless of the sentence length; and the Community Prisoner Mother Program (CPMP), where inmate mothers serve the remainder of their prison term provided that they have at least ninety days remaining and no more than five years. Both programs provide enhanced visitation programs, counseling, reunification support, and skills training. In Connecticut, Community Solutions Inc. provides community-based alternatives to incarceration, including residential treatment and work-release programs for mothers who are pregnant or caring for preschool children. Their programs provide six months of residential support for pregnant offenders through the final trimester of pregnancy and the first three months after birth. This list is by no means exhaustive. For more information, *see* NATIONAL INSTITUTE FOR CORRECTIONS, SERVING CHILDREN AND FAMILIES OF ADULT OFFENDERS: A DIRECTORY OF PROGRAMS (2005), *available at* http://www.nicic.org/pubs/2005/020200.pdf; CENTER FOR CHILDREN OF INCARCERATED PARENTS, NATIONAL SURVEY OF RESIDENTIAL MOTHER-CHILD CORRECTIONAL PROGRAMS (2001), *available at* http://www.e-ccip.org/ [hereinafter CENTER FOR CHILDREN OF INCARCERATED PARENTS].

63. CENTER FOR CHILDREN OF INCARCERATED PARENTS, *supra* note 62.

64. Rios v. Rowland, Civ. No. 330211 (Super. Ct. of Cal. 1985).

65. ABUSE OF WOMEN IN CUSTODY 2001, *supra* note 46, at 26; *see also* CENTER FOR CHILDREN OF INCARCERATED PARENTS, *supra* note 62.

66. ITVS, WHEN THE BOUGH BREAKS, MOTHERS IN PRISON, http://www.itvs.org/whentheboughbreaks/mothers.html (last visited Mar. 20, 2007).

67. Martha L. Raimon, *Barriers to Achieving Justice for Incarcerated Parents*, 70 FORDHAM L. REV. 421, 424 (2001); IMPRISONMENT AND FAMILIES FACT SHEET, *supra* note 54.

68. Erica D. Benites, *Comment, In Defense of the Family: An Argument for Maintaining the Parental Rights of Incarcerated Women in Texas*, 3 SCHOLAR 193, 205 (2001) (*citing* Adoption and Safe Families Act, 103(a)(b)(E) (1997) (codified as amended at 42 U.S.C. 603, 622, 629, 629a, 629b, 645, 653, 670–675, 677–679, 679b, 901, 1305, 1320a-9, 5111, 5113); *see also* Judge Ernestine S. Gray, *The Adoption and Safe Families Act of 1997: Confronting an American Tragedy*, 46 LA. B.J. 477,

479–80 (1999) (listing the factors for which the reasonable-efforts requirement does not apply).

69. Catherine J. Ross, *The Tyranny of Time: Vulnerable Children, "Bad" Mothers, and Statutory Deadlines in Parental Termination Proceedings,* 11 VA. J. SOC. POL'Y & L. 176, 198 (2004) (*citing* U.S. Gen. Accounting Office, States' Early Experiences Implementing the Adoption and Safe Families Act GAO/HEHS-00-1 6 (Dec. 22, 1999)).

70. Philip M. Genty, *Twelfth Annual Symposium on Contemporary Urban Challenges: Damage to Family Relationship as a Collateral Consequence of Parental Incarceration,* 30 FORDHAM URB. L.J. 1671, 1677 (2003).

71. The Illinois Supreme Court overturned the relevant statute, known as "section 1(D)(m-1) of the Adoption Act," in *In re H.G.,* 757 N.E.2d 868, 872 (2001) (The court expressly rejected the state's argument that "a fit parent does not allow his or her child to languish in foster care for fifteen months." It pointed out that the case before it "aptly illustrated" that, "in many cases, the length of a child's stay in foster care has nothing to do with the parent's ability or inability to safely care for the child but, instead, is due to circumstances beyond the parent's control.").

72. The South Carolina statute adds a ground for termination where a child "has been in foster care under the responsibility of the State for fifteen of the most recent twenty-two months" and termination is in the best interest of the child, S.C. CODE ANN. § 20-7-1572(8) (West 2006). However, the courts in South Carolina have made it clear that incarceration alone is not sufficient grounds for termination of parental rights. S.C. Dep't. of Soc. Servs. v. Wilson, 543 S.E.2d 580, 584 (S.C. Ct. App. 2001).

73. 42 U.S.C.A. 671(a)(15)(D). ASFA allows an agency to forgo reasonable efforts where

(i) the parent has subjected the child to aggravated circumstances (as defined in State law, which definition may include but need not be limited to abandonment, torture, chronic abuse, and sexual abuse);

(ii) the parent has—

(I) committed murder . . . of another child of the parent;

(II) committed voluntary manslaughter . . . of another child of the parent;

(III) aided or abetted, attempted, conspired, or solicited to commit such a murder or such a voluntary manslaughter; or

(IV) committed a felony assault that results in serious bodily injury to the child or another child of the parent; or

(iii) the parental rights of the parent to a sibling have been terminated involuntarily. *Id.*

74. Genty, *supra* note 70, at 1676–77. In Alaska, a court may determine that reasonable efforts are not required where "the parent or guardian is incarcerated and is unavailable to care for the child during a significant period of the child's minority,

considering the child's age and need for care by an adult." *Id.* at 1684, n.43 (citing Alaska Stat. § 47.10.088(d) and Alaska Stat. § 47.10.086(b)(10)). In Kentucky, "aggravated circumstances" includes cases where "the parent is incarcerated and will be unavailable to care for the child for a period of at least one (1) year from the date of the child's entry into foster care and there is no appropriate relative placement available during this period of time." *Id.* (citing Ky. Rev. Stat. Ann. § 600.020(2) (b)). In North Dakota, "aggravated circumstances" includes circumstances where a parent's latest release date will occur after the child's majority if the child is nine or older, or after the child is twice her current age if the child is under nine. *Id.* (citing N.D. Cent. Code § 27-20-02(f)). In South Dakota, reunification is not required where a parent "is incarcerated and is unavailable to care for the child during a significant period of the child's minority, considering the child's age and the child's need for care by an adult." *Id.* (citing S.D. Cod Laws § 26-8A-21.1(4)). In Tennessee, "aggravated circumstances" includes "abandonment," one definition of which applies to parents and guardians who are incarcerated at the time of the institution of the proceeding to terminate parental rights, or who have been incarcerated during all or part of the previous four months and who have willfully failed to visit or provide reasonable support for their children in the four months prior to incarceration or have "engaged in conduct prior to incarceration which exhibits a wanton disregard for the welfare of the child." *Id.* (citing Tenn. Code Ann. § 36-1-102(1) (A)(iv)).

75. Cristine H. Kim, Note, *Putting Reason Back into the Reasonable-Efforts Requirement in Child Abuse and Neglect Cases,* U. Ill. L. Rev. 287, 324 (1999) (citing Ariz. Rev. Stat. Ann. § 8-533(B)(4) (West Supp. 1998); Colo. Rev. Stat. Ann. § 19-3-604(1)(b)(III) (West Supp. 1998); Fla. Stat. Ann. § 39.464(1)(d) (West 1998); Idaho Code § 16-2005(j)(3) (Supp. 1998); 750 Ill. Comp. Stat. Ann. § 50/1(D)(s), (t) (West Supp. 1998); Iowa Code Ann. § 232.116(1)(i)(2) (West Supp. 1998); La. Child. Code Ann. art. 1015(6) (West Supp. 1998); Mich. Comp. Laws Ann. § 712A.19b(3)(h) (West Supp. 1998); Ohio Rev. Code Ann. § 2151.41.4(E) (7), (8) (Anderson Supp. 1996); R.I. Gen. Laws § 15-7-7(a)(2)(i) (1996); Tenn. Code Ann. § 36-1-113(g)(6) (Supp. 1997); Tex. Fam. Code Ann. § 161.001(1)(Q) (Vernon 1996 & Supp. 2000); Wyo. Stat. Ann. § 14-2-309(a)(iv) (Michie 1997)).

76. The friend or relative with whom a parent seeks to place her child must successfully complete a home study and a favorable background check to gain approval by child welfare authorities. Tex. Fam. Code Ann. § 107.052; *see also* Tex. Admin. Code § 700.520(b) (1999) (providing Child Protection Services with the authority to request a criminal background check from the Texas Department of Public Safety or local law enforcement). The Department's policy requires that a criminal background check be conducted on every individual requesting possession of a child. *See id.* § 700.520(b)(3).

77. Tex. Fam. Code Ann. § 161.001(1)(Q).

78. Ross, *supra* note 69, at 207.

79. OR. REV. STAT. § 419B.498; *see generally* Kathryn T. Jones, Note, *Prenatal Substance Abuse: Oregon's Progressive Approach to Treatment and Child Protection Can Support Children, Women, and Families*, 35 WILLAMETTE L. REV. 797, 815–16 (1999) (citing S.B. 689, 69th Leg., 1997 OR. LAWS ch. 873, 2a(2)(a)(A) (codified as amended at OR. REV. STAT. 419B.090 et seq.)).

80. UTAH CODE ANN. § 78-3a-311(6) (West 2005).

81. N.Y. SOC. SERV. LAW § 384-b(2)(b), (7)(f) (McKinney 2005).

82. CAL. WELF. & INST. CODE § 361.5(e)(1) (1999).

83. Naomi R. Cahn, Symposium, *Battered Women, Child Maltreatment, Prison, and Poverty: Issues for Theory and Practice*, 11 AM. U.J. GENDER SOC. POL'Y & L. 355, 359 (2003) (citing Peter D. Schneider, *Criminal Convictions, Incarceration, and Child Welfare: Ex-Offenders Lose Their Children*, in EVERY DOOR CLOSED: BARRIERS FACING PARENTS WITH CRIMINAL RECORDS 53, 61 n.35 (Amy E. Hirsch et al., Ctr. for L. & Soc. Pol'y & Community Legal Servs. 2002)).

84. Ellen M. Barry, *Bad Medicine: Health Care Inadequacies in Women's Prisons*, 16 CRIM. JUST. 39, 40 (Spring 2001).

85. WOMEN IN PRISON FACT SHEET, *supra* note 4.

86. Laura Maruschak, *HIV in Prisons 2003*, 1 BUREAU JUST. STAT. BULL. (Sept. 2005).

87. AMNESTY INTERNATIONAL, NOT PART OF MY SENTENCE: VIOLATIONS OF THE HUMAN RIGHTS OF WOMEN IN CUSTODY (Mar. 1999) [hereinafter NOT PART OF MY SENTENCE], *available at* http://web.amnesty.org/library/Index/ENGAMR510191999?open&of=ENG-373; *see also* CAUGHT IN THE NET, *supra* note 19, at 47–49.

88. Jones v. Dyer, No. H-114154-0 (Cal. App. Dep't Super. Ct.); Yeager v. Smith, 404 U.S. 859 (1971).

89. NOT PART OF MY SENTENCE, *supra* note 87.

90. *Id.*

91. *Id. See generally* Barry, *supra* note 84, at 40ñ41.

92. CAUGHT IN THE NET, *supra* note 19, at 60.

93. 60 AM. J. JURIS. 2d Penal and Correctional Institutions § 30 (updated 2002) (*citing* Batton v. State Gov't of N.C., Executive Branch, 501 F. Supp. 1173) (E.D.N.C. 1980); Bukhari v. Hutto, 487 F. Supp. 1162; Glover v. Johnson, 478 F. Supp. 1075 (E.D. Mich. 1979); Hooks v. Wainwright, 775 F.2d 1433 (11th Cir. 1985) (holding that lower quality of general educational and vocational programs offered to female prisoners at women's state prisons as compared to programs offered male prisoners at men's state prisons violated the Equal Protection Clause of the Fourteenth Amendment); Mitchell v. Untreiner, 421 F. Supp. 886 (N.D. Fla. 1976).

94. *Batton*, 501 F. Supp. 1173; *Bukhari*, 487 F. Supp. 1162; *Glover*, 478 F. Supp. 1075; *Mitchell*, 421 F. Supp. 886.

95. *Glover*, 478 F. Supp. 1075; *Hooks*, 775 F.2d 1433 (holding that lack of prison

industries, work pass, and correctional camp programs whereby women state prisoners could earn good time or money as compared to men constituted a violation of the equal protection mandate of the Fourteenth Amendment); *Mitchell,* 421 F. Supp. 886; Molar v. Gates, 98 Cal. App.3d 1 (Cal. Ct. App. 1979) (holding that county's practice of providing minimum security jail facilities, including outside work assignments, for male prisoners, while denying these facilities and privileges to female prisoners, violated the equal protection clauses of the state and federal constitutions); Cooper v. Morin, 91 Misc. 2d 302, 398 N.Y.S.2d 36, *modified in part, aff'd. in part by* Cooper v. Lombard, 64 A.D.2d 130, 409 N.Y.S.2d 30 (N.Y. App. Div. 1978), *modified by* Cooper v. Morin, 49 N.Y.2d 69, 424 N.Y.S.2d 168, 399 N.E.2d 1188 (1979), *cert. denied* 446 U.S. 984 (1980).

96. *Bukhari,* 487 F. Supp. 1162.

97. *Glover,* 478 F. Supp. 1075. For subsequent history of this case, *see* Glover v. Johnson, 721 F. Supp. 808 (E.D. Mich. 1989).

98. Glover v. Johnson, 35 F. Supp. 2d 1010 (E.D. Mich. 1999).

99. *Id.* at 1017. *See also* Keevan v. Smith, 100 F.3d 644, 645 (8th Cir. 1996) (female prisoners alleged that defendants violated their equal protection rights by failing to provide them with equal access to postsecondary educational programs and prison industry employment. The Eighth Circuit relied on its analysis in Klinger v. Dep't of Corr., 31 F.3d 727 (8th Cir. 1994) to conclude that male and female prisoners incarcerated in Department prisons were not similarly situated for purposes of an equal protection analysis.); Jeldness v. Pearce, 30 F.3d 1220, 1222 (9th Cir. 1994) (Women prisoners initiated a class action lawsuit, alleging discrimination based on sex in various vocational and educational programs in the Oregon prison system. The Ninth Circuit remanded the district court's ruling that penalogical necessity applied to plaintiffs' Title IX claims because it is not a defense to Title IX, but rather just one factor to be considered in determining how Title IX is applied in prisons. The Circuit Court also held that prison educational programs subject to Title IX must be "equally" available to male and female prisoners.).

100. Francine T. Sherman, Practicing Law Institute, Effective Advocacy Strategies for Girls: Promoting Justice in an Unjust System 25–27 (2001).

101. Klinger v. Dep't. of Corr., 31 F.3d 727, 729 (8th Cir. 1994).

102. *Id.* at 730–32 (As compared to the female prison, the male prison housed six times as many prisoners; the average length of prisoner stay was two to three times longer; it was a higher-security institution; and male prisoners are more likely to be violent and predatory than female prisoners, while female prisoners are more likely to be single parents and victims of sexual or physical abuse.).

103. *Id.* at 731–32.

104. Women Prisoners of the D.C. Dep't. of Corr. v. D.C., 93 F.3d 910 (D.C. Cir. 1996), *cert. denied,* 520 U.S. 1196 (1997).

105. *Id.* at 915.

106. *Id.* at 932.

107. Todaro v. Ward, 431 F. Supp. 1129 (S.D.N.Y. 1977), *aff'd* 565 F.2d 48 (2d Cir. 1977).

108. Harris v. McCarthy, No. 85-6002 JGD (C.D. Cal. filed Sept. 11, 1985); Jones v. Dyer, No. H-114154-0 (Cal. Super. Ct. Alameda County, filed Feb. 25, 1986); Yeager v. Smith, No. CV-F-87-493-REC (E.D. Cal. filed Sept. 2, 1987). *See generally* Barry, *supra* note 84.

109. *Harris,* No. 85-6002 JGD.

110. Barry, *supra* note 84, at 196–97.

111. Rios v. Rowland, Civ. No. 330211 (Super. Ct. of Cal. 1985); and Civ. No 333240 (Super. Ct. of Cal. 1990).

112. No. H83-366 (D. Conn. filed May 9, 1983).

113. Greer, *supra* note 47, at 81.

114. *Id.* at 82.

115. Farmer v. Brennan, 511 U.S. 825 (1994); Riley v. Olk-Long, 282 F. 3d 592, 595–97 (8th Cir. 2002) (prison warden and chief of security held liable for rape of prisoner by corrections officer upon showing of deliberate indifference).

116. Hudson v. McMillian, 503 U.S. 1, 6–7 (1992).

117. Smith v. Cochran, 339 F.3d 1205, 1212–13 (10th Cir. 2003).

118. 42 U.S.C. 1997e(a).

119. Pozo v. McCaughtry, 286 F.3d 1022, 1023–23 (7th Cir. 2002).

120. Thomas v. Woolum, 337 F.3d 720 (6th Cir. 2003).

121. 42 U.S.C. 1997e(e), *unconstitutional as applied in* Siggers-El v. Barlow, 433 F. Supp. 2d 811 (E.D. Mich. 2006).

122. Greer, *supra* note 47, at 103.

123. *Id.*

124. Adnan v. Santa Clara County Dep't. of Corr., 2002 WL 32058464 (N.D. Cal. 2002).

125. Kemner v. Hemphill, 199 F. Supp.2d 1264, 1270 (N.D. Fla. 2002).

126. Thompson v. Carter, 284 F.3d 411 (2d Cir. 2002).

127. Ahmed v. Dragovich, 297 F.3d 201, 210, n.10 (3d Cir. 2002).

128. Greer, *supra* note 47, at 106–7.

129. Anthea Dinos, Note, *Custodial Sexual Abuse: Enforcing Long-Awaited Policies Designed to Protect Female Prisoners,* 45 N.Y.L. Sch. L. Rev. 281, 284 (2000).

130. Death Penalty Information Center, Women and the Death Penalty, http://www.deathpenaltyinfo.org/womenstats.html (last visited Mar. 20, 2007).

131. Victor L. Streib, Death Penalty for Female Offenders, January 1973 through December 31, 2005 (2005), *available at* http://www.deathpenaltyinfo.org/FemDeathDec2005.pdf.

132. *Id.*

133. Death Penalty Information Center, *supra* note 130.

134. Streib, *supra* note 131.

135. Elizabeth Rapaport, *Equality of the Damned: The Execution of Women on the Cusp of the 21st Century*, 26 OHIO N.U. L. REV. 581, 585 (2000).

136. *Id.* at 582.

137. *Id.* at 583.

138. Streib, *supra* note 131.

139. *See, e.g.*, McCleskey v. Kemp, 481 U.S. 279 (1987); Deborah Fins, *NAACP Legal Defense and Educational Fund, Inc., Death Row USA* (Winter 2006), *available at* http://naacpldf.org/content/pdf/pubs/drusa/DRUSA_Winter_2006.pdf.

140. AMNESTY INTERNATIONAL, UNITED STATES OF AMERICA—DEATH BY DISCRIMINATION—THE CONTINUING ROLE OF RACE IN CAPITAL CASES (Apr. 2003), *available at* http://web.amnesty.org/library/index/engamr510462003.

141. States without the death penalty include Alaska, Hawaii, Iowa, Maine, Massachusetts, Michigan, Minnesota, North Dakota, Rhode Island, Vermont, West Virginia, and Wisconsin, as well as the District of Columbia. In 2004, the death penalty statutes of New York and Kansas were declared unconstitutional. The remaining states, as well as the United States government and military, have the death penalty. *See* Death Penalty Information Center, http://www.deathpenaltyinfo.org (last visited Mar. 20, 2007).

142. Atkins v. Virginia, 536 U.S. 304 (2002).

143. Roper v. Simmons, 543 U.S. 551 (2005).

144. DEATH PENALTY INSTITUTE OF OKLAHOMA, WANDA ALLEN EXECUTED, http://www.dpio.org/inmates/Allen,_Wanda.html (last visited Mar. 20, 2007).

145. A SERMON FOR HUMAN RIGHTS DAY: KILLING WANDA JEAN, http://www.ccadp.org/wandajeanallen-killing.htm (last visited Mar. 20, 2007).

146. A.B.A. & NAT'L. B. ASS'N., JUSTICE BY GENDER: THE LACK OF APPROPRIATE PREVENTION, DIVERSION, AND TREATMENT ALTERNATIVES FOR GIRLS IN THE JUVENILE JUSTICE SYSTEM (May 2001).

147. HOWARD N. SNYDER AND MELISSA SICKMUND, JUVENILE OFFENDERS AND VICTIMS: 1999 NATIONAL REPORT 121 (1999).

148. *Id.*

149. *Id.* at 115.

150. IMOGENE MONTGOMERY, GIRLS IN THE JUVENILE JUSTICE SYSTEM 1 (2000).

151. Snyder and Sickmund, *supra* note 147, at 121.

152. Nancy Ginsburg, *Girls and the Juvenile Justice System*, 187 PRACTICING L. INST. 131, 137 (2001).

153. Marty Beyer et al., *A Better Way to Spend $500,000: How the Juvenile Justice System Fails Girls*, 18 WIS. WOMEN'S L.J. 51, 51 (2003).

154. OFFICE OF JUVENILE JUSTICE & DELINQUENCY PREVENTION, U.S. DEP'T. OF JUSTICE & GIRLS INC., PREVENTION AND PARITY: GIRLS IN JUVENILE JUSTICE (1996).

155. *Id.*

156. Beyer et al., supra note 153, at 52; Laura A. Barnickol, *The Disparate Treatment of Males and Females within the Juvenile Justice System*, 2 WASH. U. J.L. & POL'Y 429 (2000).

157. Ginsburg, *supra* note 152, at 138.

158. Robert E. Shepherd, Jr., *Girls in the Juvenile Justice System*, 15 CRIM. JUST. 44, 45 (Winter 2001); Jane C. Ollenburger and Kathy Trihey, *Juvenile Justice: Differential Processing and the Illusion of Equality*, 13 HAMLINE J. PUB. L. & POL'Y 229, 239 (1992).

159. Levick and Sherman, *supra* note 7, at 12. *See also* Alvin W. Cohn, *Juvenile Focus: Federal Probation*, 68-DEC FED. PROBATION 60, 62 (2004); Ginsburg, *supra* note 157, at 134; Anne Bowen Poulin, *Female Delinquents: Defining Their Place in the Justice System*, 1996 WIS. L. REV. 541, 565 (1996).

160. OFFICE OF JUVENILE JUSTICE & DELINQUENCY PREVENTION, JUVENILE FEMALE OFFENDERS: A STATUS OF THE STATES REPORT (Oct. 1998), *available at* http://ojjdp.ncjrs.org/pubs/gender/contents.html [hereinafter JUVENILE FEMALE OFFENDERS].

161. Beyer et al., *supra* note 153, at 143.

162. Juvenile Justice and Delinquency Prevention Act, 42 U.S.C. § 5601 (2002), *cited in* JUVENILE FEMALE OFFENDERS, *supra* note 160.

163. OFFICE OF JUVENILE JUSTICE & DELINQUENCY PREVENTION, U.S. DEP'T. OF JUSTICE, & GIRLS INC., PREVENTION AND PARITY: GIRLS IN JUVENILE JUSTICE (1996).

164. *Id.* at 24.

165. FEMALE INTERVENTION TEAM, *available at* http://www.djs.state.md.us/fptf (last visited Mar. 20, 2007).

166. GREENE, PETERS, AND ASSOCIATES, GUIDING PRINCIPLES FOR PROMISING FEMALE PROGRAMMING: AN INVENTORY OF BEST PRACTICES (1998), *available at* http://www.ojjdp.ncjrs.org/pubs/principles/contents.html.

167. Sylvia A. Law, *Commercial Sex: Beyond Decriminalization*, 73 S. CAL. L. REV. 523, 525 (Mar. 2000).

168. *Id.* at 529–30.

169. Ann M. Lucas, *Race, Class, Gender, and Deviancy: The Criminalization of Prostitution*, 10 BERKELEY WOMEN'S L.J. 47, 48–49 (1995).

170. *Id.*

171. *Id.*

172. 63C AM. J. JURIS. 2d Prostitution § 5 (2004) (citing State v. Allen, 424 A.2d 651 (Conn. Super. Ct. 1980); State v. Hicks, 360 A.2d 150 (Del. Super. Ct. 1976); Lutz v. U.S., 434 A.2d 442 (D.C. 1981); State v. Davis, 623 So. 2d 622 (Fla. Dist. Ct. App. 1993); State v. Kelly, 379 NW2d 649 (Minn. Ct. App. 1986); State v. Wright, 561 A.2d 659 (N.J. Super. Ct. App. Div. 1989); *In re* Dora P., 418 NYS2d 597 (App. Div. 1979); Tisdale v. State, 640 S.W.2d 409 (Tex. Ct. App. 1982)).

173. State v. Mueller, 671 P.2d 1351 (Haw. 1983).

174. *See, e.g.*, J.B.K., Inc. v. Caron, 600 F.2d 710 (8th Cir. 1979), *cert. denied*, 444 U.S. 1016, 100 S.Ct. 667, 62 L.Ed.2d 645 (1980) (antiprostitution statute violates no fundamental rights); Kisley v. City of Falls Church, 212 Va. 693, dismissed on appeal at 409 U.S. 907 (1972) (no substantial federal question); Smith v. Keator, 285 N.C. 530 (1974), *dismissed on appeal* 285 N.C. 530 (1974).

175. People v. Mason, 642 P.2d 8 (Colo. 1982).

176. *Id.* at 12.

177. State v. Huie, 630 P.2d 382 (Or. Ct. App. 1981), *aff'd* 2638 P.2d 480 (1982).

178. People v. Thompson, 407 N.E.2d 761 (Ill. App. Ct. 1980).

179. Moore v. State, 201 S.E.2d 146 (Ga. 1973).

180. Commonwealth v. King, 372 N.E.2d 196 (Mass. 1977), discussed one such law. The Massachusetts legislature later rewrote the statute to cover the customer, too, as discussed in Commonwealth v. An Unnamed Defendant, 492 N.E.2d 1184 (Mass. App. Ct. 1986). The Hawaii statute discussed in State v. Tookes, 699 P.2d 983 (Haw. 1985) also appears to apply only to prostitutes and not to customers.

181. *See generally* Julie Lefler, *Shining the Spotlight on Johns: Moving toward Equal Treatment of Male Customers and Female Prostitutes,* 10 HASTINGS WOMEN'S L.J. 11, 17–18 (1999).

182. *Id.* at 19–22 (discussing inequality in the enforcement of law prohibiting prostitution and solicitation).

183. Plas v. State, 598 P.2d 966 (Alaska 1979); *King,* 372 N.E.2d at n.l; *see also* State v. George, 602 A.2d 953 (Vt. 1991) (declining to hold that statute that prohibits only members of one gender from sex-related conduct that could be committed by either gender is unconstitutional on equal protection grounds. Distinguishing approach from that taken in Plas, asserting that rather than read statute without the unconstitutional discriminatory language and apply it in a gender-neutral fashion, the court preferred to leave to the legislature the task of reforming a statute to criminalize conduct not presently prohibited).

184. *See, e.g., Tookes,* 699 P.2d at 988 (Haw. 1985); *King,* 372 N.E.2d at 204; *see* State v. Sandoval, 649 P.2d 485, 487 (N.M. App. 1982) (upholding law that has higher penalties for prostitution than for patronizing prostitutes).

185. *Id.*

186. *See* RICHARD POSNER AND KATHERINE B. SILBAUGH, A GUIDE TO AMERICA'S SEX LAWS 156 (Univ. of Chicago Press 1996).

187. PROSTITUTES EDUCATION NETWORK, PROSTITUTION IN THE UNITED STATES —THE STATISTICS, http://www.bayswan.org/stats.html (last visited Mar. 20, 2007).

188. Commonwealth v. An Unnamed Defendant, 492 N.E.2d 1184, 1186 (Mass. 1986); Riemer v. Jensen, 17 CRIM. L. REP. 2042 (Cal. 1975); *see also King,* 372 N.E.2d at 207 (proof of failure to prosecute male prostitutes would be grounds for dismissing action seeking to prosecute female prostitutes).

189. *An Unnamed Defendant,* 492 N.E.2d at 1186.

190. Minouche Kandel, *Whores in Court: Judicial Processing of Prostitutes in the Boston Municipal Court in 1990*, 4 YALE J.L. & FEMINISM 329, 340 (1992).

191. People v. Super. Ct. of Alameda County, 562 P.2d 1315, 1320 (Cal. 1977); People v. Burton, 432 N.Y.S.2d 312, 315 (N.Y. Ct. Cl. 1980); *In re* Dora P., 418 N.Y.S.2d 597 (N.Y. App. Div. 1979).

192. Julie Lefler, *Shining the Spotlight on Johns: Moving toward Equal Treatment of Male Customers and Female Prostitutes*, 10 HASTINGS WOMEN'S L.J. 11, 27–31 (Winter 1999).

193. State v. Oanes, 543 N.W.2d 658 (Minn. App. 1996) (entrapment was found where facts indicated that police officer initiated sexual activity and all affirmative contact); State v. Emerson, 10 Wash. App. 235 (Wash. App. 1973) (police agents had sex with a sex worker prior to arresting the defendant she was working for).

194. Paul Marcus, THE ENTRAPMENT DEFENSE WITH SUPPLEMENT 54 (Matthew Bender 3d ed. 2002). The majority of states follow the Supreme Court's approach to entrapment, which focuses on the defendant's mind.

195. *Id.*; *see, e.g.,* Dinkins v. United States, 374 A.2d 292 (entrapment defense unsuccessful where policeman invited a woman to engage in prostitution and she responded but did not invite activity); Wylie v. State, 2000 WL 230332 (2000) (police officers request for sex did not qualify as entrapment).

196. *Id.*; *see also* Byrd v. State, 440 S.E.2d 764 (Ga. App. 1994).

197. Marcus, *supra* note 194, at 59.

198. *Id.* at 61.

199. CAL. PENAL. CODE § 653.22; DEL. CODE ANN. tit.11, § 1321(5); KY. REV. STAT. ANN. § 529.080; N.Y. PENAL LAW § 240.37; WIS. STAT. § 947.01.

200. *See* Papachristou v. City of Jacksonville, 405 U.S. 156 (1972) (striking down an ordinance that prohibited "rogues and vagabonds" and "common night walkers," "persons wandering or strolling around without any lawful purpose or object . . . persons neglecting all lawful business and habitually spending their time by frequenting houses of ill fame. . . .").

201. *See* Coleman v. City of Richmond, 5 Va. App. 459, 364 S.E.2d 239 (Va. App. 1988); City of Cleveland v. Mathis, 136 Ohio App. 3d 41 (2001) (invalidating loitering for prostitution statutes).

202. *Id.* at 295–96. *But see* City of Milwaukee v. Burnette, 2001 WI App 258 (2001) (affirming an injunction that enjoined prostitutes from engaging in prostitution-related activities, including "[w]aiting at bus stops for more than one cycle of busses [*sic*] or waiting at bus stops with no money or bus transfers on their person or standing at pay phones for lengthy periods of time without making an actual telephone call." The appellate court did not affirm a provision of the injunction that barred prostitutes from "[s]tanding, sitting, walking, driving, gathering or appearing anywhere in public view within 25 feet of any other [person subject to the injunction] engaged in any of the above listed activities.").

203. Susan E. Thompson, *Prostitution: A Choice Ignored*, 21 WOMEN'S RTS. L. REP. 217, 242–43 (Summer 2000).

204. BARBARA MEIL HOBSON, UNEASY VIRTUE: THE POLITICS OF PROSTITUTION AND THE AMERICAN REFORM TRADITION 156 (1988).

205. NEV. REV. STAT. ANN. § 244.345 (West 2001). The population limit was subsequently increased to four hundred thousand. Nevada imposes criminal penalties on street prostitution, pimping and pandering, and the location of brothels near schools and churches. NEV. REV. STAT. §§ 1.030, 1911, 244.345 (1913).

206. *See* Nye County v. Plankinton, 587 P.2d 421 (Nev. 1978).

207. *See* NEV. REV. STAT. ANN. § 201.354 (West 2001).

208. *See* Nicole Bingham, *Nevada Sex Trade: A Gamble for the Workers*, 10 YALE J.L. & FEMINISM 69, 88 (1998).

209. Law, *supra* note 167, at 560.

210. *Id.* at 561–62.

211. Thompson, *supra* note 203, at 247.

212. *Id.* at 244.

213. *Id.* at 247.

214. Mimi H. Silbert and Ayala M. Pines, *Victimization of Street Prostitutes*, 7 VICTIMOLOGY 122, 127–28 (1983) (The sex workers surveyed ranged in age from ten to forty-six. Seventy percent of the women were under twenty-one. The 148 women surveyed had suffered 192 rapes.).

215. Reliability of prostitutes as witnesses is frequently an issue in rape cases. *See* Tracey Wilkensen, *Victim of Alleged Rape May Have Fled Because of History as Prostitute*, L.A. TIMES, Nov. 17, 1990, § B at 3.

216. People v. Varona, 143 Cal. App. 3d 566 (Cal. Ct. App. 1983) (reviewing court found that it was abuse of discretion to exclude alleged rape victim's history of having pled guilty to prostitution). In a particularly offensive case, a judge found that a prostitute could not be raped. The judge dismissively referred to the rape the woman had suffered as a "breach of contract." *See Metro Digest/Local News in Brief: Man Cleared in 1986 Rape Sentenced in 2 Assaults*, L.A. TIMES, Jan. 10, 1991, § B at 2 (Judge Alson found that the essence of the case was a "breach of a contract between a whore and trick.").

217. FLA. STAT. § 796.09 (West 1993); *see also* Margaret A. Baldwin, *Strategies of Connection: Prostitution and Feminist Politics*, 1 MICH. J. GENDER & L. 65, 70 (1993).

218. Law, *supra* note 167, at 584.

219. PROSTITUTES EDUCATION NETWORK, PROSTITUTION IN THE UNITED STATES: THE STATISTICS, *supra* note 187.

220. Law, *supra* note 167, at 550.

221. In a case brought by the ACLU of Illinois in August 1989, an Illinois trial court held that forced testing of prostitutes violated the Fourth Amendment and

equal protection. However, those cases were overturned on appeal. People v. Madison, No. 88-123613 and People v. Adams, No. 87-281577 (Aug. 3, 1989), *rev'd* 597 N.E.2d 574 (1992).

222. Love v. Super. Ct., 276 Cal. Rptr. 660 (Cal. Ct. App. 1990); People v. Adams, 597 N.E.2d 574 (Ill. 1992).

223. *See generally* Law, *supra* note 167.

# IX

# TANF/Welfare

I n 1996, Congress passed the Personal Responsibility and Work Opportunity Reconciliation Act (PRWORA), making sweeping changes to the nation's welfare laws. The PRWORA "reformed" welfare by eliminating the federal welfare program Aid to Families with Dependent Children (AFDC) and replacing it with a more punitive, time-limited system called "Temporary Assistance to Needy Families" (TANF). TANF made two major changes to the old system. First, it eliminated the federal guarantees of income assistance to poor families and of childcare assistance to adults engaged in paid work. Second, it imposed a strict set of work requirements and time limits on recipients, designed to reduce the number of people receiving welfare and push families into paid employment as quickly as possible.

With the passage of the PRWORA, Congress ended sixty-one years of guaranteed federal assistance to the nation's poorest children and replaced it with individual block grants to the states. States choosing to participate—all currently do—receive a fixed sum of money from the federal government that does not change according to the number of people receiving welfare. They can use that money to provide cash assistance and other services to low-income families in their jurisdiction. States have much more flexibility in designing their welfare programs under the PRWORA than previously and are only required to follow a limited set of federal regulations, spend some of their own money, and create a program that is reasonably calculated to accomplish TANF's purposes.[1] According to Congress, these are

- to "provide assistance to needy families so that children may be cared for in their own homes or in the homes of relatives";
- to "end the dependence of needy parents on government benefits, by promoting job preparation, work, and marriage";

- to "prevent and reduce the incidence of out-of-wedlock pregnancies"; and
- to "encourage the formation and maintenance of two-parent families."[2]

Because the PRWORA gave states so much discretion to craft their own welfare systems, the specific details of what is required and available under TANF programs depend on the state in which an individual lives. To give the fullest and most accurate account of the rights of women under TANF, this chapter would have to discuss each state's rules in detail—a project that is unfortunately beyond the scope of this book.[3] This chapter focuses instead on the baseline rights and obligations that women (and men, in the small percentage of cases where they are the adult recipients of TANF) have in every state, under federal law or the U.S. Constitution. Individuals may, however, be entitled to more protections than are available under federal law, if, for example, their state constitution has a provision requiring the state to provide for the needy. Given the importance of local and state laws in this area, individuals should consult a local legal aid office or other legal service provider for specific advice on their rights and obligations.

Furthermore, PRWORA only authorized funding for TANF through September 2002. Since then TANF funding has been temporarily extended several times, while Congress debates legislation to reauthorize TANF. As of this writing, the Senate and the House of Representatives are considering different versions of the reauthorization bill, both of which build on the original TANF provisions while changing certain aspects and funding levels. Both proposals and conference agreements include major restructuring of the current TANF work-participation requirements and would severely limit the flexibility afforded states that was a key aspect of the 1996 law. However, it is still too early to tell the effect that these changes will have on the lives of poor families, especially given the disconnect between other provisions of the House and Senate versions of the bill.[4] This chapter discusses the current TANF provisions.

Finally, this chapter focuses on the TANF program because it is the main source of income support for poor women and families. But TANF alone is not a solution to family poverty. Many policy changes would be required to truly lift all women and their families out of poverty, including improved access to quality childcare, affordable, secure housing, unemployment and health insurance, the Earned Income Tax Credit, food assistance, and paid family and medical leave. Additionally, many other programs provide some assistance to poor women, and women should be aware that they and their families may have rights to other kinds of federal assistance that cannot be covered in this chapter, including Food Stamps, Medicaid, and (if they or their children are severely disabled) Supplemental Security Income (SSI). For in-depth discussions of these programs and recipients' rights under them, consult the ACLU's most recent edition of *The Rights of the Poor*.[5]

### How does poverty affect women?

Women, especially single mothers, are at a disproportionate risk of poverty in this country as a result of caregiving responsibilities, inadequate access to decent childcare, and the continuing obstacles that women face to obtaining high-wage employment. Approximately 28 percent of all single-parent families headed by women live below the poverty line, compared to only about 13.5 percent of single-parent families headed by men.[6]

Not surprisingly, because women are more likely than men to be the primary caretakers of children, women make up 90 percent of adult recipients of TANF, reflecting these poverty rates and the fact that TANF is only available to poor families with children.[7] Women thus are disproportionately affected by the punitive policies and due-process failures that characterize the current welfare system. The percentage of women affected by TANF is also significant. In 1996 more than 8 percent of all mothers in the United States were receiving welfare benefits. This number has decreased as the welfare rolls have shrunk (to about 4 percent in 2000), but this still represents more than 1.5 million women[8] and doesn't reflect the steady rise in child poverty levels and poverty levels for single mothers since 2000.[9] TANF, its implementation, and its pending reauthorization are therefore important women's issues.

### What were the results of the 1996 welfare reforms?

States made four major changes to their welfare systems after the 1996 PRWORA was passed.[10] First, they adopted a "work first" approach to welfare, designing programs that would move people quickly into work, at the expense of long-term education and skills development for welfare recipients. They also made their work requirements stricter. For example, most states used the new leeway offered by the federal government to limit exemptions from work requirements for parents of young children to only those parents who had children under one year old. Some states went so far as to eliminate the exemption for parents of young children altogether.

Second, states changed their programs to allow welfare recipients to benefit more from paid work. Thirty-one states expanded their "income disregards" for calculating welfare benefits, allowing people to keep more of their cash TANF benefits as they began to earn wages at work. Other states adopted their own Earned Income Tax Credit (EITC) programs to supplement the support that low-income working parents receive from the federal EITC.[11]

Third, states adopted sanctions—i.e., the reduction or termination of benefits—to punish families who failed to fulfill any program requirements, including work obligations. Thirty-six states adopted the harshest form of sanctions, sometimes called "full family sanctions." In these states, the entire family can be denied benefits if a parent or caretaker does not meet work requirements or other program requirements. States also established lifetime time limits for adults receiving TANF benefits, as required by federal law. Most states prohibit adults from receiving TANF benefits for more than five years total during their entire lives. Ten states chose shorter time limits.

Fourth, states established procedures to inform welfare caseworkers and recipients about the new changes in the welfare system. For example, they created orientation programs for new recipients that emphasized the temporary nature of welfare and the expectation that almost all recipients were expected to look for jobs and quickly enter paid employment.

### What effect have these changes had on poor women and families?

The effect has been mixed. Between August 1996 and March 2003 the total number of families with children receiving TANF benefits fell by 53.7 percent, a drastic decline by any measure.[12] Caseloads have dropped more or less steadily since the passage of PRWORA, with federal representatives boasting in early 2005 that "[m]ore Americans are leaving welfare and entering the economic mainstream."[13] Some of this decline may have reflected the unprecedented economic prosperity of the late 1990s when the overall poverty rate also declined, as well as the limited success of some of the reforms. It is also true that more are working. For example, the employment rate for all single mothers rose from 59 percent in 1994 to 74 percent in 2001.[14] However, since 2000, years marked by an economic downturn in the United States, poverty rates have risen each year, with more and more children and single mothers falling well below the poverty line,[15] in spite of dropping welfare rolls. Advocates have pointed to these trends as causes for concern that perhaps the safety net that TANF is supposed to provide to the most vulnerable members of society is failing.[16]

Unfortunately, declining welfare rolls do not necessarily indicate an improvement in the lives of welfare leavers. An Urban Institute report on welfare leavers found several trends. Most of the women who leave welfare are employed in low-wage jobs, primarily in the service sector. Women leaving welfare are employed in jobs similar to those that other low-income mothers have, but are less likely to have employer-sponsored health insurance. One-third to one-half of those leaving welfare report that they have serious trouble finding the money for food, and one in five leaving welfare has serious trouble paying her rent. Overall, welfare leavers report more trouble paying for food and rent than other low-income mothers.[17] More recent reports echoed these findings, but also noted that given the tighter job market since 2000, more and more welfare leavers are having to subsequently reapply for welfare or are at risk of serious hardship because they are not working, do not have a working spouse, and are not receiving any government cash assistance.[18]

There is also some concern that welfare reform has only exacerbated racial and ethnic disparities in wealth and access to employment. Two-thirds of adults who receive public assistance are members of a minority group.[19] Despite efforts to push welfare recipients into work, people of color may be less likely to leave the rolls, perhaps because of the discrimination that persists in the labor market.[20] Some small-scale studies also suggest that people of color may be less likely to receive information about supportive services from caseworkers.[21]

Finally, delegating extensive decision-making power to the level of states and agencies seems to have exacerbated the arbitrariness of the welfare system.[22] There is evidence that the changes have resulted in widespread due process violations.

### Is there a federal constitutional right to welfare?

No. The Supreme Court has held that the U.S. Constitution does not guarantee a right to welfare.

Some justices have argued that the Constitution only provides "negative rights" that protect an individual from governmental overreaching and interference, such as freedom of speech. In contrast, "positive rights" would place duties on the government to provide services and assistance to its citizens, such as welfare and education. The conclusion that the Constitution does not provide citizens with positive rights has led federal courts to hold that there is no government duty to provide equal educational opportunity,[23] protection against private acts of violence,[24] police protection,[25] and fire protection.[26] Consistent with this theory, the Supreme Court has held that the Constitution does not require the government to provide any form of welfare to its poorest citizens.[27]

### Is there a state constitutional right to welfare?

It depends on the constitution in each state, and its interpretation by the state's courts. Some state constitutions do contain language recognizing an obligation of government to provide certain types of assistance to the needy. However, in most states, courts have never ruled on what, if any, assistance the state constitution requires governments to provide.

A few states have ruled that there is no duty for state or local governments to provide welfare under their constitution.[28] Others have created some rights to aid by passing a law, but the state has considerable discretion over who receives benefits and how much to provide.[29] Several states have constitutional provisions authorizing a state or local government to provide welfare assistance, without guaranteeing a right to welfare,[30] while other state constitutions refer to a government duty to provide care for needy citizens without specifying what kind of care or the extent of that duty.[31] Of these states, at least one has refused to grant a right to welfare even where the provision is fairly explicit.[32]

In contrast, New York has recognized a clear state constitutional right to welfare, but its courts have been unwilling to read this provision as a guarantee to a specific level of assistance.[33] West Virginia's Supreme Court also has held that its state constitution requires the state to provide some degree of assistance to the poor, but cash assistance can be time-limited as long as needy persons remain eligible for other forms of state assistance.[34]

### Who is eligible for TANF benefits?

In one respect, TANF is no different from previous federal welfare programs. It is designed to provide assistance only to the poorest families who have, or are about to have, children.[35] The PRWORA defines a "child" as someone under the age of eighteen, or under nineteen if she or he is a full-time student in secondary school or vocational/technical training. States can make certain "good cause" exceptions to this rule. However, income-eligibility rules vary by state and take into account factors such as wages, assets (e.g., a car, a house, etc.) and other resources, and family size. Certain income, and some assets, such as an automobile, can be "disregarded" for the purposes of determining income.

Both married and unmarried parents are eligible for TANF benefits, although one of the overt goals of TANF is to encourage two-parent families.[36] Finally, states can only provide TANF benefits to U.S. citizens and "qualified" immigrants who have been in the United States for at least five years. (See below for information about immigrant eligibility for TANF.) Not all poor families are automatically eligible for benefits. Eligibility will depend on how a state designs its welfare program.

### What happens if a state's TANF block grant runs out?

TANF funds are given as a single, fixed lump sum based on the number of people who were receiving welfare benefits in each state when Congress passed the PRWORA in 1996. Therefore, there has been concern over possible consequences if there is a sharp increase in the number of people needing income assistance. If, for example, hard economic times push more people onto the welfare rolls, federal funding will not, as a rule, increase. States would be free to make up shortfalls with funding from state or local budgets, but this puts a greater burden on states at a time when their budgets would probably be shrinking. States could also attempt to secure emergency federal grants or loans. Finally, if states are facing budget crises, they are likely to design their programs so that there are more barriers to obtaining benefits or so that more families are sanctioned off the program. These are the fastest and most punitive means of decreasing welfare rolls in light of budgetary constraints.[37]

However, since the rolls have continued to remain below the pre-1996 levels, the block grant system has had an unexpected effect. When the number of welfare recipients dropped dramatically after the PRWORA's passage, unexpected funds were available to states to fulfill the aims of TANF. This surplus has allowed proactive states to develop new programs to support poor children and working families. Should the numbers of people applying for and receiving benefits increase in any of these states, these special programs will probably be the first to have their budgets cut.

### How much income can a family have and still be eligible for TANF?

Federal law requires that each state must design its program to help "needy" families with children, but the states define what qualifies as "needy."

Therefore, the amount of income a family can have and still be eligible for TANF is very state specific.

### How much cash assistance will a family receive? Will that change over time?

The amount of cash assistance that a family receives depends primarily upon total family income, the number of children and other dependents in the family, and the state in which the family resides. Most states will reduce the amount of cash assistance that a family receives as their income increases, because adults in the family are required to eventually obtain paid employment.

### How does a family apply for TANF benefits?

To apply for TANF benefits, the head of the family should contact the department of human or social services in her county or city. She will need to fill out an application form, often with a caseworker, and usually must show some documentation, such as identification, etc. One can always call the welfare office first to find out what documents she should bring to apply, or contact a local legal aid, legal services, or welfare assistance organization for help with the application process.

### Does a state have to provide cash benefits under TANF?

No. In fact, the PRWORA gave states the option of eliminating welfare benefits altogether. However, no state has considered this option wise enough to make use of it, and all states provide some type of cash benefits, in addition to in-kind benefits and services such as job training and other assistance.

### For how long can an eligible family receive benefits?

According to federal law, states cannot provide TANF benefits to a family that includes an adult head of household or his or her spouse who has received welfare assistance for sixty months (approximately five years). This limit is calculated in total over the recipient's lifetime.[38] Those months when an individual receives only noncash assistance from a welfare-to-work program do not count toward the federal sixty-month limit. Children and minor parents are exempt from the time limit except minor parents who are the heads of household (or spouse). States also have the option to set shorter time limits on TANF benefits. Connecticut, for example, has a 21-month lifetime time limit for TANF recipients it deems "employable."[39]

**Can states make exceptions to the sixty-month cap on benefits?**

Yes. States may exempt up to 20 percent of their caseload from the time limit for reasons of "hardship," or if the family includes an individual who has been battered or subjected to extreme cruelty.[40] However, states are not required to provide such relief. States are also free to continue benefits to other individuals who have reached the sixty-month time limit, but only with state or local money.

**Can a family be penalized if a child does not attend school?**

Yes. According to the PRWORA, states may—but do not have to—sanction families if they fail to ensure that their school-age children attend school as required by the law of their states.[41] As of 2003, thirty-four states had such policies.[42] States may also offer school bonuses or financial incentives to parents whose children have good attendance or high school achievement, but only a few states use such bonuses.[43]

**Can states impose random drug testing upon recipients of public assistance?**

No, even though federal law allows states to test TANF recipients for drugs and to sanction those who test positive.[44] The Supreme Court has held that state-mandated drug tests invade constitutional rights to privacy and qualify as "searches" under the Fourth Amendment.[45] This means that drug tests can only be justified where the state can demonstrate a "special need" for them so substantial that it overrides the Fourth Amendment's usual requirement of an "individualized suspicion" of wrongdoing.[46] By 1999, only one state—Michigan—had opted to impose routine, suspicion-less drug tests on TANF recipients,[47] and that law was subsequently struck down as unconstitutional.[48]

**Are there any special provisions for victims of domestic violence?**

Yes. States can choose to adopt a special program, called the "Family Violence Option," to serve the needs of those who are or have been victims of domestic violence. States that choose this option must screen recipients for domestic violence and refer those who need them to support services. They can also waive TANF program requirements for recipients, when the requirements might put them at a greater risk of domestic abuse or unfairly penalize them for the abuse they suffered. (For more information on domestic violence and its impact on women, see chapter 5, "Violence against Women.")

**Do victims of domestic violence have the right to have their information kept confidential?**

Yes. For victims of domestic violence in states that have adopted the Family Violence Option, the state must have a procedure in place to safeguard their confidentiality, primarily for safety reasons.[49] For other recipients, federal law requires that states take reasonable steps to restrict the disclosure of information about recipients of TANF benefits.[50] The PRWORA, however, did not specify the meaning of "reasonable steps."

**What happens if a woman has another child while receiving benefits?**

That depends upon the state in which she lives. Traditionally, there would be a small increase in the amount of a welfare grant when a new child enters the family. However, in the 1990s states began to implement what are known as "family caps" or "child exclusions," which essentially prohibit increasing the welfare grant to cover the new child. Under TANF states could choose whether or not to implement family caps, and several states did so.[51]

The theory behind family caps is to discourage recipients from having children, which requires that women know about the policy in the first place. Therefore, to meet this purpose and the requirements of due process, states must provide adequate information and advanced notice about any family cap policy to recipients. For example, in one case, California's Department of Social Services (DSS) was sued for wrongly denying benefits for new children and not providing adequate notice of the policy. DSS settled the case, agreeing to give more notice and to stop denying benefits to families with new children who had not been adequately notified about the cap at least ten months before the child's birth. They also agreed not to apply the cap to the children born to teen parents when the mother becomes the head of her own household.[52]

Critics argue that child exclusions are unconstitutional because they unfairly discriminate against children on the basis of the circumstances of their birth. The Supreme Court has previously found that policies denying children certain benefits because their parents were unmarried or not legal U.S. residents are unconstitutional.[53] These policies punish children in an attempt to influence conduct by their parents; this is generally considered an impermissible exercise of state power.[54] Family caps are comparable in this respect.

Family caps also burden privacy rights by interfering with women's fundamental right to choose how and when to have children, and whether to continue with their pregnancies. The Supreme Court has held that the Constitution prevents states from unduly burdening a woman's right to make decisions about whether or not to give birth[55] and that the government may not try to discourage disfavored populations from having children.[56] Furthermore, once the government decides to provide public benefits, it may not selectively deny those benefits in order to infringe on a constitutional right, including the right to choose when and if to have children.[57]

Nevertheless, courts that have considered these arguments have not been persuaded that family caps violate the U.S. Constitution.[58] They may, however, violate some state constitutions.[59]

Finally, some states have tried to both deny benefits to new children *and* keep any child support payments made to that child, in order to reimburse the state for the benefits the family receives. At least one court has found that this violates both the PRWORA and the Constitution.[60]

### What happens if a recipient family moves?

If a family moves to a state where they meet the eligibility requirements of that state, they should be able to receive benefits there. They cannot be denied benefits solely because of the move. In fact, in *Shapiro v. Thomson*,[61] the Supreme Court held that it was unconstitutional to deny welfare benefits to individuals who recently moved into a state or locality, because to do so violates the fundamental right to travel, and the state in this case could show no compelling state interest to justify this. The Court reaffirmed this principle thirty years later in *Saenz v. Roe*, finding that states could not impose durational residency requirements upon recipients, nor could states penalize new citizens of the state by limiting their cash assistance to the amount they had received in their previous states.[62] States may not penalize newcomers even on a short-term basis, for example, by denying them cash assistance for sixty days.[63] Such requirements not only violate the right to travel but also violate the Equal Protection Clause of the Constitution.[64]

### Are immigrants eligible for TANF?

It depends. "Unqualified" immigrants include both undocumented immigrants and other immigrants permitted to stay in the United States on a temporary basis; unqualified immigrants cannot receive TANF benefits. Under federal law, only "qualified" immigrants can receive TANF benefits, and only under certain circumstances. The definition of a qualified immigrant is very technical and those wishing to explore their options should speak with an attorney familiar with public benefits and immigration law.

Generally, according to the Immigration and Naturalization Act (INA), a "qualified" immigrant is defined[65] as an immigrant who is a lawful permanent resident (a "green card" holder); was granted political asylum[66] or was admitted as a refugee;[67] has been "paroled" into the United States for at least one year;[68] has been granted a stay of deportation;[69] was granted conditional entry pursuant to section 203(a)(7) of the INA, as it was in effect before April 1, 1980;[70] or meets the definition of a "Cuban or Haitian entrant."[71] The Attorney General is also permitted to make certain "battered" or abused noncitizens (and sometimes their children) who meet very specific conditions eligible for programs like TANF. (For more information see chapter 5, "Violence against Women.")

States may choose to give qualified immigrants TANF benefits, but only if they became "qualified" at least five years before applying for benefits. This five-year waiting period is mandatory for most immigrants, but states can choose to make exceptions for those granted asylum, refugee status, or a stay of deportation, or for Amerasian, Cuban, or Haitian entrants.[72]

These policies deny immigrant families benefits that their tax dollars support, and threaten the welfare of poor families and children, but courts have refused to override Congress's decision to exclude certain noncitizens from benefits.[73] Congress itself can resolve the matter, but is unlikely to do so. Both the House and Senate versions of the TANF reauthorization bill have kept these exclusions in place.

### If the head of family is not a citizen, but the children are citizens, can the family receive benefits?

Yes. Many immigrant families include children who are U.S. citizens, either through birth or because one parent was a U.S. citizen when the child was born.[74] These children are eligible for TANF benefits regardless of the citizenship of their parents. However, many immigrant parents in mixed-status families are not aware that they can receive these benefits for their children,[75] and many state agencies have not been eager or able to actively inform them of that right.

### Do recipients have the right to services in their own language?

Probably yes, if their English is limited and if a significant number of people affected by the TANF program in the area also need services in that language.[76]

Title VI of the Civil Rights Act of 1964 is the primary legal source of the right to multilingual services. It states that "[n]o person in the United

States shall on the ground of race, color or national origin, be excluded from participation in, be denied the benefits of, or be subjected to discrimination under any program or activity receiving Federal financial assistance."[77] Federal regulations and guidance memos have interpreted this guarantee as requiring federally funded programs, including TANF agencies, to provide meaningful access to individuals with limited English proficiency.[78] Therefore, these agencies should provide the necessary TANF documents in different languages, after "considering the scope of the program and the size and concentration of such populations."[79] For example, a welfare office that serves many Haitian immigrants who have limited English proficiency must provide written materials or other translation services in both English and French Creole.[80] Welfare offices also are not allowed to ask individuals to bring in friends or relatives as interpreters.[81] However, these provisions are oriented towards access to services only. Bilingual speakers (who are proficient in English) do not necessarily have a right to services in the language of their choice.[82]

### Can convicted criminals receive benefits?

The federal government mandates that states deny benefits to people convicted of any of three types of crimes:

1. *Drug-related felonies*: As a general rule, states must refuse TANF or Food Stamps benefits to individuals who have been convicted of a drug-related felony, unless the state passes a law choosing to opt out of the ban.[83] The ban does not apply to other members of the household, or to the individual's Supplemental Security Income (SSI), Social Security benefits, or Medicaid/Medicare. For individuals with three or more felony convictions this is a lifetime ban, meaning they will never be eligible for TANF or Food Stamps.[84]

2. *Welfare fraud*: States cannot give TANF assistance to any individual convicted in state or federal court for lying about his or her address in order to receive TANF benefits, SSI benefits, and/or Food Stamps from two or more states at the same time. These individuals are banned from receiving benefits for ten years after the conviction.[85]

3. *Fugitive felons*: States may not provide TANF assistance to fugitives trying to avoid being prosecuted or arrested for a felony, or to convicted criminals who are in violation of parole or probation requirements.[86]

### Can teen parents receive TANF?

Yes. However, there are two special restrictions placed on unmarried parents who have not reached the age of eighteen. First, they are required to live in the home of a parent, legal guardian, or adult relative. The state can exempt teen parents from this requirement if they have no such parent, guardian, or relative, if no relatives will allow the teen to live in their homes, or if the teen or the teen's child has been abused or is at risk of abuse in that home.[87] Finally, the state can also make exceptions necessary to serve the best interests of the child. In such cases teens can be permitted to live in alternative, appropriate, adult-supervised environments, or in their current living arrangement if the state considers it appropriate.

Second, there are educational requirements for unmarried teen parents. They can only receive TANF benefits if they have completed a high school education or received a GED, if they are attending a school or program that will result in a high school diploma or its equivalent, or if they are participating in a state-approved alternative education program. Teens with an infant under the age of twelve weeks are exempt from this requirement.[88]

### Does the welfare program encourage marriage or a particular family structure?

Yes. Three of the explicit goals of the PRWORA are to promote marriage, to prevent and reduce the incidence of out-of-wedlock births, and to encourage two-parent families.[89] The PRWORA also requires that states take action to reduce the numbers of out-of-wedlock pregnancies, especially teen pregnancies.[90] PRWORA even includes an incentive program allowing the federal government to award bonuses to the top five states with the greatest decrease in out-of-wedlock births each year, without increases in abortions.[91]

In light of this pro-marriage mandate in PRWORA, many states have taken the step of removing eligibility restrictions that once made it very difficult for couples to receive benefits. However, promoting marriage alone will not serve the interests of women, and indeed may harm them if, in effect, it becomes harder for women to leave abusive relationships. Both versions of the TANF reauthorization bill have set aside up to $300 million per year in funding for marriage-promotion programs, showing that welfare reform will continue to emphasize the creation of marriage incentives, rather than facilitating choice by simply eliminating disincentives to marriage. It is important, then, that the focus of any pro-marriage programs be on creating and supporting healthy marriages, while simultaneously protecting a woman's ability to leave partners who are abusive.

Finally, when passed, the PRWORA included millions of dollars for "abstinence-only-unless-married" programs. Such abstinence programs counsel *only* abstinence, and censor other information that can help women make healthy, safe choices about sexual activity. They do not include safe, medi-cally supported information about family planning and STDs, and have a particularly negative impact on lesbian and gay youth. Furthermore, many of the leading abstinence-only curricula address the issue of homosexuality with overt hostility, or only discuss it in terms of promiscuity and disease.[92] No evidence exists to suggest that abstinence-only programming delays sexual activity among teens, although there is ample evidence that comprehensive sexuality education—that is, education that teaches about both abstinence and contraception—reduces sexual risk taking and pregnancy among young people.[93] Studies show that such programs "delay the onset of sex, reduce the frequency of sex, reduce the number of sexual partners among teens, or increase the use of condoms and other forms of contraception" among sexually active teens.[94] Nonetheless, both reauthorization bills include extended funding for abstinence-only education.

### Can the state require a woman to cooperate in establishing the paternity of her child, and in collecting child support payments from the father?

Yes, if she wants TANF benefits, and she does not have "good cause" to refuse to cooperate. Federal law requires that states deny at least 25 percent of the amount of assistance to any individual who does not cooperate with the state in establishing the paternity of her child and in establishing, modifying, or enforcing child support orders.[95] States can choose to pass welfare laws that deny more benefits, or even take away benefits altogether from individuals who do not cooperate.[96]

"Cooperating" means that recipients must, at a minimum, provide the name of the father and any other information about the father that the state requires, appear at hearings and interviews about child support, and allow their child to be genetically tested to establish paternity. States can establish additional requirements.

Each state has different standards of what it considers "good cause" for not cooperating, although most include circumstances such as a history of domestic violence or the anticipation of future domestic violence. However, states can and sometimes do require extensive evidence to support such claims. Finally, women who lack basic information about the father of their children are put into a difficult position by the statute, but most courts have found that these women cannot be penalized for lack of cooperation due to lack of knowledge about the father.[97]

**What happens to the child support funds when a mother receives both TANF benefits and child support?**

This depends on the state. Under federal law, states must require that any family that receives assistance assign child support and alimony rights to the state, meaning that all child support and alimony funds (up to the total amount of the family's grant)[98] go directly to the state and the state is in charge of collecting payments. In this way states can reimburse themselves for supporting that family. This also means that if the payments do not begin until after the family leaves welfare, the state can still collect back payments from the noncustodial parent.

Depending on the state, individuals may have the right to have some of the child support money collected "passed through" to them, and the state can only keep child support payments due during the time when the recipient is receiving state assistance.[99] Prior to 1996, states could "pass through" up to fifty dollars per month of collected child support payments to families receiving AFDC funds. Under the PRWORA, states are given discretion over how much money to pass through, if any, and at least half the states have chosen to keep any collected child support.[100]

Fifteen states have retained the traditional rule of passing through up to fifty dollars to families and disregard that child support payment when determining TANF eligibility.[101] A few states have slightly amended this concept to retain some funds.[102] Six states pass through all support collected.[103] Among these states, five use some or all of the collected child support to calculate how much the family will receive in benefits.[104] One state, Wisconsin, passes all support collected to the family and disregards the full amount in calculating benefits.[105]

Welfare agencies must inform recipients about child support options and must collect and disburse child support payments in a proper, timely, and efficient manner.[106] Recipients have a right to a hearing to challenge child support payment decisions.[107] Finally, courts have found that a child's Social Security survivor's insurance benefits do not count as "child support" for the purposes of TANF.[108]

New mechanisms for child support included in the 1996 legislation have resulted in a dramatic increase in the amount of child support collected by the states. States now take measures, including withholding child support from the noncustodial parent's wages or unemployment benefits, intercepting federal and state tax refunds, reporting past-due support to credit bureaus or the Department of Motor Vehicles (which will suspend a driver's license for nonpayment), intercepting lottery winnings, bringing contempt of court cases, referring out-of-state past-due cases for federal prosecution, and using private collection agencies. In 2000, the Child Support Enforcement (CSE) program collected almost $18 billion, an increase of 49 percent since 1996.[109] Unfortunately, when states simply use this money to reimburse themselves for the costs of the families' welfare benefits, the families themselves do not benefit. State programs that allow child support payments to be passed directly to the recipient family (without reducing its welfare assistance) have found that this can significantly raise family income, and therefore help children.

### Are there mandatory work requirements under TANF?

Yes. The PRWORA requires each caretaker or parent to work whenever the state determines that he or she is ready to work, or after her or his first twenty-four months of assistance (whichever comes first). After the first two months, however, anyone who is not working, according to the federal definition of work, must be assigned to community service.[110] The state can set the hours and definition of community service work, or opt out of the community service provision altogether.[111]

The PRWORA requires that a certain percentage of a state's recipient families participate in work programs in order to meet federally mandated participation rates. States failing to meet this requirement without reasonable cause[112] risk losing federal funding, meaning that they must spend more of their own state funds on welfare benefits. This is a very strong incentive for states to make sure their recipients work and to sanction those who do not. From 1996 to 2000, Congress steadily increased the numbers of TANF recipients who had to participate in work-related activities. By 2002 states had to ensure that at least 90 percent of two-parent families had at least one adult member participating in work programs and that 50 percent of all families were participating in work activities.[113]

Finally, the current reauthorization proposals for TANF include higher mandatory work-participation rates and new rules about what work activities can be considered for purposes of the federal participation requirements. The 2006 Budget Reconciliation Bill included provisions that require each state receiving TANF funds to meet a 50 percent participation rate for all families receiving assistance, and a separately calculated 90 percent participation rate for two-parent families, effective October 1, 2006.[114] Advocates note that these changes remove from states flexibility to establish welfare policy and are likely to have an extremely negative impact on those who remain on the rolls and have the greatest barriers—mental illness, developmental delays, disabilities, etc.—to obtaining and maintaining jobs.

### How many hours must a parent or caretaker work per week?

Federal law does not set the number of hours an individual has to work to receive TANF, but it does say that if a state wants to count an individual toward the *state's* requirements, the recipient must be working for at least thirty hours per week or, for a single custodial parent, twenty hours per week.[115] Adults in a two-parent family must work a total of thirty-five hours per week (or fifty-five hours per week if they use federally funded childcare) to be counted. Many states tend to require at least this many hours of work from all or most of their recipients, because as mentioned above, failure to meet mandated participation requirements under PRWORA will result in a loss of funding.

Reauthorization may change this requirement. The 2006 Budget Reconciliation Bill included TANF provisions that mandate an increase in the total number of families that must be participating in work activities.

### What "work activities" count toward individual work requirements?

Each state may come up with its own definition of what "work" counts toward the federal requirement of thirty hours per week. That means that states are free to allow individuals to attend school or job training as part (or all) of their individual work requirements. But states may also define work activities much more narrowly and declare that only paid work counts. Federal regulations have clarified this point, noting that the PRWORA's list of what counts as work only describes the work that states are allowed to count towards the federal work-participation requirements.[116] Therefore, a state could, for example, allow full-time college students to count their hours towards their individual work requirements for state law purposes. However, full-time college attendance is not part of the definition of work under the PRWORA, so the state would not be able to count those recipients as "working" for the purposes of meeting the state's federal work-participation goal.

Furthermore, it is important to note that, as a result of the "work first" orientation of the PRWORA, there has been a substantial decrease in the number of recipient families who participate in education and training activities.[117] PRWORA encourages states to push people into work quickly, often at the expense of education. Many advocates have urged Congress to address this problem during the reauthorization, noting that better education and training is a more permanent means of helping a family leave welfare and move out of poverty.

### What can a state count as "work" for the purposes of its federal work-participation goals?

According to federal law, at least twenty hours per week (out of thirty) of the minimum average must come from any of these specific activities:

* unsubsidized employment;
* subsidized private sector employment;
* subsidized public sector employment;
* work experience;
* on-the-job training;
* job search and job readiness assistance (for no more than four consecutive weeks and up to six weeks total in a year);
* community service programs;
* vocational education training (not to exceed twelve months for any one recipient); or
* childcare for the child of someone doing community service work with the TANF program.[118]

The remaining ten hours of required work can come from the above activities, or they can come from

* job skills training directly related to employment;
* education directly related to employment, for recipients who do not have a high school diploma or the equivalent; or
* satisfactory attendance at secondary school or in a GED course for those who do not have a high school diploma or the equivalent.[119]

No more than 30 percent of individuals who satisfy the work requirement through vocational education or in educational activities can count towards the state participation rate.[120] Different limitations apply to work done by parents under the age of twenty who are the heads of households. If they regularly attend school or the equivalent or participate in at least twenty hours per week of education related to employment (such as a vocational school or training program) they can count these educational activities towards the state participation rate.[121]

## Are there penalties if a parent or caretaker does not fulfill the work requirement?

Yes. If a recipient fails to meet her or his work requirement without "good cause," the state must reduce or terminate assistance to that person or his or her family for that month. The state must take away at least as much assistance as the family received for the person, but *can* take away more or even all of the family's assistance. States define good cause and on the basis of that definition decide for themselves when to punish people for not fulfilling their work requirements.[122]

## Are some people exempted from work requirements?

Yes. TANF allows states to exempt two categories of individuals from work requirements: single parents who have a child under one year old[123] and members of families who have been subjected to domestic violence (using the Family Violence Option).[124] However, states are not required to exempt either of these groups from work requirements; they are merely given the option to do so. States can also choose to temporarily exempt other groups from work requirements, and interested individuals should investigate their specific state's program requirements and exemptions.

Federal law also bars a state from reducing or terminating assistance to single parents of children under six if the parent proves that she or he cannot obtain appropriate childcare. The parent's inability to find appropriate childcare must be for one of the following reasons:[125]

- appropriate childcare within a reasonable distance from the individual's home or work site is unavailable;
- informal childcare by a relative or under other arrangements is unavailable or unsuitable;
- appropriate and affordable formal childcare arrangements are unavailable.

Federal law allows states to define the terms above, so the specific circumstances that qualify as proof of unavailable childcare may differ from state to state. States are required to inform families about the inadequate-childcare exception and how to meet its requirements[126] and when determining whether a parent fits this exception must take into account the best interests of the child.[127] However, this safeguard only protects parents from being sanctioned. It does not guarantee childcare, or grant them more time toward the sixty-month limit.

**Can a woman get help paying for childcare?**

This depends on state law. Under the former Aid to Families with Dependent Children (AFDC), the federal government guaranteed that parents who worked outside of the home would receive childcare subsidies. TANF eliminated that guarantee, despite the additional work requirements. However, if states want to provide childcare benefits, they are entitled to money from the federal government to help pay these benefits.[128] Federal money for childcare programs was authorized with the TANF legislation. The subsequent Child Care and Development Fund (CCDF) and its implementing regulations include several requirements that states receiving federal funding for childcare must meet. CCDF funds may only be provided to care for children under three years of age, or under the age of nineteen in the case of children who are physically or mentally incapable of caring for themselves, or who are under court supervision.[129] States must use these funds for families earning below 85 percent of the state median income, and a significant portion of the funds must be given to families who currently receive cash assistance, are in transition, or are at risk of returning to welfare.[130] States can also use CCDF funds to provide childcare support for low-income families that do not receive TANF.[131]

However, funds are extremely limited, especially given that PRWORA's focus on work increases the need for childcare without necessarily increasing the supply. As a result, no state serves all eligible families. In fact, nationally only one in seven children eligible for federal childcare assistance receives it.[132] As with TANF, states have wide discretion as to how to administer their childcare subsidy programs, and there is considerable diversity in the way states have chosen to design their programs.

**What kind of childcare does the state have to provide?**

According to the CCDF and its regulations, states must allow parents to use their childcare subsidy to purchase any kind of legal childcare that the parent chooses, such as family care, in-home care, or daycare.[133] The regulations also specifically permit the use of childcare subsidies to enroll children in religious childcare programs.[134] In most cases, such programs are not allowed to discriminate in admissions against any child on the basis of religion.[135] States are also forbidden from establishing different eligibility rules for parents according to the kind of childcare they choose.[136] Finally, most states have set up a sliding scale to determine individual subsidies, so parents are expected to contribute some of their income to daycare, and the amount a parent has to pay from her or his own pocket increases if her or his salary rises.

States must provide parents and caretakers with information that will "promote informed child care choices," including information about the full range of childcare providers in the area, and the health and safety requirements for childcare providers.[137] The state must certify that the daycare centers and in-home childcare providers comply with federal and state health and safety requirements.[138] Finally, federal requirements mandate that childcare subsidies must be sufficient to allow children receiving benefits to access childcare comparable to that available to children not receiving subsidized childcare. In reality, the quality of that care may vary greatly. For example, one national study found that over one-third of childcare programs were rated inadequate, meaning that quality was poor enough to harm children's development. A Philadelphia study found that only two out of ten centers were rated as good, with the rest being rated minimally adequate or inadequate.[139]

### What kinds of discrimination do TANF recipients face?

Evidence suggests that TANF recipients sometimes face serious discrimination on the basis of sex, race, and disability. Such discrimination is illegal and adversely affects recipients' ability to access benefits, education, and employment.

For example, some caseworkers steer female TANF recipients into jobs traditionally held by women, which typically pay the lowest wages.[140] In order to have equal opportunity to advance out of poverty, women must have access to traditionally male jobs, such as electrical work, carpentry, firefighting, or truck driving, that often pay better and have more career potential. Women must also be granted access to educational and training programs for nontraditional jobs. Finally, TANF recipients are extremely vulnerable to sexual harassment, another serious form of sex discrimination that can directly limit women's access to equal education and work.

Racial minorities also sometimes receive disparate treatment at the hands of caseworkers. One study in northern Virginia found that women of color were less likely than white women to receive information about available childcare and healthcare services, to be offered assistance with transportation to their jobs, and to be encouraged to enter education programs.[141] Other evidence suggests that a larger share of African-Americans than whites who left welfare did so because they suffered administrative sanctions,[142] and African-Americans are less likely to receive government support in the months after they leave welfare.[143] All of these reports suggest that significant racial discrimination exists in the way welfare programs are administered.[144]

Finally, individuals with physical, psychiatric, developmental, and learning disabilities, addiction disorders, and chronic health conditions make up a significant proportion of TANF recipients and often face barriers to employment and independence.[145] Many welfare advocates have begun to focus on treatment of people with disabilities receiving TANF. Some of these recipients may not qualify for Supplemental Security Income, but, without some accommodations, may find it impossible to comply with federal work requirements, much less access benefits. For instance, a 2001 survey by the Urban Institute found that 17 percent of TANF recipients reported a work limitation and 28 percent were in poor mental health.[146] Other studies have found that 20 to 30 percent of welfare recipients tested were learning disabled, and one state study identified almost 70 percent of welfare recipients as having learning disabilities not previously identified.[147]

People with disabilities may need special programs so that they can understand and meet federal requirements, but such programs may not be available. TANF agencies may also make stereotyped assumptions about an individual based on his or her disabilities when making program assignments. Finally, people with disabilities are extremely vulnerable to sanctions because of the lack of appropriate supports, inability to understand sanction notices and rules, and other factors related to the disability, health condition, or illness.[148]

### What legal remedies address discrimination in welfare?

Federal antidiscrimination laws require that federally assisted programs be administered in a way that does not discriminate on the basis of race, color, national origin, disability, sex, age, religion, or political belief.[149] The PRWORA specifies that TANF programs are subject to federal antidiscrimination laws that prohibit discrimination by race, color, national origin, age, and disability. Specifically, it states that the following laws apply to TANF programs: the Age Discrimination Act of 1975, Section 504 of the Rehabilitation Act of 1973, the Americans with Disabilities Act of 1990, and Title VI of the Civil Rights Act of 1964.[150]

Title IX, though narrower in scope than Title VI of the Civil Rights Act (prohibiting discrimination on the basis of race) and the Americans with Disabilities Act or Section 504 of the Rehabilitation Act (prohibiting discrimination on the basis of disability), prohibits gender discrimination in federally funded *educational* programs and applies to welfare programs. Therefore, those agencies cannot discriminate against clients in the educational context.

In terms of employment, other nondiscrimination laws, such as Title VII of the Civil Rights Act (which forbids sex and race discrimination in public and private employment) and the Americans with Disabilities Act (which forbids discrimination on the basis of disability in public and private employment and in public services, including public transportation, public accommodations, telecommunications, and other areas) apply to *employers* in the public and private sectors, whether or not they receive federal funding.[151]

According to guidance from the Office for Civil Rights, these antidiscrimination laws require that:

- No recipient of federal funds can treat people differently, either directly or indirectly, on the basis of their race, color, or national origin. Thus agencies cannot intentionally discriminate and also cannot use procedures that have the *effect* of discriminating by race, color, or national origin. Unless such policies can be shown to have a legitimate nondiscriminatory objective, they are forbidden. For example, agencies may not restrict training or work assignments on the basis of race or national origin by assigning people of color to lower-paying jobs or to jobs that provide fewer opportunities for permanent work. They may not require more documentation of immigration status from a particular racial or ethnic group or only ask people who speak with an accent for proof of citizenship.

- TANF programs may not exclude, deny, or provide different services to individuals on the basis of age. For example, they may not discourage older recipients from applying for computer services jobs, or refuse to allow people under thirty to work in a school because they are not mature enough. They also may not provide referrals to employers who discriminate by age.

- TANF agencies and employers covered by the Americans with Disabilities Act of 1990 may not refuse services to people with disabilities as long as they are "qualified," meaning they meet the essential eligibility requirements of the job or services without "unreasonable modifications" of rules and procedures. TANF recipients who are disabled may be particularly disadvantaged by work requirements and time limits. As a result, some states exempt disabled individuals from work requirements and time limits. Although states may offer such exemptions, they cannot refuse to allow disabled TANF recipients to participate in educational programs, training programs, or jobs because of their disability. States must also ensure that disabled individuals have equal opportunity to take advantage of all jobs and programs, by eliminating unnecessary rules or standards that present obstacles to disabled people. For example, TANF employees cannot refer recipients to jobs that exclude people who have had back injuries without assessing the individual's capabilities; cannot provide information about referrals only on the telephone, without provisions for communicating with people who are hearing impaired; and must accommodate people with vision impairment by, for example, providing them with instructional materials in Braille during educational programs. Agencies must also make sure that their buildings are accessible to people with disabilities, in as integrative a fashion as possible.[152]

• Educational programs and activities associated with TANF programs cannot discriminate on the basis of sex. This means, for example, that they cannot steer women away from job training in electrical repair work, or steer men away from cosmetology jobs. This also means, for example, that women must have equal access to qualified trainers. For instance, a culinary training program cannot have a practice of placing male students in food preparation programs with experienced chefs while sending female students to food serving and meal planning programs with less qualified teachers. It also means that women have the right not to be sexually harassed in educational programs. For instance, a trainer cannot threaten to report a woman to the welfare agency as noncompliant or fail her from the course if she refuses to date or have a sexual relationship with him or her.

Finally, the U.S. Constitution also forbids discrimination on the basis of sex, and applies directly to state agencies, including welfare agencies. In addition, state laws and constitutions may provide individuals with additional rights (for example, in some places employers cannot discriminate on the basis of sexual orientation). Here, as elsewhere, a woman should always check with her local legal aid provider or legal services organization to find out exactly what rights and protections she has under these laws.

**What other rights do "workfare" workers have?**

In 1997, the U.S. Department of Labor issued a guide to the states, reaffirming that workfare workers (or those who work in exchange for welfare benefits) are protected by the same federal employment and antidiscrimination laws as other workers.[153] The Equal Employment Opportunities Commission has also clarified that antidiscrimination laws apply to temporary workers and that "welfare recipients would likely be considered employees in most of the work activities described in the new welfare law, including unsubsidized and subsidized public and private sector employment, work experience, and on-the-job training programs."[154] It is important to note, however, that some workfare programs and placements may not qualify as "work" for the purposes of federal and state worker protection. Whether or not an individual is considered a "worker" will depend on the labor laws of the state.[155]

If workfare workers are considered "employees" under the applicable state law, then the Fair Labor Standards Act (FLSA) applies and those workers must be paid at least the applicable minimum wage as well as overtime. The FLSA has a very broad definition of "worker," so many if not most welfare recipients engaged in workfare are covered by it. However, individuals engaged in activities that are not typically considered "work" may not be covered, for example, those who are pursuing educational activities or job-search activities.[156] Those recipients receiving training are probably *not* covered by the FLSA if they are receiving training similar to that given in a vocational school; the training is for their own benefit; the training does not displace regular employees; the employers do not benefit from the training; the trainee is not entitled to a job when the training is complete; and both trainee and employer understand that the trainee is not being paid.[157] Only some federal benefits can be counted as wages for the FLSA minimum wage requirements.[158]

Workfare workers are also covered by federal health and safety regulations under the federal Occupational Safety and Health Act (OSHA). However, in many states OSHA does not apply to state employees, so the protections workfare workers have may depend on who their "employer" is.[159]

Workfare workers have access to the same unemployment insurance benefits that other workers do, if they are "employees" according to state unemployment law. A few states have explicitly extended unemployment insurance protections to workfare employees.[160] There are some exceptions. For example, federal law allows states to exempt hours worked in "work relief" or "work training" programs for the state (but not for private employers) from calculations for unemployment insurance. Community service, for example, might be considered "work relief" and therefore not count toward unemployment benefits.[161]

Title VII, which prohibits sex and race discrimination in employment, may also apply to workfare workers, although its applicability is not explicit. Provided the worker qualifies as an "employee" as defined by federal and/or state law, the worker should be protected from discriminatory treatment. Problems arise when courts refuse to consider the workfare participants as legitimate employees, such that they may work alongside full-time employees not receiving welfare and do the same work, but have none of the protections.

Workfare participants may also have rights to unpaid medical leave under the Family Medical Leave Act, which provides for job-protected unpaid leave for an employee under certain specified circumstances. However, only employees who have worked with the same employer for at least twelve months and for at least 1,250 hours are eligible for FMLA leave. Most women who work and receive TANF are part-time workers and recent entrants to the workforce and thus are unlikely to qualify for leave under the FMLA. Even if they are eligible, they are likely to be unable to afford to take unpaid leave.[162]

Finally, all other state and federal employment laws should apply to workfare workers as long as they meet the definition of "worker" or "employee" present in the laws. For example, where state or federal law provides that employees may not be fired unless there is just cause, written charges have been filed, and they have been granted a hearing, welfare recipients should also have these rights.[163]

### Does a welfare recipient have a right not to be sexually harassed at work?

Yes. Welfare recipients, like other low-income workers, are particularly vulnerable to victimization at work. Because they are required to work in order to receive their benefits, being fired from a job can often mean the risk of sanctions for noncompliance. Thus the loss of a job would be compounded by a complete loss of any income. Women who are sexually harassed at work are therefore often forced to remain in positions where they continue to be harassed. A 2000 survey by the Applied Research Center found that one in six female workfare participants had experienced sexual harassment in her work placement.[164]

Those who are "working" under the definitions of Title VII and state antidiscrimination laws are protected from sexual harassment in the workplace. In other words, they have the right to be free from demands for sexual favors by employers, employees, or customers and the right to be free from hostile, offensive, or intimidating behavior based on sex that is so severe and pervasive that it creates a hostile working environment that interferes with their ability to work. Both the EEOC and the Department of Labor have indicated that Title VII protects workfare participants if they qualify as "employees" within the meaning of state and federal laws.[165] The Office for Civil Rights of the U.S. Department of Health and Human Services has issued guidelines to TANF caseworkers stating, "Federal civil rights laws, including . . . Title VII of the Civil Rights Act of 1964 . . . continue to apply to States and other recipients that provide funds, employment, training, food stamps and other benefits under the PRWORA."[166] Finally, the Second Circuit has ruled that workers in New York's workfare program (WEP) are "employees" within the meaning of Title VII of the Civil Rights Act of 1964 and could sue for sexual harassment, sex discrimination, and racial discrimination they experienced in their workfare assignments.[167]

Unfortunately, there still seems to be some confusion as to whether a workfare participant is an "employee" for purposes of Title VII, due in part to a pre-PRWORA Tenth Circuit decision that concluded that workfare participants under AFDC were not "employees" for purposes of the Fair Labor Standards Act.[168] (For more information on sexual harassment and sex discrimination, see chapter 2, "Employment: Discrimination and Parenting Issues.")

### What is an "individual responsibility plan"?

The 1996 welfare reforms were based on the notion that individuals should move from welfare to work as quickly as possible. Federal law therefore requires states to assess the work skills, prior experience, and employability of all recipients who are over the age of eighteen. If states choose, they can then require recipients to work with agencies to develop "individual responsibility plans." All states have some version of these, which when signed are usually called either "personal responsibility contracts" or "employability plans."[169] Furthermore, all states require individuals to sign either a personal responsibility contract or an employability plan; seventeen states require both.[170] These plans are agreements between the individual and the welfare agency, and they outline what that individual must do to move into employment, and ideally what the agency must do to help recipients meet their goals. These plans also typically include various provisions, such as the number of hours a recipient must work and what educational or childcare services the applicant needs to prepare for work. They can also include expected obligations such as immunization of children, ensuring the children attend school, or attendance in counseling or drug treatment programs.

While individual responsibility plans can be a useful way to establish goals and responsibilities, it is important that they take into account the barriers that individuals face in achieving these goals.[171] In addition, many states make recipients sign plans that do not include any discussion of the agency's responsibilities, a practice that contradicts the congressional recommendations and unfairly establishes one-sided notions of responsibility.[172]

### Can a recipient be penalized for not following his or her individual responsibility plan?

Yes. If she or he does not have good cause for not following the plan, a state can reduce or refuse assistance to the recipient or the recipient's family.[173] States can define for themselves what constitutes "good cause" and determine applicable penalties for noncompliance. At least one court has found that states cannot penalize someone for not fulfilling the requirements of a work plan, if the agency does not consider the recipient's known barriers to work when formulating the plan,[174] or if the agency does not assist with or respond to requests to overcome obstacles to fulfilling work requirements, such as transportation problems.[175]

### Do recipients have rights to a hearing and other kinds of "due process" before their benefits are taken away?

Yes. "Due process" rights, guaranteed under the Fifth and Fourteenth Amendments of the U.S. Constitution, and by various federal and state statutes, protect individuals' right to be treated fairly. In the welfare context, this means, for example, that recipients have the right to information about available benefits and eligibility requirements, the right to apply for benefits, the right to be given reasons for any sanctions imposed upon them, and the right to an opportunity to tell their side of the story to an unbiased decision maker.

The foundation of due process rights in the welfare context is the landmark 1970 case *Goldberg v. Kelly*.[176] In that case, the Supreme Court held that states had to provide recipients with advance notice and an opportunity for a hearing before terminating their benefits. The protections of due process in this area are crucial; as the Supreme Court noted, "termination of aid pending resolution of a controversy over eligibility may deprive an *eligible* recipient of the very means by which to live while he waits."[177] Crucial to that case was the Court's finding that because welfare recipients had an "entitlement" to benefits, they had a "property interest" in these benefits that was protected by the Fourteenth Amendment. The PRWORA declares that the TANF program is not an "individual entitlement"[178] and therefore raises the possibility that recipients no longer have due process rights under the federal Constitution. In fact, after PRWORA's passage, some states claimed that they were no longer obligated to provide notice and hearings to recipients prior to an adverse action. Others began to deny recipients benefits while they were awaiting a hearing, pushing families into dire need before determination of the correctness of the department's decision. This kind of summary treatment may still violate the Constitution and the requirements of PWRORA.

However, courts that have considered this question have found that TANF recipients do indeed have a "property interest" in cash assistance, and that due process protections still apply.[179] That means, as a matter of constitutional law, states should provide some procedural safeguards for individuals whose benefits are being terminated or altered. In the most general terms, that means states must provide standards and consistency in their welfare program, adequate notice about any changes in TANF benefits, and fair hearings at which individuals can challenge decisions they believe are wrong or unfair.[180]

There are also statutory protections for due process. The PRWORA requires that each state submit a plan to the Department of Health and Human Services that establishes "objective criteria for the delivery of benefits and the determination of eligibility and for fair and equitable treatment, including an explanation of how the State will provide opportunities for recipients who have been adversely affected to be heard in a State administrative or appeal process."[181] As a result, all states provide some form of appeals system through fair hearings.

Finally, many states, most notably Wisconsin, are contracting out the administration of their welfare programs to private corporations. This raises numerous questions, including whether or not constitutional due process protections apply against these private corporations. There is no clear legal answer to this question yet,[182] but as in other areas, advocates urge courts to find that requirements binding upon states are also binding upon state contractors.

### Does an applicant have a right to information about benefits?

Yes. Federal statutes and regulations require that states provide accurate and timely access to assistance programs like Food Stamps and Medicaid.[183] Individuals also have a due process right under the Constitution to accurate information about state-funded benefits.[184]

### What should a woman with a disability do if she needs a special accommodation?

The Americans with Disabilities Act (ADA) requires welfare agencies to provide a variety of different types of assistance to applicants with disabilities. These agencies are required to provide an "equal and meaningful opportunity to participate in and benefit from cash assistance and other public benefits,"[185] "cannot design or administer a program in a way that has a discriminatory effect,"[186] and must make "reasonable modifications in policies and practices to avoid discrimination."[187]

A woman with a disability who needs special accommodations can request them when she applies for benefits or jobs. Sometimes simply an oral or written request by the applicant and/or her advocate can ensure that she receives the assistance needed. If she is denied benefits or sanctioned for reasons related to her disability, she can request a fair hearing to appeal the decision. In those agencies with fifty or more employees, a woman denied a modification or treated unfairly because of her disability can file an ADA grievance with the ADA coordinator at the agency. If she believes that the welfare agency is violating the ADA, she or her advocate can file a complaint with the federal Office for Civil Rights for the Department of Health and Human Services, which has the authority to enforce several federal civil rights laws, including the ADA. Finally, if a woman believes that she has been unlawfully discriminated against because of her disability, she can file a lawsuit in federal court under Title II of the ADA or Section 504 of the Rehabilitation Act.[188]

A full exploration of disability rights and an individual's options and remedies under the Americans with Disabilities Act and Section 504 of the Rehabilitation Act is beyond the scope of this chapter and this book. Those needing more information should contact their local disability rights advocacy organization, legal services group, or legal aid society. The website for the National Center for Law and Economic Justice, http://www.nclej.org, also contains a number of resources regarding disability rights and welfare advocacy and is an excellent resource for advocates and individuals with disabilities.

### What can a woman do if she is denied benefits or if her benefits are stopped suddenly?

She can request a fair hearing, or her state's equivalent, to review the decision. As discussed above, federal law requires all states to have some procedure in place "to provide opportunities for recipients who have been adversely affected to be heard in a state administrative process,"[189] although as with all aspects of TANF administration, federal law does not specify the exact procedures for requesting a fair hearing and the rules around them vary from state to state.

Fair hearings are generally adversarial-style administrative hearings in front of an impartial review officer, requested by clients to challenge any denial, discontinuance, or reduction in aid. Their purpose is to protect clients from arbitrary or unlawful government action by correcting agency errors and mistakes.[190] Those requesting the fair hearing can present evidence to a hearing officer who will in turn determine whether the adverse action (denial, discontinuance, or other sanction) was appropriate given the circumstances. From time to time merely requesting the hearing will cause agencies to review their actions and discover any errors, or may result in informal resolution of the problem outside of the administrative hearing.[191]

It is always a good idea for a woman to consult with a welfare advocacy organization or legal services attorney when requesting a fair hearing. Sometimes these hearings can require an understanding of complex evidentiary requirements and regulations. Even if an attorney or advocate cannot take the case, organizations may have useful information on the actual laws and regulations at issue, how to prepare for the hearing, and what documentation to provide.[192]

### What can a woman do if she thinks she has been discriminated against by her welfare caseworker or the agency?

There are a number of steps a woman can take if she believes that she has been discriminated against on account of her sex. Generally, she can file an administrative complaint with the appropriate agency, or file a lawsuit, or both. Since there are many factors that must be considered in determining whether to proceed and whether to file an administrative complaint or a court case, she should first consult an attorney.

If she believes that the welfare agency is in violation of a federal law, an applicant can file an administrative complaint with the Office for Civil Rights (OCR) for the Department of Health and Human Services, which has the authority to enforce certain federal civil rights laws in health and social services programs, including TANF. It is important to note, however, the limitation in filing an OCR complaint. OCR simply tries to find a solution to a problem and will negotiate directly with an agency in order to resolve any violations. It may or may not consult with the woman complaining.

She can also file a lawsuit. If she is suing under federal law, she can file the lawsuit in addition to, or instead of, an OCR complaint. For information on remedies for discrimination in an employment setting, in an educational or training program, or in housing, see chapter 2, "Employment: Discrimination and Parenting Issues"; chapter 4, "Education"; and chapter 10, "Housing."

### How can a woman file a complaint with the Office for Civil Rights?

She can file a written complaint, either online or by mail, with the Office for Civil Rights. There are several regional OCR offices, as well as a national office in Washington, D.C. Women can file online at http://www.hhs.gov/ocr or send a complaint directly to their regional offices.[193] The complaint should include the following information:[194]

- name, address, and telephone number;
- if filing for someone else, that person's name, address, and telephone number and relationship to the complainant;
- name and address of the organization or person committing the discrimination;
- what actions or policies caused or led to the discrimination;
- when the discrimination took place;
- what type of discrimination the individual or group experienced;
- signature of person complaining; and
- any other information that might be helpful.

Any complaint must be filed within 180 days of the date when the discrimination occurred. OCR may extend the 180-day period if there is "good cause."[195]

After a complaint is received, OCR will determine if it has the legal authority to investigate. If it does not, OCR has the discretion to refer the case to the appropriate agency. If it does have the authority, OCR will initiate an investigation to determine whether the alleged acts constitute unlawful discrimination and will issue a "Letter of Findings," presenting its decision on whether there has been a violation of a federal statute or regulation. If there is a violation, the agency is then allowed a specific time period, usually sixty days, to correct the violation or provide OCR with a plan of correction.

If the agency does not agree to correct its policies, OCR can hold an administrative hearing and decide to withdraw HHS funds from the welfare program, or refer the matter to the U.S. Department of Justice. In practice, however, this rarely happens.[196]

## Notes

1. 42 U.S.C. § 604(a) (2005). States may also use the funds in any manner that the state was authorized to use amounts received under the old AFDC program. *Id.* Current proposals for reauthorization may change this, sharply reducing the states' flexibility in allocating TANF funds.

2. 42 U.S.C. § 601(a) (2005).

3. For a comparison of different states' welfare laws, *see* the Economic Success Clearinghouse (formerly Welfare Information Network) website at http://www.financeproject.org/irc/win.asp.

4. For information on TANF reauthorization and an analysis of current legislation, *see* Center for Budget Planning and Priorities Special Series on TANF Reauthorization Analyses, http://www.cbpp.org/tanfseries.htm; The Center for Law and Social Policy, http://www.clasp.org.

5. Helen Hershkoff and Stephen Loffredo, The Rights of the Poor (1997).

6. U.S. Census Bureau, Current Population Survey, 2005 Annual Social and Economic Supplement, Table POV04, Families by Age of Householder, Number of Children, and Family Structure: 2004 (2005), *available at* http://pubdb3.census.gov/macro/032005/pov/new04_100_01.htm.

7. Office of Family Assistance, TANF Sixth Annual Report to Congress, Characteristics and Financial Circumstances of TANF Recipients, (2007), *available at* http://www.acf.hhs.gov/programs/ofa/character/indexchar.htm.

8. Brian J. O'Hara, U.S. Census Bureau, Current Population Reports: Work and Work-Related Activities of Mothers Receiving Temporary Assistance to Needy Families: 1996, 1998, and 2000 (2002).

9. U.S. Census Bureau, Current Population Survey, Annual Social and Economic Supplements Poverty and Health Statistics Branch, Table 2, Historical Poverty Tables: Poverty Status of People by Family Relationship, Race, and Hispanic Origin: 1959 to 2006, *available at* http://www.census.gov/hhes/www/poverty/histpov/hstpov2.html.

10. The information on these changes comes from Alan Weil, Urban Institute, Ten Things Everyone Should Know about Welfare Reform (2002), *available at* http://www.urban.org/Template.cfm?Section=ByTopic&NavMenuID=62&template=/TaggedContent/ViewPublication.cfm&PublicationID=7692.

11. These programs provide refundable tax credits, which means that eligible individuals can receive a tax refund even if their income is so low that they have little or no income tax liability.

12. Press Release, U.S. Dept. of Health and Human Servs., HHS Releases Data Showing Continuing Decline in Number of People Receiving Temporary Assistance (Sept. 3, 2003), *available at* http://www.hhs.gov/news/press/2003pres/20030903.html.

13. Press Release, U.S. Dept. of Health and Human Servs., Welfare Rolls Continue to Fall (Feb. 9, 2005), *available at* http://www.acf.hhs.gov/news/press/2005/TANFdeclineJune04.htm.

14. Olivia Golde, Urban Institute, Welfare Reform Mostly Worked (2005), *available at* http://www.urban.org/url.cfm?ID=900824.

15. Shawn Fremstad, Center on Budget Planning and Priorities, Falling TANF Caseloads amidst Rising Poverty Should Be a Cause of Concern (Sept. 5, 2003), *available at* http://www.cbpp.org/9-4-03tanf.pdf; U.S. Census Bureau, Current Population Survey, Annual Social and Economic Supplements, Table 3, Poverty Status of People, by Age, Race, and Hispanic Origin: 1959 to 2006, *available at* http://www.census.gov/hhes/www/poverty/histpov/hstpov3.html.

16. Fremstad, *supra* note 15.

17. Pamela Loprest, Urban Institute, Families Who Left Welfare: Who Are They and How Are They Doing? (Aug. 1999), *available at* http://newfederalism.urban.org/html/discussion99-02.html.

18. Pamela Loprest, Urban Institute, Fewer Welfare Leavers Employed in a Weaker Economy (Aug. 2003), *available at* http://www.urban.org/UploadedPDF/310837_snapshots3_no5.pdf.

19. TANF Sixth Annual Report to Congress, *supra* note 7.

20. *See* Harry Holzer and Michael A. Stoll, Employer Demand for Welfare Recipients by Race, Discussion Paper (Jan. 2002), *available* at http://www.urban.org/publications/310423; W.K. Kellogg Foundation Technical Paper, Racial and Ethnic Disparities in TANF: Barriers to the Viability of Low-Income Families, *available at* http://www.wkkf.org/pubs/Devolution/Pub822.pdf; *The Hidden Third Party: Welfare Recipients' Experiences with Employers*, 5 J. Pub. Mgmt & Soc. Policy 69 (Summer 1999).

21. Susan T. Gooden, *All Things Not Being Equal: Differences in Caseworker Support toward Black and White Welfare Clients,* 4 HARV. J. OF AFRICAN AM. PUB. POL. 23–33 (1998).

22. REBECCA GORDON, CRUEL AND UNUSUAL: HOW WELFARE "REFORM" PUNISHES POOR PEOPLE, *available at* http://www.arc.org.

23. San Antonio Ind't School Dist. v. Rodriguez, 411 U.S. 1 (1973).

24. DeShaney v. Winnebago County Dep't of Soc. Servs., 489 U.S. 189 (1989).

25. Jackson v. City of Joliet, 715 F.2d 1200, 1204 (1983).

26. Jackson v. Byrne, 738 F.2d 1443, 1446 (1984).

27. Dandridge v. Williams, 397 U.S. 471, 487 (1970).

28. These states include Connecticut, Moore v. Ganim, 660 A.2d 742 (Conn. 1995); Delaware, Tilden v. Hayward, 1990 WL 131162, 15–18 (Del.Ch. Sept. 10, 1990) (NO. CIV. A.11297); Illinois, Warrior v. Thompson, 449 N.E.2d 53, 58 (Ill. 1983); Beck v. Buena Park Hotel Corp., 196 N.E.2d 686 (Ill. 1964); and New Jersey, Franklin v. Dep't. of Human Servs., 543 A.2d 56 (N.J.Super. A.D. 1988) *aff'd by* 543 A.2d 1 (N.J. 1988).

29. *See, e.g.,* Arizona, Allen v. Graham, 446 P.2d 240 (Ariz. App. 1968); Idaho, Newland v. Child, 254 P.2d 1066 (Idaho 1953); Iowa, Collins v. State Bd. of Soc. Welfare, 81 N.W.2d 4 (Iowa 1957); Maine, Inhabitants of Town of Orrington v. City of Bangor, 46 A.2d 406 (Maine 1946); Nebraska, Elliott v. Ehrlich, 280 N.W.2d 637 (Neb. 1979); Nevada, County of Lander v. Bd. of Trustees of Elko General Hosp., 403 P.2d 659 (Nev. 1965); New Hampshire, New Hampshire Children's Aid Soc'y v. Morgan, 221 A.2d 238 (N.H. 1966); Ohio, Division of Aid for the Aged, Dep't of Pub. Welfare v. Hogan, 54 N.E.2d 781 (Ohio 1944); Pennsylvania, Kratzer v. Com., Dep't of Pub. Welfare, 481 A.2d 1380 (PA. 1984); South Dakota, Sioux Valley Hosp. Ass'n v. Bryan, 399 N.W.2d 352 (S.D., 1987); and Vermont, Town of St. Johnsbury v. Town of Granby, 205 A.2d 422 (Vt., 1964).

30. *See, e.g.,* California (CAL. CONST. art. XVI, 11); Georgia (GA. CONST. art. IX, § 3, ¶ I); Hawaii (HAW. CONST. art. 9, § 3); Indiana (IND. CONST. art. 9, § 3); Louisiana (LA. CONST. art. XII, §8); Montana (MONT. CONST. art. XII, §3); New Mexico (N.M. CONST. art. IX, 14); Oklahoma (OKLA. CONST. art. XXV, 1); and Texas (TEX. CONST. art. III, 51-a).

31. Alabama (ALA. CONST. art. IV, 88); Alaska (ALASKA CONST. art. VII, 5); Kansas (KAN. CONST. art. VII, 4); Michigan (MICH. CONST. art. IV, 51); Missouri (MO. CONST. art. IV, 37); North Carolina (N.C. CONST. art. XI, 4); and Wyoming (WYO. CONST. art. VII, 20).

32. *See* Bullock v. Whiteman, 865 P.2d 197 (Kan. 1993) (denying right to higher benefits based on language "as may be prescribed by law," but suggesting at some point denial of benefits could violate Constitution).

33. Tucker v. Toia, 371 N.E.2d 449 (N.Y. 1977); Matter of Bernstein v. Toia, 373 N.E.2d 238 (N.Y. 1977); Aliessa *ex rel.* Fayad v. Novello, 754 N.E.2d 1085, 1092 (N.Y. 2001).

34. West Virginia *ex rel.* K.M. v. W.V. Dep't of Health and Human Res., 575 S.E.2d 393 (W.Va. 2002).

35. 42 U.S.C. § 608(a)(1) (2001).

36. 42 U.S.C. § 601(a) (2001).

37. For more analysis of current reauthorization proposals as well as changes to TANF under the most recent Budget Reconciliation bill, see the website for the Center on Budget and Policy Priorities at http://www.cbpp.org/pubs/welfare.htm.

38. Any months that an individual lives in what the statute defines as "Indian country" or in an Alaska Native village where the unemployment rate is 50 percent or higher do not count towards the time limit. 45 C.F.R. § 264.1 (b)(1) (1999).

39. *See* http://www.dss.state.ct.us/glance.htm.

40. 42 U.S.C. § 608(a)(7)(C)(i-iii) (2001).

41. 42 U.S.C. § 604(i) (2001).

42. Gretchen Rowe and Jeffrey Versteeg, Urban Institute, Welfare Rules Databook: State TANF Policies as of July 2003, 90–91 (Apr. 2005).

43. *Id.*

44. 21 U.S.C. § 862(b) (2005).

45. *See, e.g.*, Skinner v. Railway Labor Executives' Ass'n, 489 U.S. 602, 617 (1989).

46. Chandler v. Miller, 520 U.S. 305, 318 (1997). *See also* United States v. Martinez-Fuerte, 428 U.S. 543, 560 (1976).

47. Marchwinski v. Howard, 113 F. Supp. 2d 1134, 1136 (E.D. Mich. 2000) (citing The Lindesmith Center, Drug Testing of Welfare Applicants: A Nationwide Survey of Policies, Practices and Rationales, Interim Report 2 (1999)).

48. *Id.* at 1143.

49. 42 U.S.C. § 602(a)(7)(A)(i) (2005).

50. *Id.* §602(a)(1)(A)(iv).

51. *See* Shelley Stark and Jodie Levin-Epstein, Excluded Children: Family Cap in a New Era (Feb. 1999), *available at* http://clasp.org/publications/excluded _children.pdf; CLASP, Caps on Kids: Family Cap in the New Welfare Era, A Fact Sheet (Feb. 1999), *available at* http://www.clasp.org/publications/caps_on_ kids.htm.

52. Nickols v. Saenz, No. 310867 (Cal. Super. Ct. Sept. 14, 2000); *see also In re Doe*, No. 97343038 (Cal. Dep't of Soc. Servs. Apr. 16, 1998) (finding that a county had inappropriately denied welfare benefits to a child whose parents did not receive adequate notice of the family cap policy). For more on these cases, *see* http://www. povertylaw.org/legalresearch/cases/caselist.cfm?topic=1380100&heading=Child%20 Support.

53. Plyler v. Doe, 457 U.S. 202 (1982) (holding unconstitutional a Texas statute that withheld funding for the education of children not legally admitted into the United States from local school districts); Weber v. Aetna Casualty & Surety, 406

U.S. 164 (1972) (holding unconstitutional Louisiana workers' compensation statutes that denied equal recovery rights to illegitimate children).

54. *Plyler*, 457 U.S. at 220 ( "Even if the State found it expedient to control the conduct of adults by acting against their children, legislation directing the onus of a parent's misconduct against his children does not comport with fundamental conceptions of justice.").

55. Planned Parenthood v. Casey, 505 U.S. 933 (1992).

56. Skinner v. State of Okl. *ex. rel.* Williamson, 316 U.S. 535 (1942) (striking down Oklahoma's Habitual Criminal Sterilization Act).

57. *See* Perry v. Sindermann, 408 U.S. 593, 597 (1972).

58. *See, e.g.,* C.K. v. Shalala, 883 F. Supp. 991, 1013–15 (D.N.J. 1995) (rejecting equal protection and due process challenges to New Jersey's family cap), *aff'd sub nom.* C.K. v. N.J. Dep't of Health & Human Servs., 92 F.3d 171 (3d Cir. 1996); N.B. v. Sybinski, 724 N.E.2d 1103 (Ind. App. 2000) (rejecting federal and state constitutional challenges to Indiana's family cap policy); Gates v. McIntire, No. 99-J-218 (Mass. App. Ct. May 3, 1999) (refusing a preliminary injunction against a Massachusetts family cap law, because it did not violate state and federal constitutional guarantees of equal protection and due process of law, the First Amendment's guarantee of freedom of religion, or the Massachusetts' equal rights amendment), summary at http://www.povertylaw.org/poverty-law-library/case/52200/52294.

59. *See, e.g.,* Sojourner A. *ex rel.* Y.A. v. N.J. Dep't of Human Servs., 350 N.J. Super. 152 (2002), *aff'd by* Sojourner A. v. N.J. Dep't Human Servs., 828 A.2d 306 (N.J. 2003).

60. Williams *ex rel.* Richard v. Humphreys, 125 F. Supp. 2d 881 (S.D. Ind. 2000) (finding that the excluded children whose child support payments were being assigned to the state were being deprived of a property interest in violation of the Constitution).

61. 394 U.S. 618 (1969).

62. 526 U.S. 489 (1999).

63. Warrick v. Snider, 2 F. Supp. 2d 720, 725–30 (W.D. Pa. 1997), *aff'd without opinion*, 191 F.3d 446 (3d Cir. 1999) (holding unconstitutional a sixty-day residency requirement for receipt of cash benefits from Pennsylvania's General Assistance program).

64. *Id.* at 730 (noting that there is no rational reason to apply the state's ostensible purpose—the encouragement of work—only to new residents of the state).

65. 8 U.S.C. § 1641 (2005).

66. Immigration and Nationality Act [hereinafter INA], 8 U.S.C. § 1158 (2005).

67. INA §207, 8 U.S.C. § 1157 (2005).

68. INA § 212(d)(5), 8 U.S.C. § 1182 (2005).

69. INA § 243(h), 8 U.S.C. § 1253(h), or INA § 241(b)(3), 8 U.S.C. § 1251(b) (3) (2005).

70. 8 U.S.C. § 1153(a)(7) (2005).

71. As defined in the Refugee Education Assistance Act of 1980 § 501(e), 8 U.S.C. § 1522 (2005).

72. *See* Office of the Assistant Secretary for Planning and Evaluation, Summary of Immigrant Eligibility Restriction under Current Law, http://aspe.hhs.gov/hsp/immigration/restrictions-sum.htm (last visited Mar. 28, 2007).

73. *See, e.g.,* Shvartsman v. Apfel, 138 F.3d 1196 (7th Cir. 1998) (holding that resident aliens who received food stamps and whose applications for citizenship were pending had no property rights in food stamps, and therefore had no due process rights regarding this benefit); Kiev v. Glickman, 991 F. Supp. 1090 (D. Minn. 1998) (dismissing a claim that the 1996 changes in welfare law that withdrew food stamps to legal immigrants violated the Equal Protection Clause of the Fifth Amendment, because the law was rationally related to a legitimate government interest); Cid v. S.D. Dep't of Soc. Servs., 598 N.W.2d 887 (S.D. 1999) (holding that the state could exclude aliens from welfare assistance without violating the equal protection clauses of the U.S. or South Dakota constitutions because the difference in treatment was supported by legitimate state interests: assuring that immigrants were self-reliant and supporting national immigration policy).

74. The Urban Institute has found that 78 percent of children with immigrant parents were born in the United States. Randy Capps, The Urban Institute, Hardship among Children of Immigrants: Findings from the 1999 National Survey of Americans' Families (Feb. 2001).

75. *See generally* Michael and Wendy Zimmerman, Urban Institute, All under One Roof: Mixed-Status Families in an Era of Welfare Reform (June 1999).

76. Federally funded programs have to provide written language assistance to those with limited English proficiency "[w]here a significant number or proportion of the population eligible to be served or likely to be directly affected by a federally assisted program . . . needs service or information in a language other than English in order effectively to be informed of or to participate in the program." 28 C.F.R. § 42.405(d)(1) (2005).

77. 42 U.S.C. § 2000d *et seq.* (2005); *see also* the regulations implementing Title VI, at 45 C.F.R. § 80.3(b) (2005).

78. 45 C.F.R. § 80.3(b) (2005); Office for Civil Rights Policy Guidance, Title VI Prohibition against National Origin Discrimination as It Affects Persons with Limited English Proficiency, http://www.hhs.gov/ocr/lep/guide.html; *see also* Exec. Order No. 13,166, 65 Fed. Reg. 50,121 (Aug. 11, 2000).

79. 28 C.F.R. § 42.405(d)(1) (2005).

80. Office for Civil Rights, Department of Health and Human Services, Technical Assistance for Caseworkers on Civil Rights Laws and Welfare Reform, *available at* http://www.hhs.gov/ocr/taintro.htm [hereinafter OCR, Technical Assistance].

81. OCR, Civil Rights Laws and Welfare Reform Overview, http://www.hhs.gov/ocr/overview1.htm.

82. *See, e.g.*, Garcia v. Gloor, 618 F.2d 264 (5th Cir. 1980) (holding that an English-only rule was not discriminatory where the complaining parties were bilingual).

83. 21 U.S.C. § 862–§ 862a (2005). *See generally* Amy Hirsch, Some Days Are Harder Than Hard: Welfare Reform and Women with Drug Convictions in Pennsylvania, Appendix A (1999), *available at* http://www.clasp.org/publications/some_days_are_harder_than_hard.pdf.

84. 21 U.S.C. § 862–§ 862a.

85. 42 U.S.C. § 608(a)(8) (2005).

86. *Id.* § 608(a)(9).

87. *Id.* § 608(5)(B).

88. *Id.* § 608(4).

89. 42 U.S.C. § 601(a)(2–4) (2001).

90. 42 U.S.C. § 602(a)(1)(A)(v) (2005).

91. 42 U.S.C. § 603(a)(2) (2005).

92. Martha E. Kempner, Sexuality Information and Education Counsel of the United States, Towards a Sexually Healthy America: Abstinence-Only-Until-Marriage Programs That Try to Keep Our Youth Scared Chaste 46–47 (2001).

93. According to an independent, federally funded evaluation of PRWORA abstinence-only programs, there is "no definitive research [linking] the abstinence education legislation" with the downward trend in "the percentage of teens reporting that they have had sex." Barbara Devaney et al., Mathematica Policy Research, Inc., The Evaluation of Abstinence Education Programs Funded under Title V Section 510: Interim Report 1 (2002).

94. Douglas Kirby, The National Campaign to Prevent Teen Pregnancy, Emerging Answers: Research Findings on Programs to Reduce Teen Pregnancy, Summary 16 (2001).

95. 42 U.S.C. § 608(a)(2) (2001); 45 C.F.R. §264.30 (1999).

96. At least one federal appeals court has also held that this exercise of Congress' spending power does not impermissibly coerce states into compliance or infringe upon their rights. Kansas v. United States, 214 F.3d 1196 (10th Cir. 2000), *writ of certiorari denied*, 531 U.S. 1035 (2000) (holding that TANF child support enforcement requirements did not coerce Kansas into compliance in violation of the Tenth Amendment or Congress' spending power).

97. Kelly v. Dep't of Health & Rehab. Servs., 596 So.2d 130 (Fla. App. 1992) (reversing an order denying an appellant benefits who testified under penalty of perjury that she lacked information concerning the identity of the father of her child.); P.F. v. N.D. Dep't of Human Servs., 499 N.W.2d 888 (N.D. 1993) (finding that the Department could not consider a woman uncooperative because she had provided several possible names of the father, and testified under penalty of perjury that she

had no further information); S.D. v. Dep't of Human Servs., 781 A.2d 1105 (N.J. Super. Ct. App. Div. 2001) (holding that an applicant who has provided all the information she had or could reasonably have obtained about the paternity of her child has cooperated for the purposes of New Jersey's TANF program, unless additional or contrary information is or becomes known to the agency).

98. 42 U.S.C. § 608(a)(3)(B) (2001).

99. *Id.*

100. The states that have no pass-through/disregard as of December 2003 are Arizona, Arkansas, Colorado, Florida, Hawaii, Idaho, Indiana, Iowa, Kansas, Louisiana, Maryland, Mississippi, Missouri, Montana, Nebraska, Nevada, New Hampshire, North Carolina, North Dakota, Ohio, Oklahoma, Oregon, South Dakota, Utah, Washington, and Wyoming. PAULA ROBERTS AND MICHELLE JORDAN, CENTER FOR LAW AND SOCIAL POLICY, STATE POLICY REGARDING PASS-THROUGH AND DISREGARD OF CURRENT MONTH'S CHILD SUPPORT COLLECTED FOR FAMILIES RECEIVING TANF-FUNDED CASH ASSISTANCE: AS OF DECEMBER 2003 (Feb. 2004).

101. *Id.* The states that pass through up to fifty dollars, following the AFDC concept, as of December 2003 include Alabama, Alaska, California, Delaware, Illinois, Maine, Massachusetts, Michigan, New Jersey, New Mexico, New York, Pennsylvania, Rhode Island, Vermont, and Virginia.

102. *Id.* Delaware and Maine also use fill-the-gap budgeting. Vermont passes through anything paid in excess of fifty dollars but deducts it from the TANF grant. Massachusetts has an exception, that if a child is excluded by a family cap, all child support collected is passed through, and up to ninety dollars is disregarded.

103. *Id.* The states that pass-though all child support collected to families as of December 2003 include Connecticut, Georgia, Minnesota, Tennessee, South Carolina, and Wisconsin.

104. *Id.* Connecticut disregards up to fifty dollars. Minnesota passes through all support up to court order, but does not disregard any amount for calculating benefits. Georgia, South Carolina, and Tennessee disregard an unspecified amount for fill-the-gap budgeting.

105. *Id.*

106. *See, e.g.*, Harp v. Metcalf, No. 99C-3278 (Tenn. Cir. Ct. Davidson County May 24, 2001); Emmons v. Murray, No. 91-CV-40411-FL (E.D. Mich. Aug. 26, 1997); Carpenter v. Chiles, No. 94-89-CIV-T-17C (M.D. Fla. June 28, 1995); Bonds v. Snider, No. 91-4547 (E.D. Pa. June 4, 1993).

107. *See* Harp v. Metcalf, No. 99C-3278 (Tenn. Cir. Ct. Davidson County May 24, 2001); Carpenter v. Chiles, No. 94-89-CIV-T-17C (M.D. Fla. June 28, 1995).

108. Sullivan v. Stroop, 496 U.S. 478 (1990); *see also* Head v. State, 632 N.E.2d 749 (Ind. Ct. App. 1994).

109. DEPARTMENT OF HEALTH AND HUMAN SERVICES, TEMPORARY ASSISTANCE FOR NEEDY FAMILIES PROGRAM FOURTH ANNUAL REPORT TO CONGRESS I-6 (Apr.

2002), *available at* http://www.acf.hhs.gov/programs/ofa/opreweb/ar2001/indexar. htm.

110. 42 U.S.C. § 602(a)(1)(B)(iv) (2001); 45 C.F.R. § 261.10(b) (1999).

111. 42 U.S.C. § 602(a)(1)(B)(iv); 45 C.F.R. § 261.10(b).

112. For some examples of reasonable cause, *see* 45 C.F.R. § 262.5 (1999).

113. 42 U.S.C. § 607(a)(1–3) (2005).

114. Mark Greenberg and Sharon Parrot, Center for Budget and Policy Priorities, Summary of TANF Work Participation Provisions in the Budget Reconciliation Bill (Jan. 2005), *available at* http://www.cbpp.org/1-18-06tanf. htm [hereinafter TANF Summary].

115. 45 C.F.R. § 261.35 (1999).

116. 45 C.F.R. § 261.10 at 17,767 (1999).

117. *See* Rebekah L. Smith, et al., *The Miseducation of Welfare Reform: Denying the Promise of Postsecondary Education,* 55 Me. L. Rev. 211, 224 (2003) ("After PRWORA, the percentage of welfare recipients engaged in school activities nationally declined by more than half, as single mothers were forced to abandon college in order to meet 'work-first' requirements. Levels of postsecondary enrollment for parents receiving welfare dropped by up to 82% in individual states.") (internal citations omitted).

118. 45 C.F.R. § 261.31(b) (1999).

119. *Id.* § 261.31(c).

120. 45 C.F.R. § 261.33 (1999).

121. *Id.*

122. 42 U.S.C. §607(e)(1) (2005).

123. *Id.* § 607(b)(5).

124. 42 U.S.C. § 602(a)(7) (2005); 45 C.F.R. § 260.52 (2005).

125. 42 U.S.C. § 607(e)(2) (2005); 45 C.F.R. § 261.56 (1999).

126. 42 U.S.C. § 607(e)(2); 45 C.F.R. § 261.5.

127. *See, e.g.,* Rimes v. Ohio Dep't of Human Servs., 2001 WL 65574 (Ohio App. 11 Dist. 2001) (A mother should not be sanctioned for failing to participate in work activities if her child was recently abused in private childcare and there was evidence that placement in daycare would not be in the child's best interests.).

128. 42 U.S.C. § 618(a)(1) (2001).

129. 45 C.F.R. § 98.20 (1998).

130. 45 C.F.R. § 98.50 (2005).

131. *Id.*

132. Children's Defense Fund, Child Care and Head Start Organizers Tool Kit 12 (2005).

133. 45 C.F.R. § 98.30 (2005).

134. *Id.*

135. 45 C.F.R. § 98.46 (2005).

136. *Id.* § 98.20.

137. 45 C.F.R. § 98.33 (1998).

138. *Id.* § 98.41.

139. CHILDREN'S DEFENSE FUND, CHILD CARE BASICS 2005 3 (Apr. 2005).

140. *See* INSTITUTE FOR WOMEN'S POLICY RESEARCH, WORKING FIRST BUT WORKING POOR: THE NEED FOR EDUCATION AND TRAINING FOLLOWING WELFARE REFORM, EXECUTIVE SUMMARY, A REPORT TO THE NOW LEGAL DEFENSE AND EDUCATION FUND (Oct. 2001).

141. STEVE SAVNER, POVERTY AND RACE RESEARCH ACTION COUNCIL, WELFARE REFORM AND RACIAL/ETHNIC MINORITIES: THE QUESTIONS TO ASK (July/August 2000), *available at* http://www.prrac.org/topic_type.php?topic_id=1&type_group=10.

142. Weil, *supra* note 10, at 6.

143. *Id.*

144. *See generally* Henry A. Freedman, *The Welfare Advocate's Challenge: Fighting Historic Racism in the New Welfare System*, J. POVERTY L. & POL'Y 31 (2002), *available at* http://www.nclej.org/contents/clearinghouse/freedman_article.pdf?PHPSESSID=a4e81bc590dcfca7b266f6489aa446bc.

145. Cary LaCheen, *Using Title II of the Americans with Disabilities Act on Behalf of Clients in TANF Programs*, 8 GEO. J. ON POVERTY L. & POL'Y 1 (2001); EILEEN P. SWEENEY, CENTER ON BUDGET AND POLICY PRIORITIES, RECENT STUDIES MAKE CLEAR THAT MANY PARENTS WHO ARE CURRENT OR FORMER WELFARE RECIPIENTS HAVE DISABILITIES AND OTHER MEDICAL CONDITIONS (2000), *available at* http://www.cbpp.org/2-29-00wel.pdf.

146. DAVID WITTENBURG AND MELISSA FAVREAULT, URBAN INSTITUTE, SAFETY NET OR TANGLED WEB? AN OVERVIEW OF PROGRAMS AND SERVICES FOR ADULTS WITH DISABILITIES 11 (2003), *available at* http://www.urban.org/publications/310884.html.

147. LaCheen, *supra* note 145, at 8–9.

148. *Id.*; Sweeney, *supra* note 145, at 5.

149. OCR recommendations specifically state,

Welfare providers that receive federal money may not discriminate against people on the basis of race, color, national origin, disability, or age in how they run their program or activity, or on the basis of sex in education programs. Entities may not subject persons to harassment on the basis of race, color, national origin, disability, or age, or on the basis of sex in education programs. . . . Welfare providers may not indirectly discriminate on these bases through contractors or by means of any other arrangements. Welfare providers are responsible for ensuring that their contractors administer their programs in a nondiscriminatory manner.

OCR, TECHNICAL ASSISTANCE, *supra* note 80.

150. 42 U.S.C. § 608(d) (2005).

151. OCR, Civil Rights Laws and Welfare Reform Overview, *supra* note 81.

152. It is particularly important to note here the importance of screening for disabilities. As mentioned above, a significant number of people receiving benefits are disabled or caring for a child or family member who is disabled, in addition to facing other barriers to self-sufficiency and employment. One advocate estimates that "regardless of how studies define disability, it is likely that in total, more than half of the families applying for or receiving TANF have at least one family member with a physical or mental limitation." LaCheen, *supra* note 145 at 9. Many of these disabilities go undiagnosed, meaning that in many cases individuals will be referred to inappropriate programs or unfairly sanctioned for noncompliance.

153. U.S. Dep't of Labor, Guidance: How Workplace Laws Apply to Welfare Recipients, Daily Lab. Rep. (BNA), No. 103 at E-3 (May 29, 1997, revised Feb. 1999), *available at* http://www.dol.gov/asp/w2w/welfare.htm.

154. *Enforcement Guidance: Application of EEO Laws to Contingent Workers Placed by Temporary Employment Agencies and Other Staffing Firms*, EEO Notice, No. 915.002 (Dec. 3, 1997), *available at* http://www.eeoc.gov/policy/docs/conting.html [hereinafter EEO Notice, No. 915.002].

155. For instance the Second Circuit recently ruled that workers in New York's workfare program (WEP) were "employees" within the meaning of Title VII of the Civil Rights Act of 1964 and could sue for sexual harassment, sex discrimination, and racial discrimination they experienced in their workfare assignment. United States v. City of N.Y., 359 F.3d 83, 97 (2d Cir. 2004). On the other hand, however, a pre-PRWORA Tenth Circuit Decision held that workers in Utah workfare program (GA-WEAT) were not employees of DHS for purposes of the FLSA (Fair Labor Standards Act). Johns v. Stewart, 57 F.3d 1544, 1559 (10th Cir. 1995). A few states have statutorily provided workfare recipients with legal employee status. *See generally* Nan S. Ellis, *Work Is Its Own Reward: Are Workfare Participants Employees Entitled to Protection under the Fair Labor Standards Act?*, 13 Cornell J.L. & Pub. Pol'y 1, 3. n. 12 (2003).

156. U.S. Dep't of Labor Guidance: How Workplace Laws Apply to Welfare Recipients, *supra* note 153.

157. *Id.*

158. *Id.*

159. *Id.*

160. Ellis, *supra* note 155.

161. *Id.*

162. National Partnership for Women and Families, Welfare Reform: Struggling Families Challenged by 40-Hour Work Week (Apr. 2002), *available at* http://www.nationalpartnership.org/site/DocServer/WelfareReform.pdf?docID

=1200. There may be an argument that time spent working at a workfare placement should count toward total time for purposes of the FMLA time if the woman is later hired by the placement employer.

163. However, depending upon state law and individual contracts, temporary workfare workers may not have a right to hearings or due process before they are dismissed, because they will not have the necessary "property interest" in their job. Thomas v. Peters, 2002 WL 253114, No. 99 C 7041 (Feb. 21, 2002) (holding that Illinois workfare workers had no due process rights in their employment because legitimate state rules considered them probationary employees, lacking property interest in their employment).

164. Nicola Kean, *The Unprotected Workforce: Why Title VII Must Apply to Workfare Participants*, 9 Tex. J. on C.L. & C.R. 159, 168 (2004) (internal citation omitted).

165. U.S. Dep't of Labor Guidance: How Workplace Laws Apply to Welfare Recipients, *supra* note 153; EEO Notice, No. 915.002, *supra* note 154.

166. OCR, Technical Assistance, *supra* note 80.

167. *City of New York*, 359 F.3d *passim*.

168. *Johns*, 57 F.3d *passim*.

169. Christine N. Cimini, *The New Contract: Welfare Reform, Devolution, and Due Process*, 61 Md. L. Rev. 246, 295 (2002).

170. *See* State Policy Documentation Project, Findings in Brief: TANF Applications, *available at* http://www.spdp.org/tanf/applications/appsumm.htm [hereinafter TANF applications]; State Policy Documentation Project, Personal Responsibility Contracts: Obligations, *available at* http://www.spdp.org/tanf/prcreq/index.htm [hereinafter Personal Responsibility Contracts].

171. *See* Jodie Levin-Epstein, The IRA: Individual Responsibility Agreements and TANF Family Life Obligations (Aug. 1998), *available at* http://www.clasp.org/publications/IRA.pdf.

172. Only twenty-seven states require the county or state to agree to provide services. Personal Responsibility Contracts, *supra* note 170.

173. 42 U.S.C. § 608(b)(3) (2001), TANF Applications, *supra* note 170.

174. In re [redacted], No. WWW-40/45495 (Wis. Div. of Hearings and Appeals Nov. 28, 2000); *see* http://www.povertylaw.org/legalresearch/cases/abstract.cfm?id=54291.

175. Jones v. Ohio Dep't of Human Servs., No. 98-CV-143 (Ohio C.P. Belmont County July 20, 1999).

176. 397 U.S. 254.

177. *Id.* at 264. Other courts have reinforced this holding; *see, e.g.,* Morel v. Giuliani, 927 F. Supp. 622, 635 (S.D.N.Y. 1995) (noting that for "indigent persons, the loss of even a portion of subsistence benefits constitutes irreparable injury").

178. 42 U.S.C. § 601(b) (2001).

179. Reynolds v. Giuliani, 35 F. Supp. 2d 331, 341 (S.D.N.Y. 1999), *aff'd without opinion* 198 F.3d 234 (2d Cir. 1999); Weston v. Hammons, 2001 Colo. J. C.A.R. 3563 (Colo. App. 2001); Damavandi v. Wing, No. 402371/99 (N.Y. Sup. Ct. Jan. 3, 2001).

180. There are additional (but untested) legal theories that could provide remedies even if the reasoning behind *Goldberg* no longer applied. For example, those who are cut off without adequate notice or process may also be able to pursue due process challenges based upon contract theories. Christine C. Cimini, *The New Contract: Welfare Reform, Devolution, and Due Process*, 61 MD. L. REV. 246 (2002).

181. 42 U.S.C. § 602(a)(1)(B)(iii) (2001).

182. Michele Estrin Gilman, *Legal Accountability in an Era of Privatized Welfare*, 89 CAL. L. REV. 569 (2001).

183. There are explicit statutory rights to information about food stamps, 7 U.S.C. § 2020(e)(2)(B)(i) (2005) ("a State agency . . . shall provide timely, accurate, and fair service to applicants for, and participants in, the food stamp program") and Medicaid, 42 U.S.C. § 1396a(a)(8) (2005).

184. Reynolds v. Giuliani, *supra* note 179 (holding that plaintiffs have a property interest in their food stamps, Medicaid, and cash assistance, and that "allegations concerning various practices at job centers, such as providing false or misleading information to applicants about their eligibility, arbitrarily denying benefits to eligible individuals, and failing to provide notice of hearing rights, state a viable due process claim under [28 U.S.C.] § 1983").

185. 28 C.F.R. § 35.130(b)(1)(ii) (2005).

186. *Id.* § 35.130(b)(3)(i).

187. *Id.* § 35.130(b)(7).

188. For more detailed information about options under the ADA, *see* CARY LACHEEN, WELFARE LAW CENTER, USING THE AMERICANS WITH DISABILITIES ACT TO PROTECT THE RIGHTS OF INDIVIDUALS WITH DISABILITIES IN TANF PROGRAMS: A MANUAL FOR NON-LITIGATION ADVOCACY (2004), *available at* http://www.nclej. org/contents/Upload/ADA2004_manual_full.pdf [hereinafter ADA MANUAL].

189. 42 U.S.C. § 602(a)(1)(B)(iii) (2004).

190. Vicki Lens, *Bureaucratic Disentitlement after Welfare Reform: Are Fair Hearings the Cure?*, 12 GEO. J. ON POVERTY L. & POL'Y 13, 30 (2005).

191. *Id.* at 48–49.

192. *Id.*

193. To find the address for regional offices *see* http://www.hhs.gov/ocr/ or call OCR at 1-800-368-1019 (voice) or 1-800-537-7697 (TDD). The website includes a complaint form as well.

194. OFFICE FOR CIVIL RIGHTS, DEPARTMENT OF HEALTH AND HUMAN SERVICES, FREQUENTLY ASKED QUESTIONS WITH ANSWERS ABOUT CIVIL RIGHTS, http:// www.hhs.gov/ocr/ (last visited Mar. 28, 2007); OFFICE FOR CIVIL RIGHTS, DEPART-

MENT OF HEALTH AND HUMAN SERVICES, FACT SHEET: HOW TO FILE A DISCRIMINA-
TION COMPLAINT WITH THE OFFICE FOR CIVIL RIGHTS, http://www.hhs.gov/ocr/
discrimhowtofile.html (last visited Mar. 28, 2007).

195. *Id.*

196. ADA MANUAL, *supra* note 188.

# X

# Housing

Shelter, like food and clothing, is a basic human need. In spite of this, securing housing remains a struggle for many women. However, housing discrimination is largely understood as a problem experienced along racial lines, and there is a tendency to ignore the biases women face as tenants and the power landlords hold due to the shortage of affordable housing.[1]

Women who rent housing are especially vulnerable to sex discrimination, in part because these women are disproportionately poor. Approximately 28 percent of all single-parent families headed by women live below the poverty line, compared to only about 13.5 percent of single-parent families headed by men.[2] Poor women often spend more than 25 percent of their income on housing; about 25 percent of single mothers spend over half their income on housing.[3] Furthermore, single mothers with children are the fastest-growing segment of the homeless population,[4] and while many factors have contributed to this growth, domestic violence has been cited as a primary cause. Women often leave their homes to flee their attackers, and in some instances victims of domestic violence are unfairly evicted because of the actions of their abusers.[5]

The unavailability of affordable housing also makes poor women particularly susceptible to sexual harassment and exploitation by landlords. The means of sexual intimidation that landlords can employ are unique. A landlord can invade a woman's "safe haven" without notice, often because he will have a passkey to the apartment. For example, a woman might wake up and find her landlord at the foot of her bed, or the landlord might walk in while she is in the shower.[6] Many women keep silent about such harassment because of embarrassment, fear that a landlord will retaliate through continued abuse or eviction, or concern that reporting the harassment may create an obstacle to obtaining housing in the future.[7]

When women face problems in securing housing, it can have devastating effects on them and on their children. Fortunately, there are legal tools to solve some of the problems that women face.

### Are there laws against sex discrimination in housing?

Yes. The Fair Housing Act (FHA), also referred to as "Title VIII," makes it illegal to discriminate against someone based on sex in the sale or rental of a residence. Additionally, the FHA prohibits discrimination against someone because she is pregnant or has children, i.e., discrimination based on "familial status." Finally, it protects against other forms of discrimination not discussed in this book.[8]

Sex discrimination occurs when a landlord treats a person differently because of gender or because she is a woman (or he is a man.) Familial-status discrimination occurs when a landlord (or seller) treats a renter (or buyer) less favorably because she or he has children. The FHA specifically bans housing discrimination against a parent or guardian living with one or more children under eighteen, as well as discrimination against someone living with and taking care of one or more children with his or her parent's or guardian's written permission.[9] Finally, the law bans discrimination against pregnant women or anyone in the process of obtaining custody of a child under eighteen.[10]

Many states have also passed their own fair housing laws that may offer additional protections to women facing sex discrimination in housing.

### What types of sex discrimination does the FHA prohibit?

The FHA prohibits both intentional and disparate-impact discrimination. Intentional sex discrimination occurs when a landlord treats a tenant or a potential tenant differently based on sex, or when someone selling a home treats a buyer differently based on sex. For instance, if a landlord charges women higher rents than he or she charges men, or imposes rules on female tenants that he or she does not impose on male tenants, that landlord is discriminating on the basis of sex. Disparate-impact discrimination can occur when a landlord has policies or practices that tend to harm women more than they harm men (or vice versa). This may be unlawful sex discrimination, whether or not the landlord intended to discriminate on the basis of sex when adopting these policies.

## What acts count as discrimination under the FHA?

A landlord or individual discriminates when he or she refuses to rent to, negotiate with, or sell a home to a person on the basis of his or her sex or familial status.[11] A landlord is also not allowed to use eviction policies that treat women differently from men or families with children differently from families without children.[12] Landlords cannot refuse to rent to families because of the age or sex of the children or put all families with children on a single floor in an apartment building.

The FHA also forbids "steering," which happens when a landlord or real estate broker tries to influence a woman to accept housing other than the housing she desires because of her sex or familial status.[13] He or she may try to accomplish this by discouraging the woman from inspecting, purchasing, or renting the housing that she seeks.[14] One example of steering would be telling a woman with children that she really wouldn't "fit in" with other residents of the community because the other residents are mostly single and childless.[15]

Finally, landlords cannot place advertisements or otherwise communicate a preference for tenants based on a tenant's sex or familial status.[16] An exception to this rule is made for schools, which may maintain separate housing for males and females.[17]

A landlord may ask a tenant to fill out a housing application or submit to credit approval procedures. That landlord may not, however, have different standards, qualifications, applications, or procedures for women and men, or for individuals who have children and individuals who do not.[18]

## What residences are covered by the FHA?

The FHA prohibits discrimination in traditional rental apartments, single and multifamily homes, condominiums, mobile home parks, nursing homes, homeless shelters, and cooperative apartments.[19] A building that was originally intended for another use but has become a residence, such as a factory converted to an apartment building, is considered a residence under the FHA. Finally, the FHA also covers the sale and purchase of vacant land for the construction of a residence.[20]

## Are there residences not covered by the FHA?

The FHA does not prevent some private landlords and homeowners from discriminating. Under the FHA, a private homeowner may legally discriminate in selling or renting a single-family house when that landlord (1) does not own more than three homes, (2) does not use a real estate agent or broker to sell or rent the house, and (3) does not place discriminatory advertisements for the house.[21] The FHA also does not protect tenants in apartment buildings with four or fewer apartments if the owner of the building lives in one of the apartments.[22]

In addition, religious organizations that sell or rent dwellings can often discriminate against individuals who do not belong to that religion. Private clubs that provide housing as part of their primary purpose are allowed to give preference to their members and exclude nonmembers under certain circumstances.[23]

Even when the FHA allows landlords to discriminate, state and local fair housing laws may not. If a woman believes she has been a victim of discrimination, she should always check with a housing or civil rights attorney.

### Who can be sued for discrimination?

In general, companies, individuals, and governmental agencies that own or manage housing have to follow the FHA.[24] Therefore, they may not discriminate on the basis of sex or familial status and can be sued if they do so. In many instances, a company, individual, or government agency acting as an employer may also be sued for the act of an employee who discriminates in renting or selling a dwelling. This is true even if the employer did not tell the employee to discriminate.[25] For example, if a single woman applies to rent an apartment and the building manager refuses to rent to her because she is single, even though he or she rents to single men, the company employing the building manager may be held legally responsible for that manager's behavior.

In addition, real estate brokers may not discriminate on the basis of sex or familial status and can be sued if they or their employees do so.[26] Loan agencies must also follow the FHA, and therefore may not discriminate in determining eligibility for mortgages.[27]

### How do courts determine whether housing discrimination has occurred?

Under the FHA, a court can look at a property owner's intent, or the effects of a property owner's actions, or both, when determining whether a property owner's actions are discriminatory and illegal. A property owner demonstrates discriminatory intent when he or she *purposely* treats a woman differently because of her sex or familial status. Furthermore, even if a woman's sex or her familial status is not the *only* reason for treating her differently, the property owner's behavior violates the law.[28] That owner's actions may also violate the law if they have a discriminatory effect on women—for instance, if a landlord's policy results in preventing many more women from renting apartments than men. Even if the property owner did not intend such an effect, this may violate the law.[29]

If a woman believes her landlord intentionally denied her housing or otherwise treated her differently because of her sex, because she was pregnant, or because she had children, she can present a case in court by showing that the landlord treated men, or people who were not pregnant, or people without children, differently. If a woman is denied rental or purchase of a residence she must show (1) that she applied for and was qualified to rent the residence, (2) that she was rejected, and (3) that the residence remained available.[30] Once she has done so, the landlord has a chance to show that he had another reason, other than the tenant's sex, pregnancy, or familial status, for his actions. The woman may then offer evidence that the legitimate reason given by the landlord is not the motivating factor or, for that matter, the only factor for the discriminatory behavior or that the reason given is merely a pretext invented to justify the sex discrimination.[31]

If a woman believes that her landlord's actions had the effect of discriminating against her, whether or not that landlord intended to do so, she can make her case in court by showing that the actions have a harsher effect on women than men or on families with children than on families without children. For example, if a landlord had a policy of refusing to rent apartments to people who had sought orders of protection against batterers, such a policy would have a discriminatory effect on women, because women are much more likely to be the victims of domestic violence and to seek protective orders than men. Even if the policy applied to men who had sought protective orders, and even if the landlord had not intended to discriminate against women in adopting the policy, a woman could establish her case by showing that the policy had a much greater impact on women than on men. The landlord could then respond by showing that there was an important business reason for the policy, although a legitimate business reason may not necessarily be an acceptable justification for the policy. Even with a legitimate business reason, that discriminatory practice or policy violates the law if there is a viable nondiscriminatory policy that the landlord could adopt that would accomplish the same goal.[32]

Finally, it is important to note that courts routinely adopt standards used in employment discrimination cases under Title VII to analyze housing discrimination claims. Thus, much of the law and theory developed around employment discrimination will be adapted, with varying degrees of success, to the housing discrimination context. See chapter 2, "Employment: Discrimination and Parenting Issues," for more information on sex discrimination in employment.

### What happens if a landlord claims that he or she has a legitimate reason for discriminatory behavior?

A landlord has violated the FHA if his or her actions were in any way motivated by an animus or prejudice against women or if the policy on which those actions are based has a disparate impact on women. This is true even in "mixed-motive cases," where a landlord may be able to show that he or she had a legitimate reason on which to base his or her decision, in addition to the unlawful reasons of sex, pregnancy, or familial status. Thus, if a woman can show either intentional or disparate-impact discrimination, even if the landlord had a legitimate reason for his behavior, the landlord is still liable for his or her actions under the FHA.

## Sexual Harassment and Housing

### Is it illegal for a landlord to sexually harass a tenant or prospective tenant?

Yes. Sexual harassment is a form of sex discrimination and is therefore illegal under the FHA.[33] When a landlord or any of the landlord's employees sexually harass a woman, they disrupt her life in the place where she should feel safest. Poor women are often at the greatest risk of sexual harassment by their landlords because they have few housing options and may feel that they must accept the harassment in order to keep their home. Women may experience harassment from their landlords, building managers, real estate agents, or others who work in the building in which they live. The law sometimes describes sexual harassment as either "quid pro quo" or "hostile environment" harassment, though sometimes sexual harassment will include elements of both categories.[34]

### What is quid pro quo sexual harassment?

"Quid pro quo" means "this for that." This type of sexual harassment occurs when a landlord, or someone who works for a landlord, such as a building superintendent, requests sexual favors in return for housing.[35] Quid pro quo sexual harassment occurs, for example, when a landlord tells a woman that she can only rent an apartment if she agrees to go on dates with him or if she has sex with him. It also occurs when a landlord seeks to evict a woman or otherwise retaliates against her because of her refusal to have a romantic or sexual relationship with him.[36] Furthermore, regulations adopted by the U.S. Department of Housing and Urban Development (HUD) make clear that the FHA prohibits quid pro quo sexual harassment.[37] Quid pro quo sexual harassment is illegal even if it only occurs once.[38]

To prove a quid pro quo sexual harassment claim, a woman must show that her landlord (or landlord's employee) conditioned any of the "terms, conditions, or privileges" of her tenancy on her submitting to sexual requests, or deprived her of any "term, condition, or privilege" of tenancy because she refused his requests.[39] In addition to the landlord, the harasser himself can usually be held personally liable for any discriminatory acts he commits.[40]

Even where there is a legal reason to evict a woman, if a landlord evicts a woman in part for her refusal to provide sexual favors, he has committed quid pro quo sexual harassment.[41] Courts disagree as to how serious the harm to the woman must be to prove she has suffered quid pro quo sexual harassment.[42] For example, one court has held that a woman proved her case by showing that a landlord did not make promised repairs in her apartment after she rejected his sexual advances, while other courts have suggested that to prove her claim, a woman must show that the landlord has taken some step that has a more substantial effect on her tenancy.[43] While most cases of quid pro quo sexual harassment involve the eviction of a woman for failing to submit to a landlord's sexual demands, a landlord has violated the law even if a woman submits to his demands, but does so unwillingly.[44]

**What is "hostile environment" harassment?**

A woman can sue her landlord for creating a "hostile environment" when the landlord or his employee unreasonably interferes with the use and enjoyment of her home through offensive conduct because of her sex.[45] The harassment must be " 'sufficiently severe or pervasive' to alter the conditions of the housing arrangement."[46]

This conduct can be explicitly sexual, but it need not be.[47] For example, if a landlord touches a tenant sexually against her will, or repeatedly makes unwelcome sexual comments, it may be hostile-environment harassment. If a landlord repeatedly calls a woman vulgar names such as "bitch" or "whore" or makes threats against her, this too may be hostile-environment harassment. One way to show that harassment that is not explicitly sexual is in fact motivated by gender is to submit evidence that other female tenants are similarly harassed, while male tenants are not.[48]

To establish a "hostile environment" harassment claim, at least one court has held that a woman must show that

(1) the conduct [to which the plaintiff was subjected] was unwelcome; (2) it was based on the sex or other protected characteristic of the plaintiff; (3) it was sufficiently severe or pervasive to alter the plaintiff's living conditions and to create an abusive environment; and (4) the defendant knew or should have known of the harassment, and took no effectual action to correct the situation.[49]

The law is not currently clear, however, as to whether the fourth prong of the test—that the landlord knew or should have known about the harassment—is required in every instance.[50]

In assessing a hostile-environment claim, courts will consider how often the behavior occurred, whether threats were made against the tenant, and whether the behavior was psychologically harmful to the tenant. However, there has been no clear resolution as to the degree of severity necessary to prove a hostile environment claim in the housing context. While some courts have required that the harassment be ongoing and consist of multiple acts committed over a period of time, others have placed greater emphasis on the fact that the harassment took place in the home, suggesting that any harassment in that context may in fact be more damaging and harmful to the woman.[51]

## DISCRIMINATION AGAINST VICTIMS OF DOMESTIC VIOLENCE

**Can a landlord evict someone or otherwise discriminate against someone because she is the victim of domestic violence?**

Probably not. Several recent decisions have indicated that discrimination against a person based on her status as a victim of domestic violence may be a form of impermissible sex discrimination that violates the Fair Housing Act and, in many places, state law.[52] In addition, the Violence Against Women Act of 2005 prohibits many kinds of discrimination against those victims of domestic violence living in public housing or housing subsidized under the federal Section 8 program.[53] For more information see chapter 5, "Violence against Women."

## DISCRIMINATION AGAINST WOMEN WITH CHILDREN

**May a landlord refuse to rent or sell a residence to a woman because he thinks that the residence might be dangerous for her children?**

No, the FHA does not allow a landlord to decide for a woman whether a particular residence is suitable for her and her children, even if the landlord has good intentions. For example, a landlord (or seller) may not refuse to rent (or sell) to a woman because the property has some feature that might be dangerous to children, such as a swimming pool or lead paint.[54] Likewise, a landlord may not refuse to rent or sell an upper floor unit to a woman out of safety concerns for her children.[55]

**May a landlord ask for a larger security deposit from families with children or charge them more rent?**

No, a landlord may not make any greater demands on a family with children than he or she would make of any other person seeking to rent a residence. A landlord may not ask for a higher rent or security deposit, nor add any conditions in the terms of sale or rental other than those normally included for any other individual.[56]

**Are there exceptions to this policy of nondiscrimination against women with children?**

Yes. A landlord may have a general "adults-only" rule *only if* the housing qualifies as "housing for older persons."[57] Under this category a landlord may refuse to rent to a woman with children in housing that is (1) specifically provided for elderly persons by a state or federal program; (2) intended for and solely occupied by persons aged sixty-two or older; or 3) intended for persons aged fifty-five and over, with at least 80 percent of the rental units occupied by persons aged fifty-five or over.[58]

In addition, a landlord may place reasonable limits on the number of people who can live in a particular residence.[59] This limitation should be based on neutral factors, not related to the family status of the tenants—for example, a landlord may consider the number and size of sleeping areas or the overall size of the residence.

## THE RIGHT OF ASSOCIATION

**May a landlord refuse to rent or sell to a woman because she associates with people of a different race?**

Absolutely not. A woman has a right to associate with a person of any race without that affecting her housing. For example, a landlord may not refuse to rent to a woman because she is involved in an interracial relationship. If a landlord does so, he is illegally discriminating on the basis of race and is in violation of the FHA.[60]

## ENFORCEMENT AND REMEDIES

**What can a woman do if she has been discriminated against?**

There are several ways that a woman who believes that she has been discriminated against can enforce the provisions of the FHA.[61] First, she may file an administrative complaint with HUD,[62] or contact a HUD-certified state or private fair housing agency.[63] She may also sue directly in state or federal court.[64] Under the FHA, a woman need not choose between filing an administrative complaint and filing a complaint in court.

**May a landlord evict a woman for filing a complaint under the FHA?**

No, a landlord cannot punish a woman for filing a claim under the FHA. The FHA prohibits a landlord from "coerc[ing], intimidat[ing], threaten-[ing], or interfer[ing] with any person" on account of her exercising her rights under the FHA, and its implementing regulations specifically include retaliation for making a complaint as one form of prohibited conduct.[65] Any landlord who evicts a tenant in retaliation after she makes a complaint violates the FHA.

**How can a woman file a claim with HUD?**

A woman should file a claim with her HUD regional office. The locations of all HUD regional offices can be found online at http://www.hud. gov or by calling 800-669-9777/800-927-9275 (toll-free TDD phone). The complaint can be filed in person, over the phone, or online at the HUD website. The complaint must be made within one year from the time when the discrimination occurred.[66] When a woman files a complaint, she will be called the "complainant," while the person or company she is complaining about is called the "respondent."

A complaint that is filed in writing should contain all the information the woman has about the discrimination she has suffered. It is important for her to be as specific as possible in making the complaint. A woman should also try to include the name of the person who discriminated against her, the name of that person's employer, if applicable, the dates on which the discrimination occurred, and the names of any witnesses.

In addition to contacting HUD, a woman may initially contact a "certified state or local agency" or local nonprofit agency that addresses housing discrimination. Certified state agencies are those approved by HUD as providing services and/or enforcing fair housing laws that "are substantially equivalent to those created by and under [the FHA.]"[67] Local nonprofit agencies may receive funding from HUD via the Fair Housing Initiatives Program (FHIP) to combat housing discrimination, and can also provide help with matters related to housing discrimination.[68]

**What happens after a complaint is filed with HUD?**

HUD is required by law to investigate a complaint and within one hundred days to a make a final investigative report stating whether there is reason to believe that discrimination occurred. During that period, HUD will contact the respondent to get his or her side of the story. If HUD cannot meet the 100-day deadline, HUD is required to inform the complainant and the respondent of the reasons why it cannot. If a woman needs immediate assistance, HUD may be able provide help as soon as the complaint is filed. In such a case, HUD may authorize the U.S. Attorney General to obtain a temporary injunction in court, if intervention is necessary to prevent an immediate harm and there is substantial evidence that the FHA has been violated.

If the discrimination occurs in an area with a state or local public housing agency that has been certified by HUD, the complaint will be referred to that agency.[69] HUD may continue its investigation, if that agency consents. Furthermore, if HUD refers the complaint but the state or local agency does not begin to investigate within thirty days of the date of the referral or investigates but fails to follow through with any further proceedings with "reasonable promptness," HUD may intervene and resume or begin its own investigations.[70]

When HUD investigates a complaint, it will try to settle the dispute by helping the parties to reach a "conciliation agreement."[71] The agreement can provide for money damages or other kinds of relief, and HUD must approve the conciliation agreement for it to be valid.[72] If HUD later determines that a party has broken the agreement, it will refer the matter to the Justice Department, which can file a suit against the individual breaching the agreement.[73]

If the parties do not reach a conciliation agreement and HUD determines that discrimination has occurred, it must issue a formal charge of discrimination against the landlord (or against whomever discriminated).[74] If it does not find any discrimination, HUD will dismiss the complaint. However, even if the complaint is dismissed, a woman can still file an individual complaint in state or federal court.

If HUD formally charges the landlord with discrimination, either the tenant or the landlord may request that the case be transferred to federal court within twenty days of the date on which the charge was issued.[75] Otherwise, the case will be heard by an Administrative Law Judge (ALJ), who can award damages and other relief. The ALJ must hold a hearing within 120 days after HUD has issued charges and has an additional sixty days after the hearing to reach a decision.[76]

### Should a woman choose an administrative hearing?

There are both advantages and disadvantages to an administrative hearing. An administrative hearing is similar to a trial in court but is less formal. For this reason, a woman without a lawyer may find the process less intimidating than a trial. A woman who chooses an administrative hearing has rights similar to those she would have in a trial. She has the right to be present at the hearing, to be represented by a lawyer, and to question witnesses. Going through the hearing process can also be less costly and faster than a trial in federal or state court.

However, although an ALJ can order that a landlord pay a woman for any damages she suffered because of the discrimination, an ALJ cannot force a landlord to pay her punitive damages. (These are damages that do not compensate an individual for injuries, but instead are meant to punish the landlord for discrimination, regardless of the injuries of the individual who was discriminated against.) Instead, an ALJ has the authority to order different civil penalties based on the number of times that landlord has violated the FHA: $11,000 for the first violation, $27,000 for the second violation within five years, and $55,000 for the third violation within seven years.[77]

**Should a woman choose to file a complaint in court?**

A woman can file a fair housing case in federal or state court regardless of whether she has also filed a complaint with a federal or state agency. She must bring her court case within two years of the discrimination, but the two-year period does not include any time the woman spent going through HUD or state agencies.

In addition, as mentioned above, if HUD issues a charge of discrimination based on her administrative complaint, either she or the respondent can transfer the case to federal district court within twenty days. At that point, the U.S. Justice Department will file a lawsuit on her behalf;[78] however, the complainant is not automatically a party to that lawsuit. Instead, the Justice Department, which brought the case on her behalf, is the complaining party. However, she may choose to participate in the lawsuit formally by "intervening" as a party.[79]

Under the FHA, if the court finds that discrimination occurred, it can issue an order requiring the landlord to stop the discriminatory behavior. The court can also order the wrongdoer to take steps to prevent future discrimination, such as training employees about fair housing rights.[80] Finally, if the court finds that discrimination occurred, it can award actual and punitive damages to the individual who was discriminated against, and may require the landlord to pay for the complainant's costs and attorney's fees.[81]

## STATE FAIR HOUSING LAWS

**What protections are available under state laws?**

State and local laws may offer additional protections to women facing sex discrimination in housing.[82] Some states and cities protect individuals from types and acts of housing discrimination until recently not covered by federal law, such as discrimination against a woman based on her status as a victim of domestic violence.[83] Furthermore, some states also have laws that specifically restrict a landlord's ability to use occupancy limits to discriminate against families. For instance, Washington State law allows state agencies to review occupancy standards that require fewer than two persons per bedroom. If a landlord uses such a standard, he will have to prove that it is reasonable.[84]

However, because each state is very different, a discussion of all the protections available under state law is well beyond the scope of this book. A woman who thinks she has been discriminated against in housing should consult with a qualified attorney or legal services provider to discuss her options under both state and federal law, and determine how to proceed.

## The Equal Credit Opportunity Act

### What is the Equal Credit Opportunity Act (ECOA)?

The ECOA prohibits various sorts of discrimination, including discrimination based on sex, marital status, or the receipt of public assistance. It applies to banks and other lenders that arrange credit and financing for housing.[85] The ECOA outlaws discrimination in mortgages and home refinancing, and may also outlaw some kinds of discrimination in residential leases.[86] Its protection therefore overlaps with that of the FHA.

### What types of acts are prohibited by the ECOA?

A lender may not discriminate by requiring different applications for men and women, or for married women and single women, and it cannot treat these groups differently when it reviews the applications.[87] In addition, a lender may not inquire into the marital status of a woman applying for a loan or mortgage by requiring her to choose "Miss" or "Mrs." on an application.[88] A lender may not ask a woman whether she intends to have children, whether she uses birth control, or whether she is pregnant.[89] However, a lender may inquire into a woman's marital status in order to determine its rights as a creditor and may require the signatures of both spouses, if applicable, for certain types of financing.[90]

The ECOA also prohibits lenders from discouraging or discriminating against applicants solely on the basis of their receipt of public assistance, such as welfare benefits.[91] However, a lender may look at an individual's receipt of public welfare in considering her income level or credit risk and may deny an applicant on the basis of her income level or credit risk.[92]

### Does a woman have a right to know why an application for credit has been rejected?

Yes. When a woman has been refused credit, such as a mortgage, she is entitled to a report stating the reasons. The creditor may do one of two things: it may (1) supply a list of specific written reasons along with the rejection or (2) notify the woman that her application has been rejected and that she has the right to receive a written explanation describing the specific reasons if she so requests.[93]

## How is the ECOA enforced?

Women who have been discriminated against by a lender can bring suit under the ECOA in court. If a woman wins her case, she can recover any money she lost as a result of the discrimination, punitive damages of up to $10,000, attorneys' fees, and other related relief.[94]

The ECOA can also be enforced through suits brought by the Attorney General of the United States.[95] A woman who has been discriminated against must bring her suit within two years of the discrimination.[96]

## NOTES

1. In 1988, upwards of twelve thousand housing discrimination complaints were received by fair housing agencies. HUD, the DOJ, and civil rights agencies processed approximately forty-nine hundred of these cases. The majority of complaints were initiated by single females and female-headed households of all races. Shanna Smith, *Women and Housing Discrimination, in* UNLOCKING THE DOOR: KEYS TO WOMEN'S HOUSING (McAuley Inst. Sept. 2000).

2. U.S. CENSUS BUREAU, CURRENT POPULATION SURVEY, 2005 ANNUAL SOCIAL AND ECONOMIC SUPPLEMENT, TABLE POV04, FAMILIES BY AGE OF HOUSEHOLDER, NUMBER OF CHILDREN, AND FAMILY STRUCTURE: 2004—BELOW 100% OF POVERTY—ALL RACES, *available at* http://pubdb3.census.gov/macro/032005/pov/new04_100_01.htm.

3. HARVARD JOINT CTR. FOR HOUSING STUDIES, THE STATE OF THE NATION'S HOUSING—2004 14 (2004).

4. NAT'L COALITION FOR THE HOMELESS, NCH FACT SHEET #3, WHO IS HOMELESS (2006), *available at* http://www.nationalhomeless.org/publications/facts/Whois.pdf (families with children are estimated to make up 33 percent of the homeless population).

5. ACLU WOMEN'S RIGHTS PROJECT, DOMESTIC VIOLENCE AND PUBLIC AND SUBSIDIZED HOUSING (2005) *available at* http://www.aclu.org/FilesPDFs/ACF831B.pdf; NATIONAL COALITION FOR THE HOMELESS, NCH FACT SHEET #7, DOMESTIC VIOLENCE AND HOMELESSNESS (2006) *available at* http://www.nationalhomeless.org/publications/facts/domestic.pdf ("In addition, 44% of the 27 cities surveyed by

the U.S. Conference of Mayors identified domestic violence as a primary cause of homelessness" (citing U.S. CONFERENCE OF MAYORS SURVEY (2004)).

6. Robin Abcarian, *Harassed at Home*, L.A. TIMES, Nov. 24, 1991, at E1; Sylvia Rubin, *Sex Harassment Close to Home*, S.F. CHRON., Jan. 8, 1992, at B3; William Litt, Charlotte Robinson, Lisa Anderson, and Nicole C. Bershon, *Recent Developments: Sexual Harassment Hits Home*, 2 UCLA WOMEN's L.J. 227, 233 (1992).

7. Regina Cahan, Comment, *Home Is No Haven: An Analysis of Sexual Harassment in Housing*, 1987 WIS. L. REV. 1061, 1066–70 (1987) (discussing reasons why women may keep silent about sexual harassment).

8. Title VIII of the Civil Rights Act of 1964, Fair Housing Act, 42 U.S.C. § 3604 (2006). The other sorts of discrimination that are forbidden are discrimination on the basis of race, color, religion, national origin, or disability.

9. This includes foster parents. Gorski v. Troy, 929 F.2d 1183 (7th Cir. 1991); *see also* Andujar v. Hewitt, No. 02 CIV. 2223(SAS), 2002 WL 1792065 (S.D.N.Y. 2002).

10. 42 U.S.C. § 3602(k) (2006).

11. 42 U.S.C. § 3604(a) (2006); 24 C.F.R. § 100.50–100.90 (2006).

12. 24 C.F.R. § 100.60(b)(5) (2006); *see also* Betsey v. Turtle Creek Assoc., 736 F.2d 983 (4th Cir. 1984).

13. 42 U.S.C. § 3604(a), (c) (2006); 24 C.F.R. § 100.70 (2006). *See generally* Fair Hous. Cong. v. Weber, 993 F. Supp. 1286, 1293 (C.D. Cal. 1997) (42 U.S.C. § 3604(a) forbids steering by its terms, which make it unlawful to "otherwise make unavailable" a dwelling on prohibited grounds) and Llanos v. Coehlo, 24 F. Supp. 2d 1052, 1056–58 (E.D. Cal. 1998).

14. 24 C.F.R. § 100.70(c)(1) & (2) (2006).

15. *Id.* § 100.70(c)(3).

16. 24 C.F.R. § 100.70(d)(4) and § 100.120 (2006). The Equal Credit Opportunity Act specifically prohibits gender discrimination in the provision of mortgage and credit for housing purposes. 15 U.S.C. § 1691(a)(1) (2006); *see also* Matthiesen v. Bank One Mortgage Corp., 173 F.3d 1242, 1245–1246 (10th Cir. 1999).

17. 42 U.S.C. § 3604(c) (2006); 24 C.F.R. § 100.75 (2006); 20 U.S.C. § 1686 (2006); 45 CFR § 86.32(c)(2) (2006); Wilson v. Glenwood Intermountain Properties, 876 F. Supp 1231 (D. Utah 1995), *vacated and remanded at* 98 F3d 590 (10th Cir. Utah) (Fair Housing Act's gender discrimination bar did not apply to conduct of landlords in segregating university students by sex, as Civil Rights Act expressly sanctions segregation of college students by gender; implementing regulations clarify that educational institutions may segregate their students by gender in both on- and off-campus student housing.).

18. 24 C.F.R. § 100.60(b) (2006) ("Prohibited actions under this section include but are not limited to . . . (4) using different qualification criteria or applications, or sale or rental standards or procedures, such as income standards, application

requirements, application fees, credit analysis or sale or rental approval procedures or other requirements. . . .").

19. *See* Garcia v. Condarco, 114 F. Supp. 2d 1158, 1159–60 (D. N.M. 2000).

20. 42 U.S.C. § 3602(b) (2006) ("Dwelling" means any building, structure, or portion thereof that is occupied as, or designed or intended for occupancy as, a residence by one or more families, and any vacant land that is offered for sale or lease for the construction or location thereon of any such building, structure, or portion thereof.).

21. 42 U.S.C. § 3603(b)(1) (2006). If a private homeowner chooses to advertise the property he or she is selling or renting, he or she must not include any discriminatory preferences or limitations in the advertisement.

22. *Id.* § 3603(b)(2).

23. 42 U.S.C. § 3607(a) (2006). In the case of the religious organization exemption, the organization may only limit the rental or sale of dwellings if the dwellings are owned for other than a commercial purpose and only on the basis of religious affiliation, unless membership in the religion is restricted on account of race, color, or national origin. *See, e.g.,* Bachman v. St. Monica's Congregation, 902 F.2d 1259 (7th Cir. 1990). In the case of private clubs, the exemption only applies if the "lodgings" (which is a more limited term than "dwellings" and probably means only short-term residences) are not owned for commercial purposes, and the exemption only permits a club to discriminate in favor of members. *See, e.g.,* United States v. Columbus Country Club, 915 F.2d 877 (3rd Cir. 1990), *cert. denied,* 501 U.S. 1205, 111 S. Ct. 2797 (1991).

24. 42 U.S.C. § 3603 (2006).

25. Meyer v. Holley, 537 U.S. 280 (2003) (holding that traditional principles of vicarious liability should govern courts' decisions); *see also* Walker v. Crigler, 976 F.2d 900 (4th Cir. 1992).

26. 42 U.S.C. § 3606 (2006).

27. 42 U.S.C. § 3605 (2006).

28. *See* Assoc. of Relatives & Friends of AIDS Patients v. Regulations & Permits Admin., 740 F. Supp. 95 (D. P.R. 1990).

29. *Id.; see also* Dreher v. Rana Mgmt., Inc., 493 F. Supp. 930 (E.D.N.Y 1980).

30. McDonnell Douglas Corp. v. Green, 411 U.S. 792, 802 (1973); Robinson v. 12 Lofts Realty, Inc., 610 F.2d 1032 (2nd Cir. 1979) (finding racial discrimination).

31. *See McDonnell Douglas Corp.,* 411 U.S. 792; Sabree v. United Brotherhood of Carpenters & Joiners Local No. 33, 921 F.2d 396 (1st Cir. 1990); Marbly v. Home Props. of N.Y., 205 F. Supp. 2d 736 (E.D. Mich. 2002).

32. *See* Griggs v. Duke Power Co., 401 U.S. 424 (1971); Pfaff v. U.S. Dep't. of Hous. & Urban Dev., 88 F.3d 739 (9th Cir. 1996). *But see* Huntington Branch, NAACP v. Town of Huntington, 844 F.2d 926, 934 (2d. Cir. 1988), *aff'd,* 488 U.S. 15 (1988) (Supreme Court declined to rule on the appropriateness of disparate-

impact analysis in the case since the parties had conceded its applicability). For further discussion as to the conflicting authorities on the proper model by which to prove discriminatory effect cases among the circuit courts, *see* John E. Theuman, Annotation, *Evidence of Discriminatory Effect Alone as Sufficient to Prove, or to Establish Prima Facie Case of, Violation of the Fair Housing Act,* 100 A.L.R. Fed. 97 (2003).

33. Honce v. Vigil, 1 F.3d 1085 (10th Cir. 1993); Beliveau v. Caras, 873 F. Supp. 1393, 1397 (C.D. Cal. 1995) ("[I]t is beyond question that sexual harassment is a form of discrimination."); Krueger v. Cuomo 115 F.3d 487, 491 (7th Cir. 1997) ("This court has recognized that sexual harassment in the housing context can violate the Fair Housing Act.").

34. In fact, the Supreme Court has held that harassment need not fit neatly into one or the other of these categories to be against the law. *See, e.g.,* Burlington Indus., Inc. v. Ellerth, 524 U.S. 742, 751 (1998) ("The terms quid pro quo and hostile work environment are helpful, perhaps, in making a rough demarcation between cases in which threats are carried out and those where they are not or are absent altogether, but beyond this are of limited utility.").

35. *See* Meritor Savings Bank, FSB v. Vinson, 477 U.S. 57, 65–66 (1986) (defining "quid pro quo" in the employment context).

36. *Honce,* 1 F.3d at 1089; Grieger v. Sheets, 689 F. Supp. 835 (N.D. Ill. 1988) (Plaintiff had stated claim for sexual harassment where landlord refused to make repairs in apartment after plaintiff rejected his sexual demands.), *related case at* Grieger v. Sheets, No. 87-C-6567, 1989 WL 38707 (N.D. Ill. April 10, 1989) ("quid pro quo" claim survived summary judgment where landlord refused to make repairs after tenant rejected his explicit demands for sex).

37. 24 C.F.R. § 100.65(b)(5) (2006).

38. Shellhammer v. Lewallen, 1 Fair Housing-Fair Lending (P-H), ¶ 15,472 (N.D. Ohio 1983) (unpublished opinion), *aff'd per curium,* 770 F.2d 167 (Table), 1985 WL 13505 (6th Cir. July 31, 1985) (unpublished opinion); *see also* Beliveau, 873 F. Supp. 1393.

39. *Grieger,* 1989 WL38707, at *2.

40. 42 U.S.C. 3602(d) (2006). *See generally* Nicole A. Forkenbrock Lindemyer, *Sexual Harassment on the Second Shift: The Misfit Application of Title VII Employment Standards to Title VIII Housing Cases,* 18 Law & Ineq. 351, 238 (2000) (discussing how the FHA extends liability to individuals).

41. *Shellhammer,* 770 F.2d 167.

42. *Cf. Grieger,* 689 F. Supp. at 840; *Shellhammer,* 770 F.2d 167.

43. *Shellhammer,* 770 F.2d 167. *But see* DiCenso v. Cisneros, 96 F.3d 1004, 1008–9 (7th Cir. 1996).

44. NOW Legal Defense and Education Fund, Sexual Harassment in Housing: A Primer 2 (2003) *available at* http://www.legalmomentum.org/pub/kits/SexHarassinHousingLRK0120.pdf.

45. *See Honce*, 1 F.3d at 1090; *Shellhammer*, 770 F.2d 167; *Williams*, 955 F. Supp. at 496 (enumerating factors of test to be applied in a hostile housing environment context).

46. *Honce*, 1 F.3d at 1090.

47. *See* 29 C.F.R. § 1604.11(a) (2006) (listing "unwelcome sexual advances, requests for sexual favors, and other verbal or physical conduct of a sexual nature" as forms of conduct that may constitute sexual harassment under Title VII); *see also Meritor Savings Bank, FSB*, 477 U.S. at 64–65; *Shellhammer*, 770 F.2d 167.

48. *Honce*, 1 F.3d at 1090.

49. Reeves v. Carrollsburg Condo. Unit Owners Ass'n., No. CIV. A. 96-2495RMU, 1997 WL 1877201, at *7 (D.D.C. Dec. 18, 1997) (citing *Williams*, 955 F. Supp. at 496 n.2); Harris v. Forklift Sys., Inc., 510 U.S. 17 (1993).

50. *Meyer*, 537 U.S. 280 at 285 (stating that "[n]onetheless, it is well established that the Act provides for vicarious liability" and applying traditional vicarious liability rules to determine liability of corporation in discriminatory acts of employee under FHA); *Burlington Indus.*, 524 U.S. at 765 (in employment context, finding employer could be liable for sexual harassment by employee regardless of notice in some circumstances).

51. *Compare Beliveau*, 873 F. Supp. at 1397–98 (noting that "one commentator has suggested that sexual harassment in the home is in some respects more oppressive" and citing Regina Cahan, *supra* note 7, at 1073. The court then found that plaintiff had a valid claim under FHA after alleging several incidents in which defendant made "off-color, flirtatious and unwelcome remarks," and one incident of offensive touching "committed (1) *in* plaintiff's own home, where she should feel (and be) less vulnerable, and (2) by one whose very role was to provide that safe environment. . . .") *with DiCenso*, 96 F.3d at 1008–9 (on facts similar to *Beliveau*, the court found that harassment had occurred but did not agree that "severe and pervasive" standard for hostile environment harassment had been met). For a more in-depth discussion of the two cases and differing interpretations of the hostile environment standard, *see* Forkenbrock Lindemyer, *supra* note 40, at 380–91.

52. *See, e.g.*, Bouley v. Young-Sabourin, 394 F. Supp. 2d 675 (D. Vt. 2005); Alvera v. Creekside Vill. Apartments, No. 10-99-0538-8 (H.U.D.A.L.J. April 16, 2001), *available at* http://www.legalmomentum.org/issues/vio/alveradeterm.pdf.

53. Violence Against Women Act and Department of Justice Reauthorization Act of 2005, Pub. L. No. 109-162, §§ 606, 607 (2006); 42 U.S.C. § 1437d(l)(5) (2006).

54. Llanos v. Estate of Coehlo, 24 F. Supp. 2d 1052 (E.D. Cal. 1998); United States v. Grishman, 818 F. Supp. 21 (D. Me. 1993).

55. United States v. Garden Homes Mgmt., Corp., 156 F. Supp. 2d 413, 423–24 (D.N.J. 2001); *Weber*, 993 F. Supp. at 1293 (C.D. Cal. 1997).

56. U.S. Dep't. of Hous. & Urban Dev. v. Lewis, Fair Housing-Fair Lending

(P-H), ¶ 25,035, 1992 WL 406530, (H.U.D.A.L.J. Aug. 27, 1992), *aff'd*, 43 F.3d 675 (Table) (8th Cir. 1994); 24 C.F.R. § 100.65(b)(1) (2006).

57. 42 U.S.C. § 3607(b)(2) (2006); 24 C.F.R. §§ 100.304–307 (2006).

58. 42 U.S.C. § 3607(b)(2); 24 C.F.R. §§ 100.304–307.

59. 42 U.S.C. § 3607(b)(1) (2006); *Pfaff*, 88 F.3d at 748 (holding that landlord may develop reasonable occupancy requirements based on factors such as the number of bedrooms and overall size of the dwelling unit).

60. *See, e.g.,* Cato v. Jilek, 779 F. Supp. 937, 940–41 (N.D. Ill. 1991) (The "broad protections" of the Act apply whether the interracial couple is unmarried, married, or engaged to be married.).

61. The secretary of the Department of Housing and Urban Development also has the power to initiate proceedings pursuant to 42 U.S.C. § 3610(a)(1)(A)(i), as does the Attorney General under § 3614(a).

62. A woman can file first with HUD under 42 U.S.C. § 3610; she may then elect to convert proceedings into a civil action if she moves within twenty days of a formal charge issued by HUD against the landlord, according to § 3612. It is important to note that filing first with HUD does not necessarily impede a woman's options to later file with state agencies or to commence a civil action. *See* 42 U.S.C. § 3610(f), § 3613(a) (2006).

63. 42 U.S.C. § 3610(f) (2006).

64. 42 U.S.C. § 3613 (2006).

65. 42 U.S.C. § 3617 (2006) ("It shall be unlawful to coerce, intimidate, threaten, or interfere with any person . . . on account of his having exercised or enjoyed, or on account of his having aided or encouraged any other person in the exercise or enjoyment of, any right granted or protected by [the FHA]."); 24 C.F.R. § 100.400(c)(5) (2006) ("Conduct made unlawful under this section includes, but is not limited to . . . (5) Retaliating against any person because that person has made a complaint, testified, assisted, or participated in any manner in a proceeding under the Fair Housing Act."); *see also Krueger*, 115 F.3d at 491 (upholding ALJ's decision that landlord's "continued campaign of harassment—an interference with . . . [plaintiff's] right to quiet enjoyment of her tenancy—and his retaliation against . . . [her] for her filing a complaint each independently violated 42 U.S.C. § 3617").

66. 42 U.S.C. § 3610(a)(1)(A)(i) (2006).

67. *Id.* § 3610(f)(3)(A).

68. For a list of state and local resources, *see* Fair Housing Assistance Program (FHAP) Agencies, HUD Fair Housing and Equal Opportunity Office, http://www.hud.gov/offices/fheo/partners/FHAP/agencies.cfm#AZ (last visited April 9, 2007). These agencies may eventually refer a woman seeking help to HUD, but they can also be a source of information and support for women facing discrimination.

69. 42 U.S.C. § 3610(f) (2006).

70. 42 U.S.C. § 3610(f)(2) (2006).

71. *Id.* § 3610(b).

72. *Id.* § 3610(b)(2).

73. *Id.* § 3610(c).

74. *Id.* § 3610(g)(2).

75. 42 U.S.C. § 3612 (2006). At any point in the proceedings following the filing of a complaint, the secretary may determine that prompt judicial action is necessary and may commence a civil action. 42 U.S.C. § 3610(e) (2006).

76. 42 U.S.C. § 3612(g).

77. *Id.*

78. *Id.* §§ 3612(o)-(p).

79. This intervention is as of right. *Id.* §3612(o)(2).

80. 42 U.S.C. § 3613(c)(1) (2006).

81. *Id.* § 3613(c)(2).

82. *See, e.g.,* Gnerre v. Mass. Comm'n Against Discrimination, 524 N.E.2d 84 (Mass. 1988) (finding that plaintiff had made case of hostile environment sexual harassment under state civil rights law, MASS. GEN. LAWS ANN. ch. 151B, § 4 (West 2006), *unconstitutional as applied by* Pielech v. Massasoit Greyhound, Inc., 804 N.E.2d 894 (Mass. 2004), *after showing that on* "four separate occasions, over a 2-year period, [landlord] had subjected her to unsolicited harassment involving offensive speech of a sexual nature. As a result of the repeated incidents of harassment, the tenant became terrified of the landlord because she did not know what he was capable of doing to her, and she changed her behavior patterns in order to avoid meeting him and to prevent his making further comments to her").

83. The Violence Against Women Act of 2005 added new protections for victims of domestic violence in government-subsidized housing. However, its provisions do not necessarily reach private actors; many state laws, however, do explicitly prohibit any type of discrimination against a woman due to her status or perceived status as a victim of domestic violence. For more detailed information about state laws addressing discrimination against victims of domestic violence and sexual abuse, *see* chapter 5, "Violence against Women."

84. WASH. REV. CODE ANN. § 49.60.222 (West 2006).

85. Equal Credit Opportunity Act, 15 U.S.C. § 1691 (2006). "Marital status" means whether an individual is married, single, separated, divorced, or widowed. *Id.* § 1691(a)(1); 12 C.F.R. § 202.2(u) (2006). For a more thorough discussion of the ECOA, *see* RALPH C. CLONTZ, FEDERAL FAIR LENDING AND CREDIT PRACTICES MANUAL (Warren Gorham & Lamont 1994); *see also* Cartwright v. Am. Sav. & Loan Ass'n., 880 F.2d 912, 925–27 (7th Cir. 1989) (applying the ECOA to a mortgage application); Thomas v. First Fed. Sav. Bank of Ind., 653 F. Supp. 1330, 1341 (N.D. Ind. 1987) (applying the ECOA to refinancing through a second mortgage).

86. Ferguson v. Park City Mobile Homes, No. 89-C-1909, 1989 WL 111916 (N.D. Ill. Sept. 18, 1989) (holding that ECOA applies to lease transactions, in this

case, lease of a mobile home lot); *see generally* Brian S. Prestes, Note, *Application of the Equal Credit Opportunity Act to Housing Leases,* 67 U. Chi. L. Rev. 865 (2000). *But see* Liberty Leasing Co. v. Machamer, 6 F. Supp. 2d 714 (S.D. Ohio 1998) (holding that ECOA does not apply to lease).

87. 12 C.F.R. §202.6 (2005).

88. Harbaugh v. Cont'l Ill. Nat. Bank & Trust Co. of Chicago, 615 F.2d 1169 (7th Cir. 1980); 12 C.F.R. §202.5(d)(1) (2006).

89. 12 C.F.R. § 202.5(d)(3).

90. *See, e.g.,* Midlantic Nat'l Bank v. Hansen, 48 F.3d 693 (3d Cir. 1995).

91. 15 U.S.C. § 1691(a)(2) (2006); 12 C.F.R. § 202.6(b)(2)(i) (2006).

92. *See, e.g.,* Saldana v. Citibank, Fed. Sav. Bank, No. 93-C-4164, 1996 WL 332451 (N.D. Ill. June 13, 1996); Gross v. U.S. Small Bus. Admin., 669 F. Supp. 50 (N.D.N.Y. 1987), *aff'd,* 867 F.2d 1423 (2d Cir. 1988).

93. 15 U.S.C. § 1691(d) (2006); 12 C.F.R. § 202.9 (2006).

94. 15 U.S.C. § 1691e (a)-(d) (2006).

95. *Id.* § 1691e.

96. *Id.* § 1691e(f).

# XI

# Public Accommodations and Private Clubs

Public accommodations are places or organizations open to the general public without special conditions or restrictions. They include not only places like public sidewalks and libraries but also privately owned facilities such as hotels, restaurants, hospitals, theaters, and sports arenas. Some states define public accommodations even more broadly. For example, the District of Columbia includes insurance companies in its definition,[1] while Ohio considers some types of trailer parks to be public accommodations.[2] Recently, lawsuits have argued that access to playing fields in city parks is a public accommodation.[3]

A public accommodation does not have to be a place. Many states consider organizations such as the Jaycees and Little League to be public accommodations, even though they are not located in a single place.[4] Because these organizations are open to the public, access to them should be governed in the same way as access to facilities in fixed locations that are open to the public. In general, an organization is more likely to be considered a public accommodation if its activities are supported or funded by the government or if it has a business or money-making aspect.

### Is there a federal law that forbids public accommodations from excluding or otherwise discriminating against women?

No. Unfortunately, the federal public accommodations laws—Title II of the 1964 Civil Rights Act and Title III of the Americans with Disabilities Act[5]—only forbid discrimination based on race, color, religion, national origin, and disability, and thus do not provide any protection to women on a uniform, nationwide basis.

**Are there any state or city laws forbidding public accommodations from discriminating against women?**

Yes: the fifty states, the District of Columbia, and many cities have passed laws, generally referred to as "public accommodations laws," that ban at least some types of discrimination in some public accommodations. In forty-four states and the District of Columbia, the public accommodations laws specifically ban gender discrimination.[6]

**Besides state public accommodations laws, are there any other laws protecting women from discrimination by public establishments?**

It depends. A woman may be able to challenge discrimination by a public accommodation under the Equal Protection Clause of the U.S. Constitution, or under a state's Equal Rights Act (ERA) or other state constitutional nondiscrimination provision. However, in order for the Equal Protection Clause and most state constitutional nondiscrimination provisions to apply, there must be some "state action" associated with the public accommodation. This means that the public accommodation must be government-owned or -operated, or that the government must be otherwise significantly connected to the establishment. Convincing courts that there is enough government involvement in privately owned public accommodations to amount to state action has been the chief barrier to constitutional litigation in this area. A few suits against discriminatory restaurants have succeeded in showing sufficient government involvement by pointing to state regulation of liquor licenses or use of the city police force to evict women.[7]

**Can public accommodations charge different prices to men and women?**

It depends. In some states, courts have held that offering discounts to one gender, such as reduced prices for "ladies' nights," does not violate the state's public accommodations law because men still enjoy full access at the regular price.[8] However, in other states, courts have found that differential prices charged by public accommodations do discriminate because they deny equal advantages and services to one gender.[9] A couple of factors that may distinguish these differing court findings are whether the price differential is specifically calculated to discourage one gender's patronage, and whether non-gender-based discounts are regularly offered as well. Courts sometimes seem concerned about whether the price differential serves to make one gender feel particularly unwelcome or unaccepted. Overall, however, it is not easy to explain the differing results across cases because public accommodations laws usually contain similar language prohibiting discrimination.

### Are there exceptions to the protection from discrimination that public accommodations laws provide women?

Yes. The main exception to public accommodations laws is that they generally do not apply to "distinctly private" organizations.[10] This means that a truly private club can legally exclude women (and other groups) if it so desires. One reason for this is that members of a genuinely private organization have a constitutionally protected right of association in deciding whom to admit to their group. This right cannot be overridden by the public interest in affording women equal access. Often, a key question in determining whether a particular organization has illegally discriminated is to figure out whether it is exempt from public accommodations laws as a private association.

### What factors do courts consider in determining whether an organization is "distinctly private" and therefore exempt from public accommodations laws?

The main factors courts usually consider are the organization's size; its selectiveness in admitting new members; the extent to which it permits the public to participate in its events; and its history and purpose. A club that is very small, highly selective, completely closed to nonmembers, and founded to enable a particular set of individuals to associate with one another would most likely qualify as a private club.[11]

### Does this mean that civic associations, fraternal orders, country clubs, and other membership organizations can exclude women?

It depends. If a civic association or fraternal order is found to be distinctly private, it can probably exclude women. If the organization is relatively large, lets in all or almost all men who seek to join, and often invites the public to its events, state public accommodations laws will probably recognize the organization as a public accommodation and forbid it from excluding women.

For example, a federal court in Michigan ruled that the Lions Club is a public accommodation even though it is a membership organization, because it is essentially unlimited in size and is not selective in awarding new memberships. Thus it was not found to be "private" in any meaningful sense,

and the Lions' exclusion of women was illegal under the public accommodations provisions of Michigan's Elliott-Larsen Civil Rights Act.[12] Similarly,
in Minnesota, the state Department of Human Rights found the Jaycees
to be subject to Minnesota's public accommodations law because they are
relatively large, impersonal, and nonselective. In addition, the U.S. Supreme
Court ruled that because of the Jaycees' size and nonselectiveness, requiring
the admission of women did not violate the members' First Amendment
rights of speech and association.[13] The Supreme Court has also rejected a
similar First Amendment challenge by the Rotary Club, thereby permitting
the operation of the California Unruh Civil Rights Act (California's public
accommodations law) to bar the exclusion of women from Rotary Clubs in
California.[14]

Courts have also found a number of "fraternal" orders, such as the Elks
Lodge and Eagles Order, to be subject to state public accommodations laws
that forbid gender discrimination. For example, in Michigan, a woman succeeded in enrolling in a local Elks Lodge when she brought a lawsuit under
the state public accommodations law. The Michigan court deemed the Elks
Lodge to be a public accommodation because it lacked genuine selectivity in
admitting new members.[15] More recently, in 2002, the Washington Supreme
Court ruled that the Eagles cannot exclude women because it is a public accommodation under state law. The court emphasized that the Order was
not automatically entitled to private-club status simply because it identifies
itself as a fraternal organization. Rather, a fact-based analysis showed that
the Eagles were not distinctly private or selective given the Order's large size
and involvement in public-oriented activities such as community service.[16]

It is important to remember that each of these decisions was based on a
particular state's public accommodations law that does not apply in other
states. Accordingly, the first test in any state is to determine the scope of
the local public accommodations law. For example, the antidiscrimination
provisions of New York's public accommodations law do not cover "a corporation incorporated under the benevolent orders law or described in the benevolent orders law" because New York defines such a corporation to be "in
its nature distinctly private." Even though a woman successfully challenged
the Elks in Michigan, so far New York courts have held the Elks to be cat-
egorically exempt from the state public accommodations law as a distinctly
private organization.[17]

**Can the U.S. Supreme Court's rulings in the Jaycees and Rotary Club cases be applied in other cases where an all-male organization asserts that the application of a public accommodations law is violating its First Amendment rights of association?**

It depends. The Supreme Court found that the Jaycees and the Rotary Club were large and nonexclusive. Smaller, more selective groups may have a stronger claim that requiring them to admit members of the other sex violates their First Amendments rights.

Two distinct kinds of associational rights can be at issue in the application of public accommodations laws. The First Amendment protects both the freedom of *intimate association* and the freedom of *expressive association.* "Intimate association" refers to a person's right to enter into and maintain certain private relationships of her or his choosing, free from government interference. Relationships intimate enough to warrant such protection include marriage, parent-child relationships, and cohabitation with relatives. In determining whether a particular group is sufficiently personal to warrant this kind of protection from government interference, courts consider factors such as the group's size, purpose, and selectivity, and whether others are excluded from critical aspects of the group.

"Expressive association" refers to a person's right to associate with others to engage in certain kinds of speech. The right to expressive association implies a right to associate with others in pursuit of a wide variety of political, social, economic, educational, religious, and cultural goals, which constitute the expressive speech. A public accommodations law might compromise a group's freedom of expressive association without implicating any right to intimate association, and vice versa.

In 1988, the Supreme Court upheld against constitutional attack a New York City law that prohibited discrimination by a private club if the club (1) has more than four hundred members; (2) provides regular meal services; and (3) regularly receives payment for dues, fees, use of space/facilities, services, or meals from nonmembers in furtherance of trade or business.[18] The Court held that the law did not on its face significantly affect individuals' rights of expressive or intimate association and that the law can be constitutionally applied to the large clubs it describes.

More recently however, in 2000, the Supreme Court held that the New Jersey public accommodations law could not be applied to the Boy Scouts to require them to admit openly gay members, because such action would abridge the group's freedom of expressive association.[19] The Court found that the Boy Scouts engage in expressive activity because their mission is to instill a certain set of values in young people. The Court stated that because the Scouts' official position is that homosexuality conflicts with their values, forcing them to admit openly gay members would significantly impair their freedom of expressive association, i.e., their ability to advocate their viewpoint that homosexuality conflicts with Boy Scout values. The Court further emphasized that a group does not have to associate for the express purpose of disseminating a certain message in order to be entitled to the protections of the First Amendment. Rather, as long as a group does in fact engage in expressive activity that may be impaired, it is entitled to First Amendment protections. The Court's ruling suggests that in some instances, even large, nonselective organizations that do not have a constitutional right of intimate association can still have rights of expressive association that trump antidiscrimination laws. It remains to be seen what impact, if any, this ruling will have on women's efforts to gain membership in all-male organizations pursuant to public accommodations laws.

### Why have women tried to gain entry into membership organizations such as fraternal orders and private clubs?

Women have sought entry into membership organizations to eradicate the stigma associated with being denied admission, and to gain the valuable business contacts that often flow from membership in such groups.[20] Where an organization is not selective in admitting new members, there is a particular shame that follows from nevertheless being denied admission solely because of one's gender. It is because of the value of membership in such organizations and the stigma of exclusion that many state legislatures have concluded that private clubs that are not genuinely selective in their admissions practice should not be permitted to discriminate solely on the basis of gender.

### Other than bringing a lawsuit, what methods are available to combat discrimination practiced by private clubs and other membership organizations?

The federal and state governments can deny these groups certain economic benefits. Some organizations receive tax-exempt status (permitting them not to pay taxes); others are allowed to receive gifts that are tax deductible for the giver (thus encouraging gifts); and still others receive direct government grants or subsidies. It is obviously unfair to provide such benefits at public expense to groups that discriminate against women. Thus, women can seek legislation to end this practice at both the state and the federal levels. While denying economic benefits does not force a club to stop discriminating, it does increase the cost to the club of discriminating. Therefore, legislation denying economic benefits provides powerful leverage for change through economic incentive.

Maryland pursued this approach in passing a law that prohibited favorable tax treatment of discriminatory clubs. The highest court in Maryland upheld the law against a challenge by a powerful country club, finding that the associational rights of the club's members were not implicated.[21] The country club was neither small nor selective enough to warrant the protection of intimate association, nor did the club claim to engage in activities warranting the protection of expressive association. Moreover, because the state is under no obligation to support discrimination by private groups, its failure to subsidize such discrimination does not unconstitutionally burden the group's associational rights.

### What should a woman do if she thinks she has been discriminated against in a public accommodation?

She should determine what protection her state public accommodations law provides, and whether she lives in a city with laws that afford additional protection. Many public accommodations laws provide for comprehensive enforcement by the same state agency that regulates employment discrimination. It is not possible to explain in this book the various procedures under all these laws, but some general advice is to call the state employment discrimination agency and ask for information about where to go and what to do next. In states where the laws do not provide adequate protection, a woman might work with others to get stronger antidiscrimination laws passed. Seeking publicity to bring the public's attention to the issue of equal access may also help bring about positive change. In 2003, for example, negative publicity surrounding Augusta National's long-standing exclusion of women brought significant pressure upon the private golf club to alter its policies, even though Georgia has no applicable public accommodations law forbidding gender discrimination.[22]

## NOTES

1. D.C. CODE ANN. § 2-1401.02(24) (2005).
2. *See* Ohio Civil Rights Comm'n v. Lysyj, 313 N.E.2d 3 (Ohio 1974).

3. For example, in Ashley Bellum v. City of Grants Pass, ACLU filed a complaint in April 2002 on behalf of group of girls age eight to eighteen who competed in a softball league seeking to obtain equal access for the girls to high-quality playing fields in the city park. The case was settled in 2003 with the city agreeing to improve the girls' playing field, providing same facilities already available on boys' playing fields. *See* ACLU Women's Rights Project, http://www.aclu.org/Womens Rights/WomensRights.cfm?ID=10402&c=172 and http://www.aclu.org/Womens Rights/WomensRights.cfm?ID=14427&c=172 for press releases and copy of complaint. A similar case, Baca v. City of Los Angeles, was brought by ACLU in 1998 and settled the next year. *See* Press Release, ACLU, ACLU-SC & CWLC Announce Settlement of Significant Lawsuit against City of Los Angeles (Oct. 27, 1999), *available at* http://www.aclu-sc.org/News/Releases/1999/100289/.

4. *See, e.g.,* Roberts v. U.S. Jaycees, 468 U.S. 609 (1984); Nat'l Org. for Women v. Little League Baseball, Inc., 318 A.2d 33 (N.J. Super. Ct. App. Div. 1974), *aff'd,* 338 A.2d 198 (N.J. 1974).

5. 42 U.S.C. § 2000a (1994); 42 U.S.C. § 12181–12189 (1994).

6. ALASKA STAT. § 18.80.210 (2004); ARK. CODE ANN. § 16-123-107(a) (West 2005); ARIZ. REV. STAT. ANN. § 41-1442 (2005); CAL. CIV. CODE § 51 (West 2005); COLO. REV. STAT. § 24-34-601(2) (West 2005); CONN. GEN. STAT. § 46a-64 (2005); DEL. CODE ANN. tit. 6, § 4504(a) (2005); D.C. CODE ANN. § 2-1402.31(a) (2005); FLA. STAT. ANN. § 509.092 (West 2005); HAW. REV. STAT. § 489-3 (2004); IDAHO CODE § 67-5901(2) (2005); 775 ILL. COMP. STAT. ANN. 5/1-102 (West 2005); IND. CODE § 22-9-1-2 (West 2005); IOWA CODE ANN. § 216.7 (2005); KAN. STAT. ANN. § 44-1009(c)(1) (2004); KY. REV. STAT. ANN. § 344.145 (Baldwin 2005); LA. REV. STAT. ANN. § 51:2247 (West 2004); ME. REV. STAT. ANN. tit. 5, § 4592 (2005); MD. ANN. CODE art. 49B, § 5 (West 2005); MASS. GEN. LAWS ch. 272, § 98 (2005); MICH. COMP. LAWS ANN. § 37.2302 (2005); MINN. STAT. ANN. § 363A.11 (2005); MO. REV. STAT. § 213.065(1) (Vernon 2005); MONT. CODE ANN. § 49-2-304 (2005); NEB. REV. STAT. § 20-134 (2005); NEV. REV. STAT. ANN. 233.010 (West 2005); N.H. REV. STAT. ANN. § 354-A:17 (2005); N.J. STAT. ANN. § 10:5-12(f) (2005); N.M. STAT. ANN. § 28-1-7 (West 2005); N.Y. EXEC. LAW § 296(2)(a) (McKinney 2005); N.D. CENT. CODE § 14-02.4-14 (2003); OHIO REV. CODE ANN. § 4112.02(G) (Baldwin 2005); OKLA. STAT. tit. 25, § 1402 (2005); OR. REV. STAT. § 659A.403 (West 2005); 43 PA. CONS. STAT. ANN. § 953 (Purdon 2005); R.I. GEN. LAWS § 11-24-2 (2004); S.D. CODIFIED LAWS § 20-13-23 (2005); TENN. CODE ANN. § 4-21-501 (West 2005); UTAH CODE ANN. § 13-7-3 (West 2005); VT. STAT. ANN. tit. 9, § 4502 (2003); VA. CODE ANN. § 2.2-3900 (West 2005); WASH. REV. CODE ANN. § 49.60.215 (West 2005); W. VA. CODE § 5-11-9(6) (West 2003); WIS. STAT. ANN. § 106.52 (West 2005); WYO. STAT. ANN. § 6-9-101 (2005); *see also* Nan D. Hunter, *Accommodating the Public Sphere: Beyond the Market Model,* 85 MINN. L. REV. 1591, 1615 (2001).

7. Seidenberg v. McSorley's Old Ale House, 317 F. Supp. 593 (S.D.N.Y. 1970) (state regulation of liquor licenses); Johnson v. Heinemann Candy Co., 402 F. Supp. 714 (E.D. Wis. 1975) (use of city police force).

8. *See, e.g.*, Dock Club, Inc. v. Illinois Liquor Control Comm'n, 428 N.E.2d 735 (Ill. App. Ct. 1981) (allowing "ladies night" at tavern); MacLean v. First Northwest Indus., Inc., 635 P.2d 683 (Wash. 1981) (allowing "ladies night" at basketball game); Tucich v. Dearborn Indoor Racquet Club, 309 N.W.2d 615 (Mich. Ct. App. 1981) (allowing lower membership fees to racquet club for women).

9. *See, e.g.*, Ladd v. Iowa W. Racing Ass'n, 438 N.W. 2d 600 (Iowa 1989) (finding "ladies day" at racetrack discriminated against men); Koire v. Metro Car Wash, 707 P.2d 195 (Cal. 1985) (law prohibited car wash and nightclub discounts to women); Peppin v. Woodside Delicatessen, 506 A.2d 263 (Md. Ct. Spec. App. 1986) (50 percent discount to any patron wearing a skirt or gown constituted unlawful sexual discrimination); Penn. Liquor Control Bd. v. Dobrinoff, 471 A.2d 941 (Pa. Commw. Ct. 1984) (finding no cover for female patrons of the bar when "go-go girls" performed was discrimination based on sex).

10. *See, e.g.*, Mich. Comp. Laws § 37.2303 (2001) (exempting any "private club, or other establishment not in fact open to the public"); N.J. Stat. Ann. § 10:5-5(l) (2005) (exempting any "institution, bona fide club, or place of accommodation, which is in its nature distinctly private"); N.Y. Exec. Law § 292(9) (McKinney 2005) (exempting any "institution, club or place of accommodation which proves that it is in its nature distinctly private").

11. *See, e.g.*, Kiwanis Int'l v. Ridgewood Kiwanis Club, 806 F.2d 468 (3d Cir. 1986) (holding a New Jersey Kiwanis club to be distinctly private because of its small size, selective admissions practice, and closure to nonmembers. The Ridgewood club consisted of only twenty-eight members, where ten individuals had been members for over twenty years, and only twenty new members had been admitted in the last decade. Each new member had to be sponsored by a current member, commit to pray and recite the pledge of allegiance at each meeting, and be formally voted in by the Board of Directors).

12. Rogers v. Int'l Ass'n of Lions Clubs, 636 F. Supp. 1476 (E.D. Mich. 1986).

13. Roberts v. U.S. Jaycees, 468 U.S. 609 (1984).

14. Bd. of Dirs. of Rotary Int'l v. Rotary Club, 481 U.S. 537 (1987).

15. Schellenberg v. Rochester Mich. Lodge No. 2225, of Benevolent & Protective Order of Elks of U.S.A., 577 N.W.2d 163 (Mich. Ct. App. 1998).

16. Fraternal Order of Eagles, Tenino Aerie No. 564 v. Grand Aerie of Fraternal Order of Eagles, 59 P.3d 655 (Wash. 2002).

17. *See* Cummings v. Watertown Lodge No. 496 Benevolent & Protective Order of Elks of U.S.A., Inc., 693 N.Y.S.2d 786 (N.Y. App. Div. 1999).

18. New York State Club Ass'n v. City of New York, 487 U.S. 1 (1988).

19. Boy Scouts of Am. v. Dale, 530 U.S. 640 (2000).

20. *See generally* Michael M. Burns, *The Exclusion of Women from Influential Men's Clubs: The Inner Sanctum and the Myth of Full Equality*, 18 HARV. C.R.-C.L. L. REV. 321 (1983).

21. Maryland v. Burning Tree Club, Inc., 554 A.2d 366 (Md. 1989).

22. *See generally* Charles P. Charpentier, *An Unimproved Lie: Gender Discrimination Continues at Augusta National Golf Club*, 11 VILL. SPORTS & ENT. L.J. 111 (2004) (Though Augusta National continues to deny women membership in its club, because of the public pressure in 2003 and the controversy around its policy, Augusta National Golf Club did drop all of its corporate sponsors for the 2003 Masters Tournament.).

# INDEX